# EGYPTIAN ART

## CALOUSTE GULBENKIAN COLLECTION

LUÍS MANUEL DE ARAÚJO

**GENERAL COORDINATION**
João Castel-Branco Pereira, *Director*
Nuno Vassallo e Silva, *Deputy Director*

**EDITORIAL COORDINATION**
João Carvalho Dias with the assistance
of Carla Paulino and Madalena Martins

**TEXT**
Luís Manuel de Araújo

**CURATOR**
Maria Rosa Figueiredo

**TRANSLATION**
Richard Trewinnard

**DESIGN E GRAPHIC COORDINATION**
TVM Designers – Luís Moreira

**PHOTOGRAPHY**
All pieces from the Egyptian Art Collection
Catarina Gomes Ferreira
except cat. no. 16 – Carlos Azevedo,
and cat. no. 31 – Reinaldo Viegas

**REVISION**
am edições / antónio alves martins
with Ana Márquez, Joana Pereira and Pedro Morais

**PRINTING AND FINISHING**
Textype

**COVER**
Stele of the scribe Iry, New Kingdom,
18th dynasty (ca. 1300 BC) – cat. no. 10

www.museu.gulbenkian.pt
www.gulbenkian.pt

1000 copies, October 2006

ISBN 10: 972-848-27-7 / 13: 978-972-8848-27-9

Legal depot: 249 501/06

# EGYPTIAN ART

## CALOUSTE GULBENKIAN COLLECTION

GULBENKIAN
CALOUSTE
FOUNDATION

1956
2006
50 years

Calouste Gulbenkian Museum

Lisbon, 2006

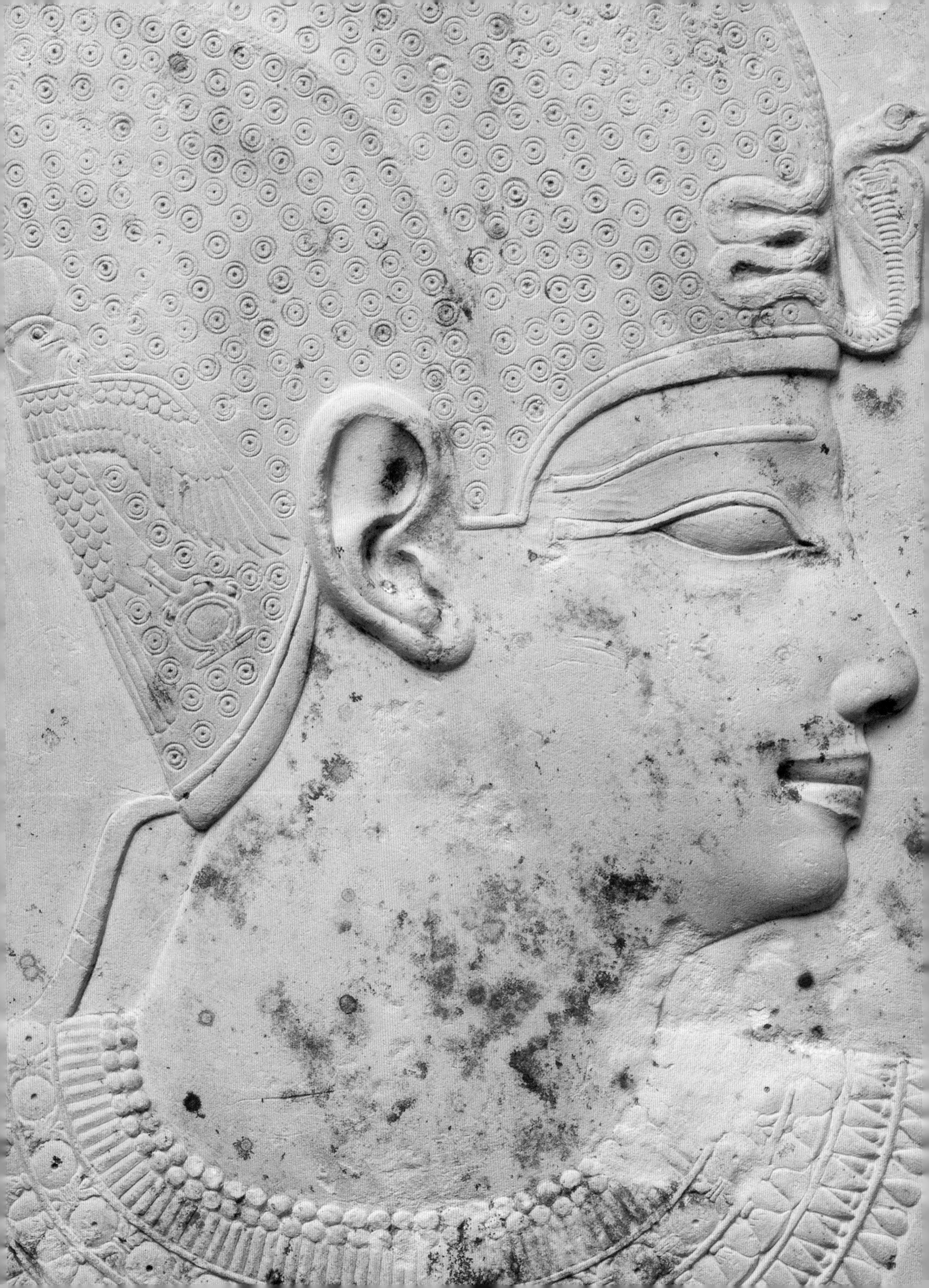

**CONTENTS**

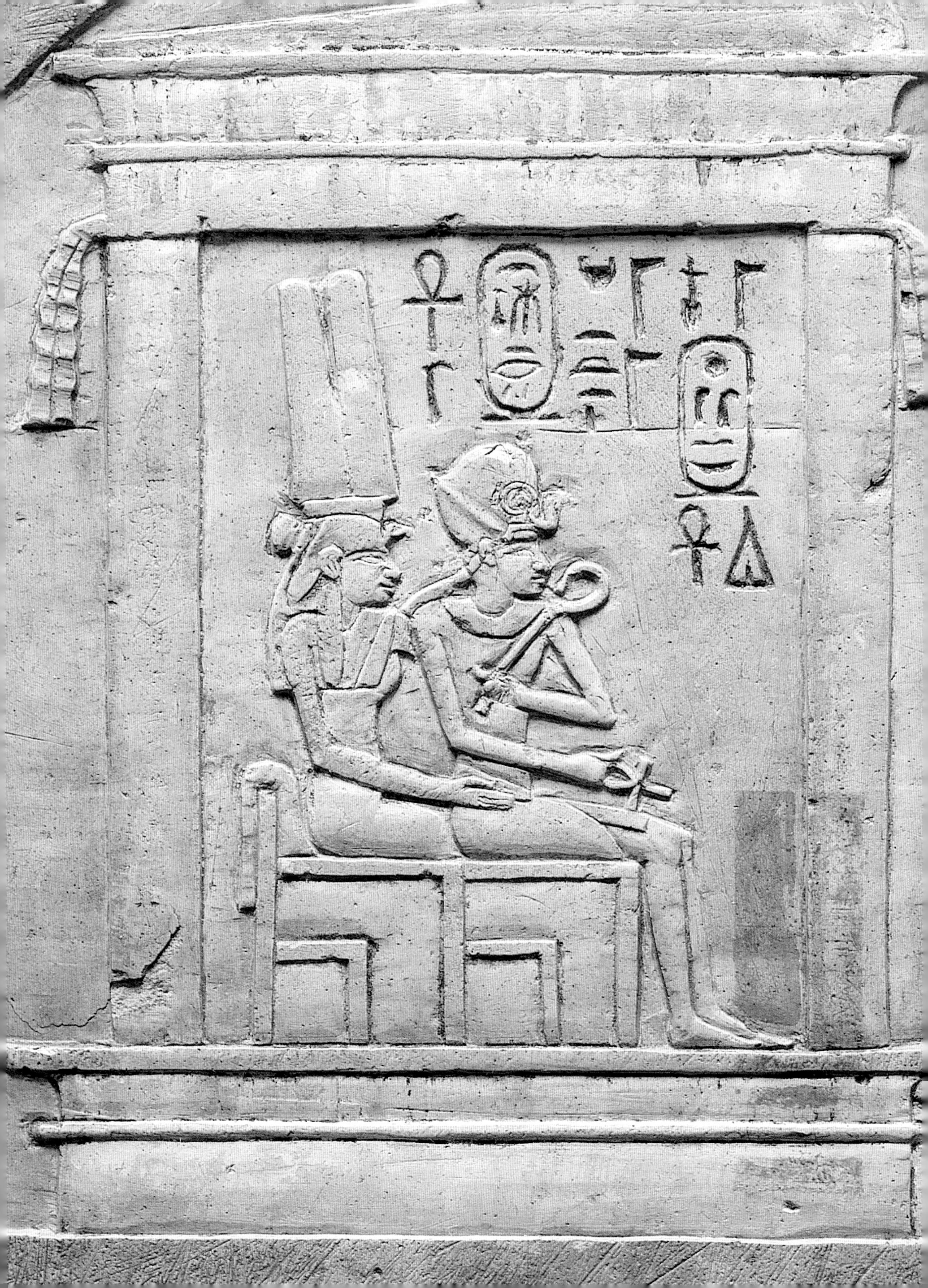

Over the years, the Calouste Gulbenkian Museum has been publishing sections of its collections in albums. Thanks both to the greater depth of information and the reproduction of complete images and details of the objects, this format enables visitors to prolong and enhance their direct appreciation of the works in exhibition.

While Egyptian Art forms the smallest section in the Museum, various generations of specialists have recognised that it is one of the most important in the entire Collection. The rarity and exceptional quality of the pieces, and the variety of their forms and iconography, coupled with the clear chronological structure of the exhibition, bring the visitor into contact with moments from a vast historical period stretching from the Old Kingdom to the Roman Period.

This positive opinion of the section was unanimously shared by experts from the British Museum (London) in 1937 and from the National Gallery of Art (Washington DC) in 1949, and was confirmed by Christiane Desroches-Noblecourt in the 1960s. In turn, Maria Helena Assam, a curator at the Museum, publicised the section when she produced a catalogue of its pieces in 1991.

The constant and rapid advances made in Egyptology, which require updated chronologies and consequently new iconographic identifications and interpretations of the objects made a new publication imperative. This in turn demanded profound knowledge of the subject and academic rigor, requirements that were magnificently met by Professor Luís Manuel de Araújo.

This work not only offers a systematic inventory of the entire Egyptian Art section in the Calouste Gulbenkian Collection, but also proposes fields for research and academic work on this fascinating artistic culture. It is hoped that the Portuguese and English versions will help extend knowledge of this culture both internally and internationally.

The enthusiasm and intellectual curiosity shown by curator Maria Rosa Figueiredo, and the rigor and dedication of editorial coordinator João Carvalho Dias deserve special mention. While these qualities are essential for the successful completion of any project, they were particularly relevant in this case, when applied to such ancient wisdom and publicised here with the clarity of those who truly understand it.

*João Castel-Branco Pereira*

DIRECTOR OF THE CALOUSTE GULBENKIAN MUSEUM

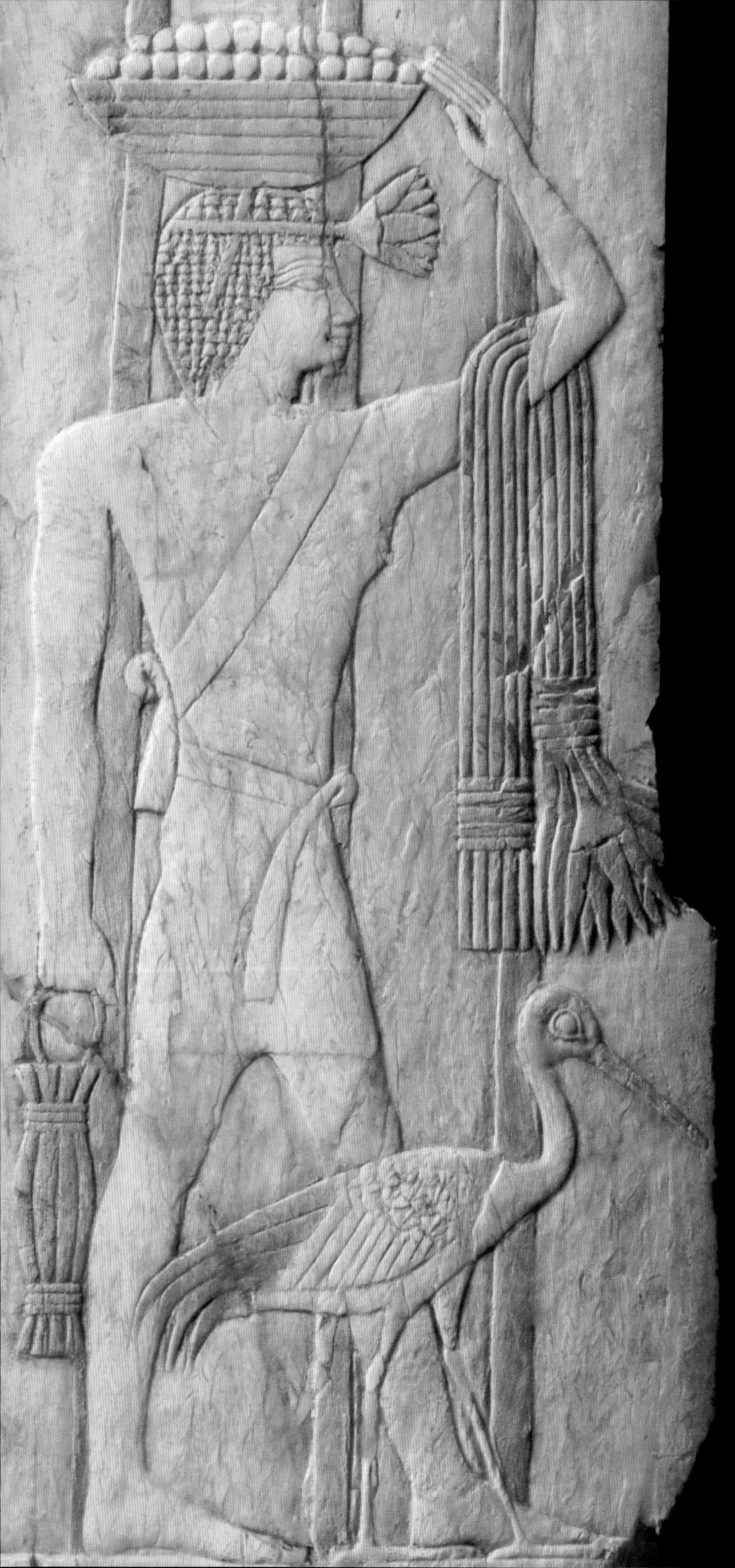

# INTRODUCTION

Although Egyptology is a relatively recent phenomenon in Portugal, it is now solidly established, especially in universities and museums. Equally, while Portugal offers no doctorates or masters degrees specifically in this field, Egyptian civilisation is studied at degree, masters and doctoral level, and open access courses held in recent years on themes from Egyptology have always attracted considerable public interest. Simultaneously, there has been an evident increase in the number of lectures, meetings, film sessions and exhibitions focusing on the Egypt of the pharaohs, as well as study visits to the land of the Nile.

Likewise, the public is more aware of the collections of Egyptian works that include many fascinating objects. Based simply on the number of pieces in exhibition, the most significant collections can be found at the Museu Nacional de Arqueologia, Museu da Farmácia, Museu da Sociedade de Geografia de Lisboa, Museu de História Natural da Faculdade de Ciências do Porto and – naturally – the Calouste Gulbenkian Museum. While the first four contain significant collections in quantitative terms, the outstanding feature of the magnificent pieces at the Calouste Gulbenkian Museum is their quality, combined with the highly appropriate atmosphere of the exhibition room in a museum that is itself set in the delightful greenery of a park.

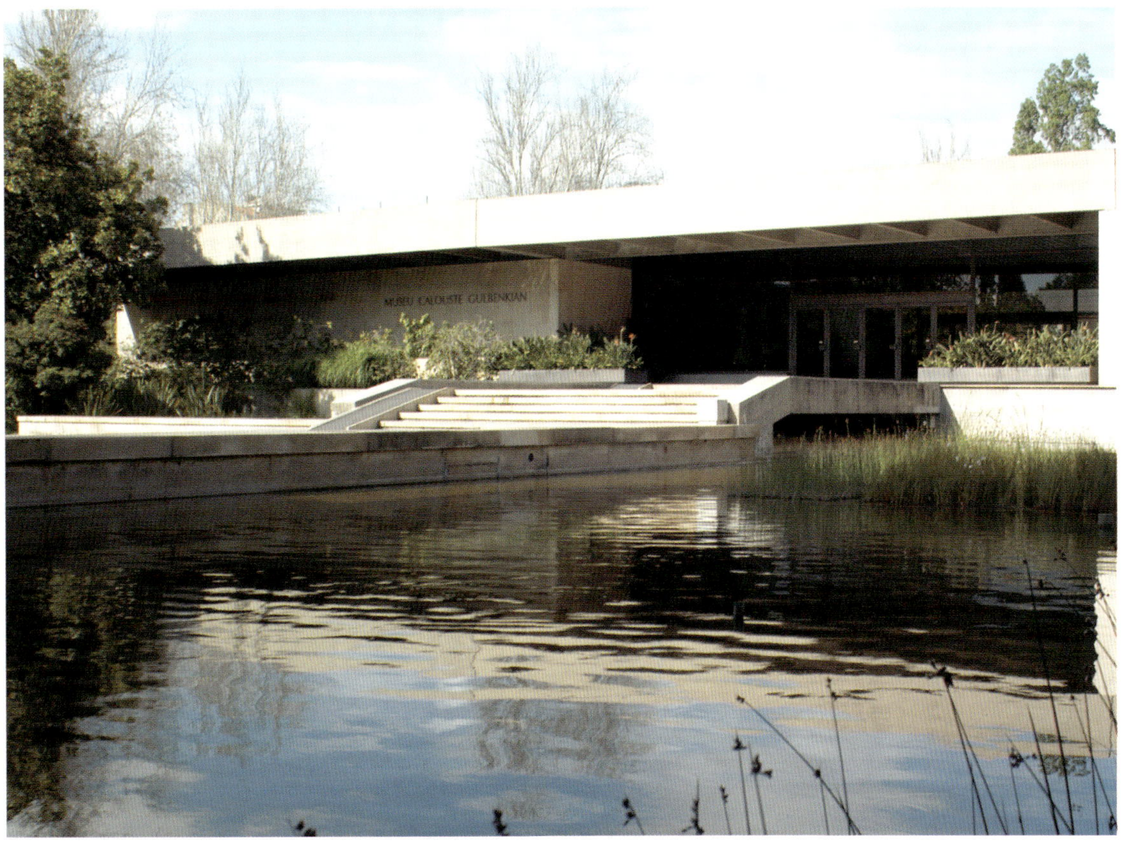

The Calouste Gulbenkian Museum, Lisbon. Façade.
Photo: Catarina Gomes Ferreira

In addition to the above, other smaller museums should also be added, as should pieces owned by private collectors. In total, this means that Portugal currently houses over one thousand objects from Ancient Egypt. The following is an updated list of the Egyptian pieces now in Portugal:

Museu Nacional de Arqueologia, Lisbon – 584 objects (309 on display)
Museu Nacional de História Natural, Faculdade de Ciências do Porto – 103 objects
Museu da Farmácia, Lisbon – 100 objects (95 on display)
Museu da Sociedade de Geografia de Lisboa – 97 objects
Calouste Gulbenkian Museum – 54 objects (40 on display)
Solar Condes de Resende, Canelas – 20 objects
Museu do Caramulo – 8 objects
Museu Nacional de Soares dos Reis, Oporto – 8 objects
Museu do Palácio de Vila Viçosa – 8 objects
Museu Condes de Castro Guimarães, Cascais – 6 objects
Museu Nogueira da Silva, Braga – 2 objects
Biblioteca Nacional de Lisboa – 2 objects
Museu Arqueológico do Carmo – 2 objects
Museu de Aveiro – 1 object
Museu Nacional de Arte Antiga, Lisbon – 1 object
Miguel Barbosa Collection – 49 objects
Sam Levy Collection – 34 objects
Fernando Freitas Simões Collection – 20 objects
Rui Assis Ferreira Collection – 18 objects
Luís Teixeira da Mota Collection – 6 objects
Amaral Cabral Collection – 2 objects
Luís Manuel de Araújo Collection – 2 objects
Sá Nogueira Collection – 2 objects
Manuel Rocha Collection – 1 object
Pedro Gonçalves Rodrigues Collection – 1 object
Mário Barroca Collection – 1 object

Egyptian or Egyptianate scarabs found in Iron Age sites in Portugal must also be added to this list. These now belong to or are part of the collections of small museums such as the Museu de Alenquer (two such pieces, one of the scaraboid type), the Museu da Universidade de Coimbra (one piece), the Museu Arqueológico de Sines (one), the Museu de Odemira (one), and the Museu Nacional de Arqueologia. Besides the scarabs on display, the Museu Nacional de Arqueologia also has three others found in Iron Age tombs in Portugal. Moreover, while carrying out excavations for IPPAR (the Portuguese Architectural Heritage Institute), archaeologist Manuela de Deus recently discovered an Egyptian or Egyptianate scarab at a site near Castro Verde.

Most of these public and private collections have already been studied and published thanks to a project run by the Oriental Institute, (Faculdade de Letras), University of Lisbon since the early 1990s. The outstanding Egyptian collection at the Calouste Gulbenkian Museum had also been studied since the 1930s by some Egyptologists, namely Sidney Smith and I. E. S. Edwards, the authors of the catalogue *Ancient Egyptian Sculpture Lent by C. S. Gulbenkian, Esq.* (London, 1937), published to accompany an exhibition at the British Museum. The pieces in question were subsequently also exhibited in the USA, at the National Gallery of Art in Washington, when I. E. S. Edwards (this time with John Walker) again wrote another catalogue: *Egyptian Sculpture from the Gulbenkian Collection* (Washington, 1949).

In 1962, the collection was studied by French specialist Christiane Desroches-Noblecourt, who came to Portugal at the invitation of the Calouste Gulbenkian Foundation. Although she returned in 1968, the expected catalogue was not published. In fact, it only came out in 1991, thanks to the dedicated efforts of the Museum's Director, Maria Teresa Gomes Ferreira. The text was the work of curator Maria Helena Assam, and the fine illustrations were created from photographs of the pieces taken by Reinaldo Viegas.

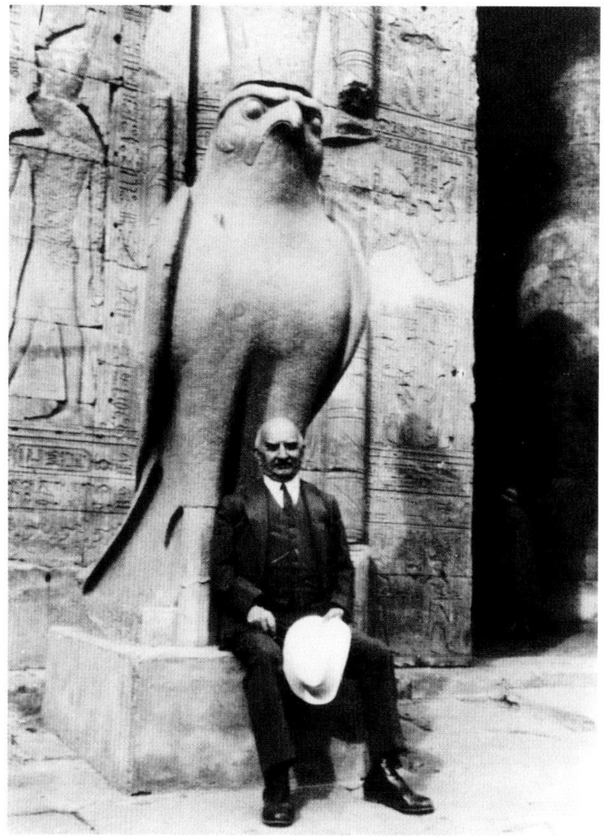

Calouste Gulbenkian at the temple of Horus in Edfu (1934).

Fifteen years on, the moment has come to publish a new catalogue that will offer a deeper analysis of the pieces exhibited in the Egyptian Room at the Calouste Gulbenkian Museum and of those in the storeroom. Particular emphasis will be given to the introductory texts so that readers can understand the main lines that define Ancient Egypt and its magnificent artwork. This volume ends with an extensive glossary and an appendix, as well as a bibliography that suggests further reading and research materials for those interested.

The catalogue numbers established by Maria Helena Assam have basically been maintained, as she provided an excellent service to the countless visitors who have, over the years, admired the Egyptian pieces collected by Calouste Gulbenkian. Owing to the decision to divide pieces that were previously considered as a whole into their individual components, a handful of alterations to the numbering system have been made. Particular and fully justified care was taken with the inscriptions on some of the objects, which are reproduced in the catalogue, with hieroglyph texts. These texts have been re-written from left to right, as normally found in Western writing, even though the original showed them in the opposite direction or written vertically. Square brackets hold parts of the text that is missing or omissions from the text, while normal brackets are used to indicate interpretations of the texts.

Having now completed the catalogue, I would like to express my heartfelt thanks to the people who supported me in this enthralling task. Deolinda Cerqueira and her colleagues from the Museum's Education Department lovingly set up "Navigating through Ancient Egypt", the mini-site on the Egyptian collection that brought an important dynamic to this process, and in which I am pleased to have been able to provide some academic guidance. In addition, working on the revision of the catalogue *7000 Years of Persian Art* (2005) and leading guided tours of the exhibition strengthened my links with the Museum. This created the environment required to present a proposal for new captions to be added to the Egyptian collection. This was accepted and several anomalies were consequently altered. It was subsequently also decided to publish this new catalogue.

During the phase of researching the collection's archives and drawing up this final text, I benefited from the kind support of curator Maria Rosa Figueiredo and the Museum staff, particularly João Carvalho Dias, who is responsible for coordinating the publication. I would like to recognise their work and thank them all, as well as the director, João Castel-Branco Pereira.

*Luís Manuel de Araújo*

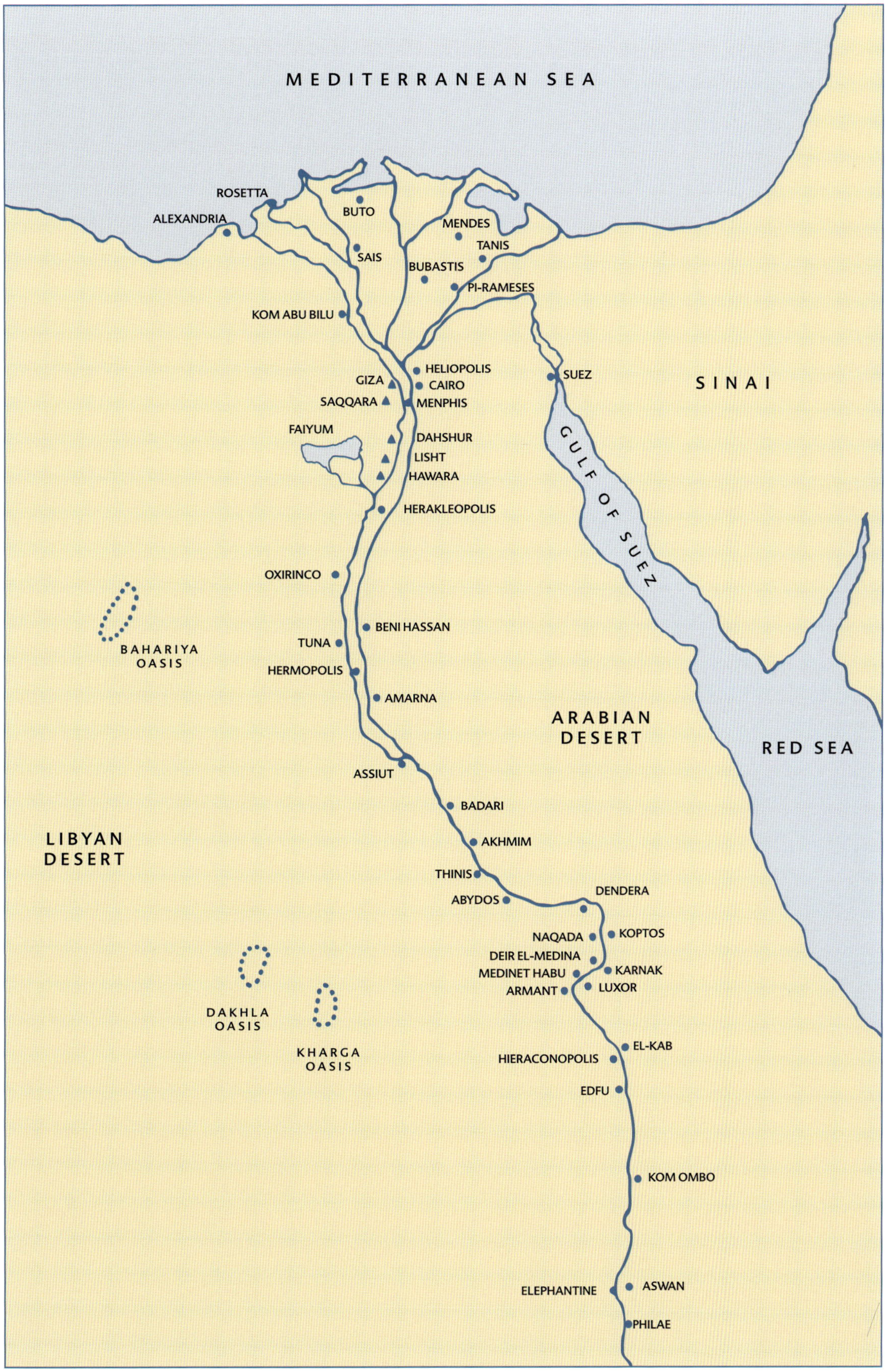


Map of Egypt showing the main locations.

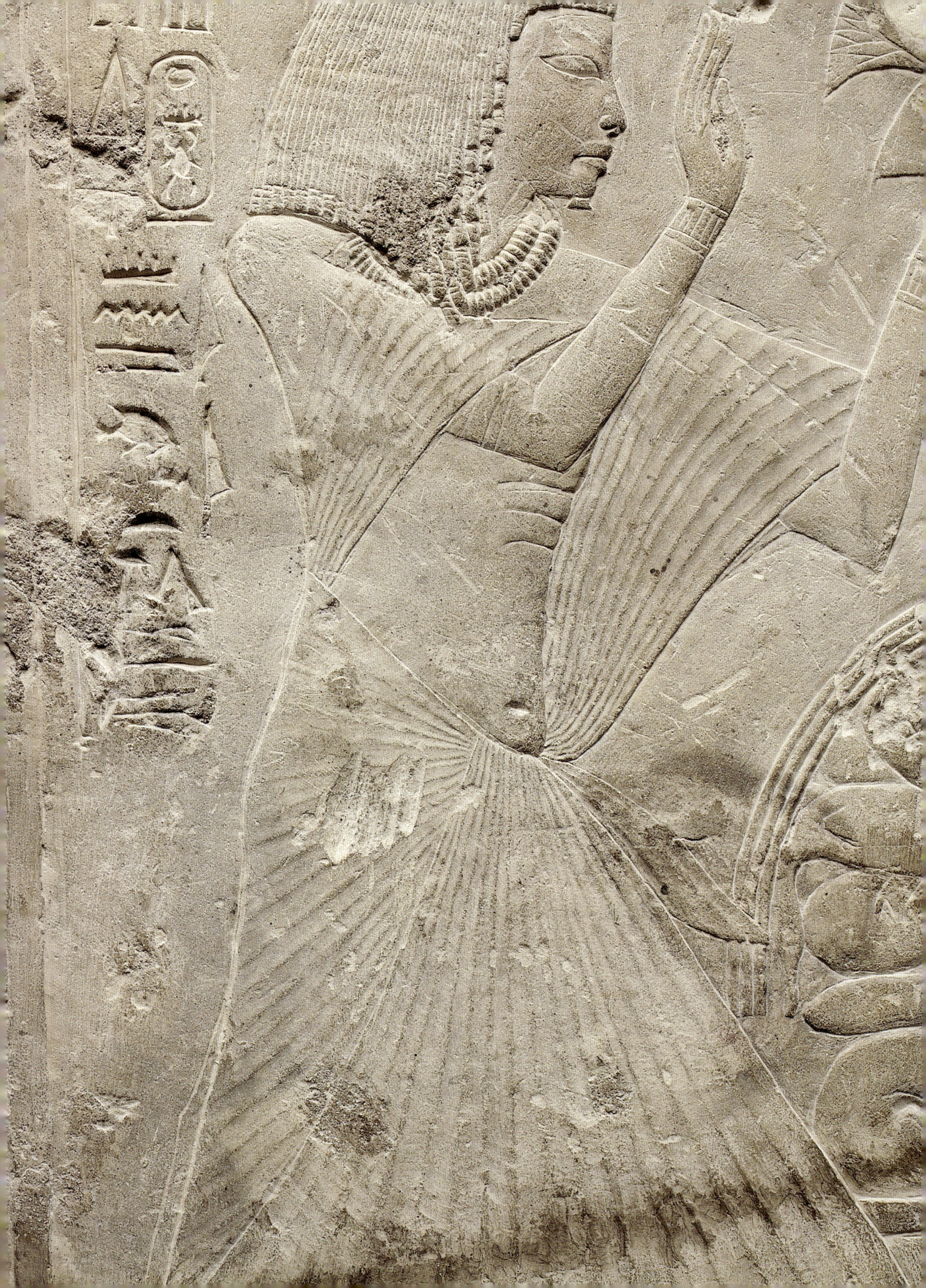

# THE HISTORY OF ANCIENT EGYPT

Ancient Egyptian civilisation was forged during the country's long prehistoric phase. The Palaeolithic period was merely a regional phenomenon in that remote age from the history of mankind; the Mesolithic witnessed the development of societies featuring agile hunters who used bows and arrows and left paintings on the rocks in the bordering deserts; and the Neolithic innovations in crop-growing, in planting and weaving flax, and in the production of pottery. The Egyptian Neolithic is commonly believed to have started around 6000 BC, the date of a polished stone axe at the Museu Nacional de Arqueologia, Lisbon, brought from Egypt by José Leite de Vasconcelos. This very early period also produced the oval houses of Merimde Beni-Salame, in the West Delta, where the dead were buried in a foetal position inside the houses and facing east, where the sun rises (Araújo, 1993: 77-82).

This phase was followed by the Badari and Naqada cultures, which left countless remains, mainly in copper, ivory, pottery and stone. It was during this phase (4500-3000 BC) that the foundations for the civilisation of Ancient Egypt were laid. There are doubts as to the important political and cultural phenomenon of the country's unification, and it is not known who actually achieved this feat. However, the southern ruler Narmer (who may be the Menes from the king-lists) is customarily identified as the first king of the unified nation, which combined Upper and Lower Egypt. Clear signs of influence from the distant land of Mesopotamia are also known during this phase when the newly unified country emerged. These Sumerian influences, specifically from the Djemdet Nasr time (3100-3000 BC), are confirmed by brick buildings with palace-style façades, by the taste for drawing mythological and composite animals (especially winged griffins and cats with snake-heads) found on palettes and knife-handles, and by the symmetrical group showing a bearded hero defeating two lions by crushing them in his arms. Pairs of entwined animals found on knife-handles and on the Narmer Palette demonstrate the existence of elements from Mesopotamia. Yet unlike Mesopotamia, where the leader was a representative of god, in Egypt he was considered to be a god in his own right.

At that time, the king of Egypt was a living Horus, a god on earth. Yet this divine vision of the king, the mainstay of the nation's unity, had nothing to do with the west's deeply-rooted and sometimes distorted Judaeo-Christian concepts of god. Rather, the king of Egypt should be seen as a figure with the broad cosmic and ritual functions that were typical of African royalty. The living Horuses who ruled in Ancient Egypt cannot be compared to the Judaeo-Christian god, who has a markedly creational and omnipotent aspect. The former were neither of these two things, at least in the cosmic sense, even though the king often bore the title *iri-khet*, or "maker of things", applied to temples, tombs and monuments, and as a bringer of peace and harmonious prosperity. Thus, the living Horus was a human and divine being, the guardian of broad powers for good, the "dynamic centre of the universe, the being in which the cosmic and the social come together, a universal integrator". In this sense, his remote origins lay in the divine African monarchies (Cervelló Autuori, 2001: 28-30). Egypt is indeed an African civilisation, and its language – formed over the centuries – is the result of the combined penetration of elements from Black

Africa and the neighbouring regions of Semitic culture (to the East) and from North Africa, via Libya and the Saharan areas (to the West). This explains why Egyptian was a Semiticised African language.

The pharaoh's very name also demonstrates that he was a deity: three of the five names from the royal titulary define him as a god – exactly as the Ancient Egyptians saw him (Shaw, 2000: 8).

Narmer was succeeded by Aha, who continued the process of political and ideological unification, and added a healthy dose of tolerance so as to maintain good relations with the Delta. He may also have been responsible for founding the city of Memphis at the strategic point where the north meets the south (Padró, 1996: 59). His successors then devoted their efforts to developing agriculture, to contacts with Nubia with trading or punitive expeditions, while there is also evidence of active navigation to Byblos and other ports in Northern Syria to purchase cedar wood, which was as high quality as the ebony that came from Nubia. It was difficult to create a peaceful atmosphere between the north and south of the country, and we are aware of periods of instability during the 1st and 2nd dynasties, perhaps the result of a latent rivalry that only diminished with the passage of time (Grimal, 1988: 65-81).

Consolidating a unified kingdom while maintaining the dual aspect of balance and complementariness was achieved by developing a flexible, centralised and efficient administrative system and by establishing a tradition with a powerful religious mark where the divine monarch was seen as the guarantee of national unity. This vision, implanted with the emergence of the Horuses, was constantly presented and would dominate the thinking of Egypt's educated elite, even in times of crisis. The dynamic development of a central government immediately eliminated many of the factors which led to the emergence of independent urban centres – city states – in the Near East, and more specifically in Lower Mesopotamia. This phenomenon did not appear in the country of the Two Lands. Egypt's various regional administrative centres did not have compact population groups, but instead featured large numbers of peasants spread along the Nile in small villages that were safe from the annual flooding between July and October. Meanwhile, the highly prestigious royal court established the cultural patterns for all of this vast country, so that the divine king were not only the centre of an enlightened and cohesive power, but also a model for behaviour (Araújo, 2001: 298).

One recent line of thinking claims that the kings from the Early Dynastic Period were buried in Abydos (near the city of Thinis from where the dynasty originates), while other studies argue that the royal tombs were built in Saqqara. Certainly, both sites have clear signs of large and imposing royal tombs. However, the suggestions made by François Daumas – that the bodies of the Horuses were buried in Saqqara and the viscera were in turn buried in Abydos (Daumas, 1987: 42-43) – have yet to be convincingly dismissed. This expresses the typically Egyptian dualist vision of the world and of things, as was abundantly clear in this initial phase of the monarchy.

It was the almost completely unknown first two dynasties that laid the foundations for solid and lasting rule by pharaohs and established the operation of a powerful administrative machine that coordinated and controlled the work of large numbers of peasants. Not only did the latter work the land, labour on the major construction work involved in building dams, canals and barns, and participate in the arduous task of transporting the building materials used on the royal tombs, but they also produced a huge volume of vessels made in a broad range of materials. One such piece – the fine alabaster cup – is the first object exhibited in the Calouste Gulbenkian Collection (cat. no. 1).

The first two dynasties established the basis for a stable and patronage-based monarchy, developing the active social relations between rulers and their subjects that originally came from the pre-dynastic Naqada Period. Besides managing the country's human resources, the monarchs' main concern was to tame the Nile and make it work for the people. This powerful force of nature, which transforms Egypt into an extensive and fertile African oasis, not only always impressed the inhabitants of Egypt, but also thrilled the foreigners who visited the region. Herodotus and others stated that Egypt was a gift of the Nile, yet it was one that was combined with the determined and concerted efforts of thousands of peasants and officials. Ultimately, in contrast to the writings of classical authors, Egypt is not a gift, but "a creation of human endeavour" (Barocas, 1987: 7).

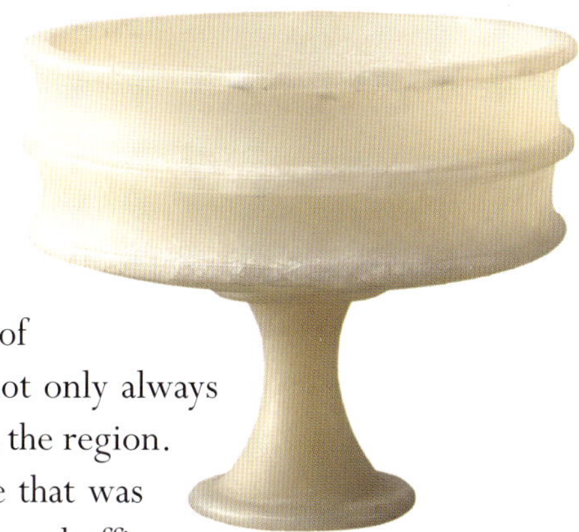

Alabaster cup, probably from the Old Kingdom (3rd dynasty?) (cat. no. 1).

The period called Old Kingdom covers the 3rd, 4th, 5th and 6th dynasties. It was during this period that the large pyramid complexes were built. The first major step came in the 3rd dynasty, around 2650 BC, with the construction of the "step pyramid" of Horus Netjerirkhet Djoser, designed by the architect Imhotep. Starting from a stone mastaba (bench-shaped tomb), several structures were added to create a pyramidal construction that would establish the paradigmatic form for kings' tombs during the following millennium. The 3rd dynasty also continued the stabilising, centripetal work started under the first two dynasties (Early Dynastic Period), which had been first attempted immediately after the unification of the Two Lands (Bard, 2000: 61-88).

The 4th dynasty saw the construction of the large pyramids in Giza for kings Khufu, Khafra and Menkaura. However, even before them, Sneferu had built a series of pyramids: two in Dahshur and possibly one in Meidum (although it is thought to be for Sneferu's predecessor – Huni – from the 3rd dynasty). The cult of the sun also attained new heights during this period, as shown by the fact that Pharaoh Djedefra introduced the formula "son of Ra" at the front of his name, a title that would continue to be used until the end of pharaonic Egypt and indeed even by the kings from the Ptolemaic dynasty. Since Horus was alive, from the 4th dynasty onwards, the king was considered to be the son of Ra and seen as a god, an idea supported by some of the most highly regarded Egyptologists.

The first 4th-dynasty king was Sneferu, who is sometimes considered to have been the most powerful monarch during the Old Kingdom. There is some truth in this: he was one of the greatest builders in all of Egypt's history. The two pyramids he had built in Dahshur and the other he completed in Meidum (possibly started by Huni, the last Horus of the 3rd dynasty) are imposing monuments that as a whole are greater in terms of the number of blocks used and the adjacent buildings than the famous Great Pyramid that his son Khufu built on Giza. While the surrounding pyramids and mastaba*s* were already empty when they were discovered, the materials found in the tomb of Queen Hetepheres, Khufu's mother, demonstrate the high levels that the decorative and utilitarian arts had achieved at that time. One of the tombs of the monarch's family members, located near the royal tomb, belonged to the Princess Merytites. A fragment of the mural from this tomb now belongs to the Calouste Gulbenkian Collection (cat. no. 2). Other monarchs from this dynasty who deserve special mention are Khafra and Menkaura, who also have pyramids on Giza, massive stone constructions that demonstrate the peak of the divine monarchy.

The most famous pharaohs from the 5$^{th}$ dynasty were its founder – Userkaf – and Sahura, Neferirkara, Kakai, Nyuserra, Djedkara, Ibesis and Unas, in order of succession, besides others about whom little is known. One characteristic of this dynasty was the cult of the sun-god Ra, which is shown by the large sun-temples that are typical of that period, although most have since disappeared. One significant political development for the administration was that important posts such as vizier ceased being given to members of the king's family and were instead awarded to senior officials whose loyalty or efficiency were rewarded with grants of land. Records show maritime expeditions as far as the Lebanon, maintaining the trade with port cities in the Levant that dated from previous eras, perhaps even from proto-history. Relations with neighbouring nations were completely peaceful, and trade fleets were sent to the coast of the Lebanon and the Red Sea to bring back the products that Egypt did not have, starting with the fine cedar wood from the Lebanon. These expeditions were complemented by prospecting work in Nubia, while there were also military expeditions (sometimes punitive) and trade missions (Málek, 1986: 65-85).

Sun-worshipping reached its peak when at least six monarchs from the 5$^{th}$ dynasty built sun-temples in Abu Gorab and Abusir, regions located between Saqqara and Giza. The 5$^{th}$-dynasty royal tombs in Abusir belong to Sahura, Neferirkara and Nyuserra, while those in Saqqara belong to Userkaf and Unas. In turn, the 6$^{th}$-dynasty kings built their pyramids in Saqqara, and – following the example of Unas, the last 5$^{th}$-dynasty monarch – had magical texts inscribed inside their tombs: the so-called "Pyramid Texts".

The most significant kings from the 6$^{th}$ dynasty were Teti, Pepy I, Merenra and Pepy II. Although the last of these had a long reign, it was not as long as has sometimes been claimed. Shortly after the dynasty began, Egypt started facing economic problems that were initially eased by doubling the frequency of the cattle census (the basis of the taxation system), and demanding greater efficiency from the bureaucratic and administrative system that was the key to running Egypt with some concept of order.

The king was helped in ruling this vast country by a group of staff who dominated the complex art of hieroglyphic writing and – for more practical and faster written tasks – hieratic script. These men, who could read, write and count, were able to receive taxes on a regular basis and carry out censuses on both cattle and people, who were called "the cattle of god". There was no written code or even written laws, so the tasks of maintaining order and collecting taxes, receiving goods and distributing foodstuffs, managing human and natural resources were associated to concepts learned at the scribes' schools (and in the great school of life through understanding a balanced and regulated daily life). Everything came down to applying the norms of *maet* to daily life. As Jan Assmann noted, *maet* was the great development that emerged from the Old Kingdom. This principle established deeply-rooted notions of practising good deeds and solidarity, leading to protection of the weak and humble, imbuing the nation's leaders with a strong commitment to implementing justice and proper ideas of harmony, balance, rectitude, generosity, tolerance and well-being – starting with the well-being of the leaders themselves.

Egyptian society is portrayed as a sort of large family that was grouped around the living god or pharaoh. He was truly the lord of the country and its inhabitants, but while the people's lives were subject to the satisfaction of the king and the senior officials, the pharaoh in turn was

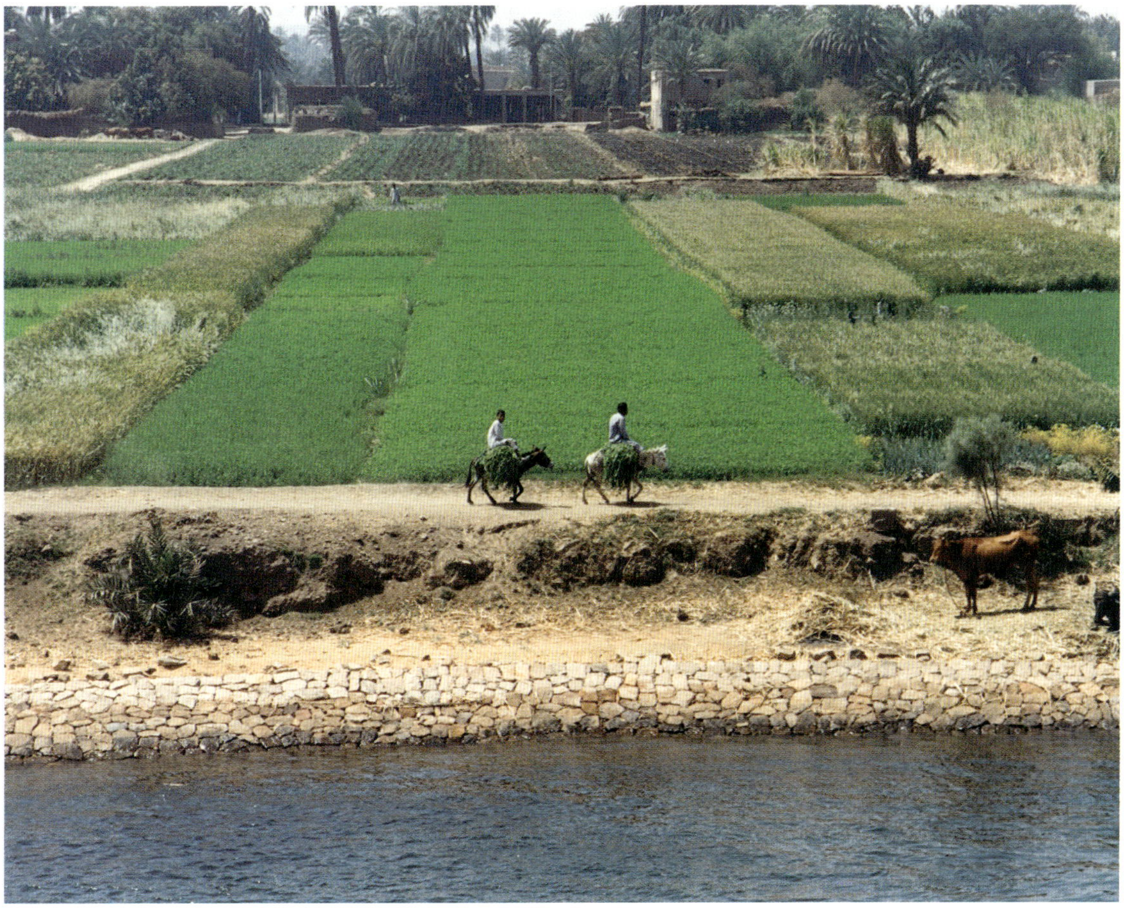

The fertile fields of the Nile today, just as they were thousands of years ago.
Photo: Telo Ferreira Canhão

also obliged to make justice rule among his subjects. The figure of the divine king was at the core of the wise and prudent court that centralised the entire administration of the country and tried to implement a normal and organised life on a nation of peasants, fulfilling the norms of *maet*, the cosmic and universal order. Ultimately, in an accurate reflection of this long historical period, the Old Kingdom would bequeath two great monuments to the future generations: the pyramid as a royal tomb and the administrative machinery.

While the pyramids bear witness to the divine royalty's great power, the mastaba*s* reveal the art and daily life of the age. Low-reliefs attained exceptional standards under the 5th dynasty, while interesting work was produced in painting, with a vast wealth of themes and colours, and sculpture created statues of kings and individuals. Some mastabas from the 4th to 6th dynasties, especially those from the Saqqara region, included a reasonable number of statues of officials in stone and wood, suggesting the intense levels of production of goods for the afterlife. In contrast, literature seems to have been less rich, although many texts must evidently have been lost. Even so, in addition to the famous "Pyramid Texts", there are texts containing knowledge that typifies the Old Kingdom. The former, long inscriptions written in beautiful hieroglyphs that were first found in the pyramid of Unas, are texts containing magical and prophylactic properties so that the king could reach the afterlife without harm and there enjoy eternity (Málek, 1986: 103-109).

Throughout the 6th dynasty, officials received large-scale rewards through grants of land. Initially, they alone were designed to enjoy the use of these lands, but ownership later became hereditary and definitive, as did their posts. The most significant position was that of provincial governor, which led to the creation of small local dynasties that became increasingly independent from the central authorities. The declining quality in works of art – in both architecture and sculpture – indicates the difficult times that came at the end of the Old Kingdom. There were probably one or two periods of famine due to poor harvests and perhaps also the result of insufficient or excessive flooding. The long reign of Pepy II may also have contributed to the dynasty's unhappy end, and the lack of a direct heir also clearly upset the political order (Daumas, 1987: 60).

In the latter years of the long 6th dynasty, the idea of unity crumbled, the once-efficient administrative machinery practically ground to a halt, the provincial governors moved away from the capital and built their tombs in the places where they had held power (often their homelands), and passed their posts down to their children. The hereditary nature of the functions is a sign of the increasing privileges associated to royal service, but simultaneously demonstrates that pharaonic power was essentially bankrupt. Charters of immunity exempted regions from supplying the goods that the crown had always previously required, and freed the lands belonging to various officials from the obligation to pay tax. Such men would have tombs in their respective regions, their own funerary clergy and vast domains that supplied foodstuffs for the deceased. The magnificent, well-planned structure of the Old Kingdom ultimately collapsed due to the grants made by the kings, who were ever less divine and had to deal by servants who were ever stronger. Thus, the administrative machine that had kept society operating in a harmonious and balanced manner for many centuries was the cause of its collapse. The system itself sowed the seed that blossomed into the chaos and social revolution that were a feature of the end of the Old Kingdom (Málek, 1986: 118-120). Writing at a later date, Ipuwer produced a very dramatic description of the social upheaval: pyramids robbed and abandoned by the funerary priests; the bodies of the deceased thrown into the river; the stones from royal tombs reused on other works; the laws rejected and broken; families being disrespected; the grain-stores empty; constant assaults; the royal palace pillaged and – the ultimate scandal – the archives destroyed. The two founding units of Egyptian society had been destroyed: the productive fields where crops grew and were prudently harvested; and the reproductive unit, where the family (particularly the royal family) was in decline (Barocas, 1987: 153-154).

The dramatic fall of the Old Kingdom brought in the era called the First Intermediate Period. This historical age, which lasted over one hundred years, is difficult to understand because of the absence of monuments to illustrate its four dynasties (according to the classical division of Egyptian history) and the shortage of documents. Maneton speaks about "seventy kings in seventy days" under the 7th dynasty, a portrayal of short-term and unstable power where the kings succeeded one another on the throne at Memphis without clear and unequivocal recognition from some of the provincial governors, who were gaining increasing autonomy and ruling their territories far from the court. Moreover, the governors were working to make the people become their subjects and thus benefit from controlled management so that there would be no hunger and order would govern. The fertile Delta regions were also much coveted by the people who came pouring in from the Sinai and the Syrian-Palestine Corridor, and there was no central power to prevent this "incursion".

After the collapse of the Old Kingdom and during the First Intermediate Period, Egyptian scholars and officials would ponder the times in which they lived, rethinking the code of values that would lead to the optimistic discovery that everyone had the right to *maet* and to enjoy eternal life with a *ka* and a *ba*. The *ka* (a metaphysical life and sexual energy, and a sort of invisible duo) had already existed in the Old Kingdom; the *ba* (the capacity for eternal movement that generates different forms for the individual), which had previously been the exclusive preserve of the king and the gods, became accessible to all those who had the right to a tomb. With the *ka* and *ba* came eternal life – provided the norms of *maet* had been fulfilled in daily life. Thus, officials upgraded their status by accompanying their bodies with the ancient royal texts that eased or guaranteed access to eternity (the "Pyramid Texts"), adapted them for their own benefit and created the "Coffin Texts". The climate was conducive to discussion of the question of divine justice (theodicy) and a type of debate-stimulating literature appeared with controversial texts which approached the theme of *maet*. Meanwhile, royal tombs such as the pyramid of King Qakara Iby (8th dynasty), which measures just 18 metres in height, are a fine illustration of declining pharaonic power, while the wall decorations in private tombs were ever more modest and of poor quality (Seidlmayer, 2000: 118-147).

The 9th dynasty and the 10th, whose most famous king was Merykara, came originally from Herakleopolis (Nen-nesut). Meanwhile, the rulers of Thebes (11th dynasty) came into conflict with the kings of Herakleopolis, starting a civil war which culminated in a golden age for Egypt with the victory of the Theban King Mentuhotep II.

The Middle Kingdom began when Mentuhotep II victoriously managed to reunify Egypt. This triumph brought an end to the rivalry between Herakleopolis and the southern city Thebes. After Narmer's unification of the Two Lands approximately one thousand years earlier, Egypt was again a single nation under one king. Yet the brilliant era that this ushered in would have to deal with problems that the Old Kingdom had never faced. Incursions by nomadic tribes from the eastern side of the Delta, where Bedouins were disturbing Egypt's contact with Syria-Palestine, were one of the issues that urgently needed to be solved. Fortification lines were built opposite the Sinai and military expeditions multiplied in the region, where Egypt also started mining the deposits of copper and turquoise in a more systematic manner.

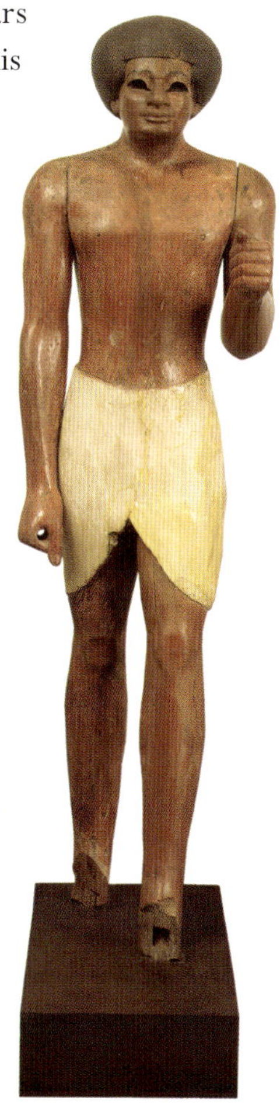

Funerary statue of the *ka* of a Middle Kingdom official (cat. no. 3).

The title given to the unifying king indicates the supremacy that the god Montu then enjoyed. He was revered in Ermant, the region around Thebes where the wooden funerary statue in the Calouste Gulbenkian Collection (cat. no. 3) may have been produced. The kings from the energetic 12th dynasty called themselves Amenemhat ("Amun is in command" or "Amun leads"), which indicates the rapid rise of the god Amun, worshipped in Waset, a provincial city that was to have a glorious future. The Greeks would later call it Thebes (although the reason for this is still unknown), and it is now called Luxor.

The 11th dynasty also carried out campaigns to regain control over trade with Nubia, which had gained autonomy in the meantime. In addition, building work on temples also restarted, exemplified by the funeral complex erected by Mentuhotep in Deir el-Bahri, which would later act as a model for Hatshepsut. However, the dynasty was not to stay in power for very long. Although the final years are not clear, several kings appear to have ruled simultaneously, and it was only thanks to the efforts of Vizier Amenemhat that the country was not again divided (Aldred, 1987: 128).

Amenemhat himself, the most senior member of the administration, seized power and became the first king of the 12th dynasty, although precisely how this happened is not known. The royal residence was moved from Thebes to an area near Lake Faiyum that was given the name Itjtawy (Amenemhat-itj-tawy in its complete form) meaning "Amenemhat the seizer of the Two Lands". This shifted the centre of power further north so as to stay in the centre of the country (the role played by Memphis during the Old Kingdom) and Egypt subsequently enjoyed a period of peace and stability. Amenemhat I built his pyramid in Lisht, to some extent using stone from ancient buildings. However, 12th-dynasty pyramids are generally of lower quality, largely because they were built in brick and small blocks of stone that were rarely properly shaped.

Amenemhat I, who seems to have been assassinated, the victim of a palace coup, was succeeded by Senwosret I. The new king carried out several expeditions and a journey to Wadi Hammamat, campaigns in Asia Minor and above all in Nubia, which was conquered as far as the second cataract and controlled by mighty fortresses. Senwosret I's pyramid is also in Lisht, while that of his son Amenemhat II is in Dahshur.

Major construction work was begun in the reign of Senwosret II (and completed by Amenemhat III) to make better use of the Faiyum region. Senwosret II's pyramid is located near Lahun, alongside the remains of a city called Kahun that was built for the workers on the pyramid. Papyruses were found there with astronomical information that has enabled a more accurate chronology for the period to be established. Amenemhat III's pyramid is near Hawara, by the ruins of a large-scale construction that was called the Labyrinth, while a second pyramid that also belonged to him was built in Dahshur. The tombs of the members of the king's family (in both Dahshur and Lahun) included pieces of gold that had belonged to princesses and queens and are genuine masterpieces of jewellery. Under the 12th dynasty, local governors gained some independence and had magnificent tombs dug into rock, particularly in Elephantine Island, Asyut, Bersha and Beni Hassan. It was only in the reign of Senwosret III that the powerful provincial governors finally submitted to pharaonic power and royal centralisation was achieved.

During this time, relations with Syria-Palestine and Nubia became more intense (to Egypt's great benefit) and the Middle Kingdom would reach one of its peaks or "golden age" (Wildung, 1984). Whereas the Old Kingdom had first created *maet* and the First Intermediate Period had debated and thematised this elevated, central concept, it was the Middle Kingdom that actually implemented it. The more humanised spirit of the sovereigns may perhaps be seen from some of the statues from the period, and from the small obsidian head of Senwosret III from the Calouste Gulbenkian Museum (cat. no. 4), a magnificent example of the king as a good shepherd, zealously caring for the justice and well-being of the Egyptians, the "cattle of god". The administration of the age expressed its loyalty to the king and participated actively in running the country, producing loyal texts and hymns to the pharaoh which complement the many royal statues that were produced and placed in highly visible spots so that they could be admired in opposition to what had been the practice during the Old Kingdom. The court and provincial workshops produced fine statues that illustrate the artists' skills, and countless decorative and utilitarian objects were left in the officials' tombs.

Proof of the fruitful cultural and trading relations between Egypt and the neighbouring regions is confirmed by the so-called "treasure of Tod", as some of this group of silver and other metal objects (dating from the reign of Amenemhat II) came from Syria and the Aegean Sea area. Moreover, a well-known literary text called *The Story of Sinuhe,* an Egyptian official who lived in

Upper Retenu (Northern Syria), records relations with the Syria-Palestine region, praising Egypt's superiority over its Asiatic neighbours.

The Middle Kingdom reached its prime under Senwosret III, whose pyramid was built in Dahshur, and his son Amenemhat III, as an effective administration governed everything and the provincial governors were totally under royal power. Art and literature also scaled new heights of brilliance, while agriculture managed to conquer new fertile lands, especially in the Faiyum region. Nubia was subjected to an intense process of colonisation and Egyptianisation, while the movements of the troublesome Bedouin tribes from the "Corridors of Sand" (Shasu) in the northern area of conflict (the East Delta) were also under control. A system of fortifications called the "Prince's Wall" was built for this purpose and proved to be quite effective, demonstrating that the kings of the Middle Kingdom paid attention to controlling their frontiers.

The end of the $12^{th}$ dynasty – in which the death of Amenemhat IV (the son of Amenemhat III) without leaving any male heir and the unstable rule of Queen Neferusobek (also called Sobekneferu) were decisive factors – put the firm and cohesive centralised government that had brought pressure to bear on the great governmental stability. The $13^{th}$ and $14^{th}$ dynasties produced a series of insignificant kings, of whom little more than their names is known, and power was once again dispersed, as had happened in the First Intermediate Period.

Then, in the middle of the $17^{th}$ century BC, groups of nomads began to penetrate into Egypt. Most of them were armed and they started to concentrate in the Delta region before gradually heading south towards Memphis. These people were the Hyksos, a word that comes from the Egyptian term *Hekau-khasut*: "rulers of foreign countries".

At the end of the $12^{th}$ dynasty, groups of Asiatic immigrants had gradually and peacefully entered Egypt, acting as labour for the large-scale constructions that were then being built under Amenemhat III. The difference was that the entrance was now violent, and the invaders overcame the Egyptian defences as they had a new type of weaponry and attacked in light, horse-drawn chariots that were hitherto unknown in Egypt. These new lords of Egypt settled mainly in the North, basing their power in Avaris, in the East Delta. They also established relations with the Nubian rulers in an apparent attempt to catch the Thebans in a pincer movement, while the Asiatic kings gradually tried to adapt in a way that clearly suggests acculturation: the Hyksos kings adopted Egyptian names and worshipped the local gods, winning over the support of the peoples from the north, especially those from the Delta.

Meanwhile, the kings of Thebes fought back, with the last rulers from the $17^{th}$ dynasty embarking on an arduous struggle against the Hyksos and their Egyptian supporters from the north, engaging in a sort of struggle for "national freedom". This violent war would only end when the $18^{th}$ dynasty came to power (Bourriau, 2000: 184-217).

The New Kingdom was one of pharaonic Egypt's golden ages, a continuation in some senses of the Middle Kingdom, from which it was separated by the turbulent Hyksos period that had such an impact during the Second Intermediate Period. Like the Middle Kingdom, the era called the New Kingdom started with a powerful recovery movement that emerged from Thebes. The expulsion of the Hyksos by Ahmose, following a programme of restoration that had started under the $17^{th}$ dynasty, signalled the beginning of the $18^{th}$ dynasty, a period in which pharaonic Egypt became a world power (Bryan, 2000: 218-271). Several campaigns were carried out in

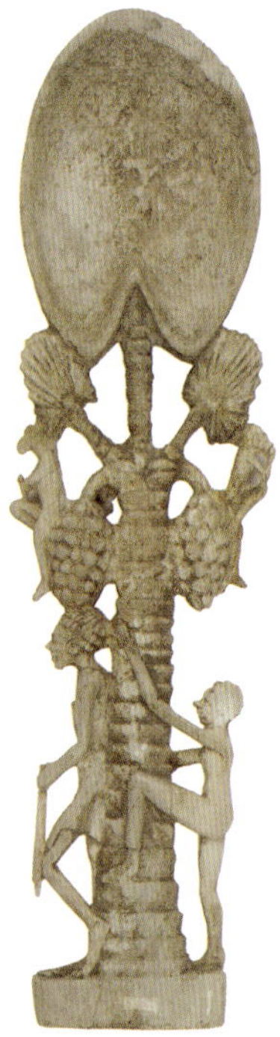

Ivory spoon for cosmetics, New Kingdom (cat. no. 9).

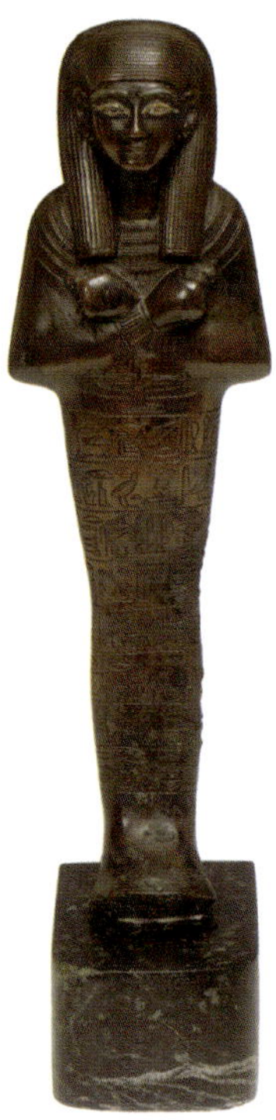

Funerary statuette of Hesmeref, New Kingdom (cat. no. 11).

Syria-Palestine and Nubia during the fruitful reign of Ahmose. His heir, Amenhotep I then extended Egypt's southern border into Nubia, and culture again flourished during his reign, exemplified by the Ebers Papyrus. This document not only provides information about some Ancient Egyptian medical knowledge, but also on the heliacal appearance of Sopdit, the star that the Greeks called Sothis (Sirius), which is extremely useful in establishing the chronology of Ancient Egypt. Thutmose I significantly expanded Egypt's possessions still further through campaigns that reached at least as far as the third cataract in Nubia and as far as the distant River Euphrates in Asia Minor. These expeditions used contingents of Nubian soldiers, and the granite head of a Nubian in the Collection may perhaps record that warfare (cat. no. 6). The small statuette of Mes (cat. no. 5), identical to many others from that age, also probably dated from the reign of Thutmose I or his predecessor Amenhotep I.

After the brief reign of the weak King Thutmose II, Thutmose III came to the throne, with Queen Hatshepsut acting as regent. She seized power and the pharaonic titulary for herself, ruling alongside Thutmose III until her death, staying on the throne for over twenty years thanks to the support of the priests of Amun and the administration. When Thutmose III finally became the sole ruler, he led victorious campaigns in Asia, bringing tribes and cities under his control and reaching as far as the Euphrates. Amenhotep II and Thutmose IV later led other expeditions to Syria, and the small head in glass paste that is part of the Gulbenkian Collection (cat. no. 8) may have belonged to one of these two pharaohs. However, Egypt lost some areas of the Asiatic region, and a peace treaty was signed with Mitanni in the reign of Thutmose IV. During the long and peaceful reign of Amenhotep III (which produced a small glass paste head in the Collection, cat. no. 7), Egypt enjoyed a period of exceptional prosperity, as shown by art from that age. Fine examples of the sophisticated work created at the end of the 18$^{th}$ dynasty include the small wooden statuettes in the Collection (cat. nos. 12, 13 and 14), the ivory "spoon" (cat. no. 9) and the beautiful funerary statuette of Hesmeref (cat. no. 11).

Following the peaceful reign of Amenhotep III, his son Amenhotep IV proclaimed Aten to be the sole god and prohibited worship of other gods, particularly Amun. Amenhotep IV changed his name to Akhenaten and shifted the royal residence to Akhetaten. Works of art produced in the peculiar Amarna style (so-called from the area's modern name), were created during this unusual period between 1364 and 1347 BC. Meanwhile, in Asia, the Hittites conquered Northern Syria and annexed the neighbouring kingdom of Mitanni, while various vassals of Egypt formed alliances with the Hittite Empire. The ruins of Amarna contain proof of intense correspondence in cuneiform script between the Egyptian court and the various states in Asia Minor. After the fleeting reign of Smenkhkara, young King Tutankhamun came to the throne, probably due to the influence of General Horemheb. During his brief, nine-year reign, he restored the religious situation to the state before Amenhotep IV and the royal city of Akhetaten was abandoned. Horemheb, who led the army, became the last pharaoh of the 18th dynasty after the brief reign of Kheperkheperura Ay. Tradition later saw Horemheb as the immediate successor to Amenhotep III, ignoring his four predecessors, who were all linked to the Amarna Period, a time that was to be forgotten and struck from history.

Under Horemheb, whose reign produced the stone fragment of the priest Ameneminet (cat. no. 15), Egypt restored some of its power in Asia, and Paramessu, the future King Rameses I, became vizier of the north and commander of the army during a period of conflict between Syria and the Hittites. The stele of the scribe Iry (cat. no. 10) may also date from that period.

The 19th dynasty started with Rameses I, who rose in the hierarchy under Horemheb and succeeded him at a late age. However, his reign was short-lived and he was succeeded by his son Sety I, whose name indicates that the god Set was increasingly popular at that time. Sety I led several victorious campaigns against tribes in Palestine and against Libya. His construction works included the great hypostyle hall in the temple at Karnak and a temple and cenotaph in Abydos, and his tomb is the largest in the Valley of the Kings. He was succeeded by Rameses II, who ruled for over sixty years and signed a peace treaty with the Hittites after a period of war that included the battle of Qadesh, whose results can be seriously questioned. Large-scale and important monuments were built during Rameses II's reign, including the temples of Abu Simbel and the Ramesseum. Under Merenptah, Egypt was attacked by Libyans and several peoples from Asia Minor (the so-called Sea Peoples), who continued their incursions into Egypt despite being defeated in the Delta. The end of the dynasty was a turbulent time, with the brief reigns of Amenmessu, Sety II and Siptah and of Queen Tausret, who tried in vain to rule as a pharaoh and imitate the brilliance of Queen Hatshepsut.

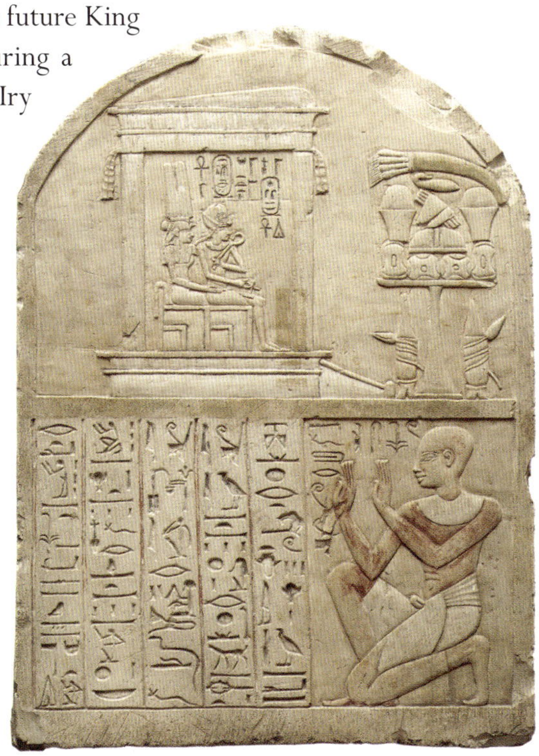

Stele of the scribe Iry, New Kingdom (cat. no. 10).

Under the New Kingdom, Nubia was a colony governed by a viceroy (the "King's son of Kush"); Canaan, Phoenicia and Syria were protectorates whose princes – many of whom were raised in Egypt – were vigilantly supervised by Egyptian officials; and the Asiatic kings sought alliances and friendship with the pharaoh and paid him tribute. At the time, profitable trade and cultural exchanges were established between Egypt and its neighbours, and peace was maintained through active diplomacy, although warfare was also employed to establish positions more forcefully. The monarch added the aura of a heroic warrior to his divine status, acting as the champion of Amun-Ra, the eminent leader of the war chariots. As in previous eras, he continued to be the dispenser of peace, well-being, generosity and justice, and thus the guarantor that *maet* was achieved. He awarded the senior administrative posts, including that of high priest of Amun, to men of his trust, who were not merely selected from among the hereditary nobles, but due to merit (and great military skills) so as to create upwards social mobility for those who could read and write.

The source of the wealth that Egypt used to support its prestige-based economy, which mainly focused on temples and tombs, came essentially from the rich area of Nubia, while the

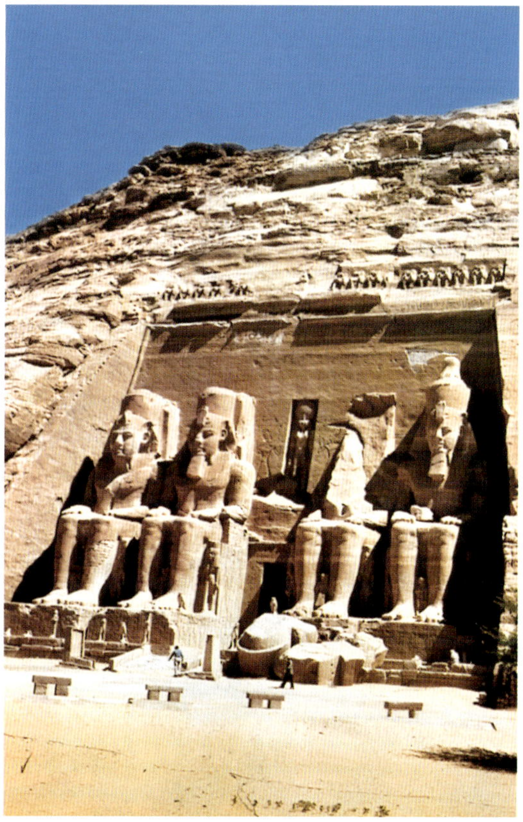

Façade of one of the rock temples at Abu Simbel, Nubia.

Syria-Palestine corridor also provided many products. The latter region was at peace for many years, thanks to constant vigilance from Egyptian garrisons and military expeditions at times of instability. Rather than the "Asiatic empire" that historiography created, it was more a "empire of transit" where the fundamental issue was to maintain peace on the caravan routes so that trade could flow.

The architecture of the New Kingdom is now clearly to be seen in some buildings such as the temples in Luxor and Karnak, as well as the funerary temples on the West Bank (Deir el-Bahri, the Ramesseum and Medinet Habu), the temples in Abu Simbel and (among others) the Osirian buildings in Abydos. Although these remains date from the reign of Amenhotep III, the taste for massive buildings reached its peak under Rameses II.

This period produced fine artwork in terms of reliefs, sculpture, painting and the decorative arts, while also signalling the peak of lyric and love poetry. The former tradition of scholar literature, stories and hymns also continued, while a major new literary form emerged: highly individual historiographical texts in praise of the triumphant monarch.

The 20$^{th}$ dynasty, founded by Sethnakht, was immediately faced by another invasion by the Sea Peoples, who attacked the multiple mouths of the Nile Delta. Rameses III drove them off at great cost, and his reign still manages to suggest an Egypt that was rich, dynamic and where there was no shortage of major constructions, such as those in Medinet Habu. From then onwards, several kings – all of whom had the prestigious name of Rameses (from IV to XI) – governed for periods of varying length and difficulties, while the high priests of Amun gradually became richer and more powerful. At the end of the final dynasty, while the pharaoh governed from the Delta, civil war broke out in Thebes between the viceroy of Nubia, Panehsy (whose name means "the Black"), and the high priest of Amun, Amenhotep. Panehsy tried to travel up the Nile and attack to the north of Thebes, but was ultimately pushed back into Nubia. Power was then assumed by one of the generals of the Egyptian army called Herihor, who was of Libyan origin. The nineteenth year of the reign of Rameses XI saw the beginning of the period called Uhemmesut or the "repeated birth" (the renaissance of Egypt after the time of chaos). Although Herihor proclaimed himself pharaoh, his act seems not to have been taken very seriously. In the meantime, Rameses XI and the New Kingdom – which had lasted some five hundred years – both disappeared.

The pharaohs of the New Kingdom were all buried in the Valley of the Kings, in Western Thebes, and their tombs – apart from the humble and secondary tomb of the famous Tutankhamun – were all pillaged. The hope that the site of the royal burials in an inaccessible and well-guarded place could be kept a secret did not work. However, some officials were more successful as they were buried in an area (wrongly called the "Valley of the Nobles") whose tombs remained untouched. Although such tombs are rare, the finds still give a fair idea of the high standard of living enjoyed by officials in this cosmopolitan era.

Administrative chaos set in and there were sacrilegious attacks on the tombs in the Valley of the Kings, the priests of Amun gained autonomy, Syria-Palestine stopped paying tribute, the administration itself became corrupt and participated in pillaging the royal tombs, an economic crisis arose that even prevented payment of the customary foodstuffs to the workers in the Valley of the Kings (who went on strike), the contingents of mercenaries in Egypt became insubordinate, there were successive disastrous floods, the grain-stores were empty and the pharaohs only ruled for short periods. Given all this, the New Kingdom finally came to an end (Van Dijk, 2000: 272-313).

Using the classical system, the following period is known as the Third Intermediate Period (1070-664 BC). This started with the 21st dynasty, whose well-known kings are buried in the perimeter of the great temple of Amun in Tanis, the capital of the north and theoretically of all Egypt. The royal tombs in Tanis contained exceptionally precious works, including the gilded mask of Psusennes I and his silver sarcophagus, which demonstrate a certain recovery in Egypt following the turbulent latter days of the New Kingdom. However, authority in the south was in the hands of the powerful high priests of Amun, who also formed a dynasty of their own. In fact, some even adopted the royal titulary around their names, framed in cartouches (Taylor, 2000: 330-368).

This period was followed by the 22nd dynasty, of Libyan origin, which was founded by Sheshonq I in 945 BC. The new dynasty was initially quite dynamic, making renewed military advances in Palestine and restarting the large-scale work on the great temple of Amun in Karnak. Another characteristic of this period was the production of countless high-quality bronze objects, as already found in the previous dynasty. Yet the existence of rival dynasties and the dogged resistance shown by Thebes to rule by the lords of Libyan origin ultimately left the country in a state of chaos. The secession of Prince Pedubast (818-787 BC) – portrayed in a superb (albeit fragmented) torso in the Gulbenkian Collection (cat. no. 16) – brought a new dynasty that ruled from Leontopolis (the source of a small bronze lion in the storeroom of the Egyptian collection). Pedubast' secession was the defining example of the squabbles in which Libyan leaders were embroiled at that time, and this 23rd dynasty was duly replaced by a rival dynasty, the 24th, led by the Egyptianised Libyan Tefnakht of Sais.

The subsequent Nubian rulers from the 25th dynasty would try to restore order to Egypt, doing so in the name of Amun and calling for the need to restore the much weakened *maet* in that unstable age. They managed to seize control over the North and establish their daughters as the official divine adoratrice (or "god's wife") of Amun in Thebes. However, the Assyrians were then advancing along the Syria-Palestine corridor and the two powers would soon come into conflict, with Memphis falling in the ensuing war. Everything came to a halt with the unthinkable sack of the temple of Amun in Karnak and the expulsion of the last Nubian ruler (Tanutamani), who sought refuge in the inaccessible area of Kush, in Upper Nubia.

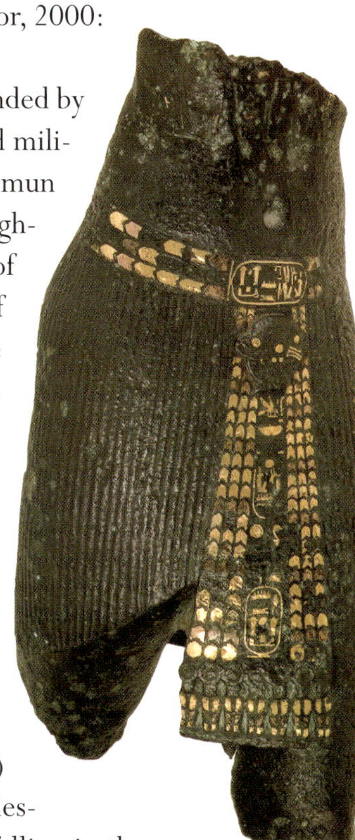

Torso of Prince Pedubast, 23rd dynasty (cat. no. 16).

Psamtek I, the ruler of Sais, forced out the last garrisons of the Assyrians and their allies, which were mostly stationed in the Delta, and then seized power throughout the country. Having initially had the support of the Assyrian occupants, they were then expelled and he embarked on a policy of absorbing his rivals either through diplomacy or force. By approximately the eighth year of his reign, he had become the lord of the Two Lands. His daughter was made the divine adoratrice of Amun, reviving a policy that the Libyan and Nubian rulers from the previous dynasties had employed and thus gaining supremacy over the Theban priests of Amun, although by that stage, they had already lost much of their former influence. Psamtek I also used the efficient services of Greek and Carian mercenaries to impose his rule, and tenaciously managed to overcome the internal and external difficulties. His name is inscribed on a limestone statuette in the Gulbenkian Collection that belonged to the senior official Bes (cat. no. 28).

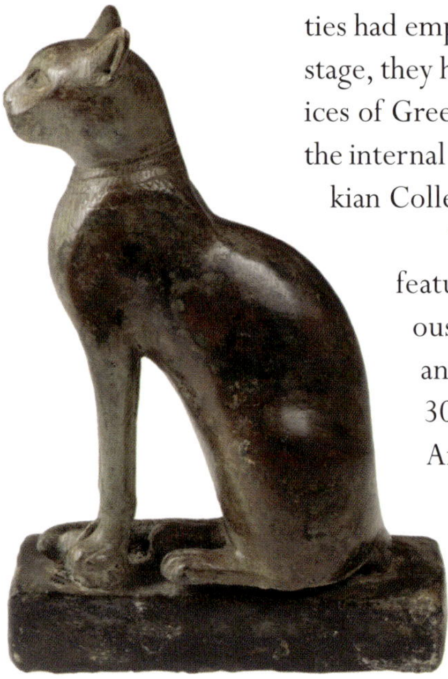

Statuette of a cat, Late Period (cat. no. 30).

The 26th dynasty, begun by Psamtek I (664-610 BC), was a period of prosperity that featured the revival of art (although this intentionally copied the art-forms from previous times), the revival of the Delta's cults and deities, the increase in zoolatry (sacred animals as hypostases of the gods), exemplified by the statuettes of cats (see nos. 29, 30 and 31) and the bull Apis (in the Egyptian collection at the Museu Nacional de Arqueologia), Greek influence, especially in the north, and the subordination of the recalcitrant priests of Amun to the power of the Saite monarchs (Lloyd, 2000: 369-394).

Psamtek I was succeeded by his son Nekau (610-595 BC), who wished to take steps in Northern Syria to prevent the advancing Chaldeans, but suffered a crushing defeat in Carchemish (Upper Euphrates). Evidently, Egyptian texts and monuments do not mention this failure, but it seems to have inspired a voyage to circumnavigate Africa from East to West. Sadly, there is no conclusive proof that this voyage took place. Psamtek II (595-589 BC) brought renewed interest in Nubia. Egyptian forces invaded and – with the help of Greek and Carian soldiers – reached as far as the fourth cataract. The highpoint of the dynasty came under Apries (589-570 BC) and Ahmose (570-526 BC), when relations with the neighbouring Greek world were strengthened and the city of Naukratis – a main centre for trade and cultural exchanges – was founded, including temples with Greek and Egyptian gods. As if to counter the growing Greek influence, a nationalistic reaction brought about repetition of art-forms from Egypt's glorious past.

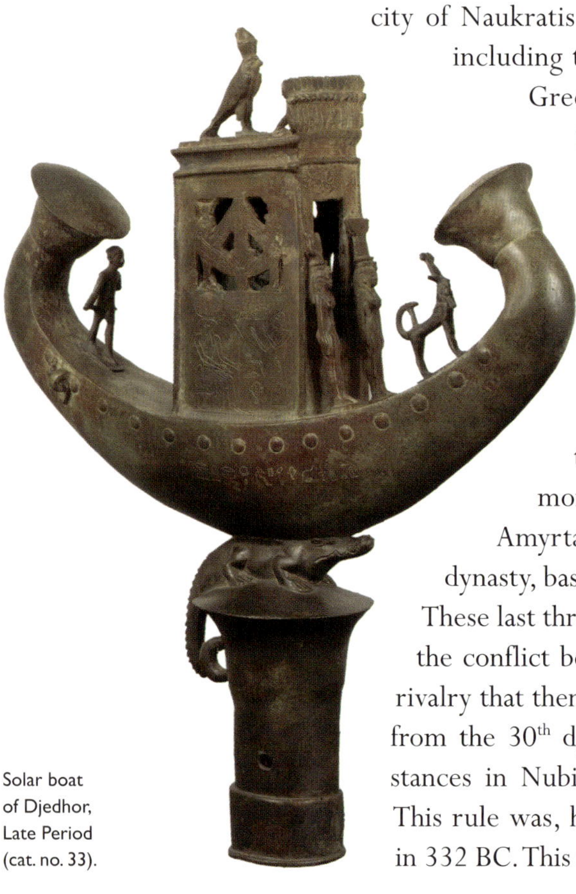

Solar boat of Djedhor, Late Period (cat. no. 33).

The Persian invasion under Cambyses at the start of the reign of Psamtek III brought the 26th dynasty to a close. The Persians conquered Egypt in 525 BC and turned the country into a satrapy within the great Achaemenid Empire. Some Egyptian officials also supported the new kings, who formed the 27th dynasty. Under Darius I, the kingdom experienced a period of peace and major constructions, but Persian control became oppressive under Xerxes. Shortly after, the Achaemenids were expelled and Egypt started its last, ephemeral moment of independence under the 28th dynasty (with just one king called Amyrtaios, who expelled the Persians with the help of Greek troops), the 29th dynasty, based in Mendes (three kings) and the 30th dynasty (also with three kings). These last three dynasties were engaged in constant fighting against the Persians, and the conflict between Egypt and Persia was the regional form of the Greco-Persian rivalry that then afflicted the entire Eastern Mediterranean. The last Egyptian pharaoh from the 30th dynasty was Nectanebo II, who disappeared under unknown circumstances in Nubia, and in 343 BC, the Persians again took control of the country. This rule was, however, short-lived as the troops under Alexander the Great arrived in 332 BC. This revivalist last dynasty left significant works of art, including the beautiful gilded funerary mask (cat. no. 32) and the solar barque of Djedhor (cat. no. 33), from the Gulbenkian Collection.

The Greco-Roman period (332 BC-395 AD) started with the end of the Persian domination of Egypt and the arrival of the Greco-Macedonian conquerors under Alexander, who founded the new capital in Alexandria, in the West Delta. When the empire was divided up after Alexander's death in 323 BC, General Ptolemy became first the governor of Egypt and then king in 305 BC, establishing the Ptolemaic dynasty that was to reign for some three-hundred years. The monarch was seen as an incarnation of two kings: one for the Greeks (the *basileus*); the other for the Egyptians (the *nesu-bit*), with the charisma of one or the other dominating according to circumstances (Sales, 2005: 307-308). Likewise, they had themselves portrayed in pharaonic poses, as clearly shown by the low-relief of a Ptolemaic ruler in the Collection (cat. no. 36).

Greek became the official language under the Ptolemaic dynasty, and the Greek influence in art, literature, the administration and military organisation continued throughout the next three hundred years, until the death of the famous Queen Cleopatra VII (30 BC). Yet even under Roman rule, the impact of Greek cultural influence was maintained. The Egyptians, the occupiers and many foreigners (namely Syrians) who moved to Egypt under the Roman Empire worshipped the traditional gods in large temples and crowded shrines, even though new deities had been introduced. The latter group included gods from the Greco-Roman pantheon, as demonstrated by the Collection's fragmented torso of Venus Anadiomene (cat. no. 40). The outstanding works of art from the Greco-Roman Period often adhered to the canons of Egyptian art, as again shown by several later objects from the Calouste Gulbenkian Collection (cat. nos. 34, 35, 37, 38 and 39).

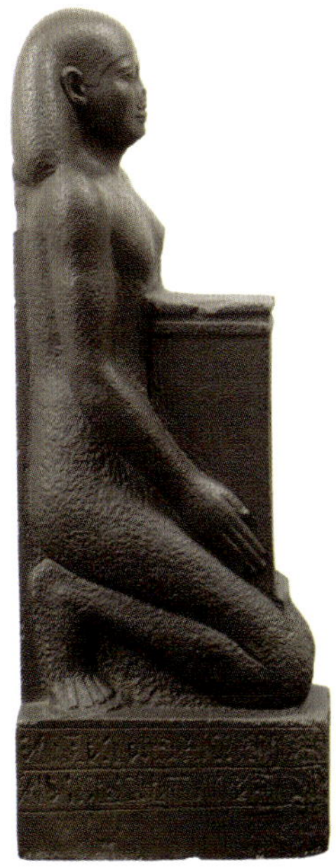

Statue of Djedhor, Greco-Roman Period (cat. no. 34).

At the request of the Ptolemaic dynasty which was then in power, the Romans gradually started to intervene in Egypt's major internal issues, and they ultimately conquered it and turned the country of the Nile into a province of the Roman Empire, albeit one with a special status as it was directly subordinate to the emperor. Much of the wheat that supplied Rome flowed out of Egypt. The Greek cultural influence was maintained under Roman rule, and many buildings that are typical of the Greco-Roman world were built across Egypt, such as hippodromes, theatres and baths. Roman influence was felt in many aspects of Egyptian life, ranging from the manufacture of simple household tools to literature, art and religion. Several emperors appeared in the low-reliefs on temples (Edfu, Kom Ombo and Philae) and statues in the traditional pose of the pharaohs, some of whom had actually been to Egypt (Vespasian, Hadrian, Septimius Severus and Caracalla).

The Greco-Roman Period is habitually divided into three complementary phases: the Macedonian Dynasty, with Alexander and his direct successors (Philip Arrhidaeus and Alexander IV); the Ptolemaic Dynasty (305-30 BC); and the Roman Period (30 BC-395 AD). The Greco-Macedonian and Roman rulers generally enjoyed the more or less tacit support of the Egyptian priests and officials, many of whom noted the benefits of working with the authorities. One of those to co-operate was the priest Petosiris, from Hermopolis, who served Alexander and left some wise words on his tomb. These words, which could have been said by one of his educated predecessors from many centuries before, emphasising the importance of achieving *maet*, which encouraged the practice of justice and solidarity among men, read as follows: "The great reward for good is eternal life".

Winged scarab, Late Period (cat. no. 19).

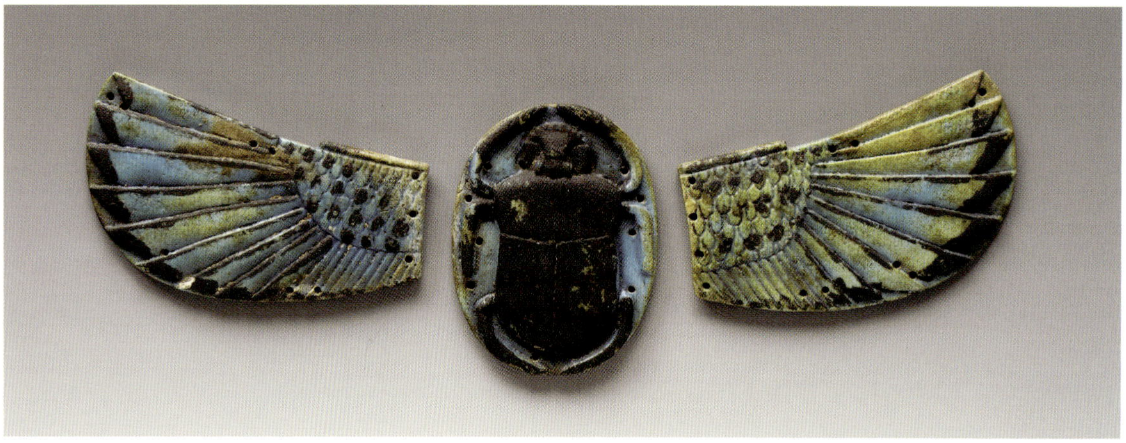

## CHRONOLOGY

| | | |
|---|---|---|
| Neolithic | | ca. 6000-4500 BC |
| Pre-dynastic Period | | ca. 4500-3000 BC |
| Early Dynastic Period | *(1st and 2nd dynasties)* | ca. 3000- 2660 BC |
| Old Kingdom | *(3rd-6th dynasties)* | ca. 2660-2180 BC |
| First Intermediate Period | *(7th-11th dynasties)* | ca. 2180-2040 BC |
| Middle Kingdom | *(11th and 12th dynasties)* | ca. 2040-1780 BC |
| Second Intermediate Period | *(13th-17th dynasties)* | ca. 1780-1550 BC |
| New Kingdom | *(18th-20th dynasties)* | ca. 1550-1070 BC |
| Third Intermediate Period | *(21st-25th dynasties)* | ca. 1070-664 BC |
| Late period | *(26th-30th dynasties)* | 664-332 BC |
| Greco-Roman Period | | 332 BC-395 AD |
| Coptic (Byzantine) Period | | 395-642 AD |

Chronology based on *Le Monde Égyptien: Les Pharaons* (3 volumes, Paris: Gallimard, 1978-1980), directed by Jean Leclant, in turn based on the work of Erik Hornung, Richard Parker and Jürgen von Beckerath.

# THE ART OF ANCIENT EGYPT

All Ancient Egyptian art – embracing architecture, statues, low-reliefs, painting and the decorative arts – was firmly based on geography, landscape, religion and political ideology. Thus, it was governed in terms of canons and *maet* by two firmly interlinked key forces: religion and royalty. In fact, although Egyptian art was clearly inspired by religion (like other activities), it was subject to the tacit approval of the pharaoh, who was seen as a genuine artistic patron and the driving forced behind the building programmes.

Created with pure, majestic lines, laden with mystery and active symbolism, and containing traces of an appealing magical force, although this art took diverse forms, it transmits a sense of the eternal and a profound feeling of calm and dignity. This was because Egyptian art – like all pharaonic Egypt's humanist civilisation – was based on the high guiding principles of *maet*. Within the aesthetic context, this can be translated as harmony, balance, truth and formal order. There was no premeditated intention of creating beauty, at least not according to our notion of beauty, which is heavily influenced by the Greco-Roman vision of the world. The Egyptians' profoundly humanised vision of the world produced an art that intentionally reflected a balanced and fruitful sense of proportion (Aldred, 1980: 13).

It is through art that Ancient Egyptian civilisation is best known today. The hallmarks of the country that most delight or enthral nowadays are the pyramids, the majestic temples, the figures of the gods, the jewels, the hieroglyphs, the sarcophagi, which all combine to form the "classical" vision of Egypt. The art produced over a period of three thousand years created these images that still today appear in a fascinating and seductive way.

Therefore, it is Ancient Egypt's unique and instantly recognisable art that still lives and attracts people, while the subtleties of the cosmogonies and divine families, the controversies surrounding the chronologies, interpretations of the texts and socio-economic questions are left to specialists and scholars. The art is enjoyed, admired and appreciated, yet curiously, the Egyptians did not create a word to define "art". Moreover, many of the objects that we look at in wonder and consider to be true "works of art" in museum display-cases were not even made to be seen! In fact, these fine objects were to be "used" for all eternity in the next world. Consequently, these pieces had a function. Whether made of gold or alabaster, bronze or terracotta, the jars, plates, bowls, rings, bracelets, necklaces, wigs, mirrors, beds, caskets, weapons, insignias, sandals, and even the sarcophagi, funerary masks, amulets and statuettes had a purpose: to serve the deceased person in the next world, even though many of them (such as the personal adornments) may have been worn or used during the owner's lifetime.

In a work published in the middle of the eighteenth century, J. Winckelmann claimed that art from antiquity went through a primitive phase (Egyptian art), a golden phase (Greek art) and a decline (Roman art). This simplistic scheme was criticised by Champollion, who plausibly argued that Egyptian art was autonomous, different and above all had different motivations and goals that the German scholar could naturally not understand. Thus, Winckelmann could never have realised that the Egyptians always remained true to their typical "aspective" vision of the world and things, deconstructing the parts to create a whole. Indeed, this is not always easy to understand since the combination of these parts gives the end result a somewhat "unreal" and sometimes "inconceivable" appearance, while emphasising a harmonious whole.

In order to understand Egyptian art, it is fundamental to comprehend what Heinrich Schäffer called *geradvorstellung*, the Egyptian method of representation based on frontal images. Emma Brunner-Traut in turn reinterpreted this as "aspective" art, so as to differentiate it from perspective vision, which Egyptian artists simply did not have. These artists showed things "part for part as it really and ideally *is*" (Schäffer, 1986: 422-424), and each part was created separately, without being seen from one single viewpoint.

Today, we admire works of Egyptian art for their harmonious proportion and the intelligent way in which they combine forms, materials and colours. This applies to jewellery, statues, sets of funerary vessels, amulets, reliefs and paintings, all of which were ultimately produced by experienced and skilled craftsmen for one sole purpose: to be useful and efficient. Moreover, the efficacy of most of these objects was further heightened by the dynamic protective power of the hieroglyph inscriptions.

In other words, the works of art that impress and delight us through their balance, grace, colour, elegance, mystery, harmony, sophistication and beauty were created by craftsmen/artists (by officials in the broadest sense) so that they could be used (i.e. work) and provide man with well-being in this and the next world. As Jean Vercoutter said, there was no intention to make them "beautiful" or "harmonious", a statement that applies equally to small objects or statuettes and to colossal statues, obelisks, steles, temples, pyramids...

These definitions can be clearly and completely applied to the art of statuary. Pharaonic Egypt had no concept of "art for art's sake", and the artist (understood in today's terms and as the Greeks already then used it) did not exist. Therefore, whether Egyptian statues portrayed a pharaoh or an official, were receptacles of life that were complemented by the living internal presence of the subject's *ka*. Since *ka* was the life force or the individual's invisible double, the statue (animated by the *ka* at its heart) became an extension of the person himself, usefully fulfilling the purpose for which the statue had been created. As Egyptian art is more of a means than an end, the artist's goal was to create statues whose essential features were accurate, so that they could – through the power of magic – be useful and efficacious. In fact, as Egyptian art was fundamentally utilitarian, it was also a magical art. Ultimately, starting from a mythological vision of the universe and moving onto a magical manipulation of the energies that gave life, the craftsman created beings that were as real as those created by nature (Yoyotte, 1970: 25).

Since (as said) Egyptian art acted as a whole, both sculpture and painting formed an integral part of architecture. The potentially most disturbing aspects for anyone who looks closely at Egyptian statues – particularly those made of stone, but regardless of whether the figure is seated, kneeling or standing – are their hieratic nature, immobility and compactness. Wall-paintings and reliefs may confuse the viewer due to the figures' unusual (even unrealistic) poses or images where the trees and houses are positioned in a rather incongruent (perhaps even "childlike") way in the space, or the crowded altars with several floating objects. Egyptian artists preferred to depict things as they were (projective geometry) rather than as they appeared (perspective geometry), and did so by capturing the perennial nature of the forms rather than their transitory appearance (Aldred, 1980: 15).

The canons for painting were the same as for reliefs, so human figures were shown according to a vision that aimed to reveal the essence of the image, often altering the object's proportions and normal appearance. There are also some typical canons that were maintained, such as darker colours for men and paler colours for women. Within painting, mural art reached its peak during the reign of Thutmose IV ($18^{th}$ dynasty), producing its finest work on Theban tombs. One paradigmatic aspect of pictorial art was the absence of time, since looking at a mural – created without any time framework – does not show either the time of day or the occasion.

From a very early stage, the forms in reliefs and paintings were dominated by an "aspective" deconstruction of the human body. Thus, the figure's face appears in profile yet the eye is depicted frontally; the chest is also seen frontally but the body then twists so that the belly is shown in three-quarters, and the arms and legs are in profile. The figure is consequently seen in three dimensions and reveals the essence of all the anatomical forms, even if figures sometimes appear to have two left feet.

Fundamentally, the art of portrayal that dominated in Ancient Egypt was essentially evocative, in keeping with the "substantially magical mechanism" (Barocas, 1987: 38) rather than descriptive or narrative. Given this intellectualisation when recreating forms, it is little wonder that the artists/craftsmen spurned perspective, since it hid and distorted reality. Fundamentally, it was important to deconstruct the objects so as to capture and understand their essence better. This procedure explains the foodstuffs floating over the altars and offering-tables, and the accumulation of images on successive levels, since the taste for symmetry and harmony was always a prime concern. In sum, it was an intellectual art-form that was guided by a highly developed system of thinking, a "true metaphysic" (Lalouette, 1996: 53).

Despite minor alterations, these characteristics would be maintained for three thousand years of creating art and tools, revealing an evolution in forms while the underlying ideas clearly survived. Some pieces do demonstrate foreign influences in the manufacture and finishing of statues, paintings and objects. However, even these always have an Egyptian background, shown by the search for aesthetic options that are in line with the vision of the universe and the development of forms that had been established in the early days, even in Egypt's prehistoric phase under the Naqada culture. Then again, the forms in statues, reliefs and paintings alike generally demonstrate a remarkable coherence. These aspects of Egyptian artwork reveal a love of timelessness and an obsession with the eternal (Daumas, 1987: 394-396).

The decorative arts, which could more accurately be called the arts of metamorphosis, complemented the other art-forms. Large quantities of objects were produced, from furniture to jewels, and with particular emphasis on tomb-goods, such as sarcophagi, funerary masks, canopic jars, funerary statuettes, amulets and scarabs, the last of which were used both by the living and the dead. All these had a protective magic and were created by craftsmen who were producing a work (*kat*) by manufacturing these objects. The Gulbenkian Collection includes fine examples of these funerary objects, while sarcophagi and canopic jars can be seen at the Museu da Farmácia, Museu Nacional de Arqueologia, Museu de História Natural (Faculdade de Ciências), University of Oporto, and the Sociedade de Geografia de Lisboa.

Egyptian craftsmen proved to be particularly skilled at creating other types of work included glass, pottery, baskets and weaving, although many of these objects have been lost as they were made of fragile materials. Nonetheless, some such pieces found in tombs bear witness to a wealth of utilitarian items produced with considerable artistic sophistication (Sales, 2000: 109-119).

Everything started in the long prehistoric phase of the Palaeolithic. Thanks to the finds made in Abasseia, Thebes-Waset, Kharga (Lower and Middle Palaeolithic), Kom Ombo and Faiyum (Lower Palaeolithic), among other areas, the well-known industry producing so-called Acheulean bifacial hand-axes and chipped-stone (Levallois-Mousterian) tools can be identified at a period between two million and thirty thousand years ago.

It is a short step from the rock paintings in Egypt's desert borderlands (part of the broader field of Saharan pictorial art) and the production of pottery to the appearance of the Badarian and Naqada cultures. These later cultures left many copper and stone tools, geometrical palettes decorated with animal forms, stone and pottery jars with a variety of decorations and a range of adornments. Beautiful polished red pottery decorated with a yellowish-white colour reveals geometrical motifs on a red ground and a taste for the stylised depiction of animals and men, while many vessels called "black-topped jars" were also produced (present in the collections of the Museu da Farmácia and Museu Nacional de Arqueologia).

The unification of Egypt (ca. 3000 BC) produced an outstanding work of art – the Narmer Palette – that had a significant political and cultural message. This schist plaque bears inscriptions on both sides and records the unification of the Two Lands, acting as a sort of birth certificate for Egypt. Since this work of art is fundamental in terms of understanding the iconography, themes, forms and ideology that would continue for a further three thousand years, I will briefly summarise previous studies (Araújo, 2001: 101-102). The famous Narmer Palette depicts a king with his symbols of power, standing in a dignified pose. His face is shown in profile, while his eyes are seen frontally, as is his chest. His trunk then turns until his legs are shown in profile, making the canonical movement of stepping forward with his left leg. Behind him is an official (in smaller scale), while the falcon Horus – representing the king himself – is in front of him. Two defeated, naked enemies in twisted poses and with no supporting base lie beneath him. The name of the monarch (Narmer) appears at the top, flanked by two cow-heads that represent the goddess Hathor. The unification of the country is recorded in hieroglyph script, which is also seen on the six papyruses in the image of his defeated enemy. Since each of the papyruses corresponds to six thousand, this states that Horus Narmer captured six thousand enemies. The reverse again bears the monarch's name at the top, flanked by the protecting goddess *Hathor*. In this case, the king appears in the foreground, carrying a pear-shaped mace and the *nekhakha* sceptre (the symbol of Lower Egypt, which he captured), marching solemnly. His officials appear in smaller scale, and he is preceded by personifications of the four provinces that helped in his campaign as he advances on a group of ten decapitated enemies. The central section shows two mythological animals held firmly by two men. As these beasts are based on Mesopotamian models, they demonstrate the Sumerian influence that can be observed when unified Egypt emerged. The lower section contains the image of a bull (the king) using his powerful horns to knock down the walls of an enemy city while simultaneously treading on his defeated adversary.

The Narmer Palette reveals some of the canons of Egyptian figurative art that would survive for many centuries and that are superbly documented by the objects in exhibition at the Calouste Gulbenkian Museum. These include an evident appreciation of the quest for balance and the almost obsessive desire for symmetrical forms; the insistence on depicting animals, which were largely seen as manifestations of power or hypostases of the deities; the interplay of proportions, where different sizes appeared according to the importance of the person portrayed; the clear preference for "aspective" depiction of things; the compulsory line at the base to support the

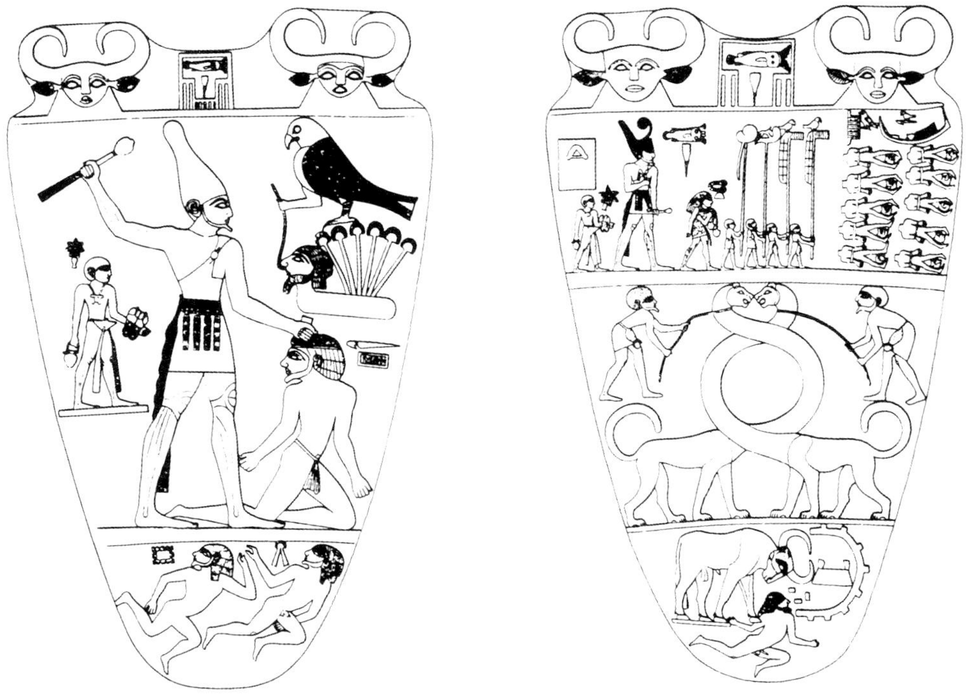

The Narmer Palette: on one side, the king wearing the crown of Upper Egypt, on the other, wearing the crown of Lower Egypt. Egyptian Museum, Cairo

figures; the use of a symbolism associated to exercising power, with crowns, sceptres, attire and other insignia. On one side, the king is wearing the white crown of Upper Egypt, while he has the red crown Lower Egypt on the other, as well as a bull's tail around his waist and the divine mace. The pointed contrast between the dignified, hieratic pose of the Egyptians and the twisted, unsupported pose of the enemy, who are portrayed as expressions of chaos, is also of note.

This famous palette is just one example of the production of countless objects from the proto-historical period found in the collections of some Portuguese museums, particularly the various pottery vessels and zoomorphic and geometrical palettes at the Museu da Farmácia and the Museu Nacional de Arqueologia.

Funerary constructions developed under the 1st (Thinite) dynasty, and large brick tombs with wooden beams were built in Abydos and Saqqara. This involved the underground image of the royal palace designed for eternity, while such tombs also extended to senior officials who also had their palaces for eternity (*per-djet*).

Egyptian architecture's specific forms make it instantly recognisable. It cannot be confused with the building work produced in other civilisations, and essentially reveals the religious nature of its tombs and temples. The early royal tombs, built between 3100 and 3000 BC, have an interrupted brick wall, adopting a Mesopotamian-influenced style that is normally called "palace façade", while other influences of the same sort also appeared, such as the cylinder seals and thematic motifs on decorating objects. Archaic architecture particularly features tombs in the typical *mastaba* form, built in large royal necropolises in Saqqara (for the king's body) and Abydos (for his viscera).

Egyptian tombs are normally divided into two parts: the private area holding the mummified body of the deceased and his goods for use in eternity; and the public space, where family members and priests (the priests of the *ka*) from the funerary cult would go. *Mastabas* originally had no funerary shrine, but simply a stele with the name of the deceased. Holes were dug near royal *mastabas* for servants and concubines, suggesting that at the time, several servants of the dead king were ritually killed so that they could accompany him on his journey to the next world. Yet the large *mastaba* of Horus Qa'a, the last king from the 1st dynasty, has no traces of any surrounding ritual tombs, while a funerary shrine appears for the first time adjacent to the tomb. This is a clear sign of Egyptian civilisation's humanist nature, putting an end to human sacrifice and progressively replacing servants of the king and major lords first with images engraved on the tomb walls, then with wooden statuettes (First Intermediate Period) and, as from the Middle Kingdom, with the typical funerary statuettes called *shabtis* or *ushebtis*, which were left in the tombs to work the land for their lords in the next world.

In artistic terms, the Old Kingdom was profoundly marked by colossal architecture of a funerary nature, the most famous of which is the pyramid shape. A major innovation appeared in North Saqqara during the reign of Netjerikhet Djoser (3rd dynasty) thanks to the mastery of royal architect Imhotep, who added five *mastabas* in diminishing size on a large initial *mastaba* to form the "Step Pyramid". The other major novelty was that the entire construction was made in stone. The funerary complex also included a large courtyard with a central altar, a north-facing funerary shrine alongside the tomb and a crypt (*serdab*) to keep the statue of the king's *ka*, two large shrines (one evoking the north; the other the south), and a series of small shrines flanking the courtyard that were designed to host the magical protective ceremony known as *sed*-festival (royal jubilee) to rejuvenate the king. Facing south, there is also a cenotaph and a long vestibule with columns decorated to look like fasces set into the walls, which start from the single door to the complex, located to the southwest. The entire complex was set inside a high stone wall that is now seriously damaged. The inaccessible crypt where the king's body was laid to rest was cut into the limestone at a depth of over twenty metres and decorated with fine faience panels and low-reliefs, a decoration that would disappear in the 4th and 5th-dynasty crypts before reappearing in the reign of Unas.

As from the 4th dynasty, the underground crypts used in the Early Dynastic Period and the one dug into the virgin rock for Djoser's burial chamber were replaced by vaults that had varying degrees of complexity. These ranged from the imposing roofing slabs on the Great Pyramid of Khufu, with the weight-relieving chambers in the higher levels, to the heavy vaulted or angled slabs in other pyramids.

This type of funerary architecture was a stone expression of three complementary types of worship: the cult of Osiris (where the king's body was buried in the earth), solar worship (shown by the tomb's pyramid form, evoking the sun's rays as they fall on the earth and the dead pharaoh's ascension to heaven) and the star cult (where the funerary shrine and entrance to the crypt face north towards the great pole star).

This type of architecture developed from the 3rd dynasty onwards, leading to the famous Old Kingdom and Middle Kingdom complexes, particularly the large pyramids in Giza: pyramids with perfect lines, a funerary temple facing east or high temple, a surrounding wall, a paved causeway and a reception temple in the valley or lower temple (Lehner, 1997: 106-135).

The 5th dynasty signalled the peak of the solar cult, with the construction of temples devoted to the sun-god Ra, who was considered to be the father of the pharaoh. The monarchs from this dynasty built pyramids in the Abusir area, apart from Userkaf (the first king) and Unas (the last), who opted instead for Saqqara, in the shadow of the already ancient step pyramid of Netjenikhet Djoser. Unas' pyramid was the first to contain mural inscriptions, the "Pyramid Texts", comprising beautiful hieroglyphs carved into the crypt walls and access corridors, a practice that would be maintained in subsequent pyramids. The royal funerary complexes were highly decorated with relief-work in the funerary temples and the paved processional causeways that led to the temple, as can be concluded from the various surviving fragments from the complexes of several monarchs, specifically Userkaf and Sahura.

The tombs of Old Kingdom officials also hold fine examples of relief-work and murals, especially in Saqqara and Giza. The sculptors had vast spaces on the tomb walls so that they could produce their compositions on several superimposed levels. Such images comprise a large-scale portrait of the tomb's owner, often accompanied by his relatives, and pleasant landscapes that are full of life and colour, with abundant flora and fauna, also including peasants and craftsmen engaging in their various activities. The proportional relationship involving the humans, animals and plants demonstrates that the artist is not reproducing scenes as they were seen, but instead idealising a world that was to be renewed in the next world. These superb low-reliefs were then painted, although most of the original colour has since been lost. The Gulbenkian Collection has a fragment of a low-relief from the tomb wall of the *mastaba* of Merytites (cat. no. 2).

The statues produced during the Old Kingdom would maintain the basics of the work created in the Early Dynastic Period, emphasising the colossal and imposing aspect while giving the works a clearly more compact feeling. Statues portraying individuals also demonstrate a sense of solidity and cohesion, showing the figures sitting in large chairs whose bases, seats and backs reveal the large rectangular block that had been hewn from the rock. The preferred stones included diorite, granite, schist, basalt, alabaster and limestone, the last of which is easier to carve. These materials were used to create statues of the rulers, as the artists tried to express the omnipotence and divinity of the monarchs from the Old Kingdom in poses of eternal and serene maturity. Meanwhile, stone and wood statues of private individuals demonstrate the search for realism as they try to capture the subject at the highest point of his life, imposes displaying an air of dynamic sobriety and dignity.

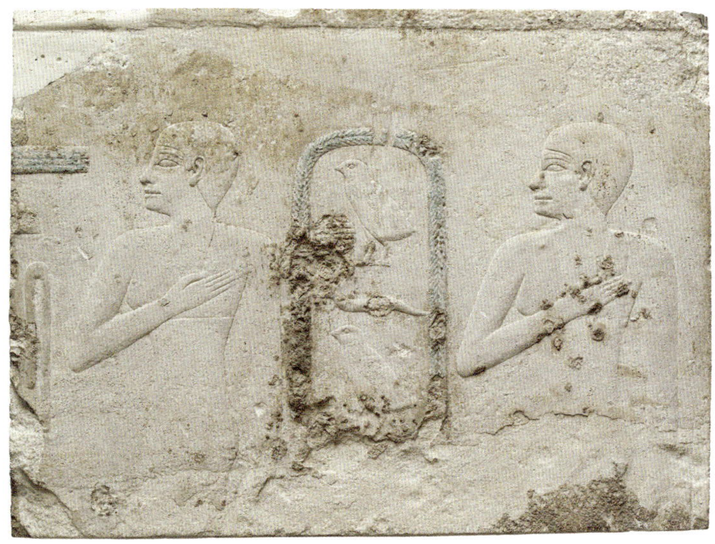

Low-relief of Princess Merytites, Old Kingdom (cat. no. 2).

The Old Kingdom also produced a large quantity of stone and pottery vessels, although there are also some in metal and other materials. Several of these objects can be found in Portuguese collections, particularly the elegant alabaster cup with bell-shaped foot from the Calouste Gulbenkian Collection (cat. no. 1). Other examples of vessels from that period are in the Egyptian collections at the Museu Nacional de Arqueologia, Lisbon, the Museu da Farmácia, Lisbon, and the Museu de História Natural (Faculdade de Ciências) University of Oporto.

Around 2040 BC, Mentuhotep II reunified Egypt, actively encouraging a political and artistic restoration. Although the new Theban rulers were "rustic" in comparison to the kings of Herakleopolis (Daumas, 1987: 62), they did pave the way for the glorious 12th dynasty. Under the Middle Kingdom, the idea of pyramid construction was revived, albeit without the scale of previous times. The ruined pyramids of Amenemhat I and Senwosret I in Lisht are a disappointment, as are those of the remaining monarchs in Dahshur (Amenemhat II, Senwosret III and Amenemhat III), El-Lahun (Senwosret II) and Hawara (Amenemhat III again). The largest are those of Senwosret III (78 metres) and Amenemhat III in Dahshur (75 metres), reflecting the fact that they were the two most powerful kings from this dynasty. However, these pyramids are nothing more than an illusion: the complex internal structure was covered with gravel and roughly hewn stone that was then finished with carefully smoothed limestone, which has since fallen off (Lehner, 1997: 168-183).

The idea of the 12th-dynasty pharaohs was to revive the glorious architecture of the Old Kingdom, continuing the programme started in Deir el-Bahri by Mentuhotep II, who had his funerary complex built in the Western Thebes region. This merged two traditions that dated back to the Old Kingdom: the pyramid form and the shrine dug into the rock. The square columns also recall the sober pillars at the reception temple in the valley, part of Khafra's funerary complex. This taste for tombs cut into the rock would continue with the provincial governors under the 12th dynasty.

The 12th dynasty also produced harmonious shrines. The finest example is the superbly graceful construction of Senwosret I in Karnak, which paradoxically combines great *maetic* beauty with a lightness in the delicately carved gigantic blocks of stone (Wildung, 1984: 63-67).

The statues from the early days of the new age that came after the turbulent and little documented First Intermediate Period left a stern image of Mentuhotep II, shown sitting on a throne and wearing his white jubilee robe, suggesting the *sed*-festival that magically brought him a sort of rebirth after thirty years of rule. This process also involved recreating statues of the divine king's *ka*, which had been kept secret under the Old Kingdom in the *serdab*, a closed and inaccessible space in the tomb (which explains how this statue survived). Yet the Middle Kingdom started exhibiting statues outside buildings (as shown by the images of Senwosret I at his funerary temple in Lisht), as well as producing royal sphinxes with human faces framed by a dense lion's mane (Amenemhat III). One characteristic of statues from this age is that the faces of the kings received particular attention, humanising the royal figure (Senwosret III and Amenemhat III) and clearly identifying his mature years or even old age. The Calouste Gulbenkian Museum has a fine example of this – an obsidian head of Senwosret III (cat. no. 4). This head inevitably summons up the hymn written in tribute to this warrior and concerned pharaoh, two facets of Senwosret III's life:

> "He has come to us,
> He has protected the Two Lands and brought peace to the Two Banks.
> He has come to us,
> He has made Egyptians live and driven off their afflictions.
> He has come to us,
> He has made the people live again and opened the breath of the people.
> He has come to us,
> He has trampled on the furthest of foreign nations,
> He has mitten the Nubians who knew not the awe he commands.
> He has come to us,
> He has allowed us to raise our children
> And to provide tombs to bury our elderly."

This fragment of a hymn is a clear indication of the king as a good shepherd and defender of his people (Lalouette, 1984: 79), an image that was superbly reflected in Middle Kingdom statuary. The artists also produced statues of queens wearing heavy wigs, and of senior officials who are sometimes shown in an innovative sculpted form called the cube statue where the figure is sitting on his buttocks with his arms resting on his knees, his clothes enveloping the body and suggesting a cube-shaped, compact appearance that is characteristic of these pieces. Another particularly significant form appears in the various wood statuettes. The finest examples include the curvaceous figure of the priestess Imeretnebes (Rijksmuseum van Oudheden, Leiden), and the funerary statue in the Gulbenkian Collection (cat. no. 3).

Low-reliefs from this age appear in the aforementioned boat shrine (unless the building was to be used for the royal coronation ceremony, as proposed by Claire Lalouette) built by Senwosret I and now rebuilt in Karnak. The excellent low-reliefs show figures of the king and the gods that accompanied him. The beautiful hieroglyphs that act as captions and harmoniously complement the scenes offer a fine example of the brilliance attained by the 12th dynasty in drawing the signs used in written script, which would continue to act as the model for subsequent eras. As also happened with architecture and statuary, reliefs from the 12th dynasty took their models from the previous dynasty, especially the dynamic style of Mentuhotep II that is clearly to be found in the painted reliefs in Deir el-Bahri. This involved strong definition of the outlines through the skilled use of light and shadow, as also seen in the large stone and wood sarcophagi from that age. Like low-reliefs, painting also established the style of the Middle Kingdom, and there is no shortage of examples from the tombs of the provincial governors with fine colours and lively scenes. Scenes from agriculture, fishing, banquets, dances, hunts and receptions were painted on fresh stucco or onto the previously created relief, while always maintaining the classical presence of the tomb's owner on a larger scale.

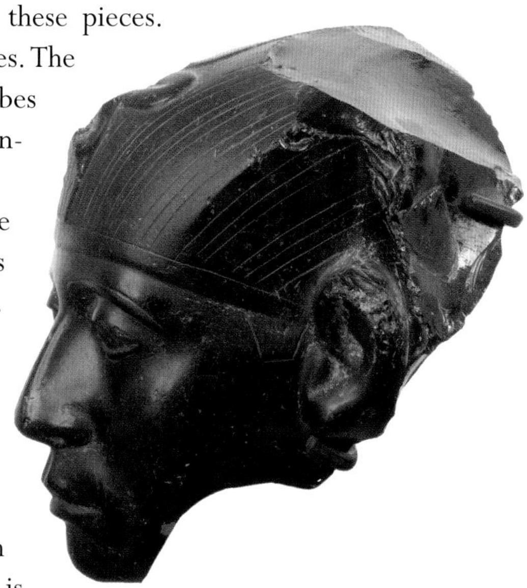

Head of King Senwosret III, Middle Kingdom (cat. no. 4).

The decorative arts emerged strongly in the Middle Kingdom, appearing in fine adornments, combs, mirrors, vessels, ointment jars, oil-lamps, boxes, caskets and countless accessories that combined highly utilitarian and magical properties, bringing together exceptional artistic beauty with the harmonious combination of material, form, colour and decoration. These aspects would survive throughout the New Kingdom, and in some cases were improved by external influences from Syria-Palestine and Crete. Meanwhile, the finest ever pieces of jewellery were produced in the Middle Kingdom (Aldred, 1978), as magnificently shown by the jewels found in the tombs of princesses buried in the Faiyum region.

Under the New Kingdom, pyramids were replaced by tombs cut into the rock, and funerary temples were built at some distance from the tomb. The construction of large divine temples proliferated, adopting a simple structure comprising an entrance flanked by tall pylons, a hypostyle courtyard, a hypostyle hall, a boat-room, a hidden shrine and possibly several rooms holding liturgical vessels, while the entire complex was surrounded by a wall. All the temples had a central axis and were perfectly symmetrical. The columns were both a structural and a decorative device whose hard stone recalled the tree-trunks used in early Egyptian history. The various types of columns were classified according to their capitals: the palm-shaped column with palm-tree leaves; the lotus-shaped column; the papyrus-shaped column; and the Hathoric column, whose capital shows the head of the goddess Hathor. The floral capital could be either open or closed, and they are normally decorated with incised or painted images and texts. Good examples can be found at the large temples in Karnak and Luxor, and at the funerary temples (now partially destroyed) in Deir el-Bahri, the Ramesseum and Medinet Habu. While the gigantic scale of the temple at Karnak (most select of places: Ipet-sut) is very impressive, the balance of the construction of the temple at Luxor (private chambers to the south: Ipet-resit) is outstanding. Thanks to its graceful proportions, the harmonious temple of Khonsu, part of the vast complex at Karnak, is seen as the model of the Egyptian temple. Other temples were also built in Abu Simbel, Abydos, Memphis and Pi-Rameses. The funerary temple at Deir el-Bahri differs from the traditional schemes in that it is made in the limestone from the massive cliff against which it stands and has rectangular columns. Similar to the neighbouring temple of Mentuhotep II, built five hundred years earlier, the latter was the basis for architect Senenmut when erecting a monument worthy of his pharaoh-queen Hatsheprut, whose reign also produced fine obelisks.

Sculpture from this period sought to produce a certain formal elegance (Hatshepsut, Thutmose III and Amenhotep II), reflecting the 18$^{th}$ dynasty's golden age of glory and hedonism. This led to the idealism shown on the faces and the bodies, which would be refined under Amenhotep III by a languid Oriental style. In turn, the Amarna Period produced unexpected statues and reliefs of Akhenaten that broke away from the canons associated to the Amun clergy. This radical aesthetic, ideological, political and religious change deliberately subverted official art while simultaneously producing fine pieces of its own, such as the graceful bust of Nefertiti. The short-lived experiment of worshipping Aten left posterity with a legacy of technical skill in working materials and an affected style that would have echoes in the reigns of Tutankhamen and Horemheb. Moreover, it would later produce works in a new style, among which the granite enthroned statue of Rameses II (Egyptian Museum, Turin) and the images of leading figures from his reign rightly merit special mention.

Low-reliefs and paintings introduced a major novelty under the New Kingdom: the image of the galloping horse pulling a lightweight war-chariot that holds the majestic figure of the king as he fires lethal arrows at the hoards of Asiatic or Nubian enemies, or at wild animals (two different aspects of the same eternal struggle against the forces of chaos). Superb low-reliefs also decorate some tombs in Thebes (e.g. Ramose, Kheruef and Khaemhat) and the tomb of General Horemheb in the necropolis at Memphis (before he became king towards the end of the 18$^{th}$ dynasty), while the painted reliefs at the temple in *Abydos* (Sety I) demonstrate an exceptionally pure idealism.

New Kingdom painting is the finest work produced in three thousand years of Egyptian art. It features fine colours, elegant lines, delicate gestures, a liking for the picturesque, a subtle taste for the exotic and a light touch of eroticism in banquet scenes, showing dances where seductive girls move their bodies in poses that break away from all the previous canons. The old theme of the large figure of the tomb-owner in a dignified pose, a legacy of the Old Kingdom, is still present, and the official is accompanied by his family, sometimes in a setting of great wealth and a range of flora and fauna that includes the customary colours and even new shades of grey, crimson and pink. The new art created during the Amarna Period also affected painting, enriching the themes with its naturalism and taste for appealing landscapes. Thousands of years later, some Theban tombs still contain fine works from this golden age of painting, which reached its peak in the reign of Thutmose IV. Examples include the paintings in the tombs of Amenemhat, Kenamun, Nakht, Menna, Horemheb, Sennefer and Nebamon, a fragment of which is now at the British Museum.

The most famous examples of the decorative arts came from the tomb of Tutankhamen, which form a small sample of the pieces that escaped the pillaging of royal tombs. The variety of furniture, vessels, jewellery, objects with a vast range of functions, statues and statuettes, weapons, etc. is astounding. The sarcophagi, gold mask, shrines, canopic jars and respective reliquary – all packed into a modest tomb in a somewhat chaotic manner – are very well known. In contrast, much of the rest from royal tombs has been lost, especially during the pillaging in the late 20th dynasty. However, some interesting objects have survived, especially from the reign of Rameses II.

Amongst the art produced under the New Kingdom, special reference should be made to the delicate adornments and statuettes in the 18th dynasty, which reveals sophisticated portrayal of both male and female figures. In fact, it was the figure of the woman that established the fashion in a period of triumphant and seductive femininity, as superbly exemplified by the small female statuettes in the Gulbenkian Collection (cat. nos. 13 and 14). Men merely followed the delicacy of female fashion, as can be seen in the relief of the funerary priest Ameneminet (cat. no. 15). The Amarna Period ultimately opened the way for a new form of portrayal in which sculptors exploited the full potential of women's attractive image and sensual forms. The exceptional quality and affectation that are clearly to be seen in sculpture would be reflected during the following dynasty in appealing lyric verses that are heavy with eroticism and exalt female beauty, as shown in the following poem:

> "Unique, beloved beyond peer,
> the most beautiful of them all!
> She is like a morning star
> that appears at the start of a good year.
> She has a luminous perfection,
> and glowing skin,
> sweet is the look from her beautiful eyes.
> Soft is the speech that falls from her lips,
> while never saying too much.
> Elegant is her neck, glorious her breasts,
> her hair is true lapis-lazuli.
> Her arms are worth more than gold,
> her fingers are as lotus flowers.
> Broad are her thighs and narrow her waist,
> her legs emphasise her beauty,
> with her graceful walk as she glides across the floor."

This lyric poem from the 19th dynasty (Araújo, 2001: 146) is ultimately a complete literary description of the two New Kingdom female statuettes in the Collection. Women's physical beauty was praised in both art and literature, and their pleated and transparent robes are a constant in love poems written in the 19th dynasty. This clearly explains the aims of a woman who wished to love and be loved when she said "I shall show you how beautiful I am in my white linen dress" (Araújo, 1995: 118).

The artistically fertile New Kingdom period is strongly represented in the Calouste Gulbenkian Museum through fine pieces recalling the many small statuettes of officials that were produced at that time, such as the statuette of Mes (cat. no. 5), or the granite head that apparently shows a Nubian (cat. no. 6). This work also includes royal figures such as the delicate head of Amenhotep III (cat. no. 7) and another depicting an unidentified pharaoh (cat. no. 8). In turn, the "spoon" for cosmetics (cat. no. 9) is paradigmatic of an age of leisure and well-being that enabled the solid, well-proportioned production of steles, such as the one of the scribe Iry (cat. no. 10). This situation also led to the production of rich collections of tomb-goods, including funerary statuettes that were designed for use in the next world, such as the fine bronze statuette made for Hesmeref (cat. no. 11). However, the tombs also housed another type of statuette that did not have the mummy-shaped pose of the *shabtis*, but instead showed people walking, such as the statuette of a young man (cat. no. 12), which demonstrates the skill and dexterity of many anonymous craftsmen who were genuine artists.

As in previous eras, artists depended directly on the palace, the temple or production centres of funerary goods. Thus, the modern concept of the artist who produces his work with total creative freedom and then sells it to interested clients quite simply did not exist. Meanwhile, the increasing prosperity and well-being that developed during this cosmopolitan period brought improved quality in the art produced (Málek, 2003: 154). Thus, the old claim that statuettes produced under the 18th dynasty were "commercial products" – let alone claims that they demonstrate "the decline of an art-form" (Smith, 1960: 7) – now makes no sense.

Jewellery was still much appreciated in the New Kingdom, which left many rings, bracelets, armbands, necklaces, diadems, earrings and mirrors in various sizes, shapes and materials. Indeed, the two female statuettes in the collection (cat. nos. 13 and 14) are shown wearing gold bracelets and necklaces.

Statue of Henut-tauy, New Kingdom (cat. no. 14).

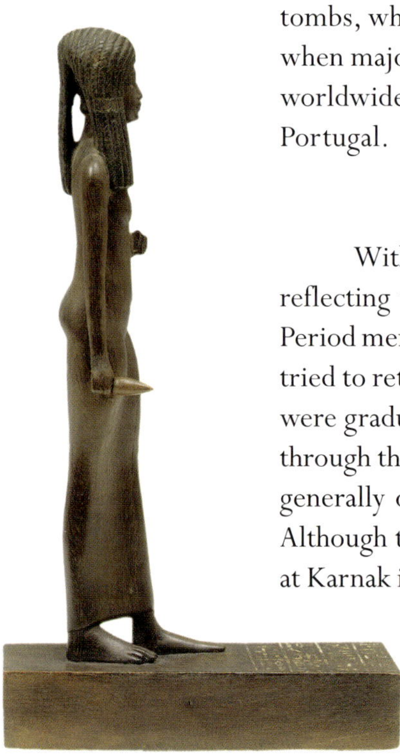

Furniture was also produced for use both in the home and expressly to be placed in tombs, while countless other vessels in a vast range of materials also date from this same period, when major art-work and utilitarian pieces were produced. Such pieces can be seen at museums worldwide, including the Museu Nacional de Arqueologia and the Museu da Farmácia in Portugal.

With the collapse of the New Kingdom, art production entered a phase of major decline, reflecting the turbulent latter days of the 20th dynasty. In some aspects, the Third Intermediate Period merely continued the trend established under the New Kingdom. Although the 21st dynasty tried to return to the previous dynamism, Egypt was in practice divided between two powers that were gradually reaching a state of balance. The only place to produce work of any note was Tanis, through the significant body of pieces found in the tombs of some Tanite kings, while the ruins are generally of little interest and artwork was largely made using materials from other locations. Although the 22nd, 23rd and 24th dynasties barely constructed anything at all, the Bubastite Portal at Karnak is far more interesting, as the 25th-dynasty's Kushite King Taharqo built a colonnade that recalls the one built by Amenhotep III at Luxor temple.

This finest work from this period came in the decorative arts, as exemplified by pieces found in the royal tombs of Tanis: the funerary masks of Psusennes I and Sheshonq II, a silver sarcophagus made for the body of Psusennes I, as well as other funerary pieces including various pieces of jewellery. Yet Third Intermediate Period statuary also included some noteworthy works, such as the beautiful gilded statue of the "divine adoratrice" Karomama (Louvre Museum) and one piece from the Egyptian collection in the Calouste Gulbenkian Museum, the torso of King Pedubast (cat. no. 16), the irreverent founder of the 23rd dynasty.

The production of art – more especially sculpture – was revived during the Late Period (26th to 30th dynasty), in what came to be called the "Saite renaissance", although this merely followed the previous dynamic introduced by rulers of Nubian origin (25th dynasty). Art from this period is characterised by the deliberate return to archaism, a movement that may be justified in terms of an instinctive reaction against foreign influences. Yet Saite and subsequent art was just a cold imitation of the great models from the past, and other than some more outstanding masterpieces, there was no true creativity. The sculptors evidently tried to capture reality and to depict the individual's physical features in the preferred hard stones, which were sometimes given an intense polish. There was also great interest in the use of bronze, both to produce statues such as the figure of the Lady Shepes (cat. no. 27) – revealing an archaic style that imitates the Old Kingdom models and can be compared to the female figures on the relief showing Merytites (cat. no. 4) – and statuettes of sacred animals. Typical examples of the latter include cats such as those in the Gulbenkian Collection: a cat with a greenish patina (cat. no. 29), another with a brownish patina (cat. no. 30) and another cat with its kittens (cat. no. 31).

Late Period art is strongly represented in the collection by fragments of the ivory panels that formed part of the covering for a casket. One shows a man bearing offerings accompanied by a cow (cat. no. 17), while the other has another man bearing offerings following an ibis (cat. no. 18). The storeroom also has a fragment with a fine hieroglyph inscription that reveals that period's appreciation of the care taken in drawing hieroglyphs, exemplifying the somewhat academic virtuosity of this "Saite renaissance", which left beautiful hieroglyph inscriptions written in a solidly sculptural calligraphic style. The Collection also includes funerary goods, which were less abundant than in the New Kingdom, including a faience winged scarab (cat. no. 19), a faience funerary adornment in the shape of a winged figure of Isis (cat. no. 20), and four statuettes showing the sons of the god Horus, who protected the internal organs of the dead: Imsety (cat. no. 21), Duamutef (cat. no. 22), Hapy with a dark face (cat. no. 23), and another Hapy with a pale face (cat. no. 24), here clearly replacing the missing figure of falcon-headed Kebehsenwef. Art from the Late Period is also superbly represented by the limestone statuette of the official Bes (cat. no. 28), a fine head of Hathor (cat. no. 25), a fragment of a faience votive sistrum, and a beautiful statuette of Osiris (cat. no. 26) in schist and gold, which records a clear revival of the cult of Osiris that began at the time and continued into the Greco-Roman Period. The 20th dynasty, the last of pharaonic Egypt before the terrible second Persian invasion and the arrival of Alexander, produced excellent works of art, exemplified by the gilded mummy mask (cat. no. 32) and the bronze processional barque of Djedhor (cat. no. 33).

Little is known of the major works of architecture from the Late Period. Such works were mainly built in the Delta region, which was chosen to house the various capitals of the dynasties that followed, from the 26th to the 30th. The cities in question were Sais, Mendes and Sebennytos, whose ruins now mainly lie under the mud and modern buildings. There is no doubt that the 26th dynasty started several construction projects that were subsequently continued, specifically in Sais, but their scale and quality are not known other than from a few blocks of stone. Finally, although

Ivory panel from a casket, Late Period (cat. no. 17).

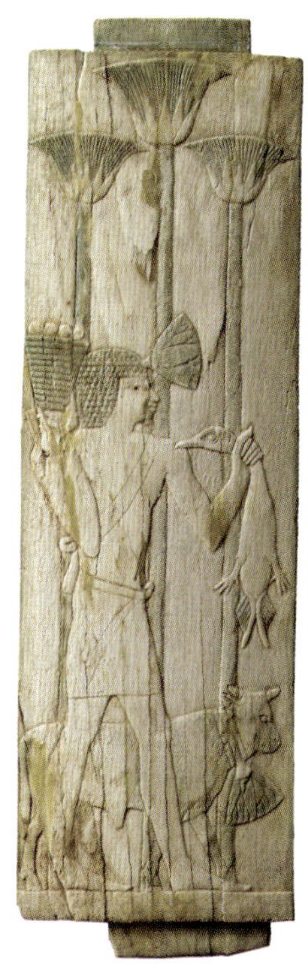

Funerary adornment with the winged goddess Isis, Late Period (cat. no. 20).

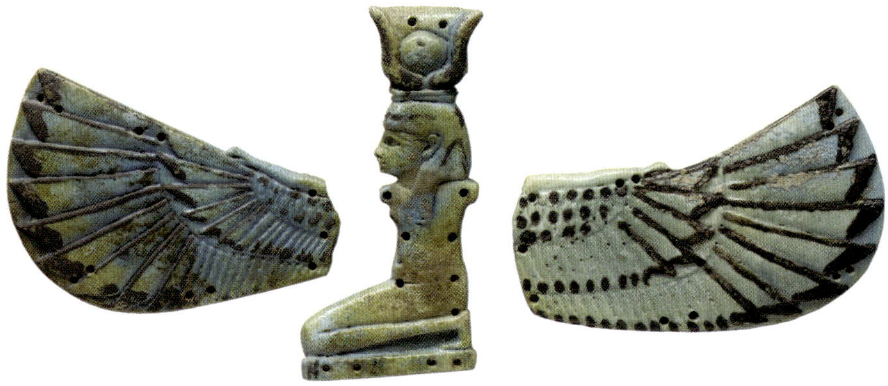

the 30th dynasty did show some dynamism in building work, this was ultimately nothing more than an initial effort for work that would undergo future development in the Ptolemaic Period.

Sculpture from this period shows an obstinate return to the past, revealing the search for the sober classicism of Memphis in the Old Kingdom and for some inspiration from Middle Kingdom and New Kingdom work. Under the 26th dynasty and the celebrated "Saite renaissance", the statues of kings, other individuals and deities were all designed to create balanced forms. The most striking feature is the technical sophistication in polishing the stone. However, the name "Saite renaissance" can be challenged, as numerous pieces that are believed to be original are in fact the result of continuous evolution since the 25th dynasty. This "renaissance" would continue to be felt in the last Egyptian dynasty before the definitive loss of independence, as the 30th dynasty (whose last king was Nectanebo II) produced some fine works of sculpture that already showed strongly idealised features.

Thousands of the bronze statuettes that are commonly found in Egyptian collections date from the Late Period. These mainly show the main gods who were then worshipped: the famous triad of Osiris, Isis and Horus, Tot, Ptah, Bes, Min, Anubis, the goddesses Bastet and Neit, and the bull Apis, among others. The Museu Nacional de Arqueologia has examples showing these gods, and such statuettes were still being produced in large quantities during the Greco-Roman Period, alongside others made in terracotta. It is symptomatic of the new age that the depiction of Amun, once so common, practically disappeared.

The production of sarcophagi, funerary masks, canopic jars, scarabs and amulets continued to fuel a prospering industry that served the afterlife, but few of these pieces can compete with the exceptional work from previous eras. Special reference can be made to the wooden sarcophagi with hieroglyph texts using signs in various colours and incrusted materials, as well as the heavy coffins in exceptionally hard stones that preserved the mummies of some senior officials from both the Saite period and later ages.

Despite losing its political independence, Egypt maintained exceptional cultural autonomy, as clearly shown by its art, especially the imposing architecture. The large and now well-preserved temples in Edfu, Kom Ombo and Philae, which date from the last three hundred years of the first millennium, continued the architectural traditions from the time when Egypt was a powerful country whose culture spread to and influenced its neighbours. Even in the Christian era, under Roman rule, construction work continued and some temples were completed. One of the novelties of the age was the construction of walls between the columns, closing and further isolating the sacred space and creating more areas for decoration. Another was the appearance of composite plant-motif capitals decorated with complex foliage, as demonstrated by one of the most characteristic works in Philae's architecture: the pavilion or shrine of Trajan, which dates from (98-117), although it should be attributed to Augustus. In this case, the unfinished decorative programme recalls the peripteral buildings of the Middle and New Kingdoms. Although few in number, the surviving pieces of private funerary architecture from the Greco-Roman Period are superbly exemplified by shrines shaped like small temples, such as the tomb of Petosirys in Tuna el-Gebel, whose internal decoration is also a model for the syncretic tastes of the age. PetosIrys' wooden sarcophagus, now at the Egyptian Museum in Cairo (Bongioanni & Croce, 2001: 253), is equally eloquent in terms of demonstrating the preference for maintaining an ancient iconography, as it features fine incrusted hieroglyphs.

The production of sarcophagi included large rectangular stone urns and anthropomorphic stone coffins, especially typical of the Late Period. This would continue during the Greco-Roman Period. However, most sarcophagi were made of wood or cartonnage, and involved abundant decoration, protecting the mummified body and its funerary mask, which was often gilded. Although the Gulbenkian Collection has no such sarcophagi, they can be found in Portugal at the Museu Arqueológico do Carmo, the Museu de História Natural (Faculdade de Ciências) University of Oporto, the Museu da Farmácia, the Museu Nacional de Arqueologia (one in wood, the other in cartonnage) and the Sociedade de Geografia de Lisboa (five from the 21st dynasty, and three inner coffin lids for mummies).

Sculpture also fundamentally followed the norms and models of the Late Period, depicting the Ptolemaic kings and Roman emperors in the pharaonic style and using the traditional iconography (*Ibidem*: 252). Other individuals, especially senior Egyptian officials working for the Ptolemaic administration, benefited from the work of the royal workshops and commissioned statues, while craftsmen continued to produce high quality adornments. The end of the Gulbenkian Collection's exhibition has fine examples of the variety and quality of Egyptian art from its final phase. The pieces in question are the basalt statue made for Djedhor (cat. no. 34), the model of a sphinx (cat. no. 35), returning to a traditional form of representing royal power that dates back to the Old Kingdom, a delicate low-relief which is a study for a pharaoh's head (cat. no. 36), the silver figure of Harpocrates (the child Horus who was so widely worshipped at the time: cat. no. 37), and a fluted breccia bowl (cat. no. 38) that – many centuries on – still bears witness to continued mastery in the art of creating vessels in hard stones, a skill that had developed in the distant pre-pharaonic times. The Ptolemaic Period also produced such exceptional works as the green schist head of an official (cat. no. 39), a highly realistic piece that appears to bear all the characteristics of a genuine portrait. The exhibition ends in chronological terms with a piece from the Roman Period: the torso of a statuette of Venus Anadiomene. Made in blue faience, the modelling and movement reveal enormous differences from works of art produced in previous eras.

Sarcophagus of the Lady Irtierut, Late Period. Museu da Farmácia, Lisbon

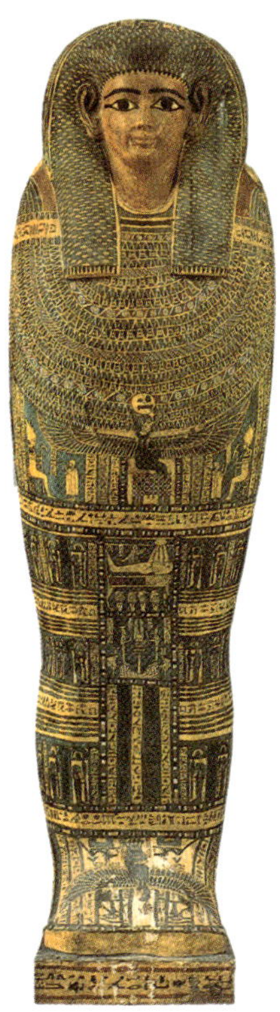

It can be concluded that there was a clear continuity of forms over the millennia of pharaonic civilisation. Comparison between the themes and techniques used to produce objects in the Early Dynastic Period and in the Late Period reveals that little or nothing had changed in many cases. Clearly, there are differences, new tastes and adaptations, but the idea of continuity and permanence is immediate and evident, as superbly illustrated by the collection assembled by Calouste Gulbenkian.

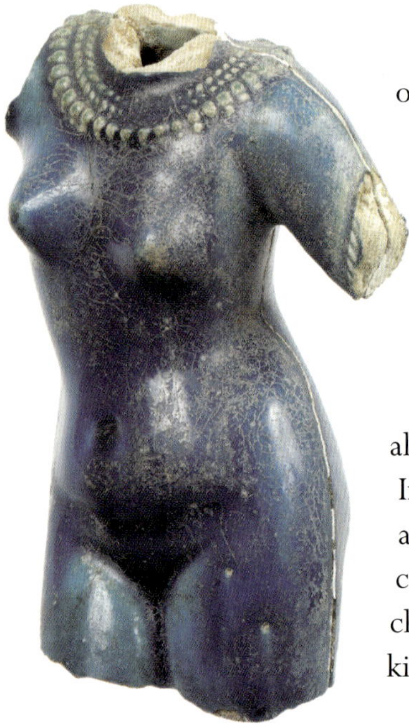

Torso of the goddess Venus Anadiomene, Greco-Roman Period (cat. no. 40).

In fact, sculpture would maintain its "law of frontality", where the body always appears on its axis, in a hieratic pose that can only slightly altered with more or les affected positions of the limbs, while the forms show a constant aspective vision of things, as can be seen in low-reliefs and paintings. Thus, the frontal position in statues and the aspective work in low-reliefs and painting are mainstays in figurative art from Ancient Egypt. Likewise, the fundamental guidelines in architecture changed little, and the late temples from the Greco-Roman Period, which are now very well preserved, would essentially adopt the ancient model.

In conclusion, the main models for architects, sculptors, painters and craftsmen can always be easily found in forms from the past, the source of inspiration for all artists. Indeed, they could deliberately make a clear ideological and political decision to copy ancient models, as happened from the 7th century BC onwards, when the 25th dynasty came to power, a feature that would continue into the Late Period, compensating for a clear Mediterranean influence on Egypt, as can also be observed in the Calouste Gulbenkian Museum's Egyptian collection.

# THE EGYPTIAN COLLECTION

The urge to collect is one of mankind's oldest instincts, and the process of gathering together works of art and antiquities is clearly one of man's noblest passions, as Dietrich von Bothmer said in the introduction to the catalogue that his brother Bernard Bothmer organised for the Christos Bastis Collection (Bothmer, 1988: 18). Indeed, the origin of many of the Egyptian sections in the great European and American institutional collections lie in donations made by private collectors who felt this passion.

The specific desire to purchase and collect antiquities from Ancient Egypt comes from the powerful feelings aroused by Egyptomania, a cultural phenomenon that still stirs appreciation and passion nowadays, and that continues to go hand-in-hand with Egyptology, a relatively young but very dynamic science (Araújo, 2001: 313).

When Egyptomania appears in its most generous and impassioned form (and provided there is the financial wherewithal), it ultimately leads those who fall under its sway to collect Egyptian antiquities. This is a costly activity for anyone who wishes to own high quality objects whose beauty and rarity invoke the brilliant cultural heritage left by Ancient Egypt. Calouste Sarkis Gulbenkian felt this emotive appeal, and had the will, the good taste and the funds required to purchase such antiquities.

In fact, Calouste Gulbenkian was merely following in footsteps that had existed for many centuries, when Greek and Roman travellers visited Egypt and returned bearing Egyptian goods. During the Roman Empire, the wealthy and cultured would travel to Egypt and bring back some antiquities, or at least some more or less exotic novelties from their travels in the land of the Nile. Then, after the Muslim conquest in the middle of the seventh century, Egypt increasingly closed itself off from Europe and became practically inaccessible. Any knowledge gleaned about the country came from the Bible, was generally written in a deprecatory tone and presented a very negative aspect.

Meanwhile, the brilliant era of the Renaissance rekindled interest in Egypt, as can be seen from the studies by the Jesuit Athanasius Kircher, who tried (without great success) to decipher hieroglyph script from his base in Rome. Simultaneously, the major restoration work undertaken by the popes in Christendom's capital led to the discovery of several obelisks buried in Rome, which stirred up great admiration for pharaonic Egypt. This phenomenon continued to grow in the seventeenth and eighteenth centuries as the number of leading figures who visited the country increased. Some of these visitors also published interesting texts recording their travels and adventures.

Egypt really opened up to Europe in 1798, thanks to the expedition led by Napoleon Bonaparte, who was accompanied by a group of scholars. The aim was to conquer Egypt both by force of arms and by in-depth knowledge of the country. Although the expedition was a military failure, it proved to be an academic triumph. This led to the publication of some works of undeniable value on Egypt, which made the country better known and also attracted still more visitors: some who wished to study the country, its inhabitants and its history, while the majority went just to traffic antiquities. It was during the Napoleonic expedition that the Rosetta Stone was discovered. This fundamental monument enabled the script of the Ancient Egyptians to be deciphered in 1822. Following an initial phase of "horizontal" archaeology, exemplified by Auguste Mariette, "vertical" archaeology emerged under Sir Flinders Petrie, confirming Egyptology's establishment as a science that continues to captivate countless admirers across the world, fuelling the appealing and enthralling phenomena of Egyptomania and Egyptophilia.

The fine collection of Egyptian objects assembled by Calouste Gulbenkian is part of this general fascination for Egyptian things, revealing his personal taste and also demonstrating – through the chronological organisation of the main pieces – the development of artistic and utilitarian work from Ancient Egypt over three thousand years. The only items missing from the collection are objects from Egypt's prehistoric period, from the Early Dynastic Period (1st and 2nd dynasties) and the Coptic Period (from the 4th century BC), although these can be found in the Egyptian collection at the Museu Nacional de Arqueologia. These absences exist because the collector was not interested in the less clearly defined historical periods, and it did not even occur to him to purchase objects – mummies and sarcophagi – whose spectacular nature are now a major attraction in Egyptian collections. This is perfectly natural, because there was a clear intention and a refined personal taste behind his collection of the four dozen fundamental pieces exhibited.

Although Calouste Gulbenkian acquired a relatively small number of Egyptian works of art, the pieces from its various periods and the high quality of some of the pieces on display do follow the evolution of art in Egypt from the Old Kingdom (some 2700 BC) to the Greco-Roman Period (1st century), only failing to include the Amarna Period.

Gulbenkian's love of and admiration for works of art from Ancient Egypt emerged long before he visited the country, as his first acquisition of Egyptian pieces dates from 1907: the fluted breccia bowl (cat. no. 38) purchased at Christie's, the highly regarded London auctioneers. This was followed in 1911 by the bronze statue of the Lady Shepes (cat. no. 27) and in 1917 by the wooden statue of Henut-tauy (cat. no. 14) and the basalt naophore statue of Djedhor (cat. no. 34). Subsequently, his purchases of Egyptian objects became more regular, occurring in all the remaining years of the 1920s: one piece in 1920, four in 1921, twenty in 1922 (the year with most acquisitions), two in 1924, one in 1925, three in 1926, one in 1928 and two in 1929, excluding those now in the storeroom.

Gulbenkian's intermediary and adviser when acquIryng some of these objects was British Egyptologist Howard Carter. Carter had famously worked for Lord Carnarvon and discovered (1922) the tomb of the young pharaoh Tutankhamen, which had also become famous due to the exceptional treasure that it contained. However, this spectacular find had no influence on Gulbenkian's purchase of Egyptian objects in that fertile year, as may at first sight seem, since the tomb was discovered in November and the acquisitions were made over previous months. Yet Howard Carter was not merely an intermediary, as he sold both a blue faience scarab (kept in the storeroom) and a head of a Nubian directly to Calouste Gulbenkian (cat. no. 6).

Before incorporation into Calouste Gulbenkian's collection, a significant number of works had been in private hands. Sixteen had belonged to the wealthy British collector Reverend William MacGregor alone. The most significant of these was the obsidian head of pharaoh Senwosret III (although it was then thought to be of his son Amenemhat III).

Curiously, it was only after all the most important pieces (now on display) from his Egyptian collection had been assembled that Gulbenkian decided to visit the country which had produced these works of art. Thus, it was only in 1934 that Calouste Gulbenkian finally travelled to Egypt, when he was 65 years old. He was agreeably surprised by everything that he saw and evidently bade farewell to the land of the pharaohs with some emotion, with fond memories of the fine days he had enjoyed on the banks of the Nile, looking at the magnificent monuments from the past. His travel diary included the following observation, among other impressions as he sailed up the Nile: "so much beauty, so much civilisation (tant de beauté, de civilisation)"...

As still happens today and was already tradition then, this important traveller had photographs taken at several moments of his time in Egypt. One of the most celebrated and memorable shows Calouste Gulbenkian sitting under a statue of the falcon-shaped god Horus, taken at the temple in Edfu. It was this image of the collector, sitting – or enthroned – under the benevolent protection of Horus that was the inspiration for the fine statue in the Foundation garden that overlooks Praça de Espanha.

In 1936, Calouste Gulbenkian decided to decentralise his art collection, loaning two extremely important pieces from the Egyptian collection – the obsidian head of Senwosret III and the gilded silver funerary mask – to the British Museum for eighteen months. His intention was also to offer visitors a fine opportunity to admire works of art from a private collection that was not normally open to pubic viewing. This generous offer was soon expanded, and he ultimately loaned the famous London museum a total of twenty-six pieces. Moreover, Gulbenkian also decided to make a donation of £150 to support the costs of organising the exhibition and publishing the respective catalogue (Perdigão, 1969: 159).

Statue of Calouste Gulbenkian,
by Leopoldo de Almeida,
in the gardens of the Foundation.
Photo: Carlos Azevedo

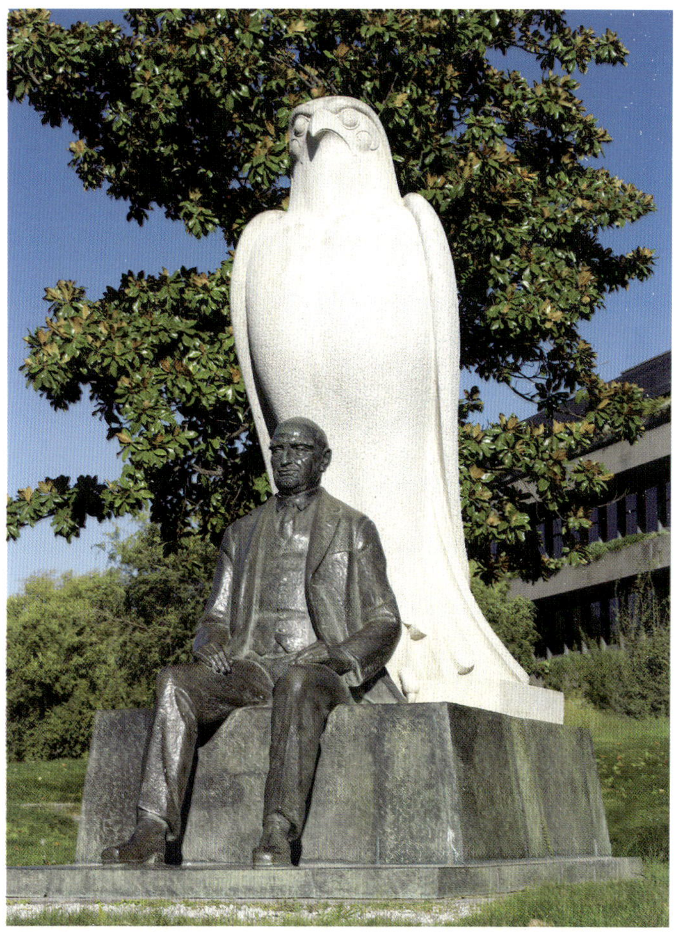

The catalogue, written by Sidney Smith and with translations of the inscriptions by I. E. S. Edwards, is still an essential tool in studying Calouste Gulbenkian's Egyptian collection. In the preface, Sir John Forsdyke (then the director of the British Museum) wrote: "Mr. Gulbenkian has formed his collection during many years from the best material that has from time to time become available, and its importance as selected series for public exhibition lies in its representative character as well as in its fine quality."

The objects went on public exhibition, and were then duly protected when London was under fierce attack during World War II. After the war was over, the pieces were again exhibited, staying in the British capital until 1949, when they went on loan to the National Gallery of Art in Washington following a request by the American government, while two other pieces were also in exhibition at the Brooklyn Museum in New York. In 1960, the works of art in the USA were moved to Portugal, which had already received a small nucleus of Egyptian antiquities previously at Calouste Gulbenkian's Paris home in Avenue d'Iéna, now the Calouste Gulbenkian Cultural Centre, opened in 1965. The Museum archives include a genuine documentary relic: the typed catalogue organised by the collector with annotations in the margins. Volume II, pp. 1-77 is of particular value for any specific study of the Egyptian collection.

Having arrived in Portugal, the Egyptian works of art were initially kept at the Pombal Palace, Oeiras. Once the entire collection had been studied (first in 1962, and again in 1968) by French specialist Christiane Desroches-Noblecourt, whom the Calouste Gulbenkian Foundation invited to come to Portugal for that express purpose, most of the Egyptian collection was first publicly exhibited in 1965. However, the Egyptian objects were removed from the exhibition in December 1967 because the area of the palace where they were located was needed to restore the works of art affected by the serious flooding that devastated Lisbon and the surrounding areas in November of that year. The six pieces of Egyptian art that had been damaged (from the storeroom in the palace's strong-room) were consolidated, cleaned and restored at the Conservation Laboratory of the Museu Monográfico de Conímbriga (Assam, 1991: 29).

When the construction and fittings of the Calouste Gulbenkian Museum in Lisbon were completed, the entire art collection – comprising hundreds of pieces – was finally transferred to its final destination. The excellent premises of the current museum officially opened its doors on 2 October 1969. Since then, the Egyptian works of art have almost entirely been in a specially-designed gallery, the first on any tour of the museum, emphasising their aesthetic quality and timeless beauty. Although the collection is relatively small, it is of exceptional artistic and educational value thanks to the outstanding quality of most of the pieces and its undeniable historical and documentary relevance. This arouses enormous interest among the countless visitors to the section, notably among many students from all levels of education (primary to university level). In fact, this explains why the fine catalogues of Egyptian art published abroad often refer to pieces from the Gulbenkian Collection as paradigms of artwork produced in Ancient Egypt.

The former Egyptian Art gallery in the Pombal Palace, Oeiras.
Photo: Mário Novaes

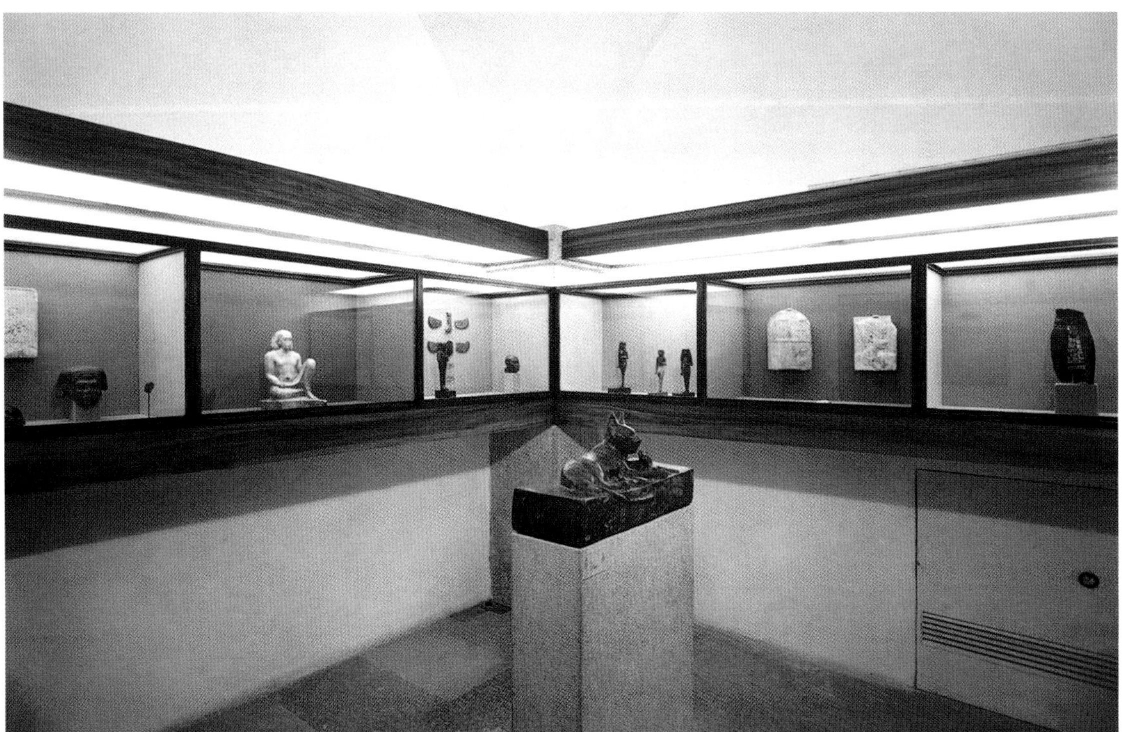

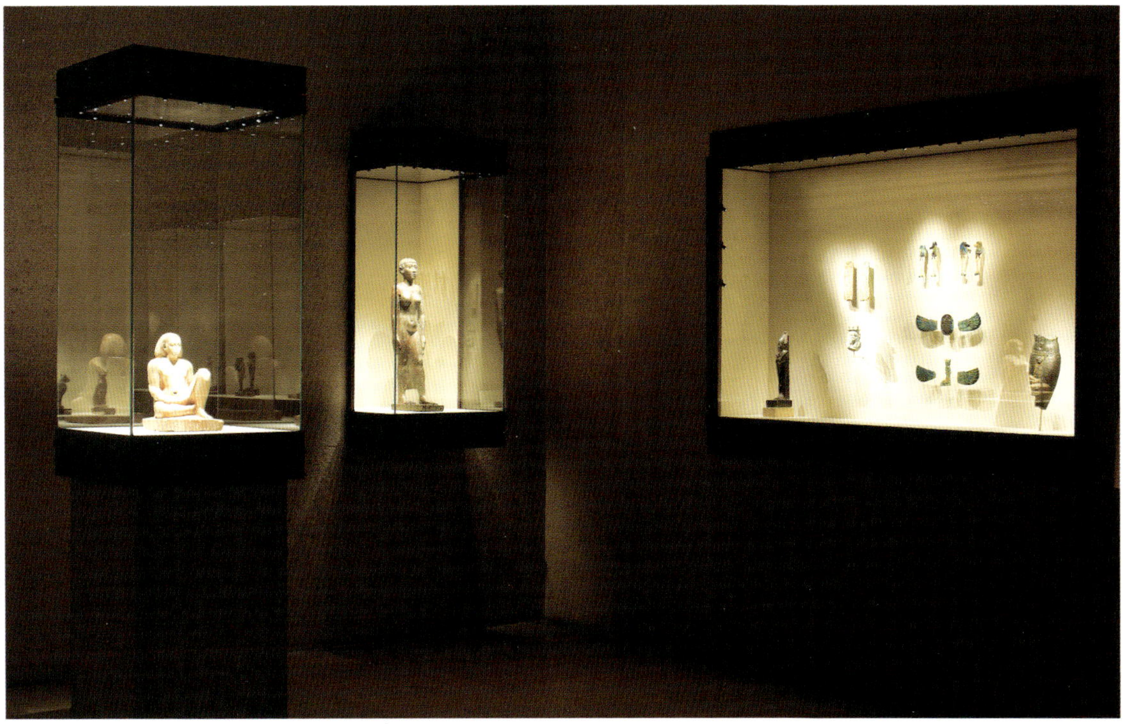

The current Egyptian Art gallery in the Calouste Gulbenkian Museum.
Photo: Carlos Azevedo

The pieces exhibited in the Egyptian antiquities room at the Calouste Gulbenkian Museum are essentially presented using the structure of the previous catalogue. Thus, after identifying the object, the entries record the material: the most widely used being stone (alabaster, limestone, granite, basalt, schist, breccia and obsidian); metal (gold, silver, bronze and copper); wood (one funerary statue, two female statuettes and a male statuette); then faience, terracotta, ivory and glass paste.

This is followed by the date and the dimensions in centimetres. It was decided that a statue would be defined as a piece of sculpture over 50 centimetres, while smaller ones should be called statuettes. The description of the object is followed by notes and comments, and finally, the entries have the inventory data (provenance, date of incorporation into the collection and inventory number) as well as the exhibitions in which the pieces have been. The information from the previous catalogue by Maria Helena Assam was extremely useful in this aspect. Fundamentally, the aim was to follow the numerical order from that catalogue, while separating out and giving individual numbers to the ivory panels and figurines of the sons of Horus, which were previously considered as a whole.

Thus, the new numbering system proposed for the Egyptian pieces in exhibition at the Calouste Gulbenkian Museum is as follows:

1 Cup, alabaster
2 Low-relief depicting Princess Merytites, limestone
3 Funerary statue, wood
4 Head of King Senwosret III, obsidian
5 Statuette of Mes, limestone
6 Head of a Nubian (?), granite
7 Head of King Amenhotep III, glass paste

8 Head of a pharaoh, glass paste and faience
9 Cosmetic 'spoon', ivory
10 Stele of the scribe Iry, limestone
11 Funerary statuette of Hesmeref, bronze
12 Male statuette, wood
13 Female statuette, wood
14 Statuette of the lady of the house Henut-tauy, wood
15 Low-relief of the priest Ameneminet, limestone
16 Torso of King Pedubast, bronze, gold and copper
17 Panel from a casket, ivory
18 Panel from a casket, ivory
19 Winged scarab, faience
20 Winged image of goddess Isis, faience
21 Statuette of Imsety, faience
22 Statuette of Duamutef, faience
23 Statuette of Hapi, faience
24 Statuette of Hapi, faience
25 Head of the goddess Hathor, faience
26 Statuette of the god Osiris, schist and gold
27 Statue of the Lady Shepes, bronze
28 Statuette of the official Bes, limestone
29 Statuette of a cat, bronze
30 Statuette of a cat, bronze
31 Cat with kittens, bronze
32 Funerary mask, gilded silver
33 Solar barque of Djedhor, bronze
34 Statue of Djedhor, basalt
35 Model of a sphinx, limestone
36 Low-relief of a pharaoh, limestone
37 Statuette of the god Harpocrates, silver
38 Bowl, breccia
39 Head of an official, schist
40 Torso of the goddess Venus Anadiomene, faience

The pieces in the Museum's storage, some of which are of origin uncertain, are as follows:

41 Alabaster bowl (heavily restored)
42 Panel of an ivory casket with hieroglyph inscription
43 Panel of an ivory casket with a man bearing offerings
44 Panel of an ivory casket with plant motifs
45 Panel of an ivory casket with plant motifs
46 Panel of an ivory casket with a man bearing offerings (lower part)
47 Lion, bronze
48 Scarab, faience

49 Funerary statuette (*shabti*), faience with hieroglyph inscription
50 Funerary statuette (*shabti*), faience, no inscrition
51 Statuette of the god Osiris, bronze
52 Statuette of the god Harpocrates, bronze
53 Statuette of an official, painted limestone
54 Statue of an official, painted limestone

# CATALOGUE

1

**CUP**

Old Kingdom (?), 3rd dynasty (?) (ca. 2700-2600 BC)
Alabaster
H: 10.5 cm; Diameter: 12 cm
Provenance: The MacGregor Collection
Date incorporated: 1922
Inv. no. 409 A

Cylindrical alabaster cup decorated with three gently protruding ridges, and with an elegant bell-shaped foot that ends in a base with a lightly rounded rim. Probably used to measure solids, it was found in a tomb north of Thebes, at a place described as being Reqaqnah, and was part of the luxurious tomb-goods of the deceased from tomb 40. The tomb dates from the 3rd dynasty (?) of the Old Kingdom, a time when fine objects were made in alabaster. No other known piece has the same shape as this cup.

The Ancient Egyptians placed copies of the objects that they used in life inside their tombs. Such copies were made using more luxurious and longer-lasting materials since they were designed for use throughout all eternity. Thus, this cup was probably based on an identical one in another material, possibly pottery or wood. Similar cups were used to hold ointments during the New Kingdom.

Close examination of the cup from bottom to top allows the viewer a better appreciation of the material's exceptional translucence.

NOTES AND COMMENTS

A date for the production of this beautiful vessel can be established thanks to the studies by Christiane Desroches-Noblecourt, who based her decision on the fact that there is a mural in the tomb of the senior official Hesyra that shows similar objects. Among other functions, Hesyra was the doctor of Horus Netjerirkhet Djoser (3rd dynasty), and his rich tomb in Saqqara was excavated and studied by J. Quibell in the early 20th century.

Large numbers of stone vessels were found in the crypts of Djoser's tomb in Saqqara – the famous "step pyramid" – and in tombs dating from the first two dynasties. However, according to the type of the pieces found (both stone and pottery) and drawn by Walter Emery, who excavated the area, none is like the form of this cup from the Calouste Gulbenkian Museum (Emery, 1972: 208-209, 217-218). In fact, comparison of the many vessels in the collections of a broad range of museums will not reveal similar forms that date from the Old Kingdom.

In 1988, the late Egyptologist Bernard Bothmer, a professor at the University of New York (Institute of Fine Arts), accompanied me to the room holding Egyptian antiquities and had no hesitation in stating that this cup came from the 18th dynasty. It is symptomatic that the catalogue published for the London exhibition, that included this cup in 1922 (Burlington Fine Arts Club), identified it as being from the New Kingdom. However, the images in books showing New Kingdom pieces from various museum collections do not include any recipient with the shape of this cup. However, some of a small group of alabaster and gold objects found in the tomb of three wives of pharaoh Thutmose III (in exhibition at the Metropolitan Museum of Art in New York) have the same type of bell-shaped foot, and one even has the same cylindrical form, albeit without the three decorative ridges.

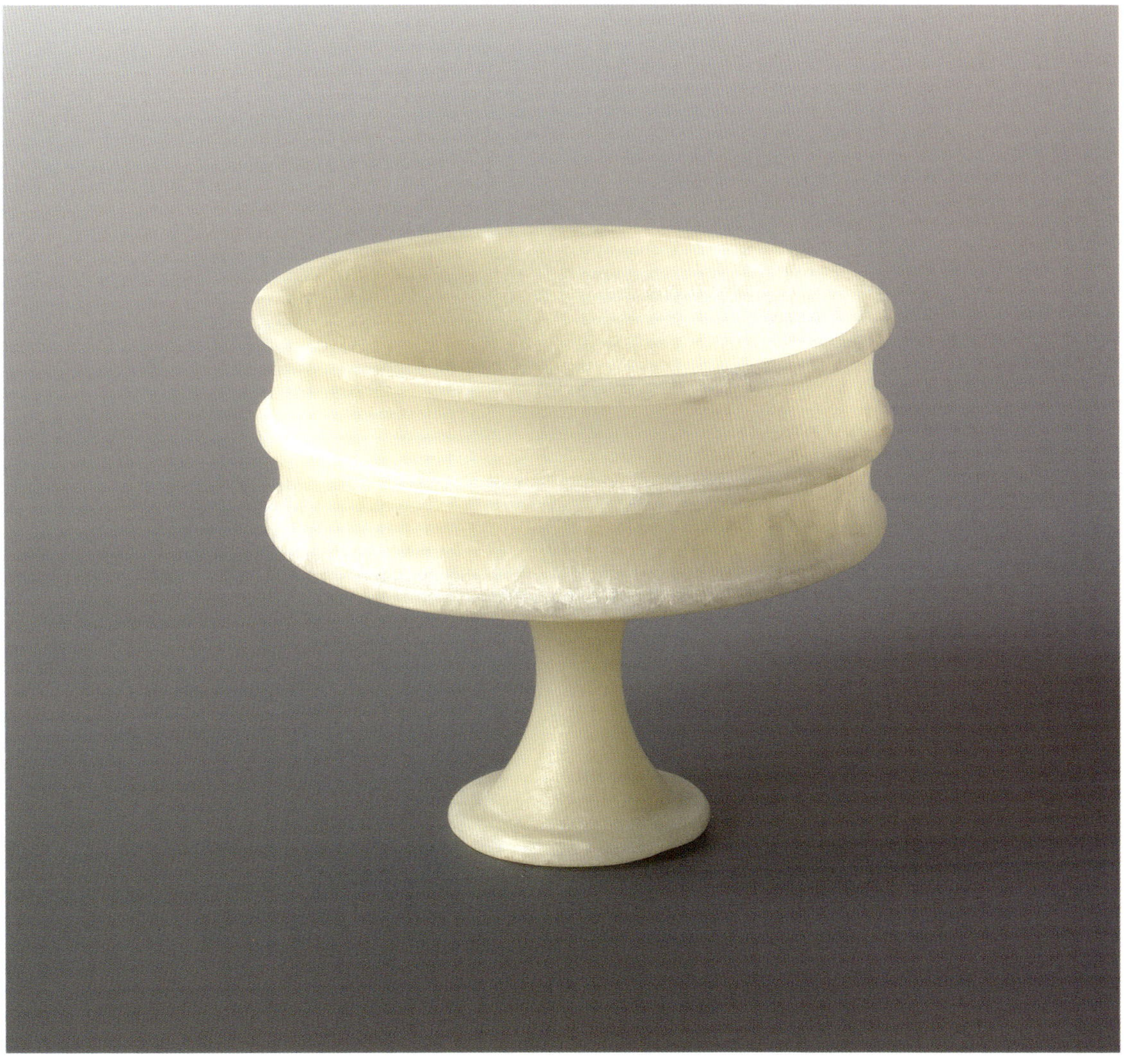

This type of foot can also be found on polychrome glass vessels (Hayes, 1990, II: 141, 194). The Metropolitan Museum also owns a small turquoise blue container with three decorative ridges and a foot, which may be included in this same typology, and this can also be observed in an alabaster cup bearing the names of Amenhotep IV and Nefertiti (*Ibidem*: 278, 294).

According to the collection records, this cup came with an alabaster plate that is now in the Museum storeroom. However, observation of the two pieces shows that this is impossible since the two objects reveal different quality and finishes (see the description of the works in the storeroom further ahead).

EXHIBITIONS

1921 – Ancient Egyptian Art. London, Burlington Fine Arts Club.

1965 – Obras de Arte da Fundação Calouste Gulbenkian. Oeiras, Pombal Palace.

2

**LOW-RELIEF DEPICTING PRINCESS MERYTITES**

Old Kingdom, 4$^{th}$ dynasty (ca. 2500 BC)
Polychrome limestone
H: 23 cm; W: 31.5 cm
Provenance: The MacGregor Collection
Date incorporated: 1922
Inv. no. 159

Fragment of a limestone low-relief taken from the tomb of Princess Merytites and her husband Akhtihetep, in Giza. During the 4$^{th}$ dynasty (Old Kingdom), Pharaoh Khufu had one of the three pyramids on the Giza plain built for his burial, while *mastabas* were built around this Great Pyramid for his wives and favourite children, including Princess Merytites. This fragment comes from one of the walls of her funerary shrine.

The piece shows two female figures flanking a cartouche composed of two cords and bearing the name of Pharaoh Khufu, part of the name of the figure on the right, in hieroglyphs. Their simple robes, with two straps, and the type of short hair both suggest the Old Kingdom style. The details of the ladies' faces are carefully drawn, showing their eyebrows, well-defined ears, noses and closed mouths with clearly outlined lips. Both are displaying a naked right breast next to their right arms, which curve forward when they would really have been hidden by the strap. They also have their open hands with very elongated fingers resting on their chests. Their bodies mirror the ideal of beauty at that time.

The canonical representation of the two figures, who are facing left before an important person who would be shown on the next block, partially reveals the use of some conventional rules in the pose for wall reliefs. Thus, the trunk is simultaneously seen from the front and in profile, the heads are in profile while the eye is seen frontally. If the figures were complete, their legs and feet would also be shown in profile.

The small block of limestone still has traces of green, the only surviving colour from the piece's original chromatic variety (since reliefs were generally painted) and the ladies' skin would originally have been in the yellowish colour given to females. The surface is dotted with small incrustations of earth.

The name of the lady on the left can partially be read in the hieroglyphs at the side: specifically the three-sided sign 𓊵 *htp* (*hotep*), where the signs 𓏏 *t* and 𓋴 *s* are components of the name Hetepheres. The name of the lady on the right is of the pharaonic type, i.e. an onomastic form that contained the name of a king. Both were daughters of Merytites and Akhtihetep.

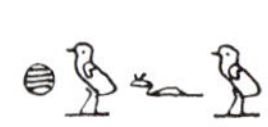

NOTES AND COMMENTS

The name Merytites means "Beloved of her father", while the name of the other lady is composed using the name of Khufu. At that time, there were several people whose names were formed using the prestigious name of the pharaoh who had the Great Pyramid built and whose full name was Khnumkhu-fui, or "The god Khnum protects me". Moreover, Khufu's mother was called Hetepheres and one of his wives was also called Merytites (Grimal, 1988: 90).

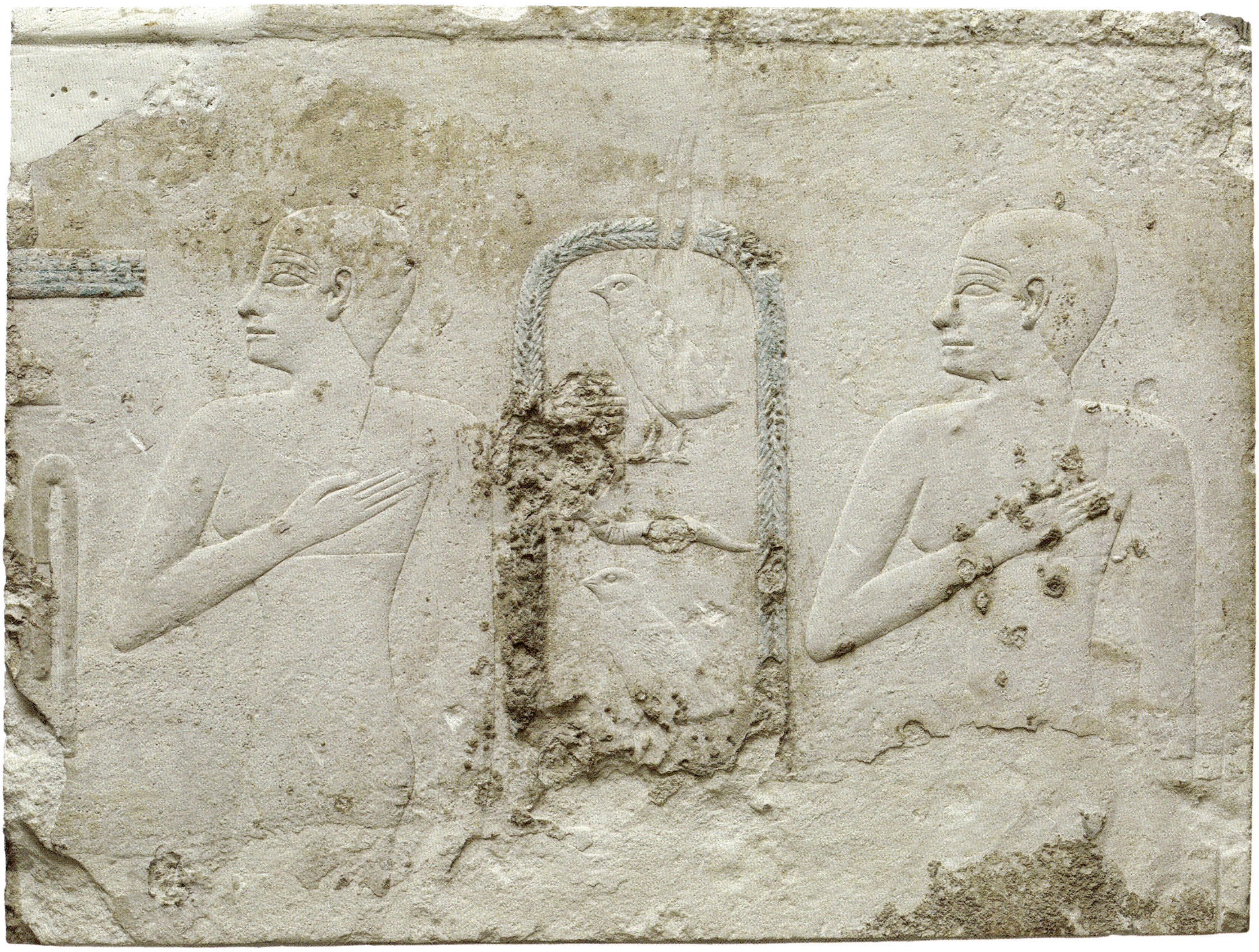

The fragment was acquired via Howard Carter in July 1922, just four months before the discovery of the spectacular tomb of Tutankhamun in the Valley of the Kings. Carter wrote a short text on this in his "Carnet Spécial" identifying the female figures as representations of the funerary assistants associated to supplying goods and foodstuffs for the cult of the dead – "procession of women symbolizing various estates". That is not the case here, because the ladies depicted do not appear to be bearing the typical offerings. Carter's erroneous opinion would be reflected in the text from the catalogue of the Burlington Fine Arts Club, which considered the image of the two ladies to be "a representation of the estates of a noble".

Similar fragments were taken from the same funerary shrine and are now in the Museo Baracco (Rome) and the Museum of Fine Arts (Boston). In the nineteenth and early twentieth century (and with the connivance of the local authorities), some European and American museums took the opportunity to bring many fragments of tomb murals from Egypt and even entire funerary shrines, not only from the Old Kingdom but also from other periods.

Egyptologist William Stevenson Smith, then part of the Harvard-Boston Expedition excavating in the Giza area, wrote a letter to Calouste Gulbenkian requesting permission to publish an image of this fragment, which was then on display in the British Museum. The letter was sent from Cairo on 28 January 1937, and Gulbenkian replied immediately (6 February), giving his consent. Smith intended to include the image of this block in a reconstitution of the funerary shrine of Princess Merytites and her husband, the official Akhtihetep (G 7650), which had been excavated by George Reisner in the eastern cemetery in Giza.

EXHIBITIONS

1921 – Ancient Egyptian Art. London, Burlington Fine Arts Club.

1937 – Ancient Egyptian Sculpture lent by C. S. Gulbenkian, Esq. London, British Museum.

1949 – Egyptian Sculpture from the Gulbenkian Collection. Washington, D. C., National Gallery of Art.

1965 – Obras de Arte da Fundação Calouste Gulbenkian. Oeiras, Pombal Palace.

1999 – "Only the Best": Masterpieces of the Calouste Gulbenkian Museum. New York, The Metropolitan Museum of Art.

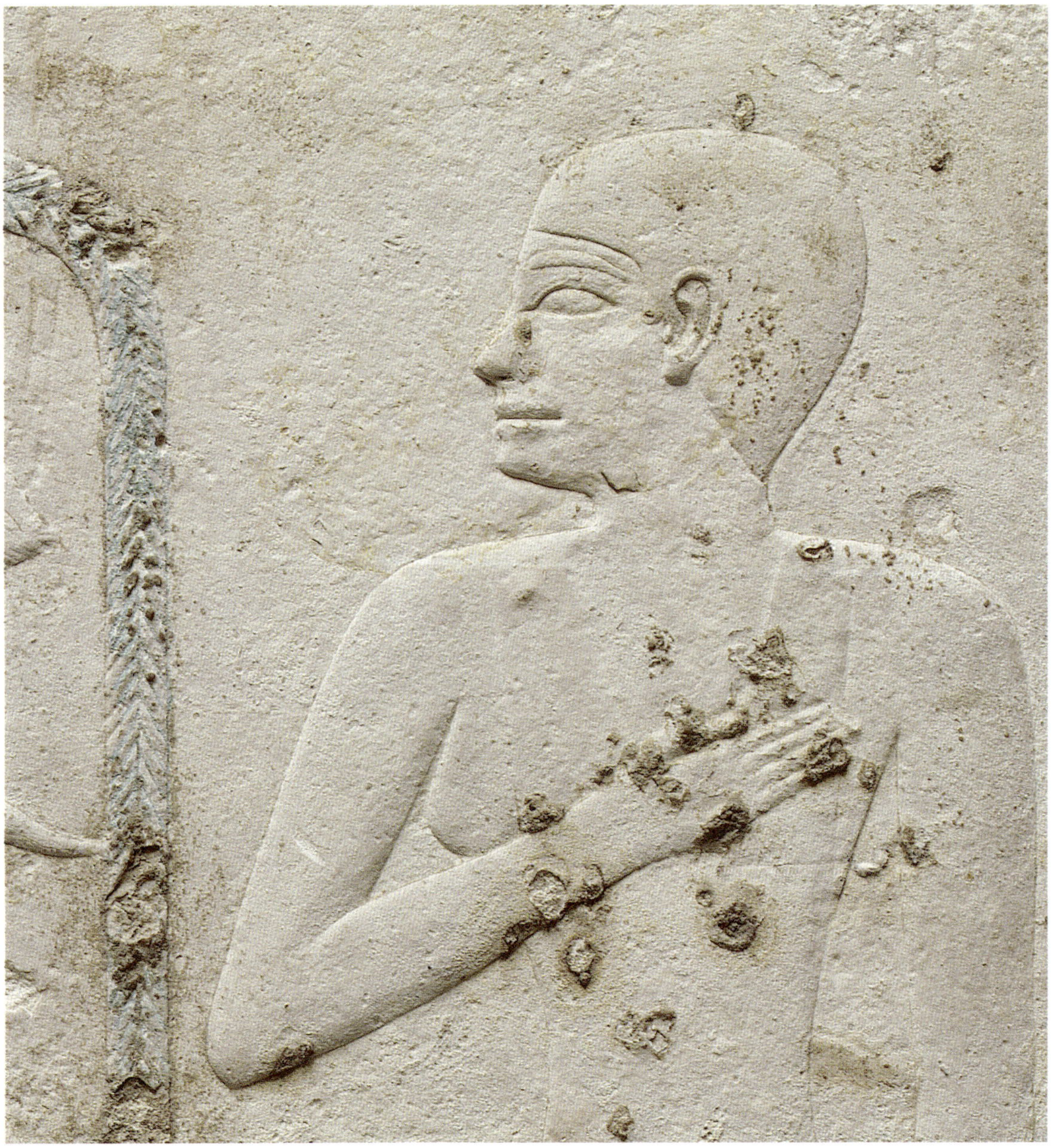

3

**FUNERARY STATUE**

Middle Kingdom, 11th dynasty (ca. 2000 BC)
Polychrome ebony
H: 69 cm
Provenance: The Paul Mallon Collection
Date incorporated: 1920
Inv. no. 142

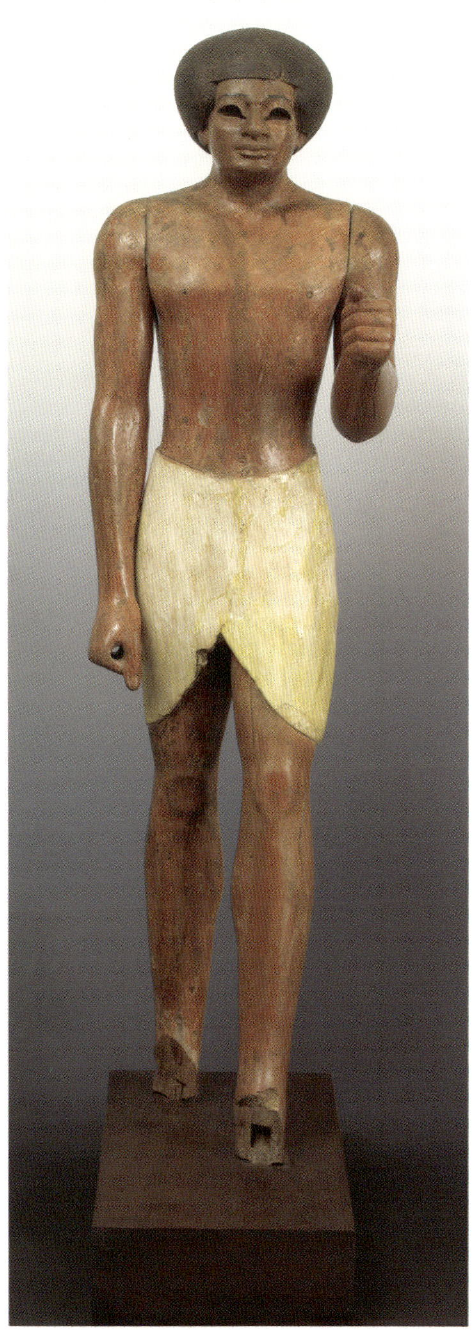

This male figure made of painted ebony was found in the Deir el-Bahri region in Eastern Thebes. The figure is wearing a simple kilt made of canvas covered with plaster. His short, black round-cut hair is indicated by small curls incised into the wood, and his earlobes are visible, although his once inset eyes have been lost. His left leg is thrust forward, his right arms is hanging down and his left is folded, and he has lost the insignia that he once held in his hands: a staff and a sceptre to symbolise his authority. His upper limbs were made separately and then attached to the dynamic and well-proportioned body (although his head seems rather small in comparison to the trunk) with small wooden pegs that can be seen on the back. The feet are now missing, while the base, which would evidently have had the name of the deceased and possibly his titles, is not original.

The pose, representing the *ka* or vital force of the deceased, obeys one of the most important rules of Egyptian art, the "law of frontality". The figure stands upright on his axis, in perfect symmetry and looking ahead. Another famous canon that also appears is the brown paint that was typically used for male figures.

NOTES AND COMMENTS

According to the documents recording the acquisition of this piece, it was found "in the small temple to the left of the large temple in Deir el-Bahri", indicating the ruins of the funerary temple of Mentuhotep II, the 11th-dynasty king who reunited Egypt at the end of the 3rd millennium. The monarch's temple, now severely damaged, stands south of the funerary temple of Queen Hatshepsut, and indeed provided the architectural inspiration for the latter temple.

Statuettes depicting the *ka* of the deceased were placed in the funerary shrines of tombs inside a closed chamber called the *serdab,* from where the *ka* could "see" anyone who entered the shrine through slits or holes in the wall. This hidden location may explain why so many Egyptian statues from such distant eras have survived intact. The *ka* was a sort of double of the deceased: a vital and sexual force that took the same form as the body but had the property of being invisible, since it was a spiritual and psychic creation.

Although many similar wooden statues are known from collections in several museums (starting with the large set in the Egyptian Museum in Cairo), this figure from the Gulbenkian Collection includes the novel feature of showing the earlobes. Other apparently unique aspects concern the eyebrows, which are drawn almost horizontally, and the lips, whose appearance differs from that found on all other statues from that period. It seems that Howard Carter's concerns as to the authenticity of this piece came from its varnish rather than these unique characteristics. In the resulting controversy, Calouste Gulbenkian maintained his position of expectation and prudence, writing to Sir John Forsdyke (then the director of the British Museum) to say, "May I be permitted to say that I am always most pleased to learn and I am never offended by criticism."The British Museum's experts later concluded that the piece was authentic, and Sidney Smith noted in his report that "The figure has been treated slightly repaired since it was found. The original loincloth was a piece of canvas covered with plaster; the part over the left leg has been made up with modern plaster and varnish. The nose and right cheek has been repainted. One arm may be of a different wood, but is, possibly, ancient work." He consequently concluded that "An attentive examination of the internal evidence fails to reveal any cause for doubt on physical or chemical grounds, but rather confirms the authenticity of the figure."

The statue had clearly undergone some restoration work after it was found, arousing the interest of leading Egyptologists such as Sir Flinders Petrie, who wrote on it in an article published in *Ancient Egypt* (1920), and Georges Bénédite, who supported its claimed authenticity in his article "Vraie ou Fausse?" (*Revue d'Art*, January-March 1924). Curiously, the experienced Flinders Petrie was mistaken in his attribution of the statue, since his article wrongly states that it was an image of pharaoh Nebhepetra (Mentuhotep II). For some years, the statue was on display in the Louvre Museum, before moving to London in 1937 to be exhibited at the British Museum (Perdigão, 1969: 160-163).

EXHIBITIONS

1922 – Paris, Louvre Museum.

1937 – Ancient Egyptian Sculpture lent by C. S. Gulbenkian, Esq. London, British Museum.

1949 – Egyptian Sculpture from the Gulbenkian Collection. Washington, D. C., National Gallery of Art.

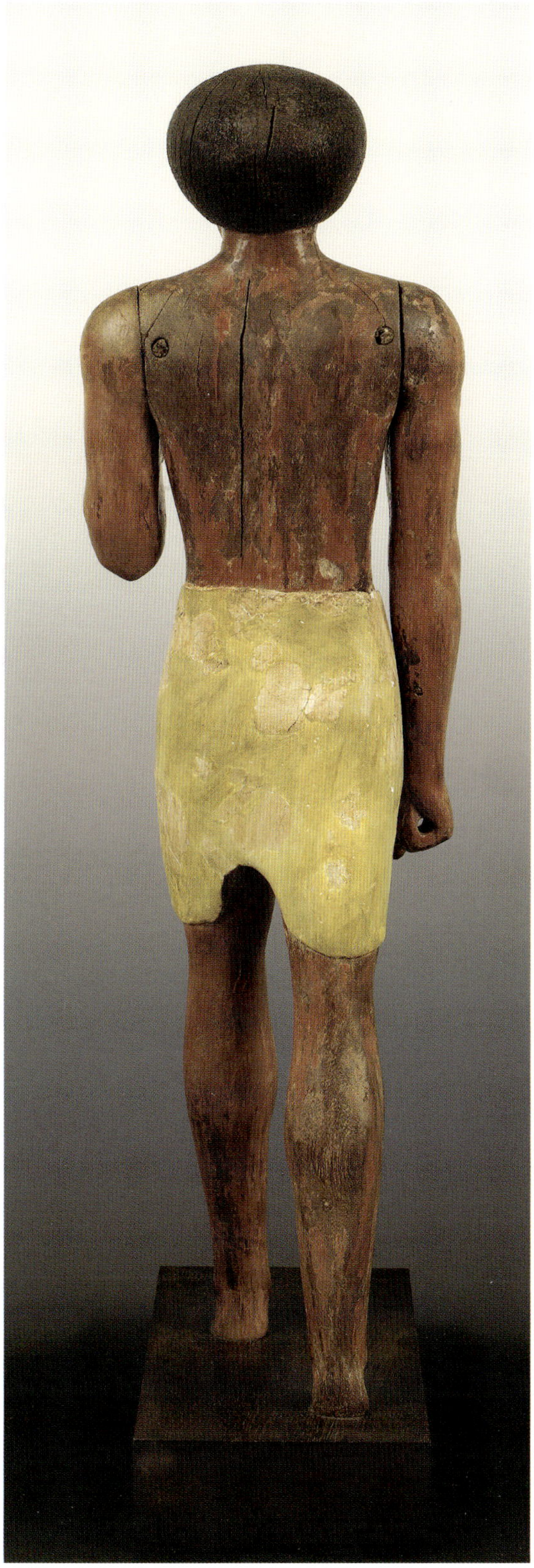

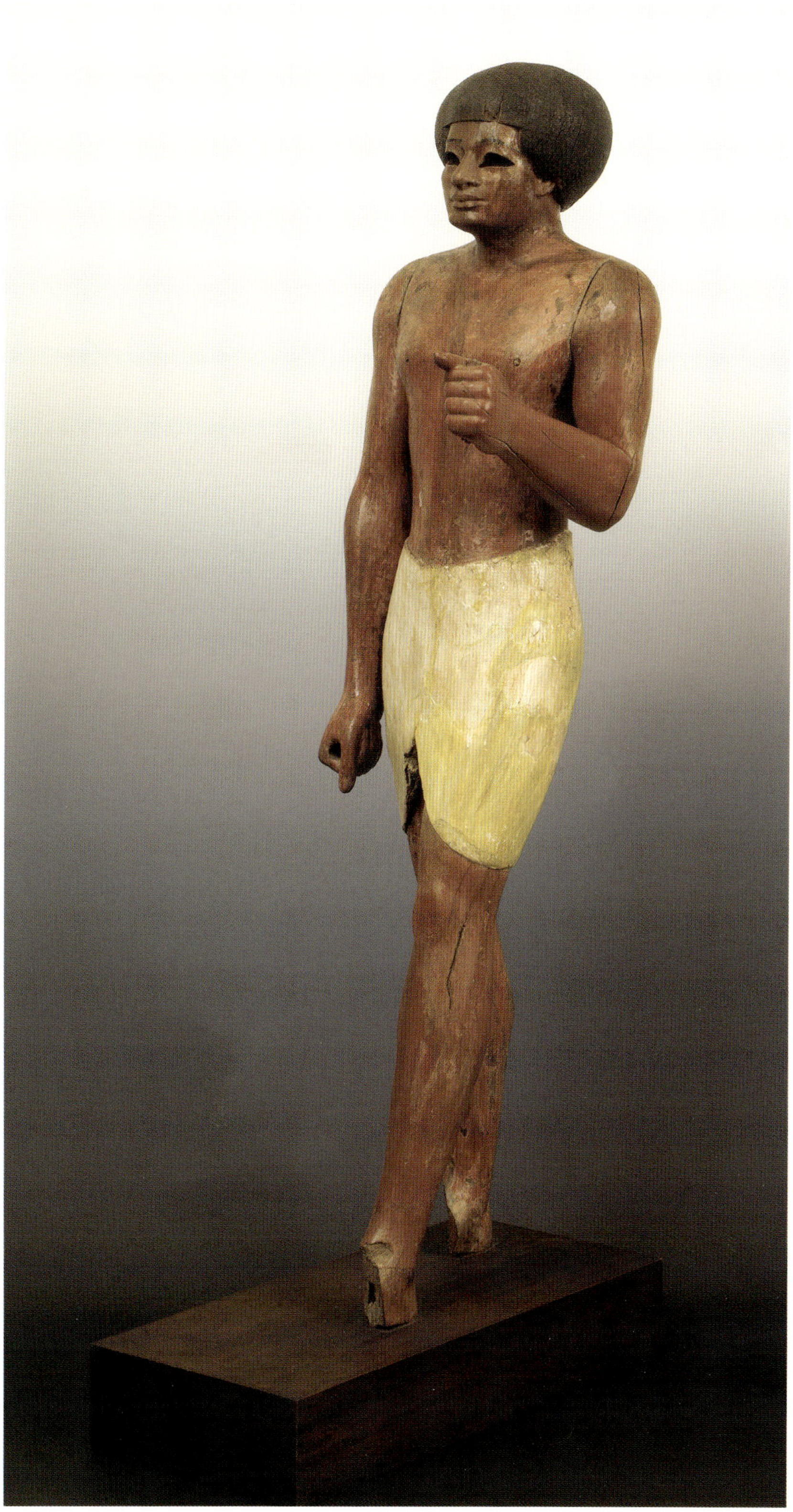

4

**HEAD OF KING SENWOSRET III**

Middle Kingdom, 12th dynasty (ca. 1860 BC)
Obsidian
H: 12 cm
Provenance: The MacGregor Collection
Date incorporated: 1922
Inv. no. 138

This magnificent fragmented head portrays King Senwosret III, under whom Egypt attained an exceptional peak. The portrait, made in obsidian and handled in a realistic manner, reveals a humanised spirit and a firm attitude, both of which were characteristics of the kings from this dynamic dynasty, who wished to be seen as the executors of *maet* (truth, justice, harmony and order), while also expressing the realism that was then in fashion.

The pharaoh is wearing a pleated headdress called a *nemsit* decorated with the descending sacred serpent (*uraeus*), which has lost its head. The headdress, which reaches halfway down the king's forehead, would continue around the back of his head and then fall onto his shoulders in horizontal folds, but this part no longer exists. His eyes, set under thick eyebrows, do not have the customary image of the iris, while the bridge of his nose is emphasised, his cheekbones protrude and the dimple between his nose and lips adds a touch of naturalism.

NOTES AND COMMENTS

Exhibited at the Burlington Fine Arts Club in 1921, even before Calouste Gulbenkian acquired the piece, this fine head immediately aroused great attention. At the time, Sir Claude Philips wrote in *The Daily Telegraph* that it was "the best piece of small-scale Egyptian art ever discovered". The exhibition of the royal head at the National Gallery of Art in Washington moved John Walker to say: "This small fragment of a statue, carved in one of the hardest and simultaneously most fragile materials known – obsidian – truly pushes back the boundaries of art. In all likelihood, the subject was Amenemhat III, who ruled in the second half of the 12th dynasty" (Perdigão, 1969: 155-158).

Some earlier studies, from the first half of the twentieth century, believed that the face portrayed was of Amenemhat III, the son of Senwosret III, but more recent analyses and opinions produced by experienced Egyptologists fairly consensually suggest that it was Senwosret III himself (also known under his Greek name of Sesostris). Other images offer very convincing support for this attribution. The striking image of the face of Senwosret III in the Gulbenkian Collection is very similar to one on a diorite sphinx of the same king now in the Metropolitan Museum of Art, New York, which also has a quartzite head of this dynamic monarch with the same features (Hayes, 1990, I: 197-198). A fragmented diorite head of Senwosret III can also be seen at the Louvre, revealing identical "embittered" features (Ziegler, 1990: 35). Another head, the remains of a statue of the king that was found at the Karnak temple in 1970 and is now at the Luxor Museum, again shows the ruler with similar features (Cairo, 1979: 32-35). The same mature and realistic appearance can be observed on the head at the Kunsthistorisches Museum in Vienna, which shows an aged Senwosret III (Satzinger, n.d., 20, print 7), and on a granite head at the Egyptian Museum in Berlin (Wildung, 1999: 15), a paternal image of the good shepherd that was exalted in the ideology of the age.

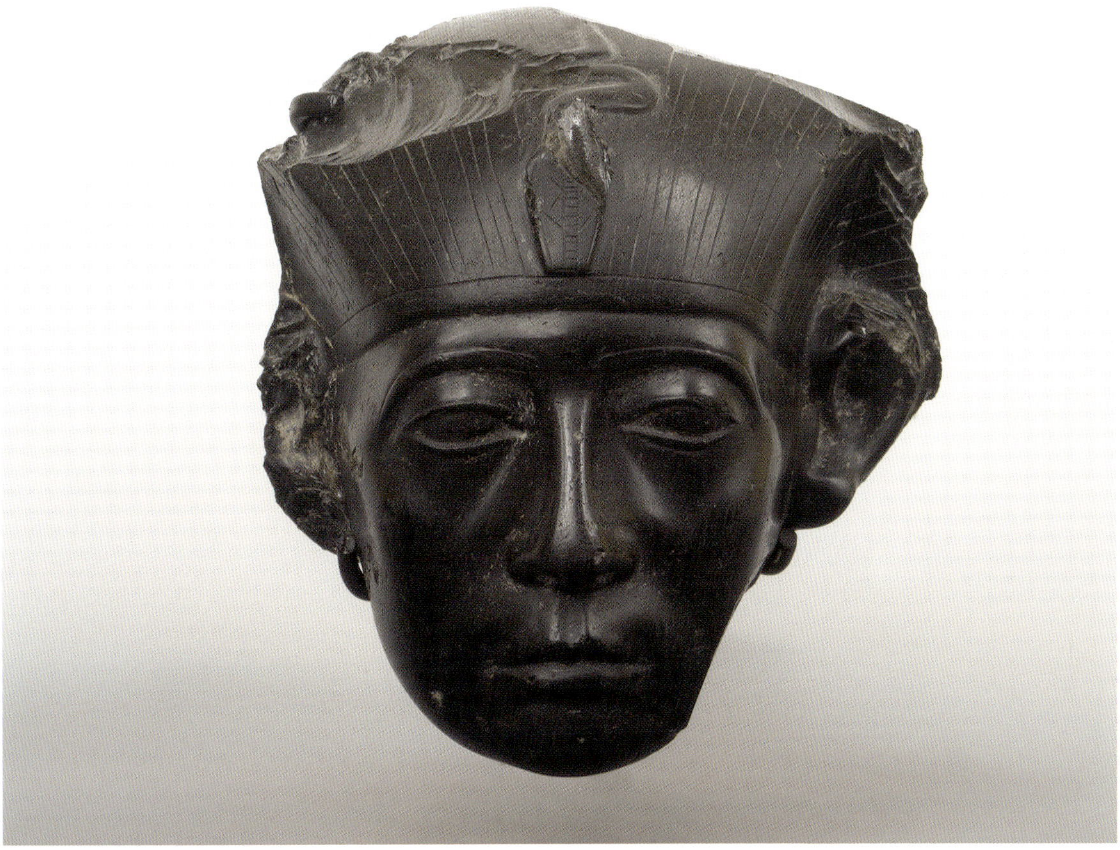

Jean Yoyotte believes that these images may illustrate a southern tendency towards realism, contrasting with work from the north, which was based on Memphite idealism. Thus, Theban realism expressed a new "humanisation of the divine" and in this case established the portrait as a "mask of wisdom" (Yoyotte, 1968: 40) or imbued it with "an exciting and painful realism" (Vandier, 1958: 214). The sculptor ultimately copied the finest and most expressive statues of rulers from the Old Kingdom, but removed that characteristic expression of self-confidence that they customarily had. Instead, he showed the somewhat concerned features of a man who took difficult decisions without being sure that they are being put into practice (Málek, 2003: 113). Yet this work is more a realistic portrayal of the king as he truly was than an expression of the spirit of the period when the statue was produced. This establishes a clear and deliberate contrast to the idealised statues from the early days of the dynasty, as can be seen in the statues that still retain traces of Memphite production that were carved for Senwosret I (Aldred, 1980: 129; Tiradritti, 1998: 91).

Crowned head of Senwosret III, Middle Kingdom, 12th dynasty. Luxor Museum

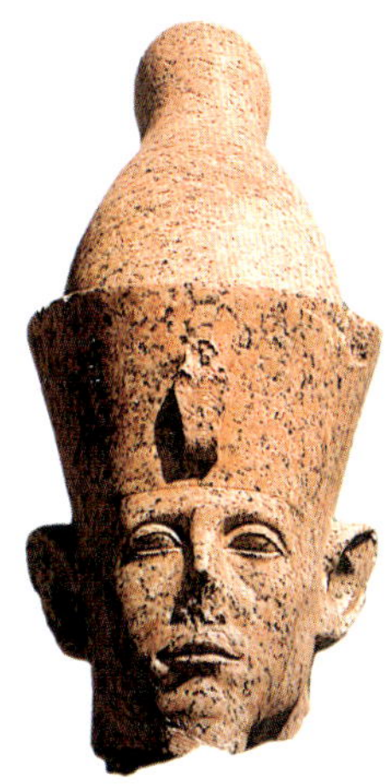

It should also be noted that the Louvre, which owns the aforementioned impressive head, also has a statue of Senwosret III as a young man (Ziegler, 1990: 35). Both statues came from Medamud, a centre for the worship of Montu, a powerful cult in the 12th dynasty. The magnificent head in the Calouste Gulbenkian Museum probably comes from the same region. In fact, there are statues of Amenemhat III – Senwosret III's successor – whose facial features can be both young and old. The face with clearly defined features on a sphinx of Amenemhat III is well known, as is another statue where the monarch is wearing a priest's robes, now at the Egyptian Museum in Cairo (Tiradritti, 1998: 132-133; Bongioanni & Croce, 2001: 507). It is enlightening to contrast the head of Amenemhat III and its dynamic and youthful features (Metropolitan

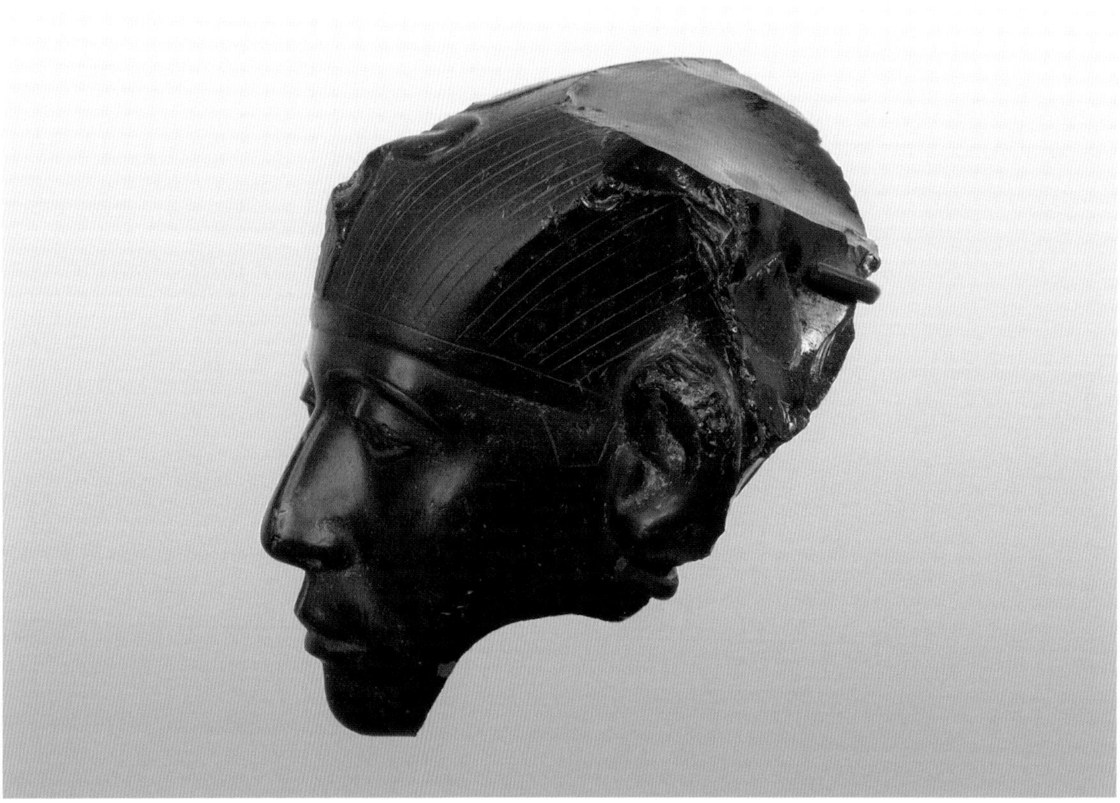

Museum of Art in New York; Hayes, 1990, I: 199) with another statue of Amenemhat III as an old man (Málek, 2003: 120). One plausible theory is that the artist opted to capture the king's youth in realistic fashion, and later produced an older image at the end of his reign so as to demonstrate maturity and wisdom. The texts written at that highly productive time could also be recalled, as they variously depict Pharaoh Senwosret III as a fierce young warrior who led the aggressive campaigns in Nubia and as a wise old man and zealous administrator who worked to encourage the principles of *maet* in daily life (Yoyotte, 1968: 40).

It is symptomatic that the mature expressiveness of the pharaoh's face also inspired the production of statues showing other individuals. Other portraits from this same period show their subjects with elderly features that offer a wise and living reflection of their lengthy experience of life (Bothmer, 1987: 2-5). However, there were also cases from as early as the Old Kingdom where the tomb-owner had himself portrayed on statues either as a young man or with an older appearance.

EXHIBITIONS

1921 – Ancient Egyptian Art. London, Burlington Fine Arts Club.

1937 – Ancient Egyptian Sculpture lent by C. S. Gulbenkian, Esq. London, British Museum.

1949 – Egyptian Sculpture from the Gulbenkian Collection. Washington, D. C., National Gallery of Art.

1965 – Obras de Arte da Fundação Calouste Gulbenkian. Oeiras, Pombal Palace.

2000 – Ägypten, 2000 v. Chr. Die Geburt des Individuums. Kunst Forum (Grundkredit Bank), Egyptian Museum of Berlin.

5

## STATUETTE OF MES

New Kingdom, early 18$^{th}$ dynasty (ca. 1530 BC)
Polychrome limestone
H: 22 cm
Provenance: The Amherst Collection
Date incorporated: 1921
Inv. no. 402

The figure shown is a man named Mes, who is portrayed in a pose that obeys the rules of the "law of frontality". He is sitting in a chair with a cubic base whose side is used to bear the inscription in hieroglyphs incised into four bordered vertical columns, two of which are damaged in parts.

His arms run alongside his body, bending at the elbows to follow his seated pose. His right hand holds a small stylised lotus flower that rests on his lap, and he has a painted two-string necklace (now rather worn) holding a hanging winged scarab. He is wearing a long kilt that reaches down to his ankles and was painted white, with a side knot at the waist made in relief.

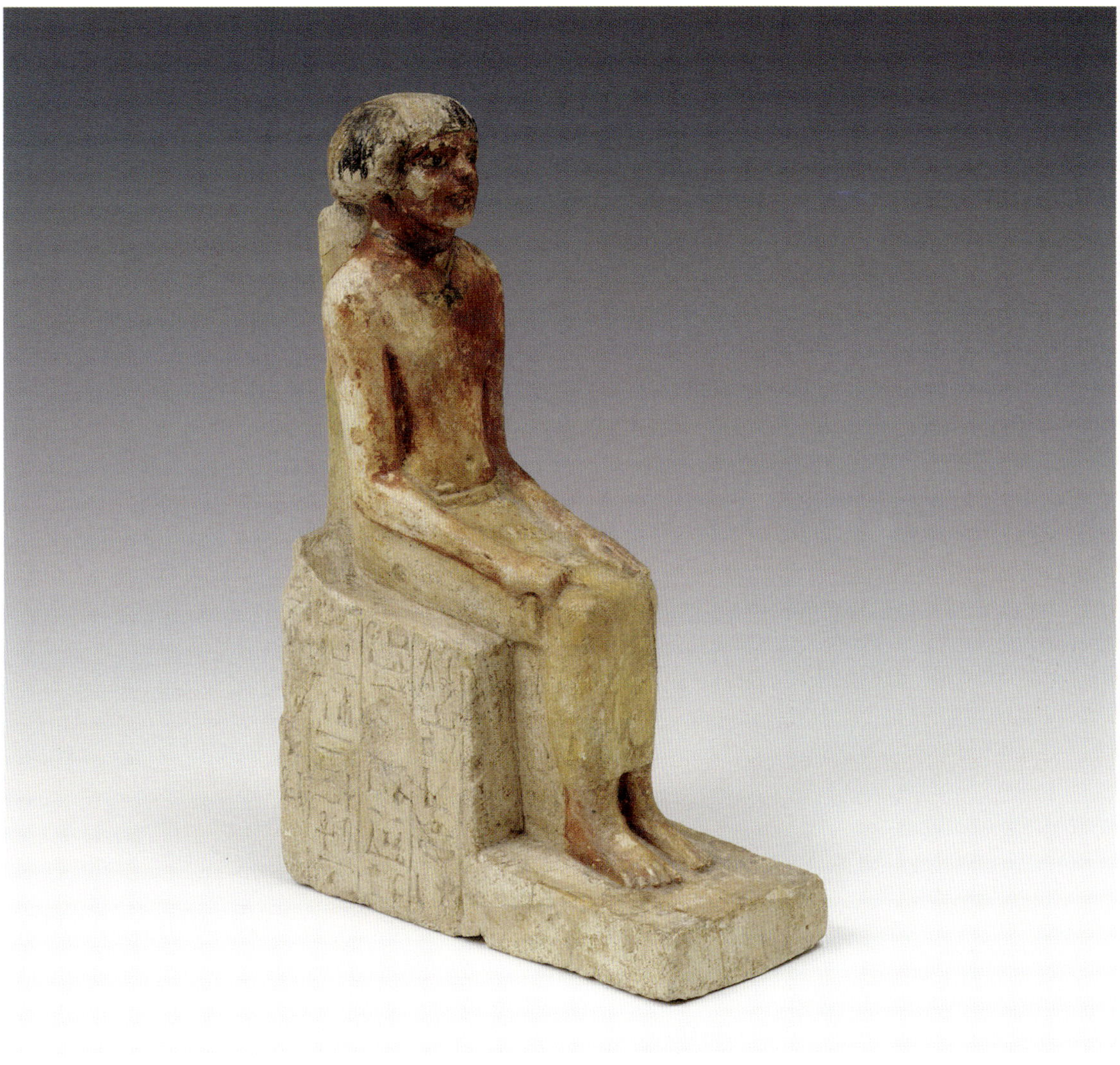

The sculpture was painted and the black of his short striated hair and the red ochre of his body can still be seen. According to the canons of painting, red was reserved for male figures. The chair where he is sitting is cube-shaped, although the form is interrupted at the back by a slight and gently curving elevation that connects it to the back pillar against which the figure rests. Unlike other known cases, this bears no inscription. The cohesive and compact aspect of the sculpture is emphasised by the connection between the legs and the front of the chair, which has the following hieroglyph inscription:

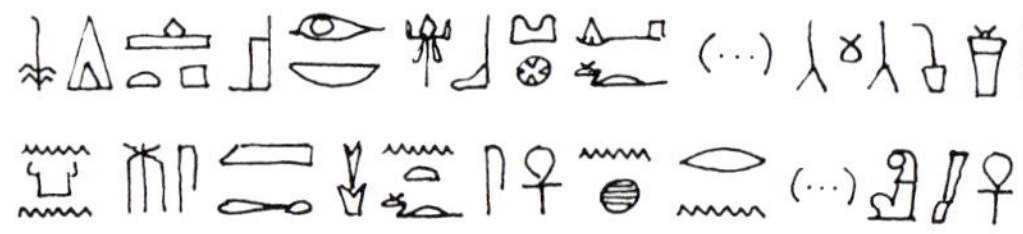

"Gift made by the king to Osiris, lord of Abydos, so that he will grant [invocations-offerings of bread, beer, beef and fowl, good and pure things], vessels, cloths, incense and ointments for the *ka* of Mes, justified. His sister, who gives life to [his] name [...] renewed in life."

NOTES AND COMMENTS

The hieroglyph inscription on the right of the chair offers a fine example of brotherly love, as the statuette was devoted to Mes by his sister, whose name does not appear in the text. It should be noted that the term "sister" often means "beloved", although it is more plausible in this context to believe that it really was his sister. The name Mes was very common in Ancient Egypt, and was the source of the Hebrew name Moses.

The hieroglyph inscription also demonstrates another truly significant aspect of the funerary texts, as it starts with the formulaic expression: "gift made by the king" (in Egyptian *hotep-di-nesu*). Theoretically, it was the king who offered the tomb and its goods to Osiris, the god of eternity, rather than to the deceased. The god would then supply the *ka* of the Osirified deceased with the "invocations-offerings" (in Egyptian *peret-kheru*, or literally "what leaves from the mouth") that were indicated in the list of products. In this case, although part of the inscription is missing, these are known to have been traditionally "bread, beer, beef and fowl" among other widely requested foodstuffs. The missing hieroglyph inscription would certainly be as follows:

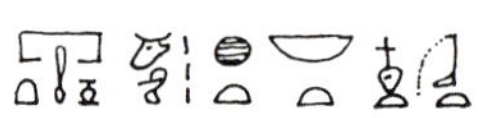

Statuette of an official,
New Kingdom, 18th dynasty.
Painted limestone, H. 25 cm.
Egyptian Museum, Turin,
inv. no. cat. 3089

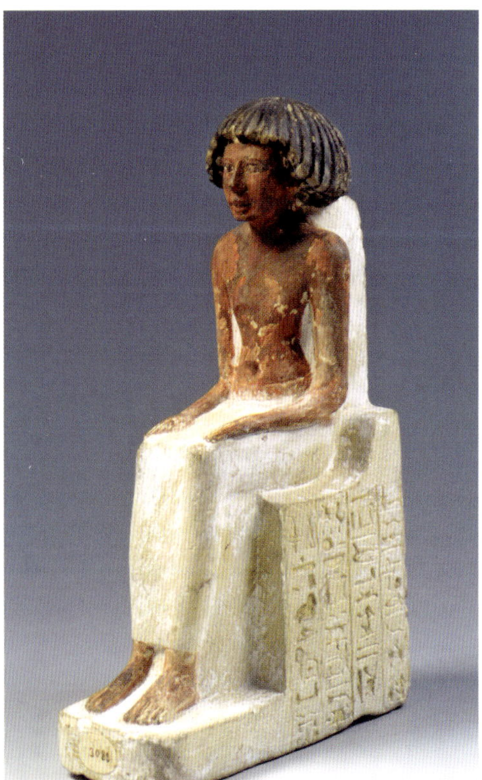

It was enough for the god to mention ("leave from the mouth") the goods required for subsistence for them to magically appear. The end of the inscription lacks the name of Mes' sister, which has unfortunately been obliterated, leaving only the indication that the name was a female one, followed by the comforting declaration: "renewed in life" (*uhem-ankh*).

This statuette was one of the works of art at the Pombal Palace in Oeiras that was affected by the major floods in 1967. Having been covered in mud, it was restored at the Conservation Laboratory at the Museu Monográfico de Conímbriga. The cleaning and treatment process used thirty litres of deionised water, followed by long and complex restoration and consolidation operations.

There is a similar sculpture at the Egyptian Museum in Turin (Seipel, 1989: 278), dated to the 18th dynasty (between the reigns of Thutmose II and Amenhotep II). The typology and period both correspond to the production of this statuette of Mes.

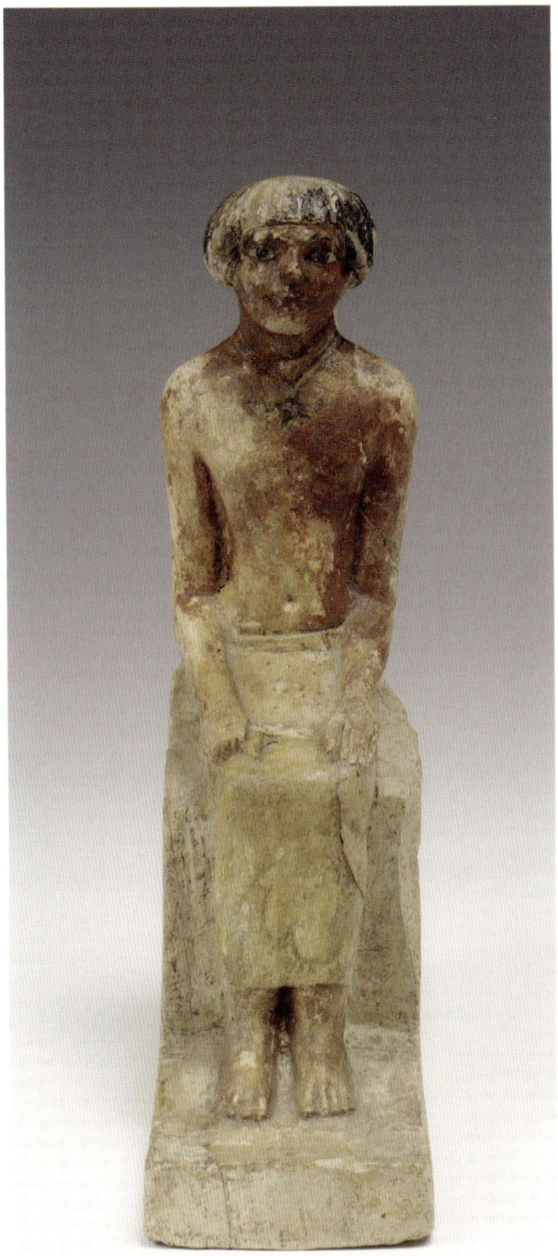

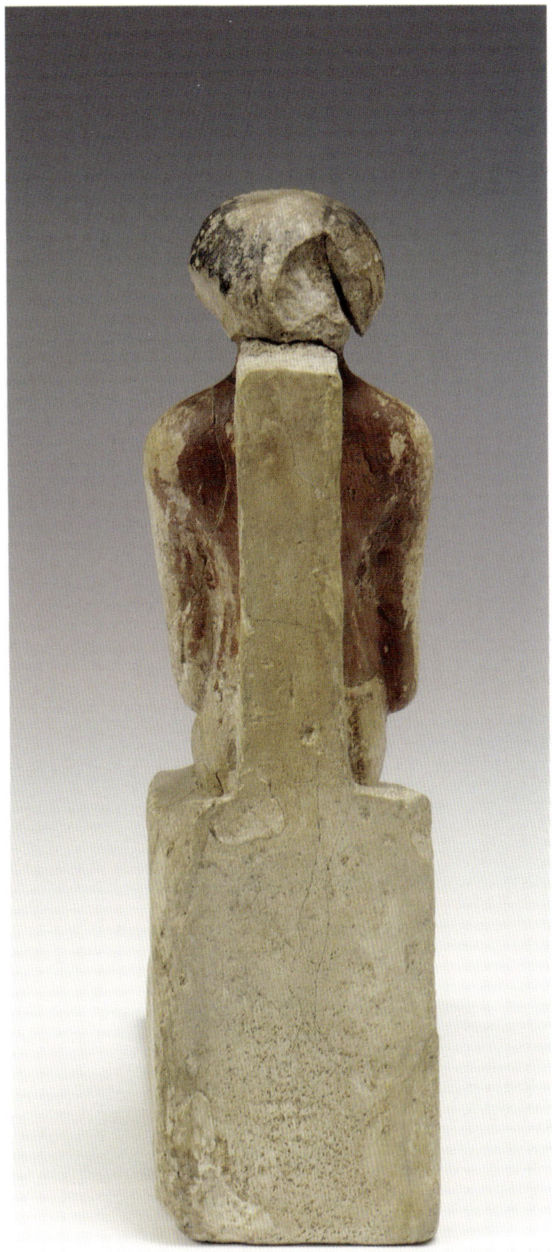

6

**HEAD OF A NUBIAN (?)**

New Kingdom, 18th dynasty (ca. 1500-1300 BC)
Black granite
H: 14 cm
Provenance: Acquired from Howard Carter
Date incorporated: 1929
Inv. no. 218

This head probably shows a man who came from the Nubian (rather than the Egyptian) ethnic group. The inhabitants of Nubia, a vast area south of Aswan, had Negroid features, including darker skin than the Egyptians. Consequently, the sculptor used black granite so as to make the portrait more realistic. The subject may have been an important official who (as was customary during the expansionist and cosmopolitan period under the New Kingdom) was made a leadership position within the military.

Rather than his own hair, he seems to be wearing the sort of wig that soldiers had at that time, which starts in the middle of his forehead and extends towards his partially lost ears. He has prominent cheekbones, no irises in his eyes, a slightly flattened nose and dilated nostrils, while his thick lips are pressed firmly together, and he has a slightly worn furrow between his upper lip and his nose. His face, which was not carved in great detail, is given a certain naturalist feel by the two clear lines that run away from his nose and by his firm protruding chin.

NOTES AND COMMENTS

Due to its apparently Negroid features, this figure has been seen as an image of a Nubian. However, there are also grounds for doubt. Contemporary images show people with very similar features, including a granodiorite statue in exhibition at the Egyptian Museum in Cairo. The figure was made for Amenhotep, the son of Hapu, a senior official from the reign of Amenhotep III, who was definitively not of Nubian origin, but from the northern city of Athribis (Huttaherib). The hairstyle and the facial features of both statues are similar (Tiradritti, 1998: 182; Málek, 2003: 170). In this case, the most relevant issue was to show signs of the subject's mature age and wisdom, which is portrayed through an interpretative process that would later also be used for some imagery from the Ptolemaic Period.

If this striking head does indeed portray a Nubian, it then summons up images of the contingents of Nubian archers who served in the army during the campaigns in the Syria-Palestine corridor. Such images of Nubian archers had been produced in previous periods, and their effective services had also been used under the Middle Kingdom after Senwosret III's campaigns in Nubia. However, Nubians from that age had never reached senior positions in the pharaonic administration. Under the New Kingdom, when there was an increase in military activities in the Syria-Palestine corridor, Nubian troops were again used as support forces, and also benefited from the demands made by the Egyptian authorities at a time when military service was a means of rapid social climbing. There can be no doubt that the statue of this anonymous person was carved due to his social status of some dignity and importance, although it is impossible to tell whether the figure was standing or sitting.

The general term used to describe the inhabitants of Nubia, as shown in Egyptian art with clear Negroid features, was *nehesiu* (meaning the blacks). Meanwhile, the Nubians were not only used for military action abroad (particularly in the Syria-Palestine corridor), but also as part of the police forces that

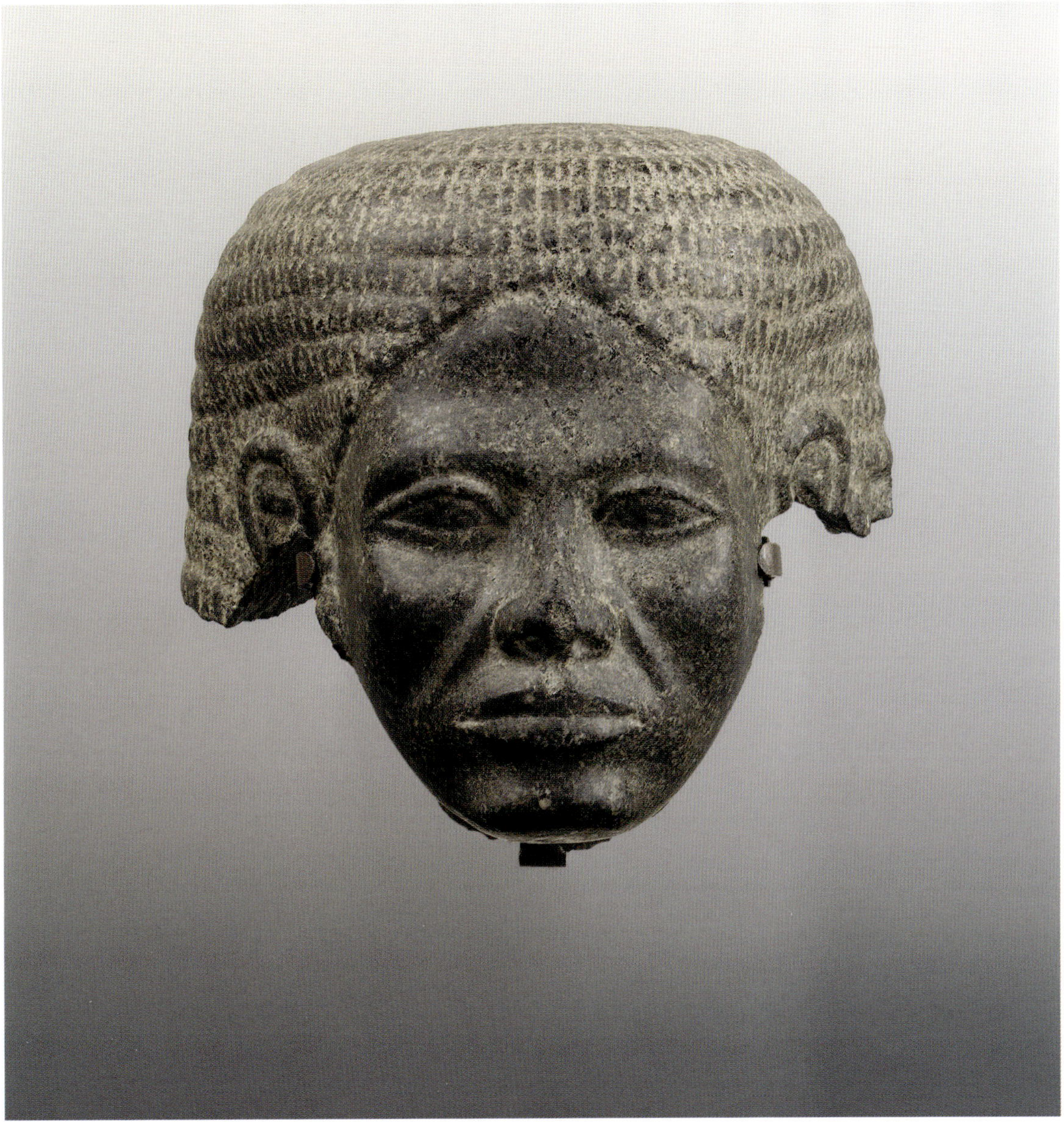

were recruited to keep the peace at home, being armed with staffs and accompanied by aggressive dogs (Araújo, 2001: 562).

EXHIBITIONS

1937 – Ancient Egyptian Sculpture lent by C. S. Gulbenkian, Esq. London, British Museum.

1949 – Egyptian Sculpture from the Gulbenkian Collection. Washington, D. C., National Gallery of Art.

1965 – Obras de Arte da Fundação Calouste Gulbenkian. Oeiras, Pombal Palace.

7

**HEAD OF KING AMENHOTEP III**

New Kingdom, 18th dynasty (ca. 1402-1364 BC)
Blue glass paste
H: 3.7 cm
Provenance: The MacGregor Collection
Date incorporated: 1922
Inv. no. 139

This delicately carved small head with almond-shaped eyes is an idealised portrait of Pharaoh Amenhotep III, who became king at the tender age of around ten. He is portrayed as an adolescent wearing the *kheprech* or blue crown, decorated with small circles. The front has three holes used to hold the *uraeus* (*iaret*), the sacred snake, which was probably made of gold and has been lost. The young king's almond-shaped eyes and eyebrows are outlined in black, a typical feature of the first period of his long reign, which lasted for almost forty years and produced in-the-round images and wall sculptures of the king. His initially boyish features were gradually transformed by time into the healthy adult face of this patron and admirer of the arts.

NOTES AND COMMENTS

Some Egyptologists believe that the reign of Amenhotep III was the peak of Egyptian civilisation (Grimal, 1988: 285-290; Padró, 1996: 274-276). The king's youthful appearance would influence the sculpture produced during that age of ostentation, which was fertile in statues and low-reliefs of officials depicted in elegant and rather affected poses. Imagery showing the monarch during the early days of his reign is well known, including a head (larger than this fragment) at the Louvre Museum (Ziegler, 1990: 46) that reveals the same almond-shaped eyes. Another in stuccoed and painted clay can be found at the Egyptian Museum in Cairo (Tiradritti, 1998: 174). The pharaoh's youthful face can also be admired in several pieces from the Luxor Museum: a study for a portrait; a small head demonstrating the typical sophistication from the early period of his reign and the colossal head in red granite (Cairo, 1979: 72-73, 76-77, 96-97). Another fascinating example is the quartzite head with the pharaoh's typical almond-shaped eyes that is now at the British Museum (Quirke & Spencer, 1992: 43). Even when Amenhotep III is depicted in large-scale statues, the sculptors always carve his gentle face with youthful, smiling lines, almond-shaped eyes and lips outlined by a small and delicate relief line (Málek, 2003: 161).

Crowned head of Amenhotep III, New Kingdom. Diorite, H. 32.5 cm. The Louvre Museum, inv. no. A25 © Photo RMN / © Hervé Lawandowski

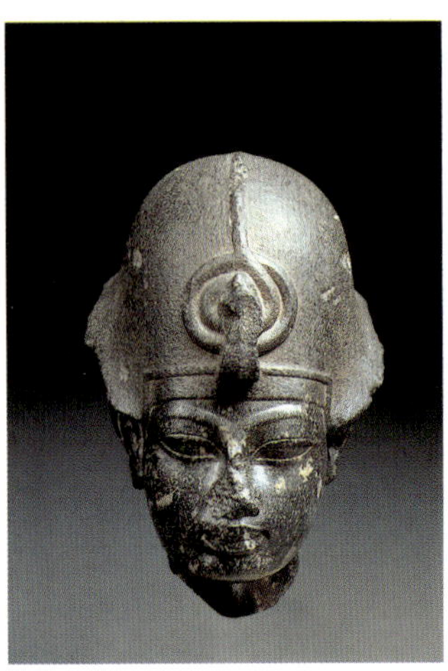

The blue crown on the king's head is sometimes called the "war crown", although this is a controversial attribution since it often also appears in scenes that have no connection to warfare. It is true that many royal images from the New Kingdom period show the ruling pharaoh in magnificent combats and wearing the blue crown, but other idyllic – almost bucolic – images also exist where several different monarchs are wearing the same crown, which was apparently introduced into Egypt by the Hyksos.

The pharaoh's name, translated as "Amun is satisfied", sometimes appears in Greek versions as Amenophis, a form that is increasingly rare and only used by a handful of Egyptologists and Orientalists nowadays. In fact, even this is incorrect, as the proper Greek form would be Amenothis (a Hellenic reinterpretation of Amenhotep), rather than Amenophis (derived from Amenemope).

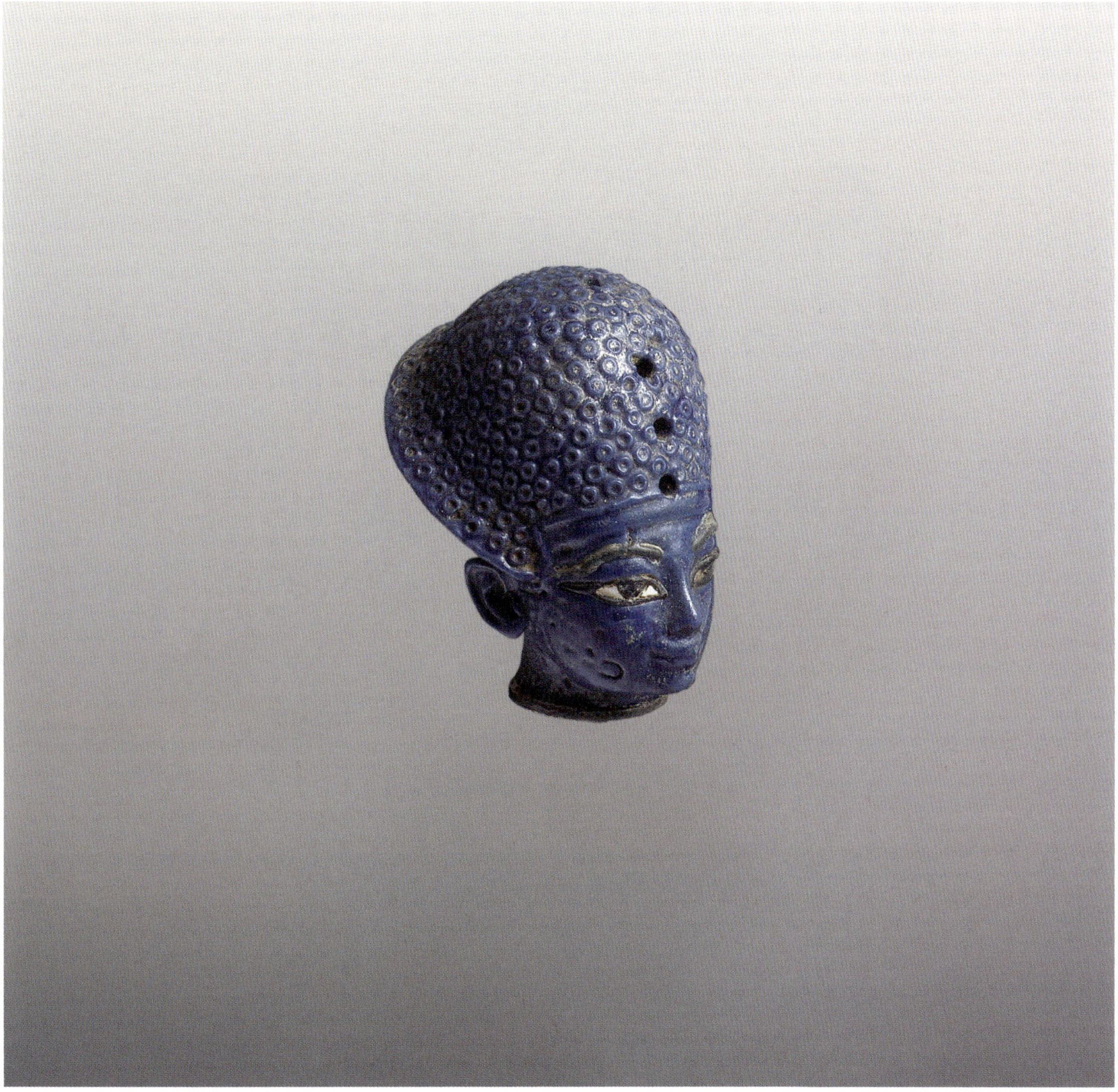

EXHIBITIONS

1921 – Ancient Egyptian Art. London, Burlington Fine Arts Club.

1937 – Ancient Egyptian Sculpture lent by C. S. Gulbenkian, Esq. London, British Museum.

1949 – Egyptian Sculpture from the Gulbenkian Collection. Washington, D. C., National Gallery of Art.

1965 – Obras de Arte da Fundação Calouste Gulbenkian. Oeiras, Pombal Palace.

8

## HEAD OF A PHARAOH

New Kingdom, 18$^{th}$ dynasty (?) (ca. 1500-1300 BC)
Blue glass paste and enamelled faience
H: 7 cm
Provenance: The Dr. Fouquet Collection, Cairo
Date incorporated: 1922
Inv. no. 48

This head of a pharaoh wearing the *kheprech* is made in blue glass paste so as to represent the blue crown. His face, in white faience, has a blue line running under his chin, representing the thread that held his beard, the symbol of royal and divine power. This would have been made in gold, as would the *uraeus* (*iaret* or sacred serpent), which was also removed from the front hole. The hole under the chin shows the location for the now-lost beard, while his hollowed-out eyes would have held fine stones to imitate his cornea and iris. The three wrinkles on his neck, a conventional way of indicating adulthood, first appeared with the aesthetic innovations brought by the Amarna Period. The original enamelling on some parts of this small head has already fallen.

NOTES AND COMMENTS

This small head of a pharaoh may depict a king from the 18$^{th}$ or 19$^{th}$ dynasty, which explains the doubt as to the proposed date. The sales catalogue from 1922 suggests that this object (no. 38) is a portrait of Thutmose III. However, since wrinkles on figures' necks appear more frequently after the Amarna Period, the figure may portray Pharaoh Horemheb (18$^{th}$ dynasty), or one of the early kings from the 19$^{th}$ dynasty.

EXHIBITIONS

1937 – Ancient Egyptian Sculpture lent by C. S. Gulbenkian, Esq. London, British Museum.

1949 – Egyptian Sculpture from the Gulbenkian Collection. Washington, D. C., National Gallery of Art.

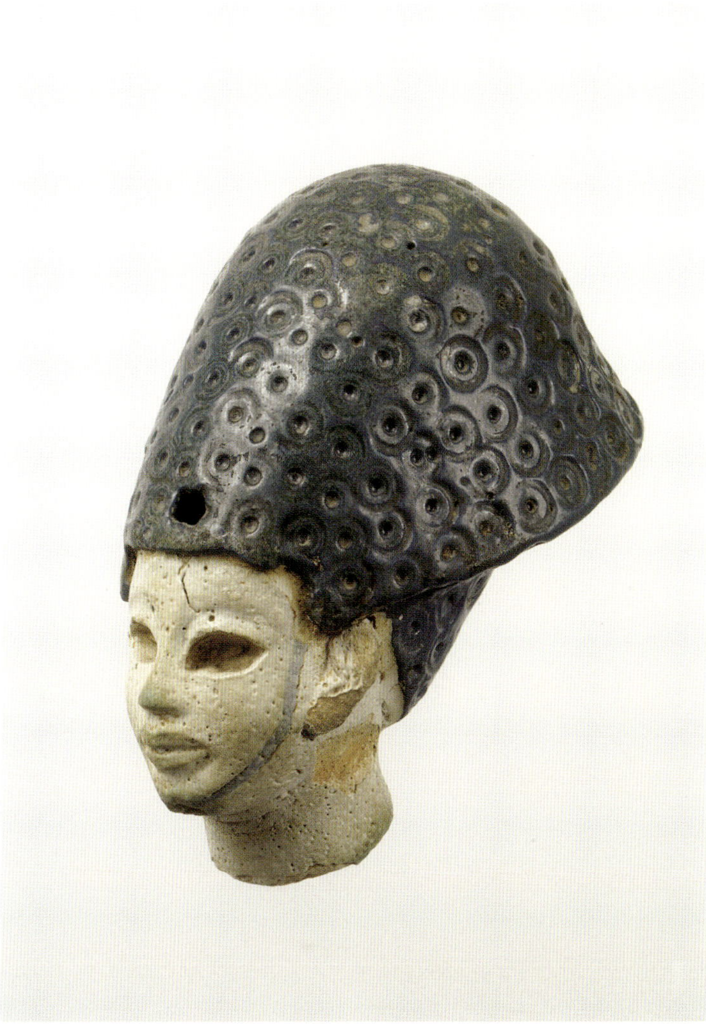

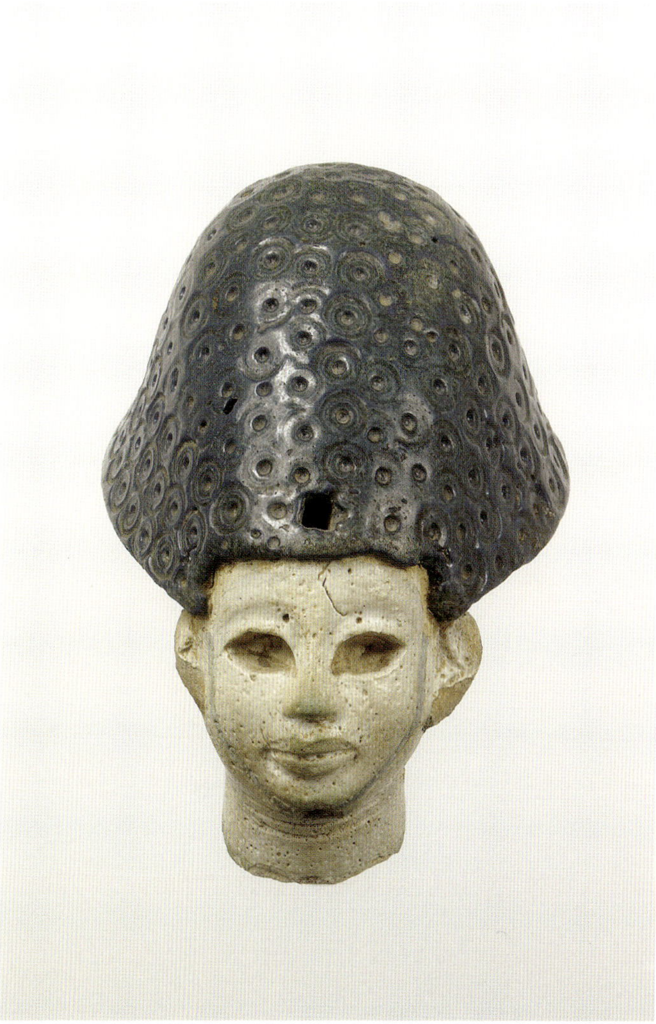

9

**COSMETIC 'SPOON'**

New Kingdom, 18$^{th}$ dynasty
Ivory
L: 20 cm
Provenance: The MacGregor Collection
Date incorporated: 1922
Inv. no. 165

This object is called a 'spoon' for cosmetics as it was used as a container for ointments. Carved in ivory, it reveals great artistic sensitivity and a sense of humour when dealing with an everyday theme. It shows a date-palm whose bowl is like a large leaf and handle is a palm-shaped tree-trunk. Leaves grow out of the thick, irregular trunk and heavy bunches of dates hang down on either side of it, while two monkeys are eating the fruit with great gusto. On one side of the trunk, an old man is holding a stick and guarding the dates, while on the other side, a bold young man is climbing the tree to steal them. This piece does not have the customary symmetry found in this type of object due to the positioning of the two figures, which were evidently carved to have an exotic and ironic purpose. The figures are Negroid, clearly Nubians, as shown by the customary ethnic details: the man's curly hair and earring, and the boy's facial features.

Small parts of the object have been lost, since the end of the bowl, the man's stick and parts of the boy's head and foot have all been broken. The material is unusual, as the typical 'spoons' for ointments from this era are almost always made of wood or other materials.

NOTES AND COMMENTS

The term 'spoon' appears between inverted commas, as is usual when describing this very typical dressing-table item a at a time when sophistication and cosmopolitan behaviour were flourishing. Concern with beauty and a well-presented body that enhanced its physical aspects gained a new dimension in this age of expansion, although the trend dated from earlier eras. The New Kingdom, and especially the 18$^{th}$ dynasty, used the large-scale production of combs, tweezers, pins, mirrors and 'spoons' (designed to help people make themselves more attractive) to give full expression to its aesthetic and decorative tastes, decorating such objects with erotic or entertaining themes.

The ivory 'spoon' in the Gulbenkian Collection, found in Tuna el-Gebel, Middle Egypt, is part of the flourishing artistic world and expresses the *joie de vivre* that led to the production of many such objects with entertaining or erotic themes. Moreover, at that time of luxury and sophistication, there was apparently no shortage of Asiatic influence from the Syria-Palestine corridor (Araújo, 1995: 79).

Many mirrors and 'spoons' show girls – some with Nubian features, either naked or wearing sophisticated clothing (Wildung, 1999: 30; Málek, 2003: 163) – or animals such as gazelles with tied legs and ducks (Hayes, 1990, II: 191). Sometimes, the girls depicted on the handles of the 'spoons' can be associated to ducks, whose bodies acted as containers for the ointments (Leclant, 1979, 2: 235-237). The collection at the Museu da Farmácia, Lisbon, demonstrates this, as it includes a 'spoon' with a naked girl, another with a gazelle whose legs are tied, and two twinned ducks. It should be noted that at the time, the duck was an erotic symbol.

Like other objects in the Collection, this one was also acquired via Howard Carter, whose records note that it was made during the Middle Kingdom, although this is highly unlikely.

EXHIBITIONS

1937 – Ancient Egyptian Sculpture lent by C. S. Gulbenkian, Esq. London, British Museum.

1949 – Egyptian Sculpture from the Gulbenkian Collection. Washington, D. C., National Gallery of Art.

1965 – Obras de Arte da Fundação Calouste Gulbenkian. Oeiras, Pombal Palace.

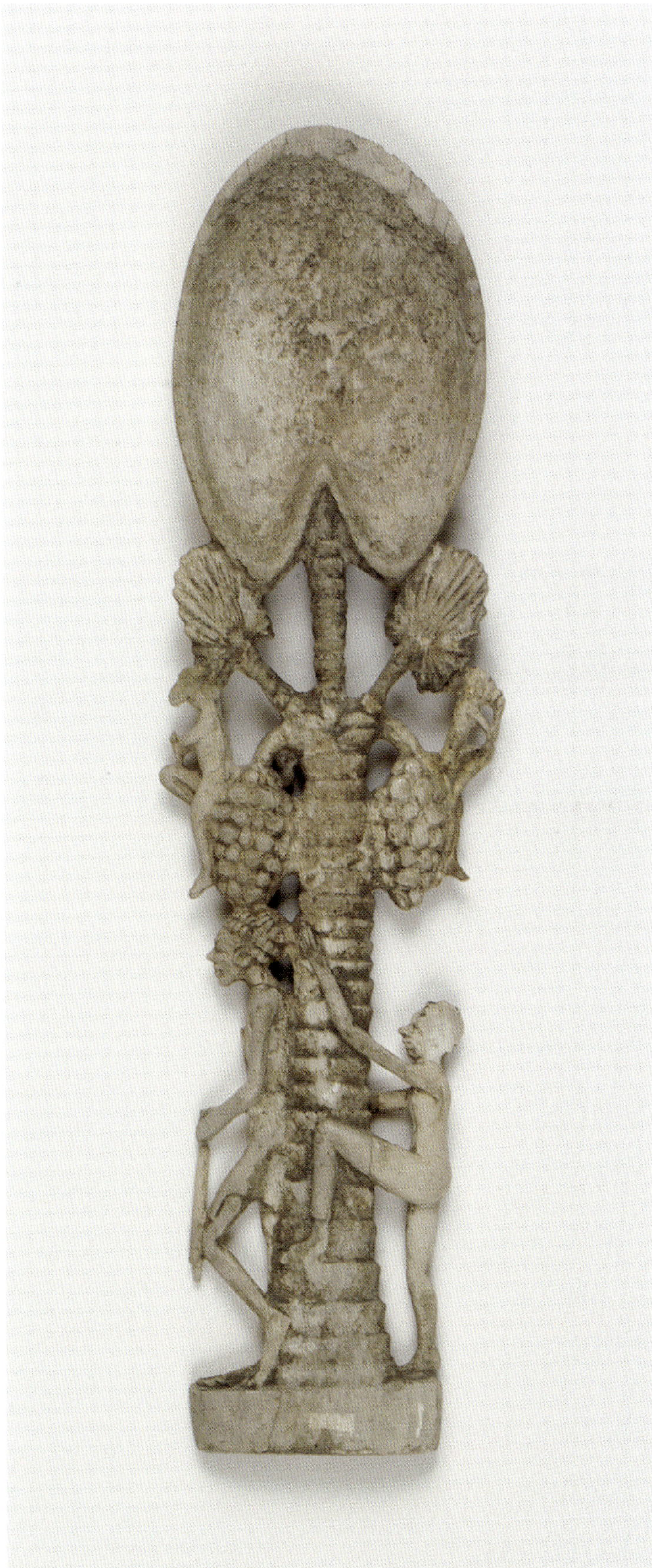

10

## STELE OF THE SCRIBE IRY

New Kingdom, 18th dynasty (ca. 1300 BC)
Polychrome limestone
H: 29 cm; W: 21.6 cm
Provenance: The MacGregor Collection
Date incorporated: 1922
Inv. no. 160

The decoration on this limestone stele with a rounded top is divided into two sections. The upper part shows a shrine where King Ahmose (the founder of the 18th dynasty) and Queen Ahmose-Nefertari are depicted sitting on their thrones. The pharaoh is wearing the *kheprech* (blue crown) and holding the *ankh* symbol in his right hand and the royal sceptre in his left. The queen, sitting next to him, is wearing a crown with tall feathers, and has her left arm around her husband in an intimate yet commonly seen gesture in images of couples. A heavily laden table of offerings stands in front of them. Jars holding liquids (probably wine) and surrounded by aquatic plants to keep them cool appear beneath, flanking the raised foot of the altar. These jars are set on two appropriate supports that form the hieroglyph sign used for the phoneme *g*.

The lower section shows the scribe Iry, kneeling and saying a prayer that appears in hieroglyphs in front of him, as if coming out of his mouth. The official's body is finely sculpted, his head is closely shaved, his eyes are almond shaped and his ear clearly outlined, while the two lines above his navel, suggesting a slight amount of fat around his belly, add a touch of the Armana style. His linen kilt, lightly bunched up on his back, is held by a belt with three folds and a knot at the front, before leading into an apron. He is also wearing another larger kilt in finer cloth that can only be seen through a light transparency at the bottom, by the ankle. His bent-over foot with a curved stylised appearance can also be seen.

The figures of the king and queen above, the scribe below, the shrine, the table of offerings and the jars are in low relief, while the hieroglyphs and vertical separating lines are incised. There are also traces of polychrome: the green stems of the offerings on the altar, the brownish tone (as established by the artistic canons) of the scribe's body, the black hieroglyphs and the separating red lines. The shrine has no side, allowing the two royal figures to be seen inside, and access to the shrine is via a gentle slope. The separation between the supporting beams and the shrine's roof has two floating decorations at the front and behind. Various objects – including bread, containers with unidentifiable fruit, chops and a duck or goose whose neck has been wrung, all crowned by plants – are piled in orderly fashion on the altar with the raised foot and broad base.

Inscription inside the shrine:

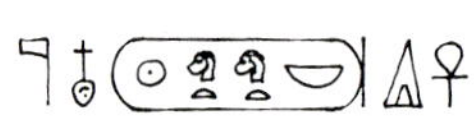

"The kind god Nebheptra, imbued with life."

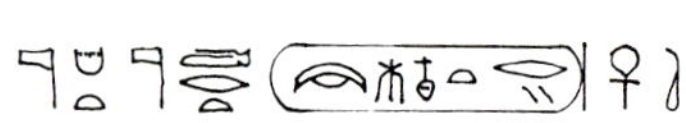

"Long live the divine wife, the hand of god, Ahmose-Nefertari."

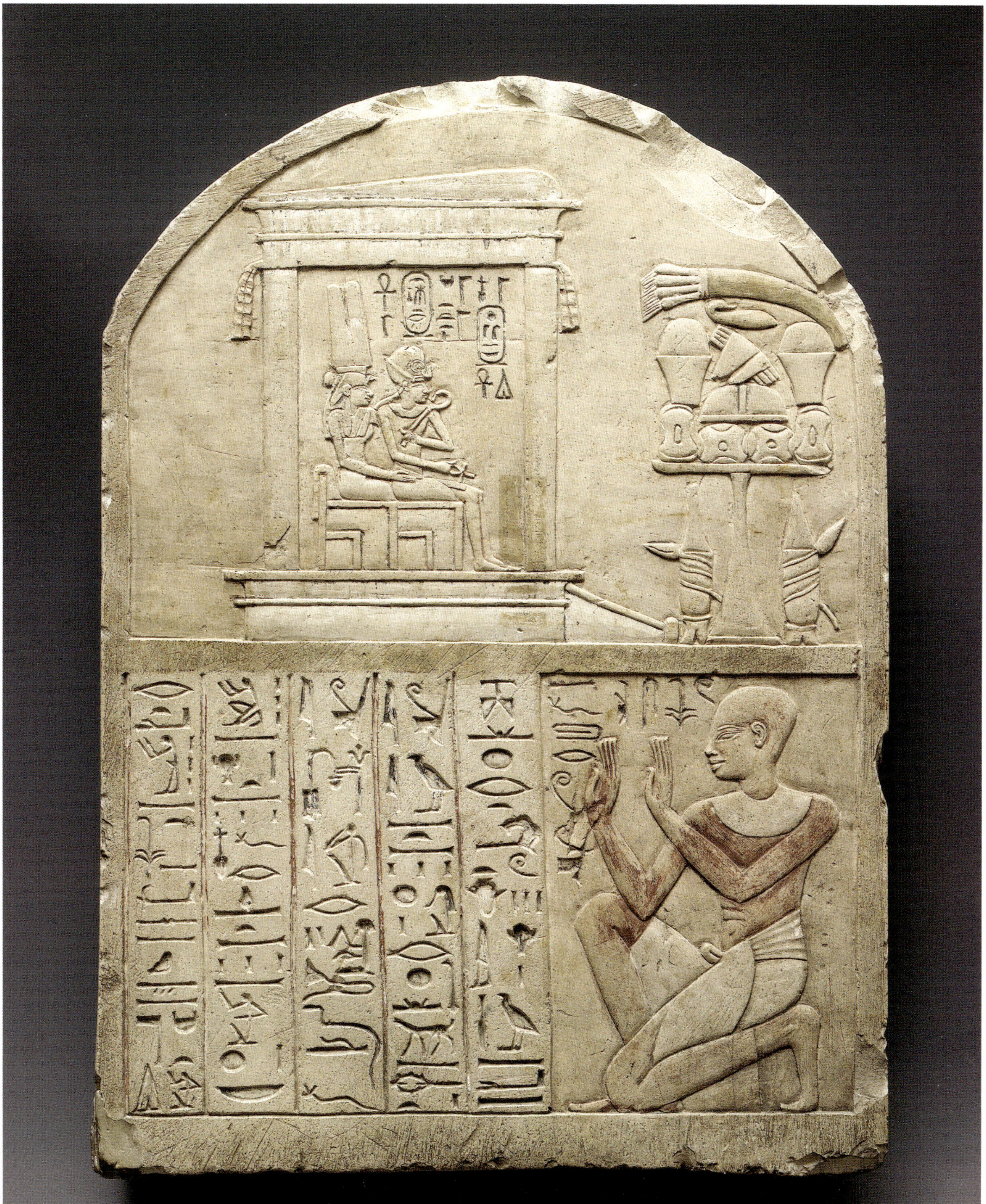

The inner part of the stele reads:

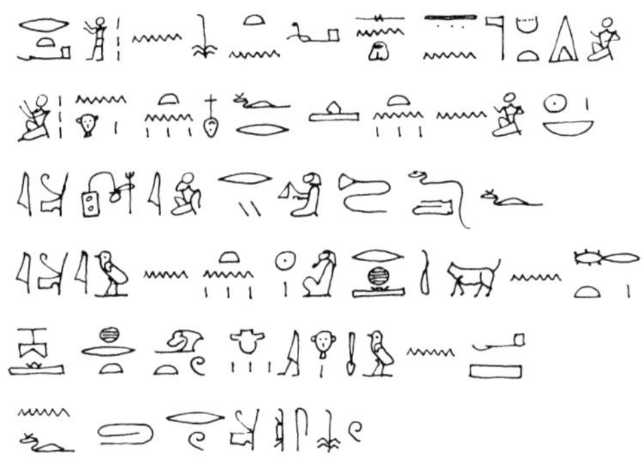

"Giving praise to the victorious king, kissing the ground for the divine spouse. I praise your beautiful face so that you will be kind to me every day. Thus speaks the scribe Iry, justified: Do you have Ra, who knows what is inside the body, who assesses the state of hearts, who responds to the voice of he who summons him and turns to he who follows him?"

NOTES AND COMMENTS

Similar figures to this one of the shaven-headed scribe Iry appear on steles from the late 18th dynasty and later periods, as can be seen, for example, at the Egyptian Museum in Turin (Seipel, 1989: 272). The shaved head, projected slightly backwards, suggests that the work should be dated to the late 18th dynasty, an attribution that is strengthened by the figure's clearly almond-shaped eye, indicating that it was produced in the reign of Horemheb, after the Amarna Period. The stele has a rounded top, a style that started to replace the former rectangular steles from the Middle Kingdom onwards. A fine example of the rectangular stele can be found in Portugal at the Museu Nacional de Arqueologia, Lisbon (Araújo, 2001a: 143). The entire stele has a relief border that is broader at the base and divides the two sections in the middle.

The shrine holding the royal couple may represent a shrine in the Thebes region, where Ahmose and Ahmose-Nefertari were venerated. In fact, the cult of these deified figures (like that of their son Amenhotep I) became a tradition in Thebes-Waset that lasted throughout the 19th and 20th dynasties. The form of the shrine (*kai* in Egyptian) corresponds to Gardiner's O 18 sign, with a vaulted roof, while the pedestal with a small slope suggests the *maetic* pedestal (Gardiner, Aa 11). In addition, the shrine strongly suggests one of the canons of Egyptian art: altering the form of reality so as to offer a better understanding of what is really shown. The shrine would actually have been closed at the side, but it is here shown as if the side were transparent so that the figures can be seen inside.

Given Egyptian art's love for projective (rather than perspective) geometry, another typical feature is the clear option to capture an aspective image of forms and things. This is shown by the depiction of the foodstuffs on the altar bearing offerings, including the deconstructed products and individualised positioning, rather than the compact accumulation where one product is hidden behind another, as would have been the true case (Schäffer, 1986: 421-446).

While the catalogue for the temporary exhibition at the British Museum (Smith & Edwards, 1937: 23) was useful when translating the hieroglyph texts on the stele, the interpretation made by Sir Alan Gardiner when the piece was still part of the MacGregor Collection (Gardiner, 1920: 188-189) was still more valuable. The text is one of supplication with a somewhat rhetorical nature, as can also be detected in the hymns to Amun-Ra, among other deities. The expression *duá*, meaning prayer or praise, appears in

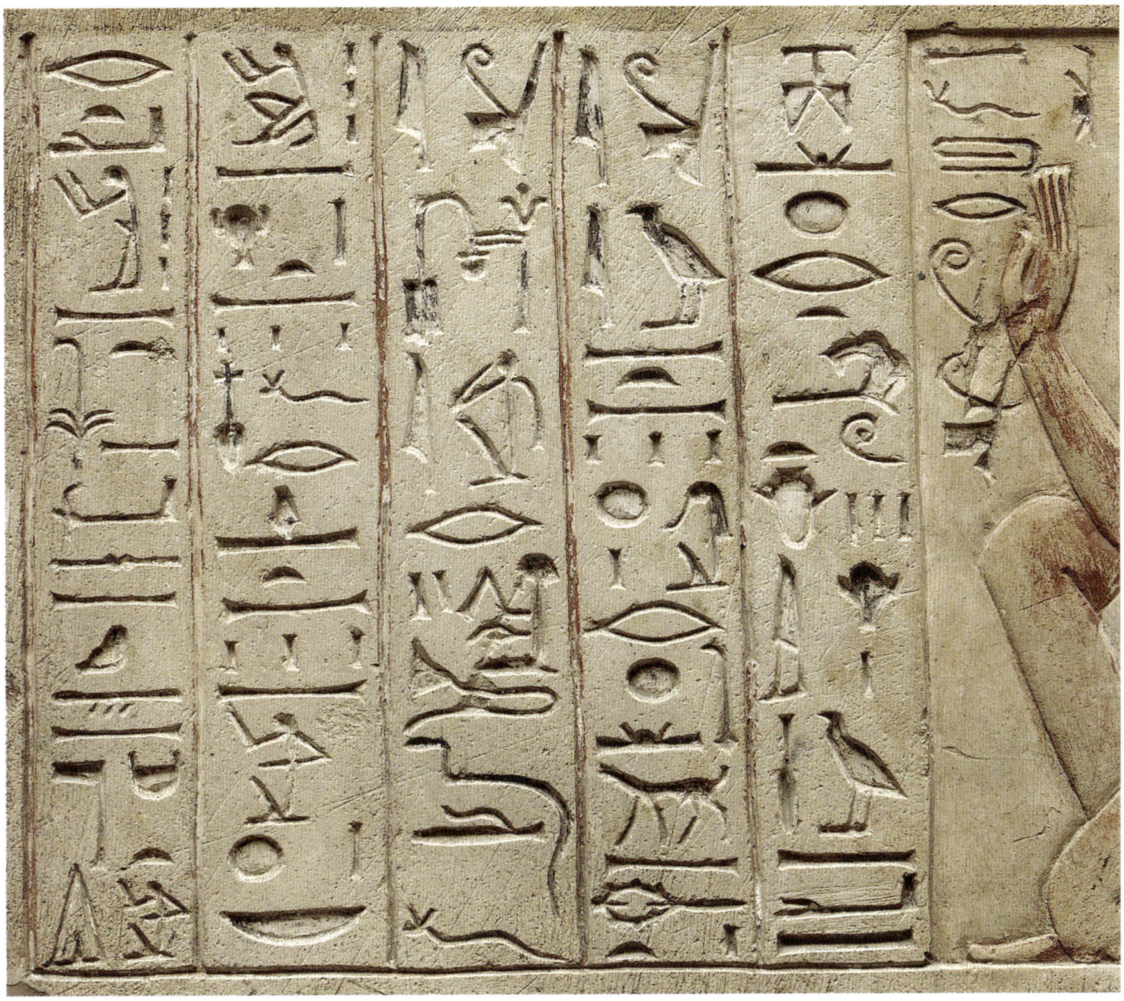

both forms here: in the former case, the sign shows a standing man followed by three lines from the plural (as they were prayers or multiple forms of praise); in the latter, the figure is kneeling in a similar pose to that of Iry, who appears on the right. The word *rekh* (know) is followed by the unnecessary sign *ti*, clearly a mistake made by the scribe.

The king and queen bear the customary titles of the age. Ahmose is called the "kind god" (*netjer nefer*), while Ahmose-Nefertari appears with two titles that have clearly connotations with Amun: "divine wife" (*hemet-netjer*) and "hand of god" (*deret-netjer*) – in this case a reference to Atum, the god who created Heliopolis and who had created the world by masturbating – a demiurgical act that was later attributed to Amun. The hand that Atum used to masturbate was instantly deified (becoming the goddess Iusaaset), and later led to the important title of the "hand of god" that was adopted by queens and priestesses.

EXHIBITIONS

1921 – Ancient Egyptian Art. London, Burlington Fine Arts Club.

1937 – Ancient Egyptian Sculpture lent by C. S. Gulbenkian, Esq. London, British Museum.

1949 – Egyptian Sculpture from the Gulbenkian Collection. Washington, D. C., National Gallery of Art.

1965 – Obras de Arte da Fundação Calouste Gulbenkian. Oeiras, Pombal Palace.

11

**FUNERARY STATUETTE OF HESMEREF**

New Kingdom, 18th dynasty (ca. 1400-1340 BC)
Bronze
H: 24 cm
Provenance: The Carmichael Collection
Date incorporated: 1926
Inv. no. 166

This fine funerary statuette, called a *shabti*, features delicate finishing and exceptional technical virtuosity. The wig is divided into three parts shown by incised lines, and the front ends fall forwards over the necklace. The hair frames a gentle face with pierced ears, clearly drawn eyes and eyebrows, a well-proportioned nose and a mouth whose finely drawn lips are outlined by a border. The figure's closed hands, featuring protruding thumbs and a broad incised bracelet, rest on the exceptional four-string necklace of the *usekh* type.

This attractive *shabti*, beautifully sculpted in bronze and showing great anatomical detail, has now lost the tools it would originally have held to work the land in the next world. The winged goddess Nut is depicted under the figure's crossed arms, and her name is written in hieroglyphs above her image, followed by a hieroglyph text, a version of chapter 6 of the "Book of the Dead", engraved in eight horizontal lines bordered by incised lines.

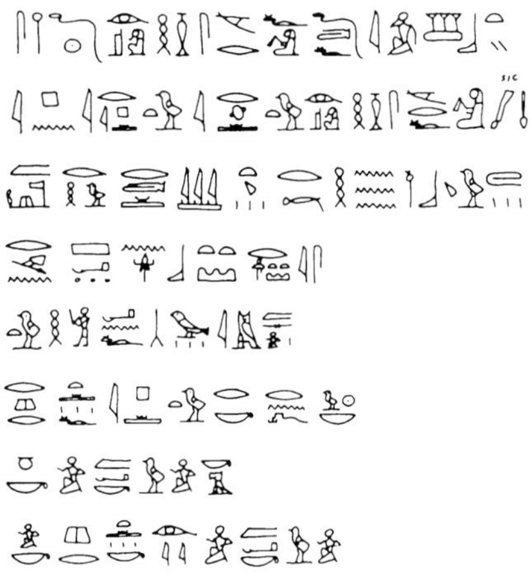

"May the Osiris Hesmeref shine. He says: Oh, this *shabti*, if Osiris Hesmeref, justified, is appointed in the sacred land (the next world) to plant the fields, fill the canals with water and carry earth (manure) from east to west, then shall the task be imposed as if to a man performing his rightful functions. If you are so appointed at any moment, you shall say: I am here! I am here to do your tasks."

NOTES AND COMMENTS

One of the most striking aspects of this funerary statuette is that it is made of bronze, which was rare at that time. *Shabtis* of the same type, but made in other materials, can be found in various collections. Given their elegance and style, interesting comparisons can be drawn with those at the Liebieghaus in Frankfurt (Gessler-Löhr, 1981: 30), the Egyptian Museum in Cairo, made for Iuia (Bongioanni & Croce, 2001: 305), the Louvre, made for the high priest of Amun Ptah (Leclant, 1979: 252; Tiradritti, 1998:

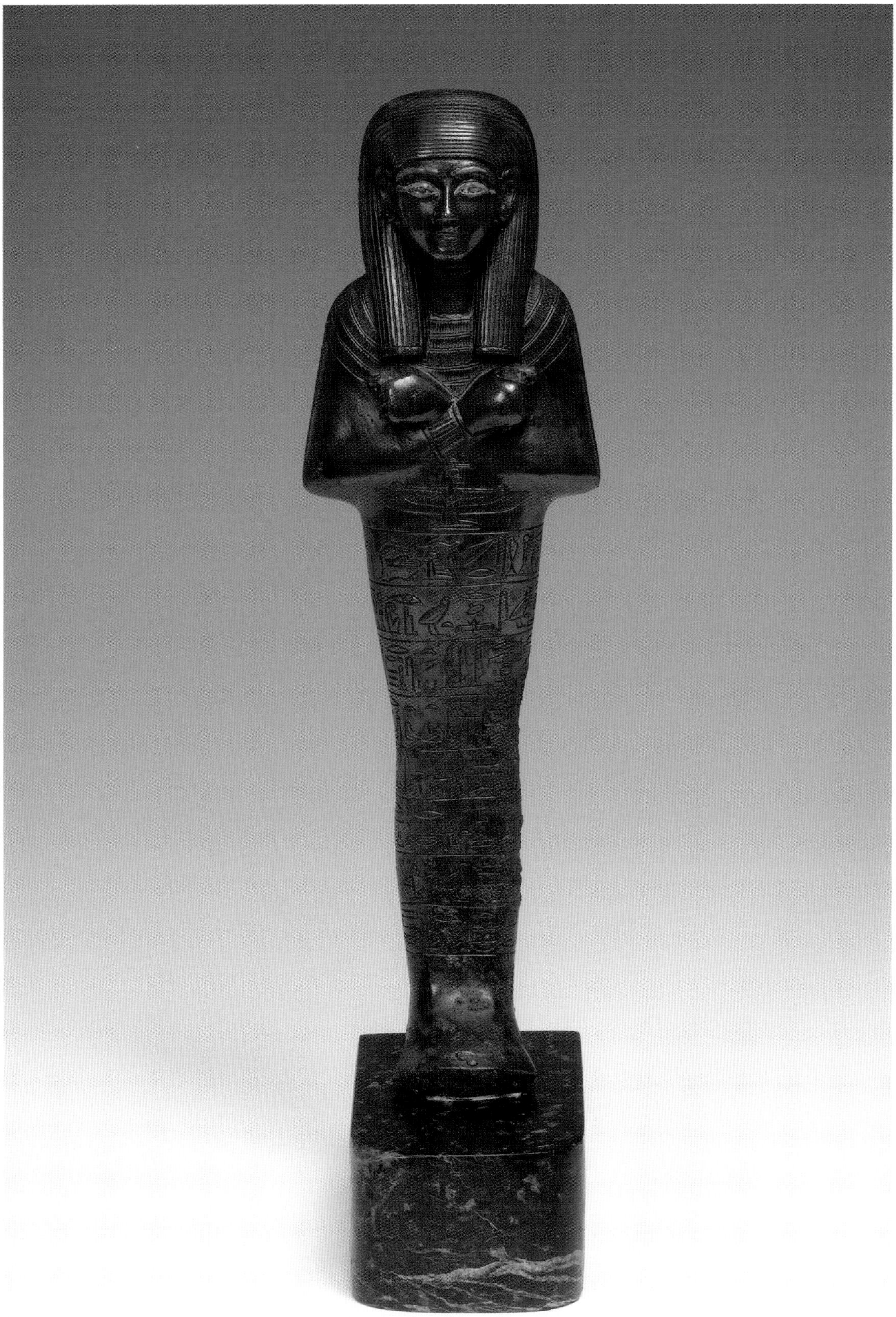

157), and a similar statuette at the Rijksmuseum Meermanno-Westreenianum, The Hague (Hosang, 1989: 94, 99), from the 18th dynasty but with a *ba* bird held to the breast. The *shabtis* made for Tutankhamun and discovered in his tomb are also very interesting (El-Mallakh & Brackman, 1978: 240, figs. 65-66). The interesting Egyptian collection at the Gaia Municipal Cultural Centre, housed in the Solar Condes de Resende in Canelas (Portugal) owns an attractive wooden statuette from approximately the same period that was made for the official Minemai. The text on the front bears the title of the doorkeeper at the necropolis at Memphis, (Araújo, 2003: 300-301).

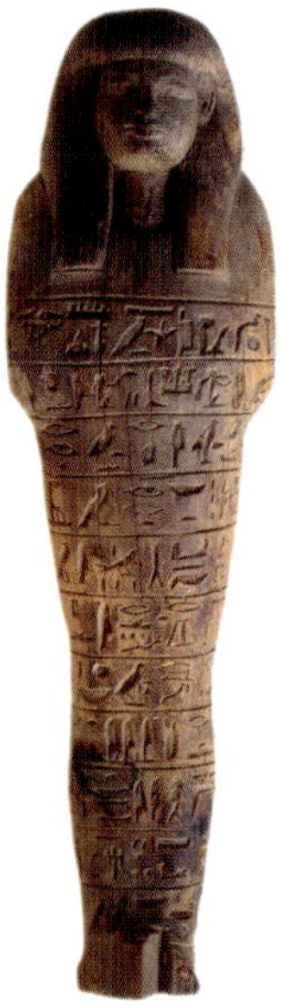

*Shabti* of Minemai, New Kingdom, 18th dynasty. Wood, H. 24 cm. Solar Condes de Resende, Canelas
Câmara Municipal de Vila Nova de Gaia, Casa Municipal de Cultura. Photo: Maria de Fátima Teixeira

The catalogue for the exhibition at the Burlington Fine Arts Club recorded that the *shabti* of Hesmeref dated from the reign of Amenhotep III, while the previous catalogue from the Gulbenkian Collection attributed it to the reign of Tutankhamun (Assam, 1991: 54). While the gentle delicacy of the facial features does indeed suggest the latter, it is equally true that it recalls Amenhotep III and imagery depicting the king from the early days of his reign. Attention should be paid to the outline around the lips, one of the characteristics of art from this monarch's age. Therefore, the date proposed here covers several decades from the reigns of Amenhotep III and Tutankhamun, evidently excluding the Amarna Period, when the few known *shabtis* were given different texts invoking Aten rather than the Osirification of the deceased, while still depicting similarly delicate features (Schneider, 1977, I: 289-290).

The version of the inscription on this *shabti* has already been published in Portuguese (Araújo, 2003: 302-303). Adapted from the version published in the temporary exhibition catalogue at the British Museum (Smith & Edwards, 1937: 23), it also considers more recent studies into this type of piece (Schneider, 1977, I: 81-82). This specific transliteration has merely changed the position of the signs 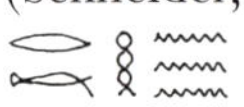 *r smḥw*, "irrigate, fill the canals with water", which was very compact and inelegant in the original. From the Middle Kingdom onwards, the name-title Osiris (here attributed to Hesmeref) was given to the deceased who were considered candidates for eternal life in the fields of the next world, which presupposes their Osirification and solarisation. In other words, they could be reborn as Osiris and travel outside the other world, sailing on the solar barque of Ra. The comforting title of "justified" (*maé-kheru*) that follows the deceased's name refers to Hesmeref's status. Having declared his innocence at the court of Osiris and Maet (reciting chapter 125 of the "Book of the Dead", also known as the "negative confession"), he was considered "just of voice" or "justified".

*Shabtis* are small mummy-shaped statuettes that were placed in tombs to replace the deceased in the work that he was supposed to perform in the next world. They simultaneously served the deceased and were his image, and were seen as such until at least the Ramessid Period. The expression comes from *shab*, the name of the wood of the *persea* tree that most funerary statuettes were made of. Even when such objects started being made in stone, terracotta, faience and other materials, they maintained their original identification as *shabtis* (Araújo, 2003: 107-109).

EXHIBITIONS

1921 – Ancient Egyptian Art. London, Burlington Fine Arts Club.

1937 – Ancient Egyptian Sculpture lent by C. S. Gulbenkian, Esq. London, British Museum.

1949 – Egyptian Sculpture from the Gulbenkian Collection. Washington, D. C., National Gallery of Art.

1965 – Obras de Arte da Fundação Calouste Gulbenkian. Oeiras, Pombal Palace.

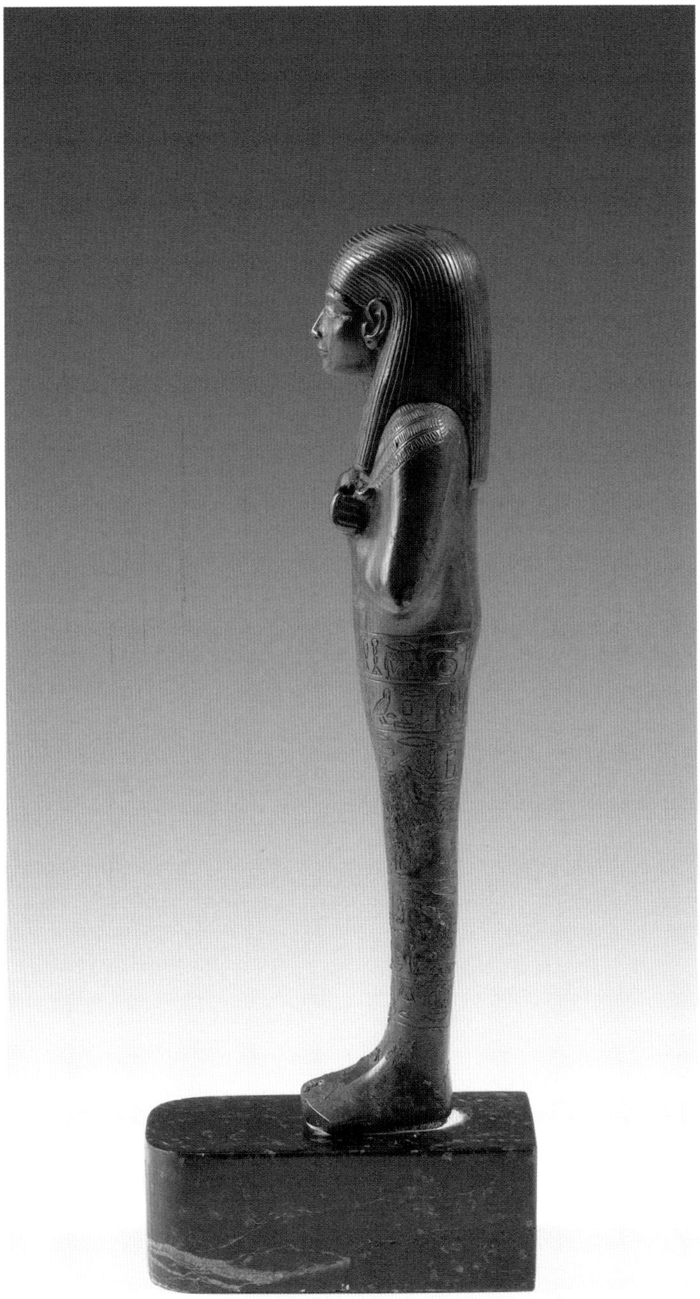

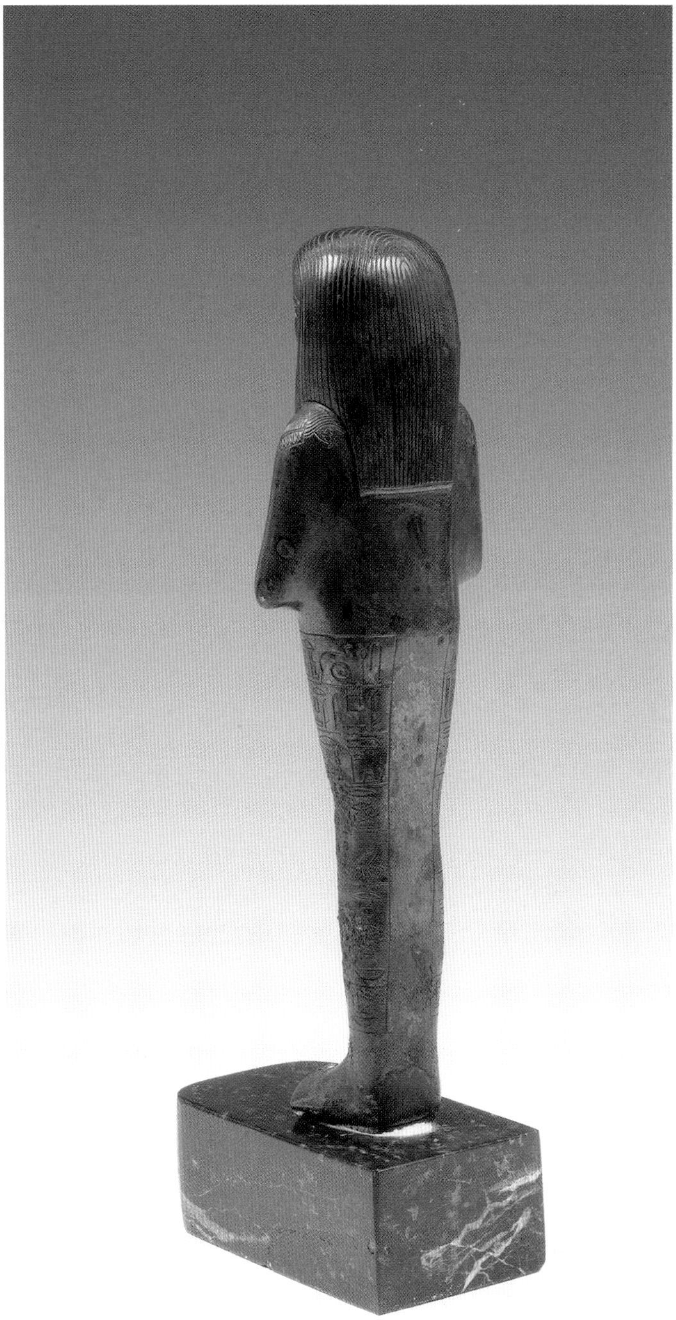

12

**MALE STATUETTE**

New Kingdom, 18th dynasty (ca. 1400-1340 BC)
Polychrome wood
H: 25 cm
Provenance: The Amherst Collection
Date incorporated: 1921
Inv. no. 121 A

This beautiful statuette shows a young man in a classical walking pose, with his left leg forward. Sculpted with great delicacy and detail, it demonstrates the high artistic standards of the time. Although the details have been lost and the eyes, nose and mouth are rather worn, the figure's face evidently has young features. The young man's short, layered hair has three levels and covers his ears, as indicated by vertical lines, and is slightly raised at the nape. In his right hand, he is holding a stem, probably from a lotus bud or – as sometimes found with officials – a symbol of authority such as the *sekhem* sceptre. He is wearing a short, white, pleated kilt, joined at the front and held at the waist by a relief knot. The lines of the pleats start from this knot, as does a band that hangs over his right leg.

His arms were made separately and later attached to the body, as can be clearly seen from the space at the shoulders and the different tone of the wood. The body has some fractures, one of which runs from the neck to the front end of the kilt. The rectangular base is original, but is fractured in several parts and bears no inscription.

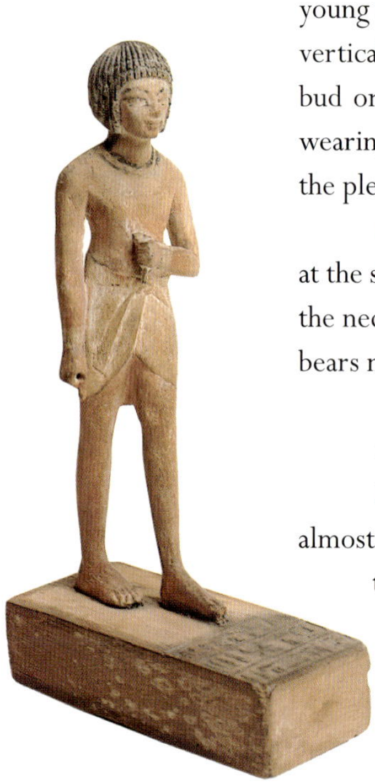

Funerary statuette, New Kingdom, 18th dynasty. Wood, H. 19.2 cm. Rijksmuseum Meermano-Westreenianum, The Hague, inv. no. 76/124.

NOTES AND COMMENTS

It is difficult to date this statuette accurately, although one factor should be considered: the wig is almost identical to one worn by Tutankhamun, so the figure is probably from the same period. However, the delicate features and the graceful and elegant appearance of the body are still similar to work from the reign of Amenhotep III, when some statuettes with short and round-cut hair were produced, albeit without the three superimposed levels found in this piece. Therefore, it seems more appropriate to propose the broader date mentioned above.

A similar statuette, with a hieroglyph inscription on the base but less delicate carving, can be found at the Rijksmuseum Meermanno-Westreenianum, The Hague (Hosang, 1989: 91, 96). This was made for somebody called Mi, and dates from the 18th or 19th dynasty.

EXHIBITIONS

1937 – Ancient Egyptian Sculpture lent by C. S. Gulbenkian, Esq. London, British Museum.
1949 – Egyptian Sculpture from the Gulbenkian Collection. Washington, D. C., National Gallery of Art.
1965 – Obras de Arte da Fundação Calouste Gulbenkian. Oeiras, Pombal Palace.

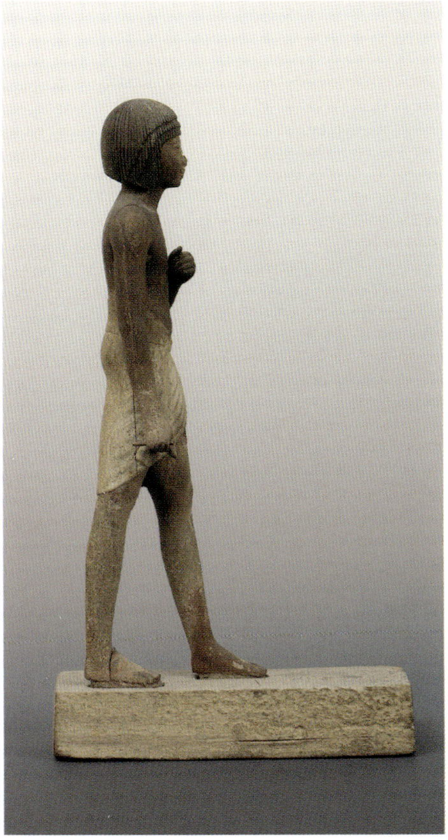

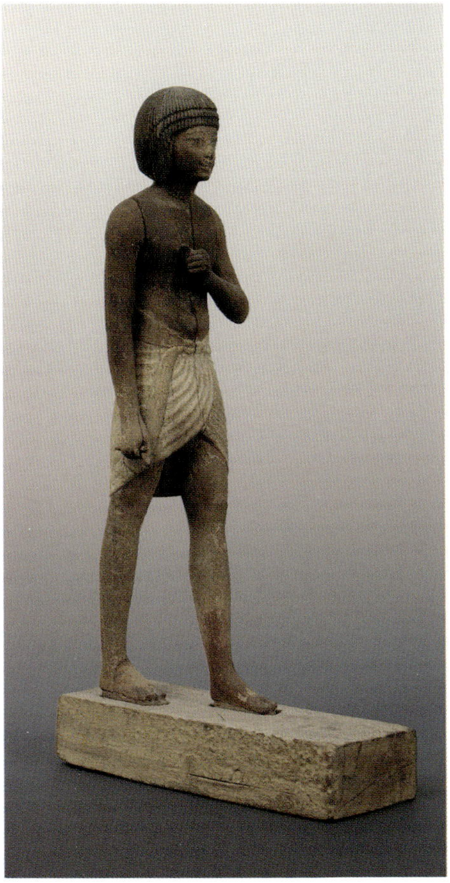

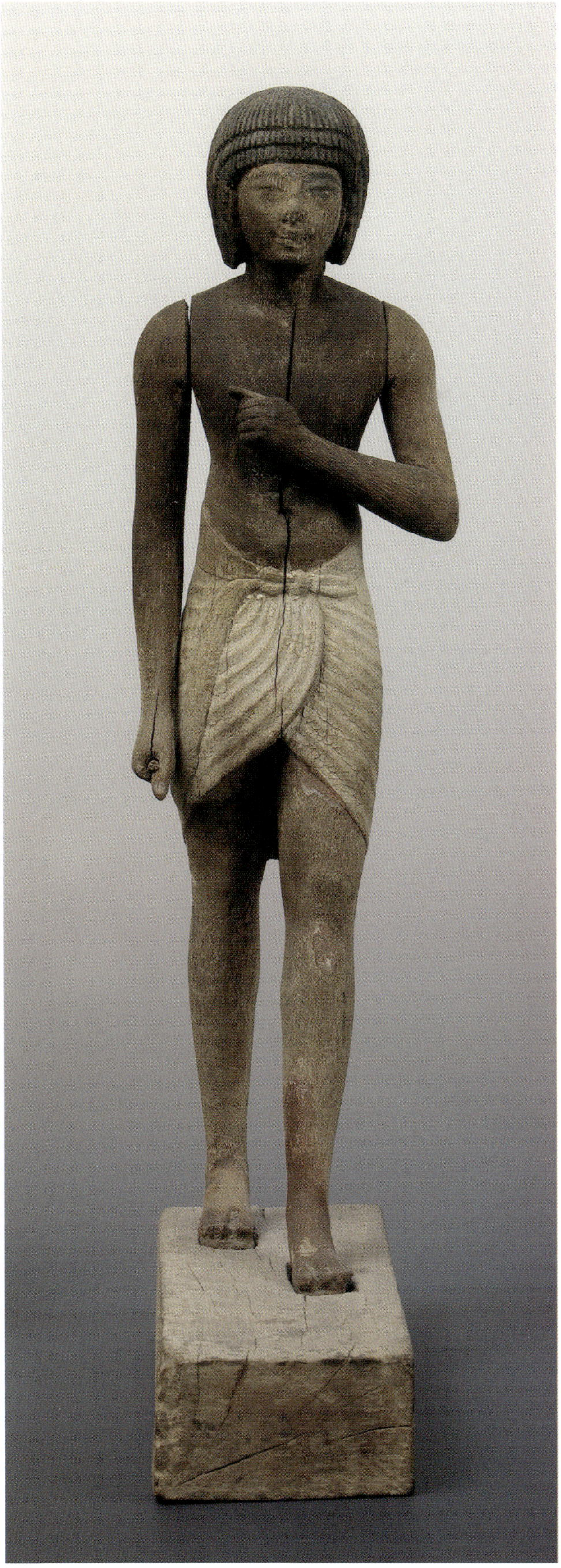

13

**FEMALE STATUETTE**

New Kingdom, late 18th dynasty
Polychrome wood and gold
H: 25 cm
Provenance: The Amherst Collection
Date incorporated: 1921
Inv. no. 121 B

Finely sculpted in wood, this female figure is wearing highly sophisticated clothes comprising a long, pleated tunic that clings to her body and a heavy wig covering down to her shoulders, crowned by a partially lost diadem. Her hair seems tightly curled and ends in interwoven fringes, with two fringes leading from her forehead until halfway down the wig. The lady's real hair appears on her forehead underneath the wig. It is painted black, as are her eyebrows and the outline round her eyes.

Her dress crosses at the front between her covered breasts, although it was customary at that time to leave the right breast exposed. The pleated tunic covers her left arm, which is bent and ends in her closed hand below her breasts, while her right arm, hanging alongside her body, is bare and seems once to have had an armband. Her wrists are decorated with gold bracelets, although her hands no longer have their original adornments, which were probably lotus flowers. The three-string gold necklace with geometrical decoration made using incised lines adds a touch of sophistication. The original rectangular base, also in wood, bears no inscription.

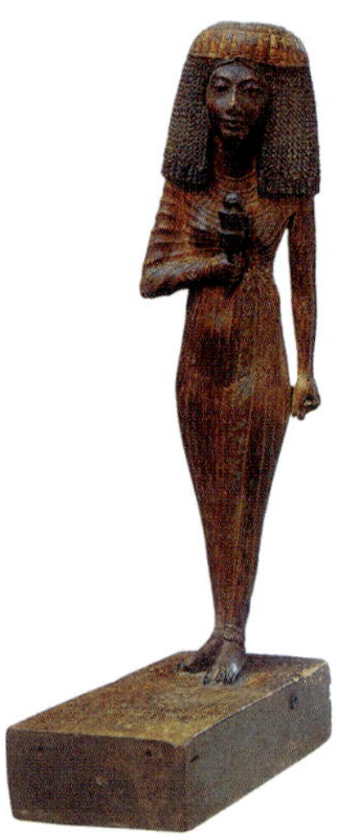

Statuette of Henutnakhtu, New Kingdom, 18th dynasty, ca. 1300 BC. Wood with traces of polychrome and gold leaf, H. 22.2 cm. Egyptian Museum, Cairo, inv. no. JE 6056=CG804

NOTES AND COMMENTS

Figurines of ladies normally show them with the left leg slightly forward, but that is not the case here. Similar statuettes – with the left leg forward, the typical wigs and pleated robes – can be found in several collections. On such piece is the figurine at the Louvre (Málek, 2003: 168), made for the Lady Toui, the high priestess of the god Min (the god of fertility and sexual energy), although it has more refined finishing and shows her right breast exposed. Likewise, the Egyptian Museum in Cairo has a fine, curvaceous statuette, made for Henutnakhtu, wearing a heavy wig with a floral diadem. This is very similar to the figure of the anonymous lady in the Gulbenkian Collection, despite clear differences in the position of the arms (Tiradritti, 1998: 185). Another elegant ebony statuette made for the Lady Tia and now at the Metropolitan Museum of Art in New York, also bears some similarities (Hayes, 1990, II: 267), as does another statuette at the Louvre showing the Lady Nay (Ziegler, 1990: 57). It can also be compared to similar images at the Brooklyn Museum, made for Mi and Tuty, and at the Metropolitan Museum of Art, New York, for the 'lady of the house' Tiye (Fay, 2004: 41-45).

Although the statuette in the Gulbenkian Collection no longer has the flowers that would originally have decorated the figure's hands, other pieces show that floral decorations were the normal adornment for these ladies, who are portrayed in all their physical beauty for eternity. These flowers enable such sculpted images to be linked to the literary imagery found in the beautiful love poems from the 19th dynasty, where the plant motifs both participate in and contribute to an erotic environment of enjoying a carefree daily life (Araújo, 2001: 276, 284). The wig is a clearly erotic adornment, as are the necklace and the seductive black paint around the eyes, as a young lover acknowledged in a poem:

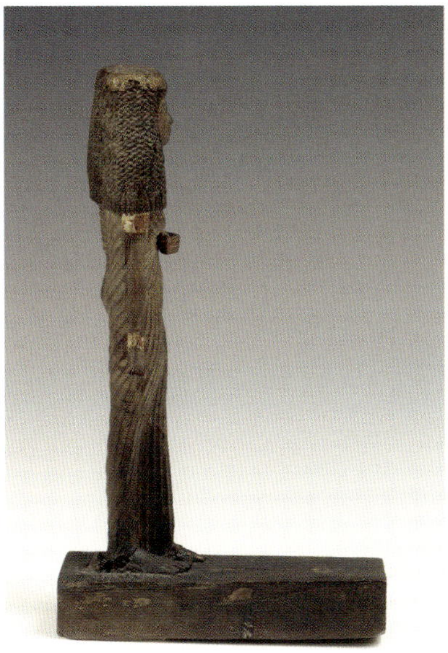

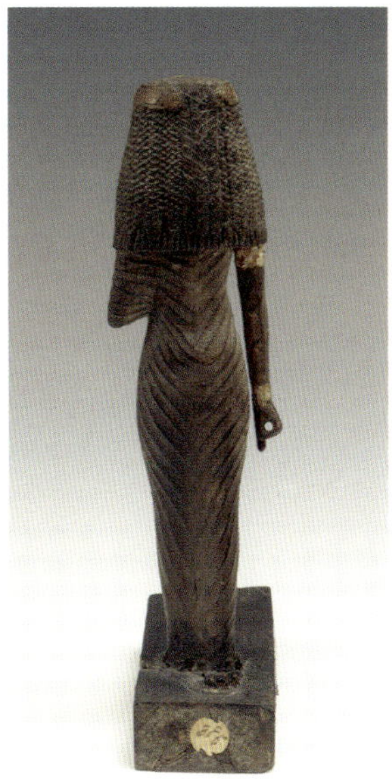

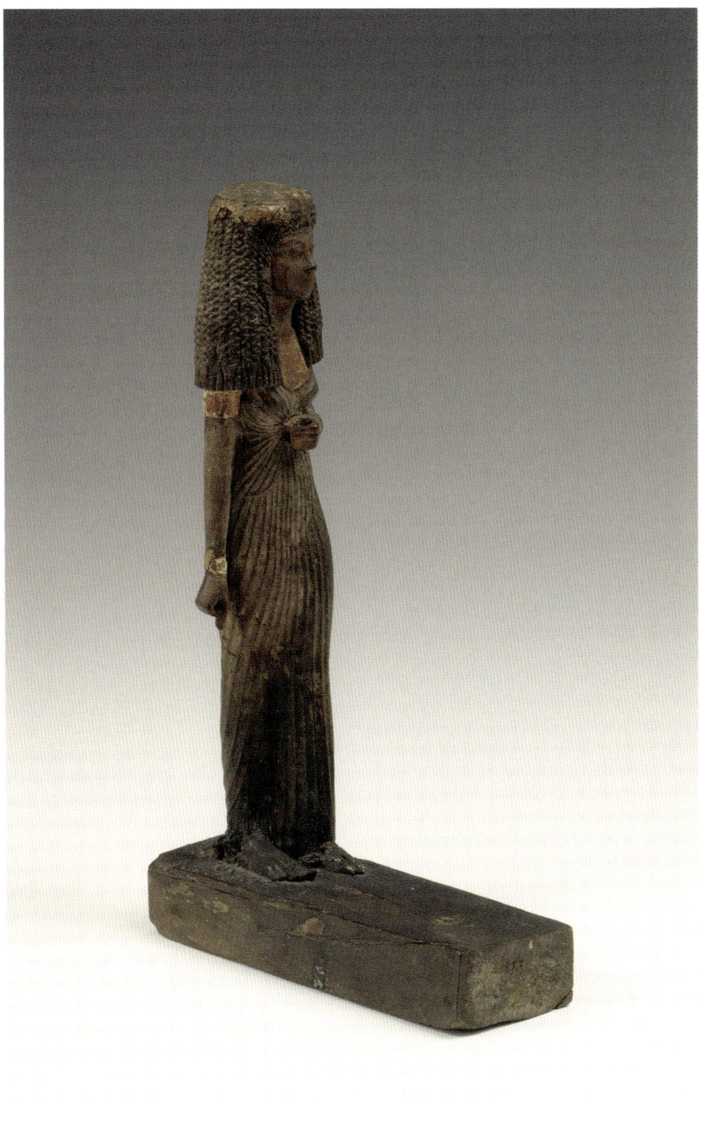

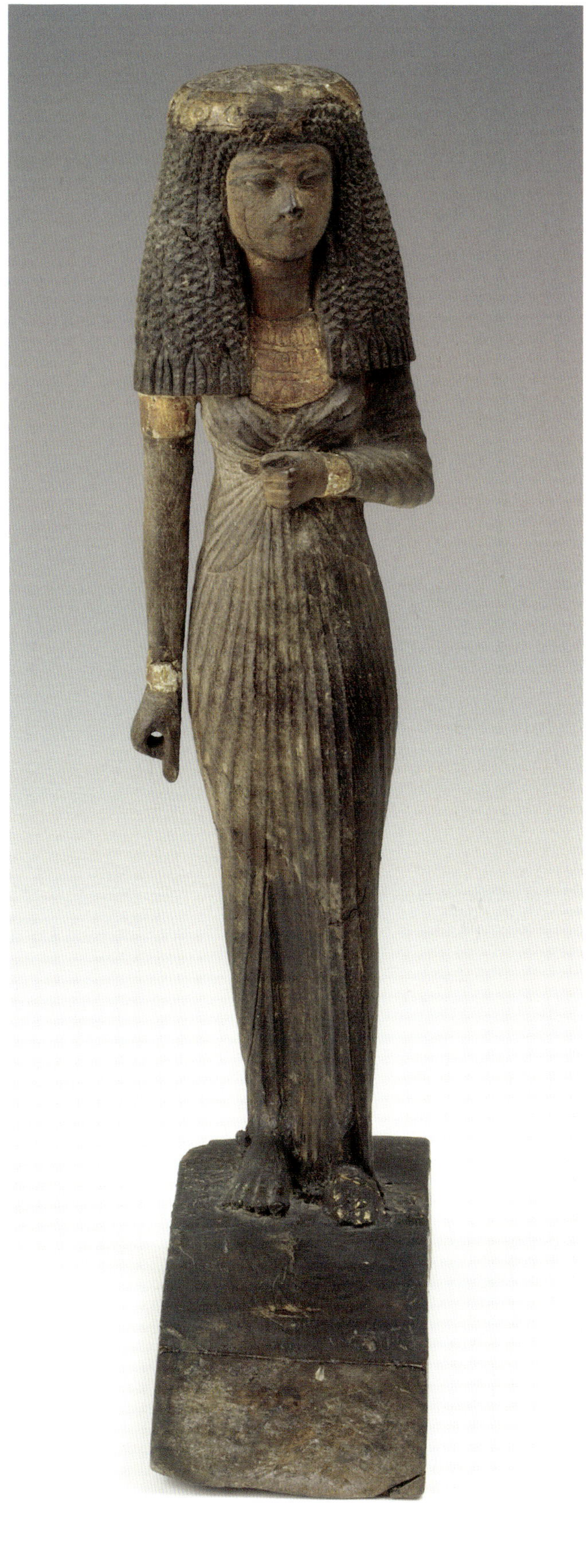

“She ties me with her hair,
She captures me with her gaze,
She binds me with her necklace.”

In similar fashion, the following ecstatic outpouring by a yearning lady demonstrates how a well-positioned wig was essential in love:

“My heart thinks of my love for you.
With my hair only half combed
I ran to seek you
And neglected my wig.
But I shall tighten more my curls
And soon I shall be ready.”

EXHIBITIONS

1937 – Ancient Egyptian Sculpture lent by C. S. Gulbenkian, Esq. London, British Museum.

1949 – Egyptian Sculpture from the Gulbenkian Collection. Washington, D.C., National Gallery of Art.

1965 – Obras de Arte da Fundação Calouste Gulbenkian. Oeiras, Pombal Palace.

14

**STATUETTE OF THE LADY OF THE HOUSE HENUT-TAUY**

New Kingdom, 18th dynasty
Polychrome wood and gold
H: 29.2 cm
Provenance: The Lord Grenfell Collection
Date incorporated: 1917
Inv. no. 129

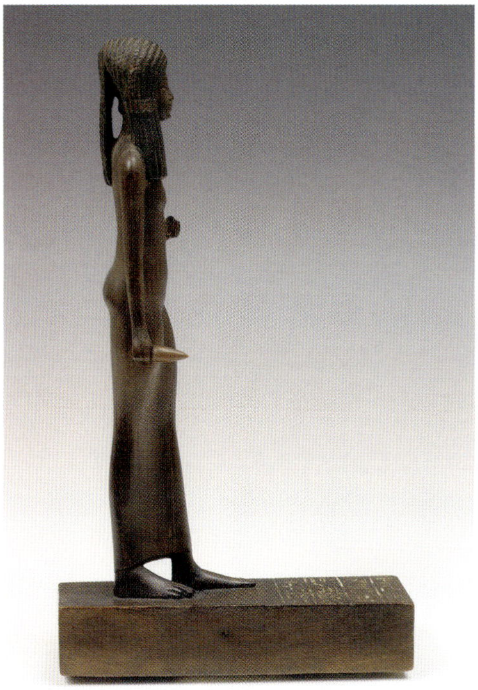

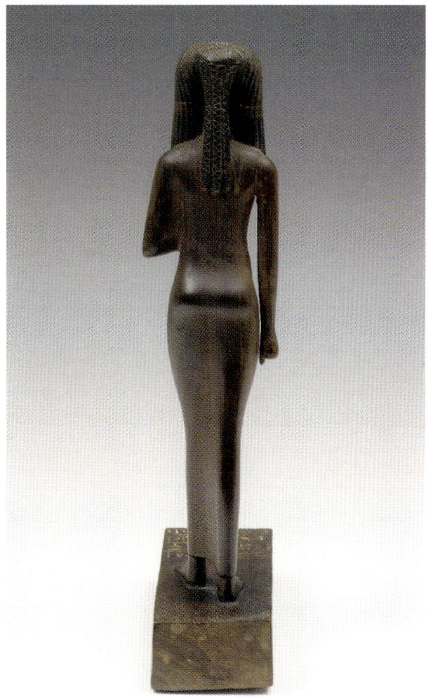

This elegantly sculpted wooden figurine, with traces of polychrome and gold, shows Henut-tauy with the title "lady of the house" (*nebet-per*). Her tightly fitting, transparent tunic emphasises her sculptural body and reveals the carver's mastery of his craft, giving the figure an erotic feel that is characteristic of the age when it was produced. She is wearing a three-part wig that hangs down over her chest and back in thick curling strands, and is held on top of her head by a band decorated with six lines in low relief. Her gentle face has clearly defined eyebrows, eyes, nose, mouth and a gently protruding chin. Her eyebrows and elongated eyes have traces of black paint around them, while her well-proportioned nose has a small fracture. The lady's own hair can be seen under the heavy wig, with a parting in the middle and coming down towards her eyebrows. She is wearing a striking necklace and a gold bracelet on her left wrist, and there are traces of another bracelet on her right wrist.

Her dress is held at the neck, and has an opening shown by a line running from her left breast down along her left leg, which is pushed slightly forward in the usual way. Since the ankle-length dress does not have the decorative fringe found in other pieces from that age, the opening – which allowed her to walk more freely – cannot initially be seen. The linen cloth covers her left breast but leaves the right one exposed, adding a touch of subtle eroticism that is heightened by the appealing curves of her waist and hips around her lower waist and clearly defined pubic area.

The figure's left arm is bent up and held next to her body, causing the cloth to fold. Her left hand (now lost) would have been set below her breasts and have held a plant, while her right arm hangs down next to her body without touching it. Her right hand is holding a lotus bud, which is also an attractive symbol of an erotic nature.

The original rectangular base bears a hieroglyph inscription written horizontally on four bordered lines. The text reads as follows:

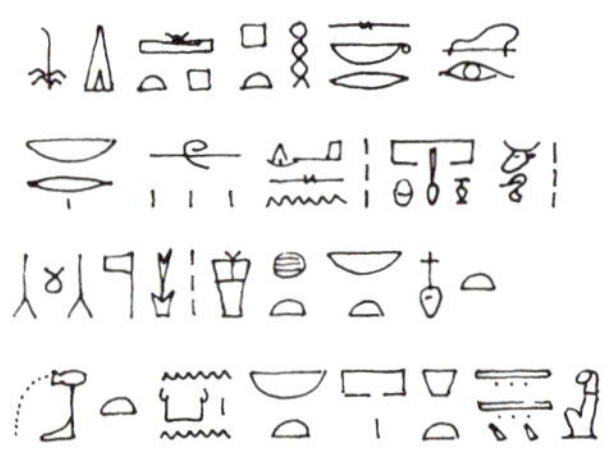

"Offering made by the king to Ptah-Sokar-Osiris, lord of Ra-setau, so that they grant invocations-offerings of bread, beer, beef and fowl, cloth, vessels, incense and ointments, all good and pure things for the *ka* of the lady of the house Henut-tauy."

NOTES AND COMMENTS

The collection's record for this magnificent statuette identifies Henut-tauy as the "superior of the cloistered followers of Min", a reference to a similar figure at the Louvre that apparently shows the same person. This questionable identification was made by Egyptologist Christiane Desroches-Noblecourt during her study of the collection in 1962, when the pieces was still in Oeiras. Following this first analysis, the catalogue of the Collection identified her as "high priestess and superior of the women devoted to the cult of the god Min" (Assam, 1991: 60), at least improving on the previous title of the "cloistered followers of Min", which was evidently inaccurate since the priestesses of Min, like those that served other deities, did not live in enclosure.

Statuette of Toui,
New Kingdom, 18th dynasty,
ca. 1370 BC. Wood,
H. 33.2 cm. The Louvre
Museum, inv. no. E10665
© Photo RMN /
© René-Gabriel Ojéda

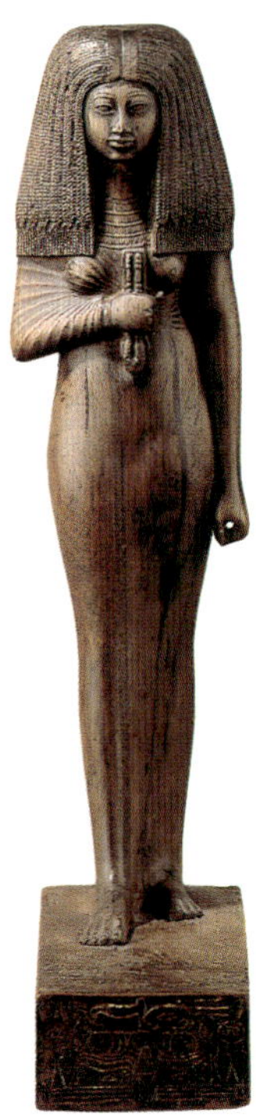

The Louvre has a fine statuette of a priestess of Min, but this relates to lady named Toui (Málek, 2003: 168), as mentioned above. The piece in question is of exceptional aesthetic and sociological interest, as it not only elevates the concept of female beauty that was then in fashion, but also bears witness to the great social importance and status that women could achieve in pharaonic Egypt, occupying prestigious positions. The statuette in the Louvre is ultimately a synthesis of the previous statuette of an anonymous woman (cat. no. 13) and the statuette of Henut-tauy. While the sophisticated wig and pleated folds of the dress on her left arm recall the former, the four-string gilded necklace, the stylish cut of the dress, her exposed right breast and advanced left leg are identical to those in the latter.

The collection's record notes that the figure was found in a "tomb in Upper Egypt", and Jaromír Málek accepts the attribution by Provenance, considering it to be "probably from a tomb in the Theban area" (*Ibidem:* 154). However, the inscription on the base suggests that it comes from the Memphis-Saqqara region, as that was where the necropolis of Ra-setau was located, and the presence of the syncretic deity Ptah-Sokar-Osiris is normal in Memphite texts. Two statuettes of this deity can be fund in the Museu Nacional de Arqueologia, Lisbon (Araújo, 1993: 239-243).

The engraved text on the base of the statuette again includes several aspects examined above (see the funerary text of the *hotep-di-nesu* type engraved on the statuette of Mes, cat. no. 5). Like that text, this one also starts with the introductory formula *hotep-di-nesu* and requests that the respective god (in this case a syncretic deity that justifies the text's use of the pronoun "they") provide the invocations-offerings (*peret-kheru*) for the *ka* of Henut-tauy. The title of lady of the house (*nebet-per*) establishes her considerable

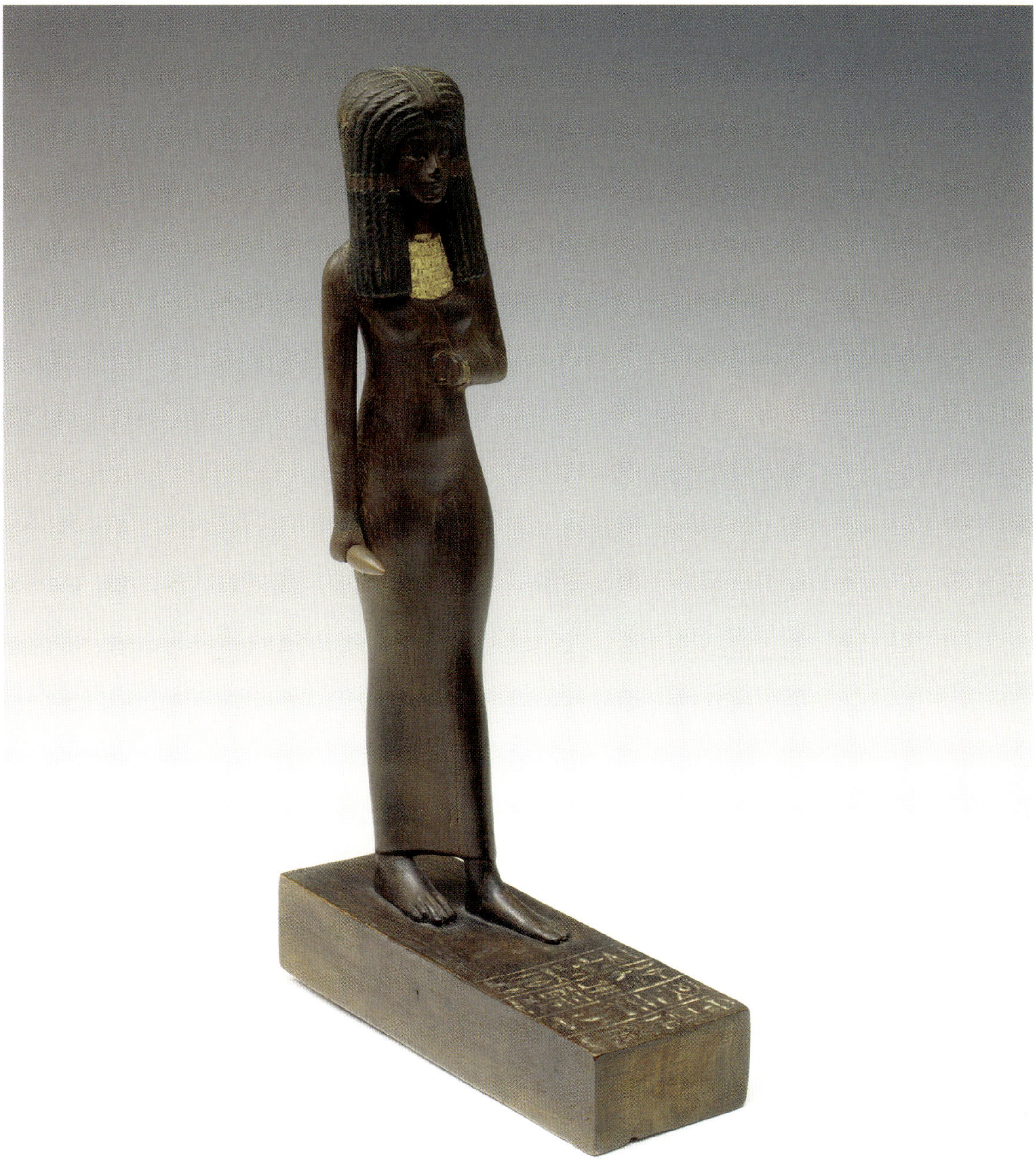

dignity and indicates the respected status that women enjoyed in Egyptian society as they took care of and maintained the home.

EXHIBITIONS

1895 – London, Burlington Fine Arts Club.

1937 – Ancient Egyptian Sculpture lent by C. S. Gulbenkian, Esq. London, British Museum.

1949 – Egyptian Sculpture from the Gulbenkian Collection. Washington, D. C., National Gallery of Art.

1965 – Obras de Arte da Fundação Calouste Gulbenkian. Oeiras, Pombal Palace.

15

## LOW-RELIEF OF THE PRIEST AMENEMINET

New Kingdom, late 18th dynasty (ca. 1320 BC)
Limestone
H: 66 cm; W: 36 cm
Provenance: Khawam Brothers, Cairo
Date incorporated: 1925
Inv. no. 205

This fragmented limestone stele depicts a funerary priest of Thutmose III offering the god delicacies placed on a tall offering table seen partially on the right. He is wearing a long, plaited wig, a double necklace, and a loose-fitting, pleated tunic, and holding a sprig of lotus flowers in his left hand. He has a small goatee beard, while his face has delicate features and almond-shaped eyes. His pose is not rigid (as in figures from previous periods) since it was designed with greater freedom, with particular emphasis on curving lines to show his slightly drooping belly and his skinny limbs. This demonstrates the clear influence of art from the Amarna Period.

A column with hieroglyph script to his left mentions Thutmose III's birth-name (Menkheperra) and the name of the person depicted (Ameneminet):

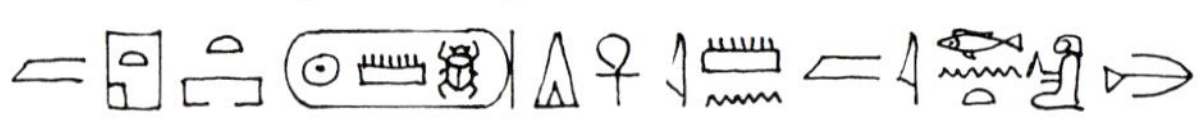

The inscription only shows the final part, reading: "...in the temple of Menkheperra, imbued with life, Ameneminet, justified."

NOTES AND COMMENTS

This stone fragment was acquired via Howard Carter, who called it "really a fine piece" in a letter to Calouste Gulbenkian dated January 1925.

The temple mentioned in the inscription may be the funerary temple of Thutmose III in Deir el-Bahri, which stands next to the large rock cliff between the famous and very well-preserved funerary temple of Queen Hatshepsut and another older one of Pharaoh Nebhepetra (Mentuhotep II) from the 11th dynasty. However, as this fragment came from the Memphis region, it may be concluded that there was a temple in that region to worship Thutmose III, and that the priest Ameneminet, part of the king's funerary cult, served there. The piece mentions the king by his fourth name (or birth-name) of Menkheperra. The name Ameneminet, a theophoric invocation of the god Amun, was very common at the time and means "Amun is in the valley". Since the name is typically Theban, this zealous official may have been moved from the south to the Memphis region where his tomb was found. There are fragments of Ameneminet's tomb at the Egyptian Museum in Cairo, and in Copenhagen, Bologna and Heidelberg. The limestone relief at the Louvre showing a couple – the official Amenmose and his wife Depet, presented as the children of Ameneminet, who is given the title of general (Málek, 2003: 215) – may also be from the same tomb or from that of a homonym. Although the figure of Ameneminet in the Gulbenkian Collection bears the title of funerary priest, it should be recalled that in general, Egyptian officials would accumulate several functions. The quality of the images and the hieroglyphs on the relief at the Louvre is higher.

The hieroglyph text in the Gulbenkian Collection was produced by a relatively unskilled sculptor. In fact, some signs are poorly carved: the anatomy of the beetle (*kheper*) inside a cartouche used to form the name of Menkheperra is highly inaccurate. The above translation of the hieroglyph text is based on the one in the catalogue of the temporary exhibition at the British Museum (Smith & Edwards, 1937: 22), although one error has been corrected here: the final signs used to declare him to be "justified" (*maé-kheru*) are not but .

The details, which are clearly based on the Amarna-Akhetaten aesthetic, suggest that this stone fragment of Ameneminet can be dated to the late 18th dynasty, during the reign of Horemheb. Symptomatically, reliefs of Horemheb from the time before he became pharaoh and was just a senior official of Tutankhamun and Kheperkheperura Ay have been found in the vast Saqqara-Memphis region, as have those of other leading figures from the age. These images have a very similar style to that of the stone fragment of Ameneminet (Pernigotti, 1994: 31-43).

EXHIBITIONS

1937 – Ancient Egyptian Sculpture lent by C. S. Gulbenkian, Esq. London, British Museum.

1949 – Egyptian Sculpture from the Gulbenkian Collection. Washington, D. C., National Gallery of Art.

1965 – Obras de Arte da Fundação Calouste Gulbenkian. Oeiras, Pombal Palace.

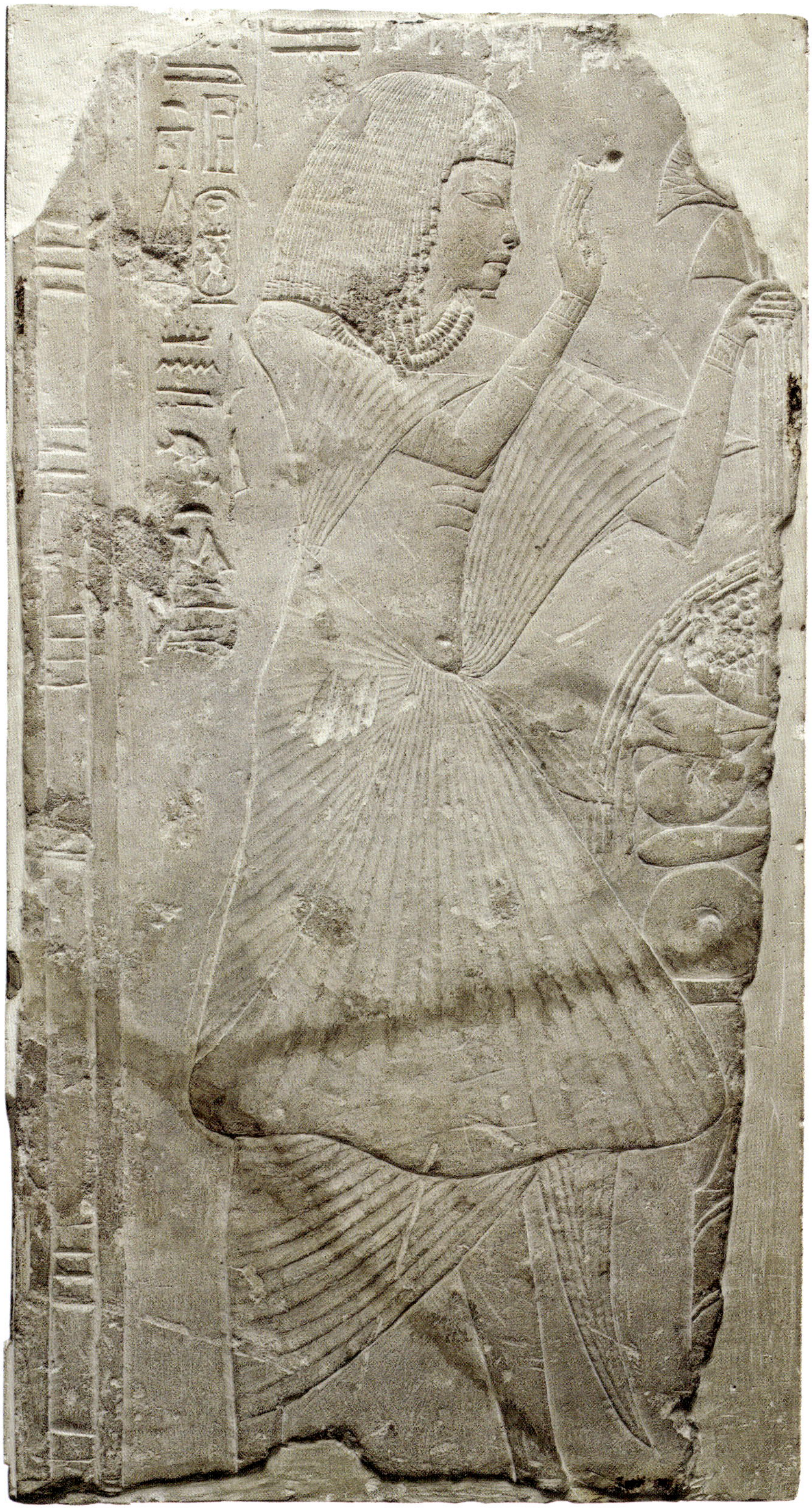

16

**TORSO OF KING PEDUBAST**

Third Intermediate Period, 23rd dynasty (818-793 BC)
Bronze incrusted with gold and copper
H: 26 cm
Provenance: The Count Gregory Stroganoff Collection, Rome
Date incorporated: 1921
Inv. no. 52

This is a fragment of a bronze statue of King Pedubast (Pedubastis in Greek), who founded the 23rd dynasty and whose name and titles are recorded in cartouches on the belt and vertical band of the figure's apron, decorated with gold and copper. His finely pleated kilt, which hangs close to his body, still has traces of gold-leaf in the folds. It flares outwards towards the bottom and ends in a frieze of seven solarised serpents in the typical raised-head position. The rest of the figure reveals that the pharaoh was shown standing and with his left leg forward, as established by the artistic canons. There is one truly unusual feature: a stylised feline head on the kilt under the belt buckle, which has a cartouche with both the king's fourth and fifth names concentrated inside the small space, while on the central band of the kilt, they are separate and bear the traditional titles.

On the buckle:

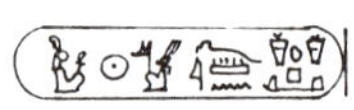

"Usermaatra-Setepenamun Padibastet-Sibastet-Meriamun."

On the apron:

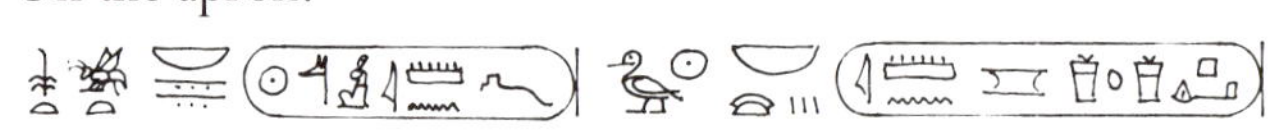

"King of Upper and Lower Egypt, lord of the Two Lands, Usermaatra-Setepenamun, son of Ra, lord of the diadems, Pedubast-Sibastet-Meriamun."

NOTES AND COMMENTS

In a letter to Calouste Gulbenkian dated January 1922, Duveen Brothers of Amsterdam guaranteed that this was "a very fine acquisition", since it was one of the finest objects from the Egyptian Collection of Count Gregory Stroganoff. The piece bears eloquent testimony to the revived and beautiful art of bronze produced in the Third Intermediate Period. This period began with the 21st dynasty, which was based in Tanis and always maintained contact with the outside world, specifically with Phoenician traders that brought (among other goods) the tin that Egypt needed to produce bronze objects.

This piece is part of the high-quality work produced in the long period from the 21st to the 23rd dynasty. One of the finest examples of such work is the statue of Queen Karomama (Málek, 2003: 282). The middle of the 22nd dynasty saw the beginning of political rivalry, as the kings of Libyan origin refused to accept the authority of the Tanite king once the promising days of Sheshonq I (the founder of the dynasty) were gone. This debilitating feud came to a head when Prince Pedubastis, from the city of Leontopolis (Taremu) in the Central Delta, rebelled in the eighth year of Osorkon III's reign and founded a new dynasty (the 23rd). Pedubastis ruled for some twenty-five years with the muted support of the clergy of Amun in Thebes, who were always keen to see the "rival" Tanite dynasty facing internal problems.

Besides being very rich in political and ideological terms, the name of the new king is exceptionally complex, adding the name of the goddess Bastet, who was widely venerated in the Delta at that time. Pedubast can be translated as "He who was given by Bastet", while Sibastet establishes him as the "Son of Bastet". The word "son" (*sa*) appears in the titles in two ways. In the first case, it is drawn as a duck which, when transformed into a phonogram, can be read as *sa*; in the second, it appears as an egg, in this case an ingenious and comprehensible ideogram for son. The honorary position before the name of Meriamun is of note, with the hieroglyph *meri* (beloved) appears after the name of the god Amun, *Imn*, although it is read before. The graphic handling of the names also shows another virtual aspect of hieroglyphic script: the name at the top uses both an ideogram and single and double consonant phonograms to create the name of Amun. The name of the Theban god is here fully justified, as Amun was not just worshipped in Tanis-Djanet but also in Thebes-Waset, and so the king guaranteed – by using his nomen related to Amun (Setepenamun) – that he had been selected by that god. Finally, not only does his praenomen Usermaatra include an invocation of Ra and Maet, it was also the nomen of the famous Rameses II.

The image of an apparently stylised cat's head at the top of the apron may indicate that King Pedubast held a ritual, priestly function, offering vessels to a deity (in this case, it would more specifically be a leopard's head). Alternatively, as also seems likely, it may be a reference to the feline goddess Bastet, also part of the royal titulary. A recent study of exceptional technical depth examined the process of manufacturing this bronze statue (Hill and Schorsch, 2005: 163-195).

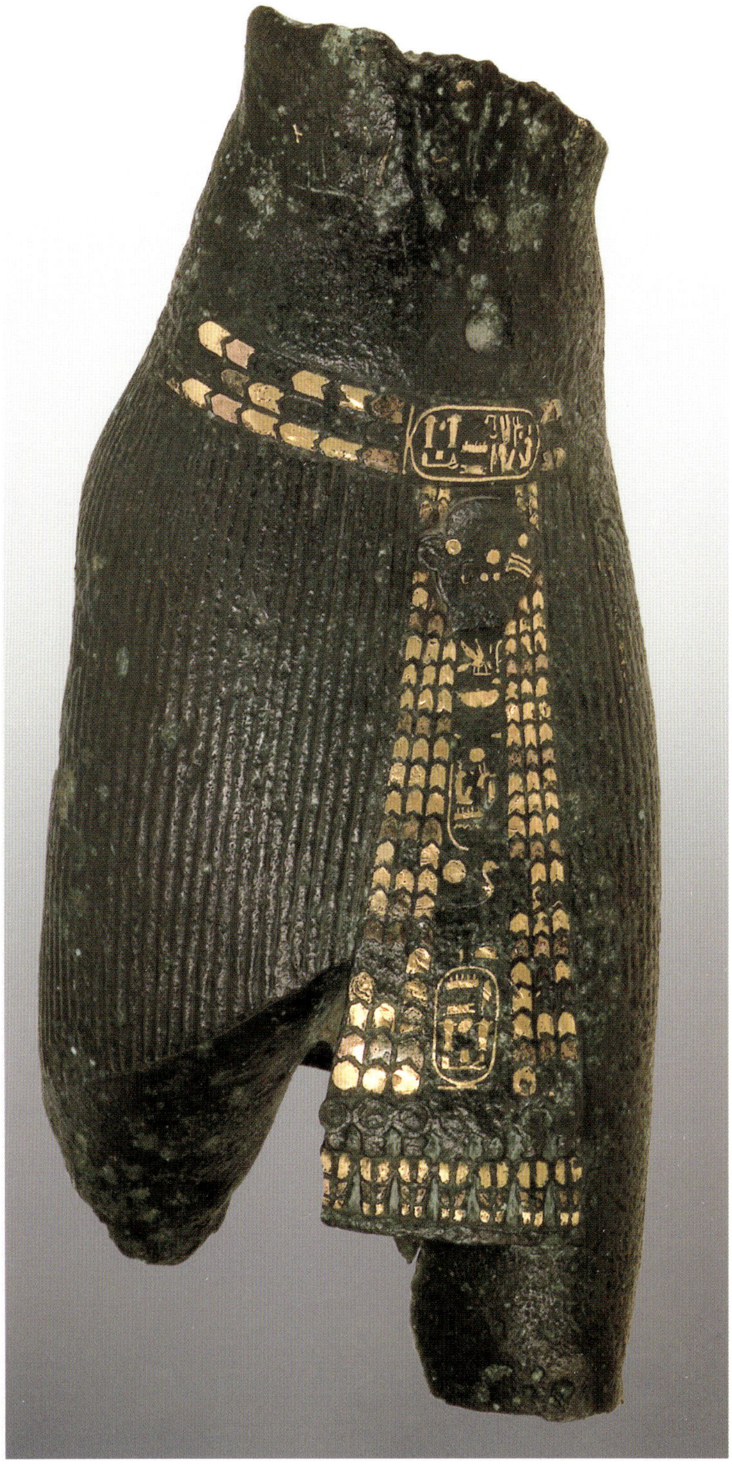

EXHIBITIONS

1937 – Ancient Egyptian Sculpture lent by C. S. Gulbenkian, Esq. London, British Museum.

1949 – Egyptian Sculpture from the Gulbenkian Collection. Washington, D. C., National Gallery of Art.

1965 – Obras de Arte da Fundação Calouste Gulbenkian. Oeiras, Pombal Palace.

1999 – "Only the Best": Masterpieces of the Calouste Gulbenkian Museum. New York, The Metropolitan Museum of Art.

17

## PANEL FROM A CASKET

Late Period, 26th dynasty (?)
Ivory
H: 15.7 cm; W: 6 cm
Provenance: The MacGregor Collection
Date incorporated: 1922
Inv. no. 164 (A)

Carved in fine low-relief, this panel (like others from the same small casket) is considered to be among the most beautiful Egyptian works in ivory. The panels decorated a casket or jewel-box, and still have traces of green polychrome. The scene depicted shows a procession of people bearing offerings, set against a background decoration of papyruses whose green has turned grey. The clearly outlined figure shows one nipple to indicate the left side of his chest, and is wearing a short, simple kilt with a belt tied at the front into a knot whose end hangs in a curve. A sash runs from his left shoulder and is tied off at the opposite side, slightly above his waist. He has short curly hair reaching down to his nape, and a lotus-flower on his forehead, held by a ribbon. His facial features are clearly defined, his eye and eyebrow are outlined, and he has a short beard. He is holding a cone-shaped basket in his right hand, which is bent up and rests on his shoulder, while his left hand is holding a bird (possibly a duck or goose) by the neck. Behind him, there is an ox with short horns: the features of its round head are sketchily drawn, the hair between its horns consists of incised lines, and it has a collar with a hanging lotus flower around its thick neck. The figures and plants rest on a base line formed by the hieroglyph *ta* (land). Above and beneath the piece, there are protrusions so that they can be attached to the now lost casket, and the panel has several vertical fractures.

### NOTES AND COMMENTS

This ivory panel, purchased via Howard Carter, is a pair for another in exhibition (cat. no. 18) and part of a set comprising a further five, now in the storeroom. It was among the objects damaged by the flooding in 1967, when it was covered in mud. It was subsequently thoroughly cleaned and restored by the Conservation Laboratory at the Museu Monográfico de Conímbriga.

The panel shows clear signs of the taste for archaic art that was typical of the Late Period, reviving forms from the Old Kingdom, namely scenes of processions carrying products as offerings. Images showing processions of people bearing such offerings are traditional in the tombs of individuals and at places of funerary worship of monarchs from the Old Kingdom period. For example, this theme was found on the walls of the severely damaged funerary temple of Sahura (5th dynasty) in Abusir, studied by Ludwig Borchardt. A fragment of a limestone wall from that monument is now at the Liebieghaus in Frankfurt (Gessler-Löhr, 1981: 8-9).

Other typical procession images often appear in Old Kingdom mastabas. One of the best preserved can be appreciated at the tomb of the senior official Ti, from the 5th dynasty (visited by Portuguese author Eça de Queirós in 1869), which shows a procession of people bearing offerings for the owner of the tomb (Barocas, 1987: 50-51).

The taste for this theme continued throughout the Middle Kingdom, as can be seen in a processional group found at the funerary temple of Senwosret I in Lisht, now part of the Egyptian Collection at the

Metropolitan Museum of Art, New York (Hayes, 1990: 186). The only difference is the sash running from his left shoulder, which may be seen as a detail in updating the image.

EXHIBITIONS

1921 – Ancient Egyptian Art. London, Burlington Fine Arts Club.

1937 – Ancient Egyptian Sculpture lent by C. S. Gulbenkian, Esq. London, British Museum.

1949 – Egyptian Sculpture from the Gulbenkian Collection. Washington, D. C., National Gallery of Art.

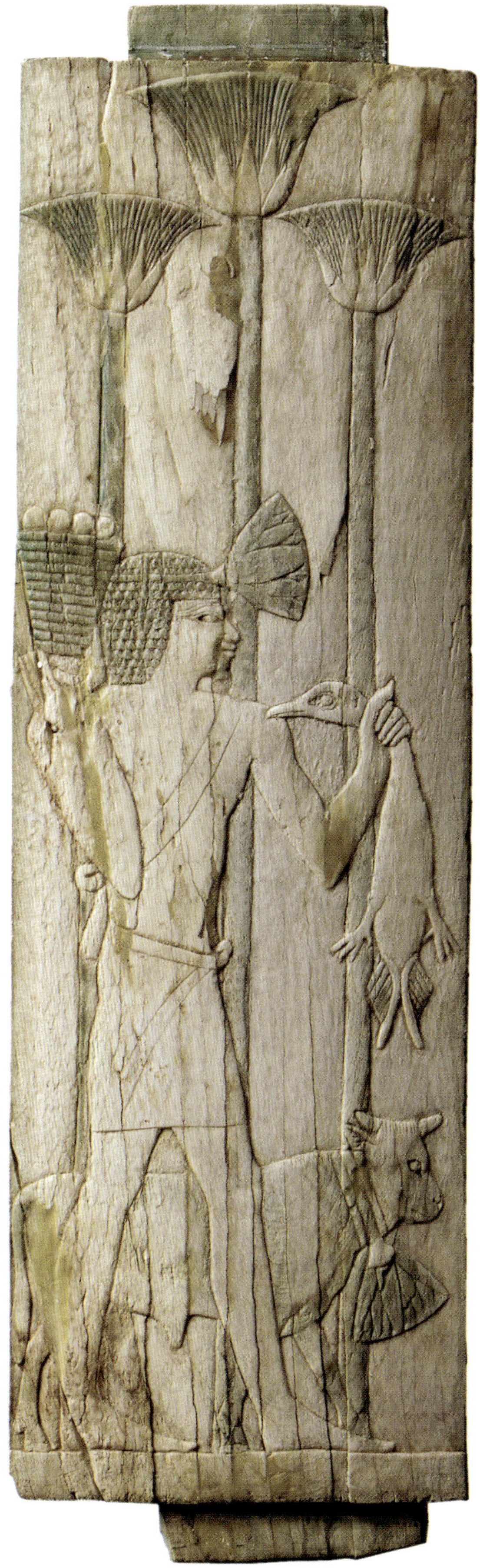

Procession in a tomb, Old Kingdom.

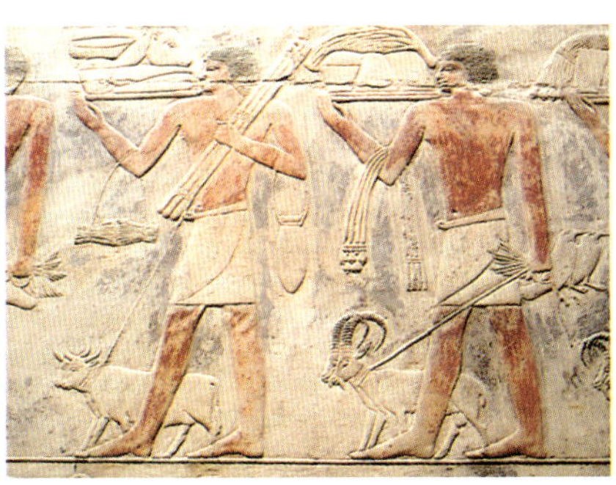

18

## PANEL FROM A CASKET

Late Period, 26th dynasty (?)
Ivory
H: 16.5 cm; W: 6 cm
Provenance: The MacGregor Collection
Date incorporated: 1922
Inv. no. 164 (B)

Carved in fine low-relief, this panel (like others from the same small casket) is considered to be among the most beautiful Egyptian works in ivory. The panels decorated a casket or jewel-box, and still have traces of green polychrome. The scene depicted shows a procession of people bearing offerings, set against a background decoration of papyruses whose green has survived, unlike the previous piece (cat. no. 17), where it has turned grey. The clearly outlined figure shows one nipple to indicate the left side of his chest, and is wearing a short, simple kilt with a belt tied at the front into a knot whose end hangs forward in a curve. A sash runs from his left shoulder and is tied off at the opposite side, slightly above his waist. He has short curly hair reaching down to his nape, and a small lotus-flower on his forehead, held by a ribbon. His facial features are clearly defined, his eye and eyebrow are outlined, and he has a short beard. His right arm is hanging down beside his body and he is holding a green rush basket in his right hand, while his left arm is turned upwards and his left hand holds – in a simple and elegant gesture – a basket (*neb*) full of fruit, suggested by twenty-two circles. Five lotus-flower stems that end in open buds are tied together and hang from the same arm. A long-legged bird that seems to be an ibis with a long beak and a clearly marked eye appears in front of the figure, walking alongside his advanced left leg. The figures and plants rest on a base line formed by the hieroglyph *ta* (land). Above and beneath the piece, there are protrusions so that they can be attached to the now lost casket, and the panel has a flaw in the bottom right corner.

### NOTES AND COMMENTS

This ivory panel, purchased via Howard Carter, is a pair for another in exhibition (cat. no. 17) and part of a set comprising a further five, now in the storeroom.

The panel shows clear signs of the taste for archaic art that was typical of the Late Period, reviving forms from the Old Kingdom, namely scenes of processions carrying products as offerings. As noted in the previous piece, processions of people bearing such offerings are traditional in Old Kingdom art. The only difference is the sash running from his left shoulder, which may be seen as a detail in updating the image.

### EXHIBITIONS

1921 – Ancient Egyptian Art. London, Burlington Fine Arts Club.

1937 – Ancient Egyptian Sculpture lent by C. S. Gulbenkian, Esq. London, British Museum.

1949 – Egyptian Sculpture from the Gulbenkian Collection. Washington, D. C., National Gallery of Art.

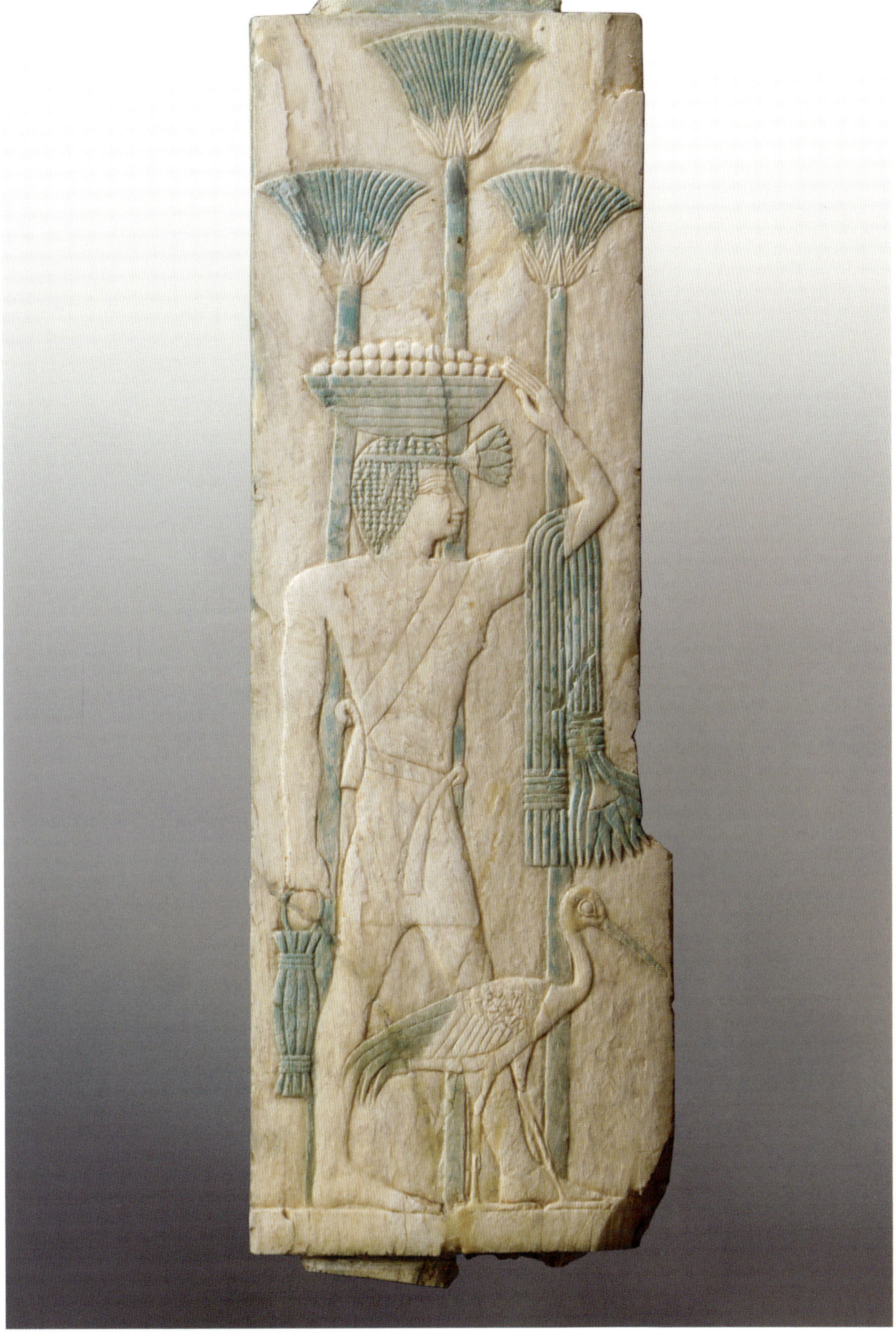

19

**WINGED SCARAB**

Late Period, 26th dynasty (664-525 BC)
Greenish faience
W: 27.5 cm; H: 8 cm
Provenance: The MacGregor Collection
Date incorporated: 1922
Inv. no. 162 A

The long wings of this faience winged scarab were made separately. Both the scarab (6.5 centimetres wide) and the two wings have holes to that the object could be sewn into the bindings on a mummy, probably around the heart. The wings are different sizes (left: 11 x 6.5 centimetres; right: 10.5 x 5.5 centimetres). The scarab's body is painted black, and the clypei are clearly defined, the prothorax is divided from the two elytrons on the shell and the legs (two front, two middle and two rear) are shown in relief. The long feathers on the wings start from a centre with a scale decoration heightened with black dots. The longest feathers at the edges have dark tips.

NOTES AND COMMENTS

The scarab was one of the most sought-after sacred animals in Ancient Egypt, possibly due to a rather prosodic question: scarab is pronounced *kheperer* (an onomatopoeic word), which is similar to the verb forms "transform", "become" and "come to be" (*kheper*). The beetle, which lays its eggs in a ball of dung kept in its hole, was greatly admired by the ancient Egyptians as the image of the spontaneous appearance of life. This was also associated to the image of the sun being born from the earth after its nocturnal journey, in which case it took the name Khepri, a god who is usually depicted as a scarab or a man with a scarab instead of a head. The Egyptians were exceptional and intelligent observers of nature and all its details, so they saw how the beetle pushed the ball of dung and they drew comparisons to the path of the sun across the heavens and its rebirth on the next day. This cyclical rebirth of the sun also invoked the rebirth of the deceased, so the scarab was consequently related to the cult of the dead (Araújo, 2001: 329). The winged scarab appears in many collections, including a painted wood example in the Egyptian collection at the Museu do Palácio de Vila Viçosa (Portugal) and the faience scarab at the Museu da Farmácia. Images of this sacred beetle (albeit without wings) can also be found in other Portuguese collections.

According to the records in the Gulbenkian Archive, this piece may have been part (along with cat. no. 20, the figurine of the winged goddess Isis and cat. nos. 21, 22, 23 and 24, the small figures of the sons of Horus), of the funerary goods of a body found in Tuna el-Gebel in Middle Egypt. The notes written by Howard Carter, via whom of the scarab was purchased, date it to the 21st-23rd dynasties, although this seems improbable.

EXHIBITIONS

1965 – Obras de Arte da Fundação Calouste Gulbenkian. Oeiras, Pombal Palace.

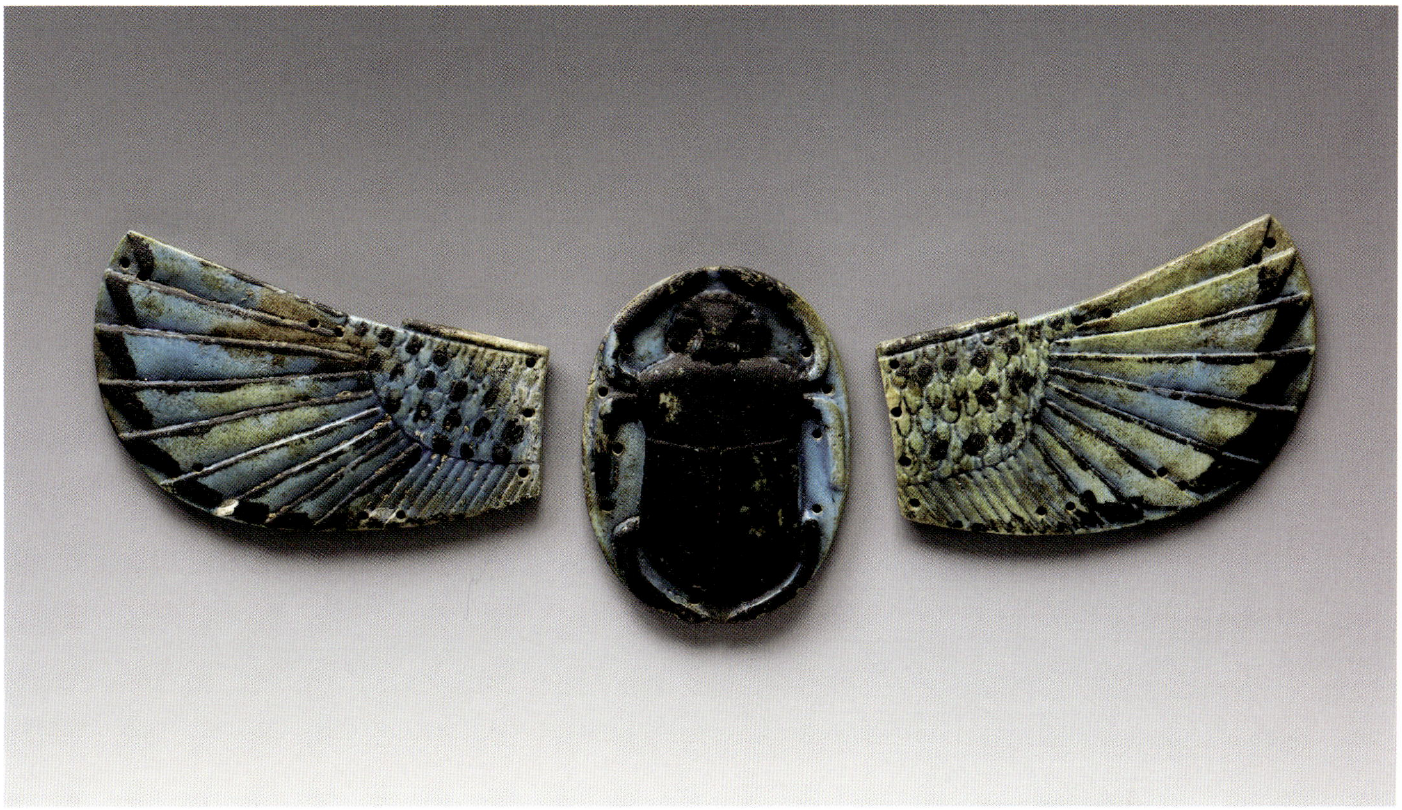

20

## WINGED IMAGE OF THE GODDESS ISIS (?)

Late Period, 26th dynasty (664-525 BC)
Greenish faience
H: 10.5 cm; W: 22.5 cm
Provenance: The MacGregor Collection
Date incorporated: 1922
Inv. no. 162 B

This funerary ornament in green faience with brownish tones portrays the goddess Isis (?) in the amulet form used in mummification rituals, i.e., with holes so that it could be sewn into the linen bands that were wrapped about the body, normally at the point where the arms were crossed. The face reveals fine anatomical details, with a clearly defined nose, mouth and ears, while her iris is indicated by a black dot. The goddess Isis, whose iconography is often similar to that of the goddess Hathor, is shown kneeling on a mat measuring five centimetres and crowned by her symbols: the solar disc framed by two lily-shaped horns standing on a small base on the figure's hair. Open wings stretch from her outstretched arms, and the feathers start from a centre with a scale decoration heightened with black dots. The largest feathers at the edges have dark dots, while the smaller ones end in black dots. The wings are of different sizes (left: 10 x 8.5 centimetres; right: 10.5 x 6 centimetres), and some parts of the surface have small incrustations of earth.

NOTES AND COMMENTS

The original caption in both the exhibition and the previous catalogue identified the goddess as Hathor (Assam, 1991: 70-71), and the two deities do indeed have very similar iconographies that are often confused. In this case, the funerary aspects are dominant, since the object was designed to be sewn into the linen bands wrapped around the mummy, probably on the front. Therefore, the figure more probably depicts the goddess Isis, who appeared more commonly on funeral materials and is often painted on the sarcophagi and shrouds around the mummies. However, for the sake of caution, the question mark must remain in front of her name.

From the Late Period onwards, similar funerary ornaments were incorporated into the traditional and complex network of pearls, made up of many tiny faience tubes and other materials that were wrapped around the shroud. Sometimes, instead of having a figurine of Isis, her image was painted onto the fabric, as in the mummy at the Museu Nacional de Arqueologia, Lisbon.

According to the archival records, this object may be part – with the winged scarab (cat. no. 19) and the small images of the sons of Horus (cat. nos. 21, 22, 23 and 24) – of the funerary goods of a body discovered in Tuna el-Gebel, Middle Egypt.

EXHIBITIONS

1965 – Obras de Arte da Fundação Calouste Gulbenkian. Oeiras, Pombal Palace.

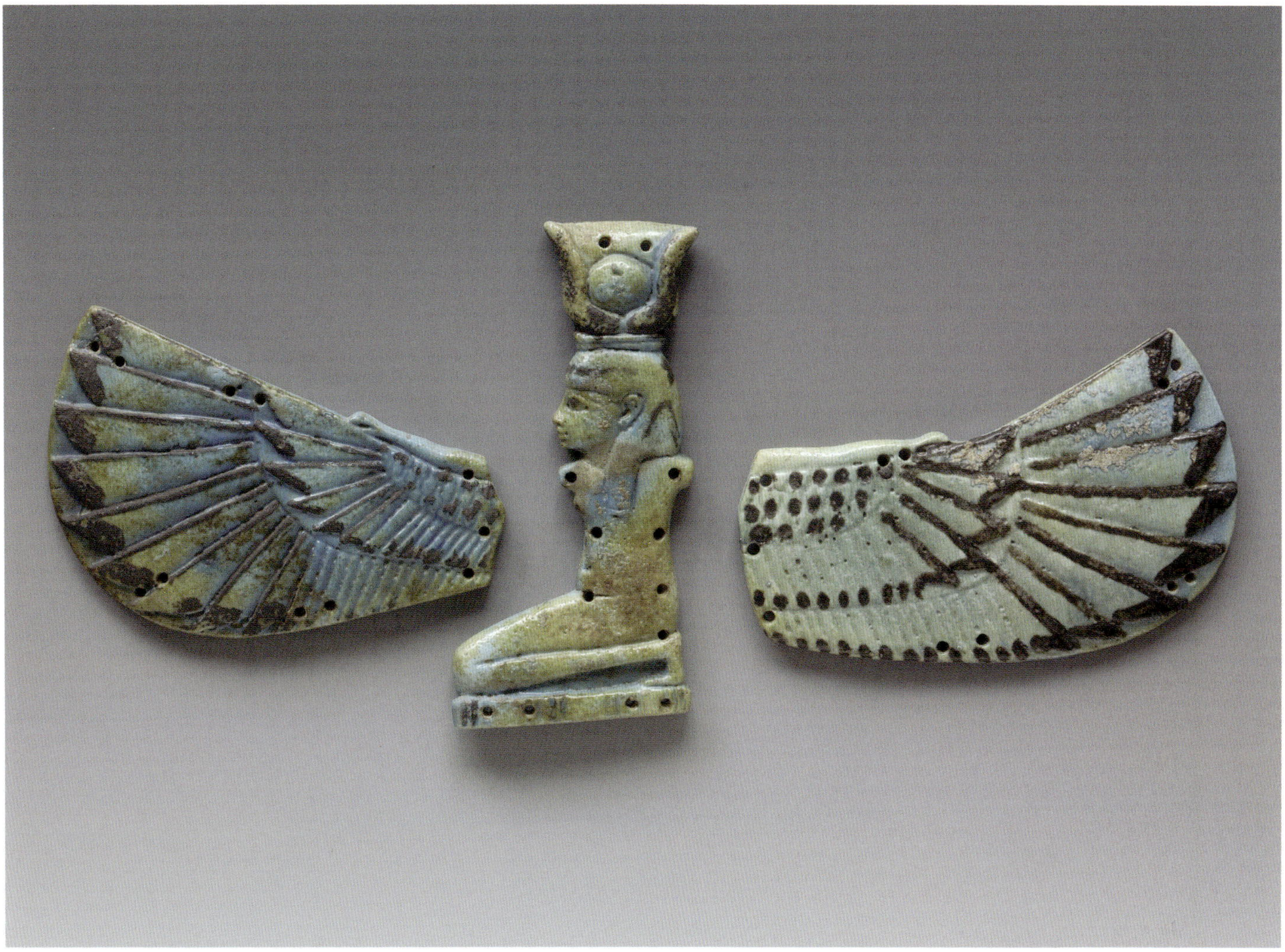

21

**STATUETTE OF IMSETY**

Late Period, 26th dynasty (664-525 BC)
Polychrome faience
H: 13 cm; W: 3.5 cm
Provenance: The MacGregor Collection
Date incorporated: 1922
Inv. no. 410 A

This flat figurine shows Imsety, one of the sons of the god Horus, with a human head and long hair that hangs over his chest and back. His body is depicted in cursory fashion, with slightly protruding buttocks, and he is shown standing on a mat held by two black lines. His face is pale, suggesting the typically hermaphrodite nature of this divine figure. His hair is mostly green, but is blue above the band on the top of his head, while black lines create a bow on the headband and there are three horizontal bands between the hair and body, which act as the starting point for two diagonal ribbons. The rear has three holes (at the head, abdomen and feet) so that the piece could be attached.

NOTES AND COMMENTS

Horus had four sons: Imsety, Duamutef, Hapi and Kebehsenuef (the last of whom is not included in this group). Imsety protected the liver of the deceased, who also enjoyed the protection of the goddess Isis. Imsety, shown here looking to the left, was related to the southwest and was normally placed alongside Duamutef on one side of the body.

According to the "Pyramid Texts" from the Old Kingdom, the four sons of Horus (more precisely Horuer, Ancient Horus) tended to the deceased during his journey to the next world, and they would continue to be seen in this role throughout the history of Egypt. They ensured that the body's main internal organs were kept in good condition, storing them all in appropriate containers except for the heart, which received separate treatment (Araújo, 2001a: 377).

From the New Kingdom onwards, images of the four sons of Horus, sometimes called the funerary genii, were also sculpted on the lids of the canopic jars that held the respective viscera which these figures protected. Jars of this type exist in the Egyptian collections at the Museu Nacional de Arqueologia, Lisbon, the Museu de História Natural (Faculdade de Ciências) University of Oporto, the Museu da Farmácia, Lisbon, and the Museu do Palácio de Vila Viçosa.

Complete set of the four sons of Horus. Third Intermediate Period, ca. 1079-800 BC. Polychrome faience, H. 14.6 cm (max.). British Museum, inv. no. EA26230 © Courtesy of the Trustees of the British Museum

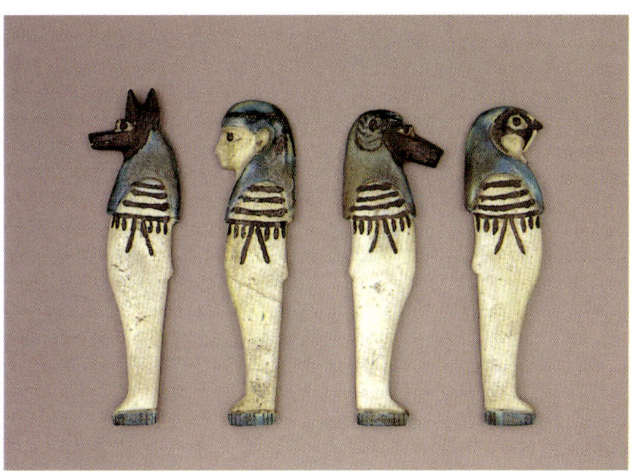

The British Museum owns a complete collection of the four sons of Horus that is very similar to those in the Gulbenkian Collection (Seipel, 1989: 187). The figures are paradigmatic of many sets of varying sizes and styles found in many public and private collections.

EXHIBITIONS

1965 – Obras de Arte da Fundação Calouste Gulbenkian. Oeiras, Pombal Palace.

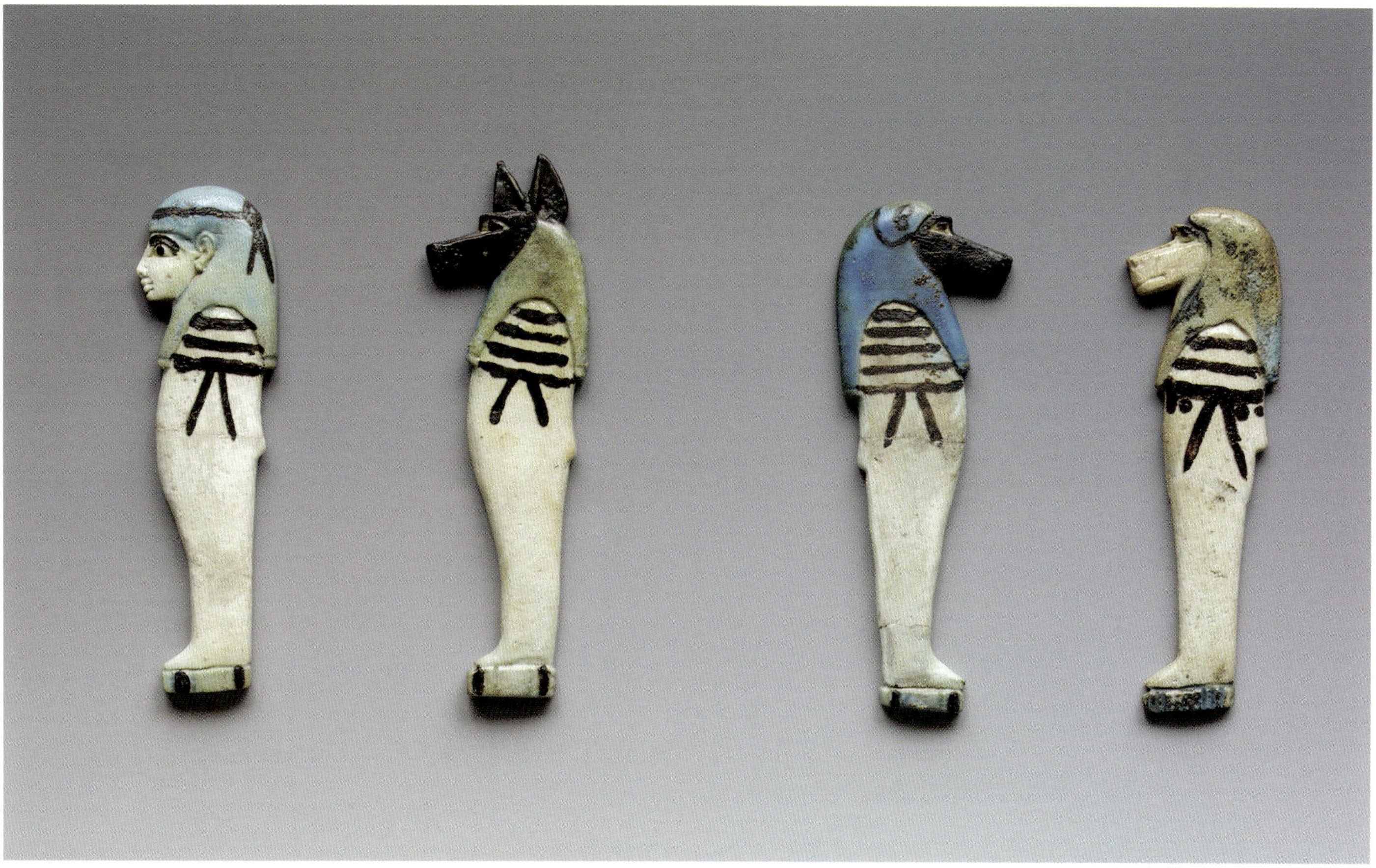

21 | 22 | 23 | 24

22

**STATUETTE OF DUAMUTEF**

Late Period, 26th dynasty (664-525 BC)
Polychrome faience
H: 14 cm; W: 4 cm
Provenance: The MacGregor Collection
Date incorporated: 1922
Inv. no. 410 B

This flat figurine shows Duamutef, one of the sons of the god Horus, with a dog's head and long hair that hangs over his chest and back, an iconography that is quite similar to that of images depicting Anubis. His body is depicted in cursory fashion, with slightly protruding buttocks, and he is standing on a mat held by two black lines. His head is black and has two typically canine ears on the top. His hair is green (and apparently was once blue), and black lines mark out the four horizontal bands between his hair and body, which act as the starting point for two diagonal ribbons. The rear has three holes (at the head, abdomen and feet) so that the piece could be attached.

NOTES AND COMMENTS

Horus had four sons: Imsety, Duamutef, Hapi and Kebehsenuef. Duamutef protected the stomach of the deceased, who also enjoyed the protection of the goddess Neith. Duamutef, shown here looking to the left, was related to the southeast and was normally placed alongside Imsety on one side of the body.

Duamutef is sometimes described as having a jackal's head, but real jackals have never existed in Egypt. Thus, the image is of a wild dog similar to those that roamed around Egyptian necropolises at the edge of the desert (Araújo, 2001a: 377).

See also the Notes and comments after the figurine of Imsety (cat. no. 21).

EXHIBITIONS

1965 – Obras de Arte da Fundação Calouste Gulbenkian. Oeiras, Pombal Palace.

---

**STATUETTE OF HAPI**

23 Late Period, 26th dynasty (664-525 BC)
Faience
H: 13 cm; W: 4.5 cm
Provenance: The MacGregor Collection
Date incorporated: 1922
Inv. no. 410 C

This flat figurine shows Hapi, one of the sons of the god Horus, with a baboon's head and long hair that hangs over his chest and back. His body is depicted in cursory fashion, with slightly protruding buttocks, and he is standing on a mat held by two black lines. His head is black, with bulging eyes and white corneas, and with incrustations on the surface. His hair is blue, and black lines mark the five horizontal bands between his hair and body, which act as the starting point for two diagonal ribbons. The rear has three holes (at the head, abdomen and feet) so that the piece could be attached.

NOTES AND COMMENTS

Horus had four sons: Imsety, Duamutef, Hapi and Kebehsenuef. Hapi protected the lungs of the deceased, who also enjoyed the protection of the goddess Nephthys. Hapi, shown here looking to the right, was related to the northwest and was normally placed on one side of the body alongside the figure of Kebehsenuef, which is missing from this group.

See also the notes and comments after the figurine of Imsety (cat no. 21).

EXHIBITIONS

1965 – Obras de Arte da Fundação Calouste Gulbenkian. Oeiras, Pombal Palace.

24

**STATUETTE OF HAPI**

Late Period, 26th dynasty (664-525 BC)
Faience
H: 13 cm; W: 4 cm
Provenance: The MacGregor Collection
Date incorporated: 1922
Inv. no. 410 D

This flat figurine shows Hapi, one of the sons of the god Horus, with a baboon's head and long hair that hangs over his chest and back. His body is depicted in cursory fashion, with slightly protruding buttocks, and he is standing on a mat held by black lines. His head is yellowish, with bulging eyee, while his facial features are anatomically more accurate than those on the previous piece (cat. no. 23). His hair is brownish-green (and was apparently once blue), and black lines mark the three horizontal bands (decorated with four pearls) between his hair and his body, which act as the starting point for two diagonal ribbons. The rear has three holes (at the head, abdomen and feet) so that the piece could be attached.

NOTES AND COMMENTS

Horus had four sons: Imsety, Duamutef, Hapi and Kebehsenuef. Hapi protected the lungs of the deceased, who also enjoyed the protection of the goddess Nephthys. Hapi, shown here looking to the left and with a more ape-like appearance than the previous piece, was related to the northwest and was normally placed alongside Kebehsenuef on one side of the body.

See also the notes and comments after the figurine of Imsety (cat no. 21).

This is an extra figurine of Hapi in this set, which lacks the figure of Kebehsenuef. The latter, normally depicted with a falcon's head, protected the intestines of the deceased, as did the goddess Serket. Like the other sons of Horus, Kebehsenuef was also related to one of the cardinal point s, in this case the northeast.

This figurine of Hapi should be looking to the right (in contrast to Imsety and Duamutef), so it must come from another set. Another clear difference is that it has four pearls decorating the last of the three horizontal bands between the body and the hair, which is not found on the other three figures from the set in the Gulbenkian Collection, while the handling of the mat on the base and the buttocks is also different.

EXHIBITIONS

1965 – Obras de Arte da Fundação Calouste Gulbenkian. Oeiras, Pombal Palace.

25

**HEAD OF THE GODDESS HATHOR**

Late Period, 26th dynasty (664-332 BC)
Green faience
H: 11 cm
Provenance: The Dr. Fouquet Collection, Cairo
Date incorporated: 1922
Inv. no. 411

Both sides of this fragment of a votive sistrum have images of the head of the goddess Hathor. The piece is part of a Hathor sistrum, a musical instrument that is associated to the cult of that goddess and acted as her emblem. It lacks the handle, which was generally shaped like a stylised lotus flower, and the top, which would end in a pylon-shaped shrine flanked by two spiral antennae set on the head of the goddess. A serpent emerges at the bottom centre of this shrine. Only the lower part of the shrine with the sacred serpent still survives. Hathor is depicted as a woman with dense hair, a four-string necklace and cow's ears, one of the typical forms found in her attractive iconography. The necklace combines several decorative elements, including incised lines, papyrus petals and lotus flowers, and ends at the top in a string of pearls and at the bottom in drop-shaped pendants. Her thick hair, one of the clearest symbols of Hathor, is decorated with bands that each consist of three relief strips ending in two-strip bands. Her smiling and friendly expression, with clearly defined eyes and mouth, although her nose is damaged on both sides, is also of note.

NOTES AND COMMENTS

A fragment from a similar votive sistrum is now part of a private collection. However, it dates from a later period (perhaps the Ptolemaic Period), is made of limestone, and the image of the shrine that is traditionally found on top of the goddess' head is still intact (Bothmer, 1988: 87-88).

Fragment of a votive sistrum of Hathor. Egypt, Ptolemaic Period, 300-100 BC. White limestone, discoloured. Private collection © Sotheby's

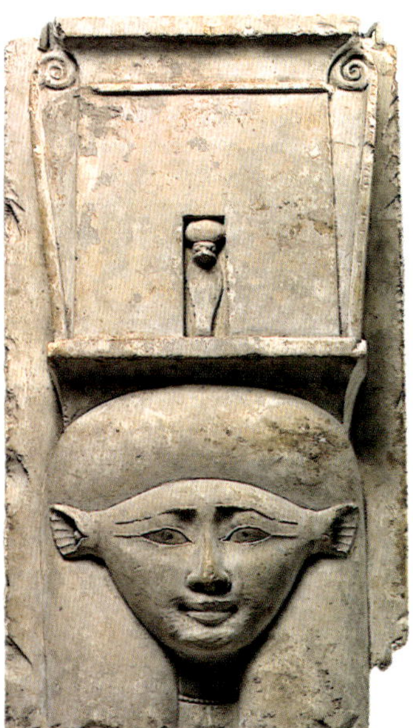

Although the head of Hathor often appears on bronze sistra, faience, stone or terracotta sculptures reproducing these votive instruments allow the goddess of love's delicate features and her characteristic cow's ears (sculpted by extending the lines of her eyes and eyebrows) to be modelled in a more elegant manner that reveals some artistic virtuosity.

Sistra that reveal the form of this musical instrument and are in varying degrees of conservation can be found in the collection of Museum of Fine Arts in Boston, amongst others (Simpson, 1987: 52-53). The Egyptian Museum in Cairo (Bongioanni & Croce, 2001: 507) also owns a fine example, while the Musée Pincé, Angers has another Hathor sistrum in excellent condition (Affholder-Gérard & Cornic, 1990: 154). All the above examples confirm that the object basically consisted of a handle, a sort of sounding box that bore the image of Hathor and ended in a shrine or other iconographic elements, and a metal blade that curved around and joined one side of the Hathor shrine (when it existed) to the other, or stood on a support in the hair of the goddess. This top part had a series of bars holding pieces of metal that produced the required sound when the instrument was shaken. It seems that the sistrum was mostly used in religious ceremonies to imitate sounds that suggested leaves being moved by the wind, thereby summoning the gentle goddess Hathor. The high esteem in which sistrum-players were held is evident from the fact that imagery from tombs or depicting festivities often shows queens and

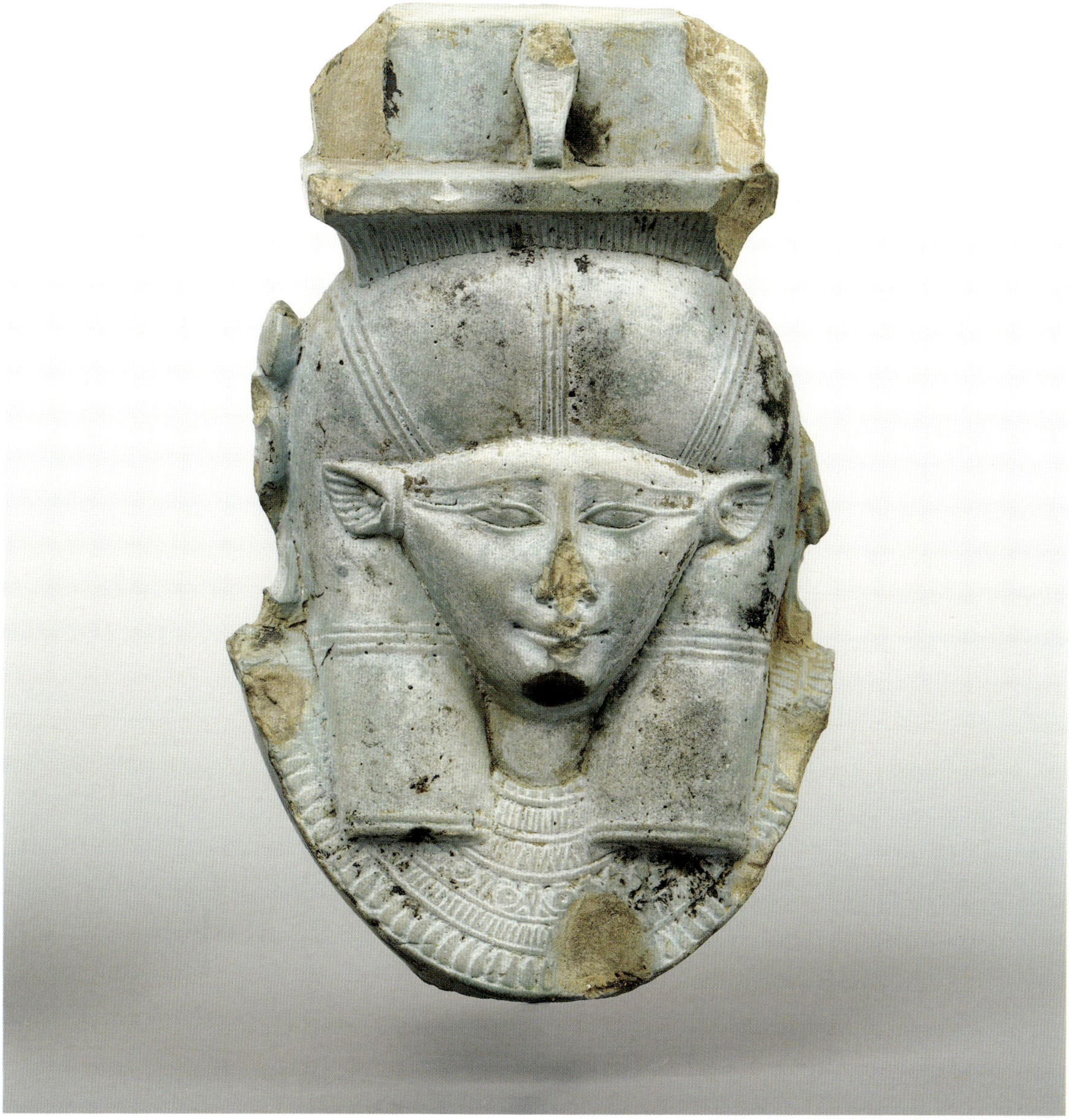

princesses shaking these instruments. In fact, even some goddesses were occasionally shown doing the same. One good example is a mural at the temple of Sety I in Abydos, where the goddess Isis is shown shaking a sistrum in honour of the deceased king.

The cow's ear on Hathor's beautiful face is also a sign in its own right from hieroglyphicic script. It corresponds to the triliteral sign *sedjem* (*sdm*), the verb "to listen". In Egyptian, the sistrum was called *sesechet* (*sššt*), a clearly onomatopoeic name.

26

## STATUETTE OF THE GOD OSIRIS

Late Period, 26$^{th}$ dynasty (664-525 BC)
Schist and gold
H: 32.5 cm
Provenance: The MacGregor Collection
Date incorporated: 1922
Inv. no. 404

This schist statuette of Osiris with gold decorations has a perfect finish. The god of death and resurrection appears in his customary form, as a mummified human figure whose hands can be seen emerging through his shroud and holding the royal sceptres: *hekat* (from Upper Egypt) in his left hand, and *nekhakha* (from Lower Egypt) in his right. He is wearing the *hedjet*, the white crown of Upper Egypt, one of the most typical symbols of royalty, decorated with two tall ostrich feathers on the side and ending at the front in the *uraeus* (*iaret*), the sacred serpent. This transforms the traditional crown of the earthly ruler into the Osiric *atef* crown that the god wore to demonstrate his royal status in the other world.

The slim figure of Osiris is standing both against a dorsal pillar that merges into his well-rounded form and on a rectangular base whose front corners are slightly curved. The gentle lines of the god's face were created in some detail, showing almond-shaped eyes and dense eyebrows, a well-proportioned nose and mouth, and protruding ears, while an incised line indicates the ribbon that started at the base of the crown and held his divine beard. Traces of the gold-leaf can still be seen on the figure's eyes, beard and the whip-shaped *nekhakha* sceptre.

NOTES AND COMMENTS

This excellent statuette is a fine example of artwork from the Late Period, not only in aesthetic terms but also in its ideological reading. The perfect finish is indicative of the high-quality bronze and stone work that was typically produced in the Late Period and that would continue into the Greco-Roman Period, particularly the Ptolemaic Period. One characteristic aspect of the age is the figure's serene, smiling face – the so-called "Saite smile" that can also be found on statues of non-royal figures. In ideological terms, the statuette refers to the well-known myth of Osiris, the husband and brother of Isis, and part of the Heliopolis Ennead. He was considered to be a good and just king that ruled over the earth to the delight of mankind, who learned the art of agriculture from him. Yet this generous god had an evil, jealous brother (Set) who murdered him, chopped his body up into several parts and scattered them across Egypt. With the help of her sister Nephthys, Osiris' pious wife Isis went in search of the pieces, reassembled his body and thereby created the first mummy, symbolising the possibility of rebirth and life after death. Despite the absence of Osiris' divine penis, which never appeared (having been eaten by a fish, the oxyrhynchus), Isis used her erotic magic to have a son – the god Horus – by her late husband. In time, Horus became the champion of good and justice, and the legitimate heir to the throne. Based on this myth, all the Egyptian kings would be living Horuses on earth (Araújo, 2005: 121-126).

There are many similar pieces in public and private collections. The Cairo Museum owns a large variety of standing or sitting figures (Tiradritti, 1998: 367) made in different materials. Among others, these include stone, more specifically schist (like the work in the Calouste Gulbenkian Collection and the green statuette at the Pelizaeus-Museum in Hildesheim), and metal (such as the bronze statuette in the

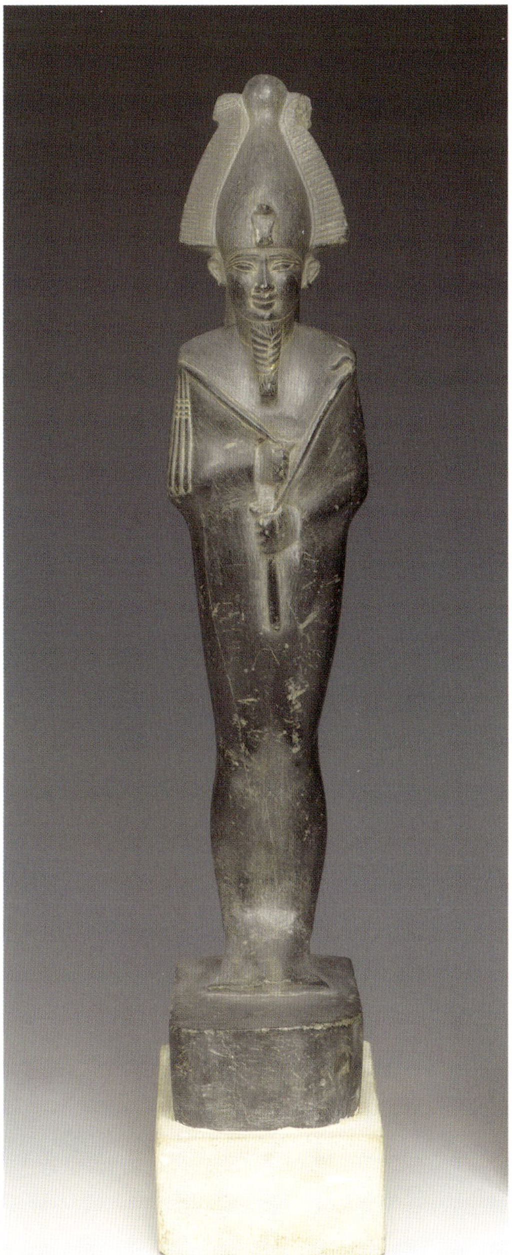

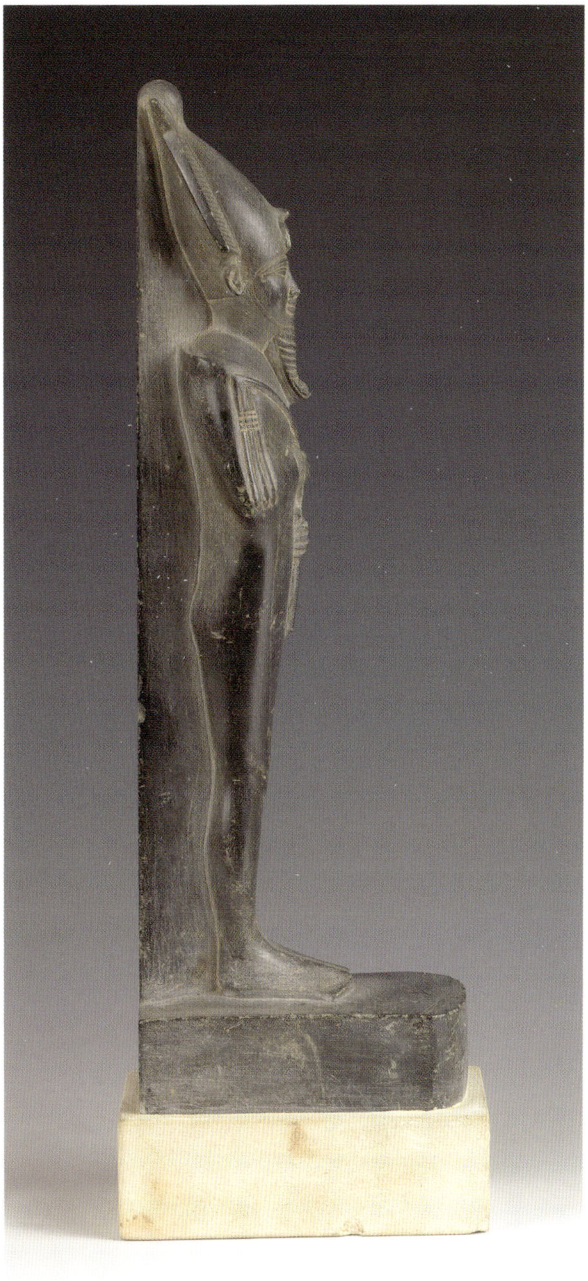

British Museum and the gold one at the Kunsthistorisches Museum, Vienna) (Seipel, 1989: 146-149). Bronze statuettes of Osiris can also be found at the Museu do Caramulo and the Museu Nacional de Arqueologia, both in Portugal (Araújo, 1993: 342-343).

EXHIBITIONS

1921 – Ancient Egyptian Art. London, Burlington Fine Arts Club.

1937 – Ancient Egyptian Sculpture lent by C. S. Gulbenkian, Esq. London, British Museum.

1949 – Egyptian Sculpture from the Gulbenkian Collection. Washington, D. C., National Gallery of Art.

27

**STATUE OF THE LADY SHEPES**

Late Period, 26th dynasty (664-525 BC)
Bronze
H: 66 cm
Provenance: The Dr. Eddé Collection, Alexandria
Date incorporated: 1911
Inv. no. 400

The hieroglyph text on the base shows that this votive statue of the Lady Shepes was dedicated to her by her daughter, the priestess Neitemhat. The lady's bronze figure is wearing a very simple and close-fitting tunic, in the Old Kingdom style, and the rather unconventional form of her smiling face, with short hair and hints of Negroid facial features, may be considered to be an attempted portrait. Like many works from this period, this one also features the "Saite smile".

The lady has a three-string necklace with incised geometrical decorations whose central elements form a zigzag pattern and end at the bottom with a string of drop-shaped pendants. Her body is well-rounded, with full breasts in the Old Kingdom style, her arms hang down alongside her body with the palms of her hands resting on her thighs, and the shape of her abdomen and pubic region are clearly visible. The tight-fitting tunic ends slightly above her ankles, while her feet are not shown with any great anatomical accuracy. Her left leg is pushed slightly forward in the traditional pose, and she is shown standing on a low, rectangular base that has a vertical hieroglyph inscription bordered by incised lines in front of her right foot.

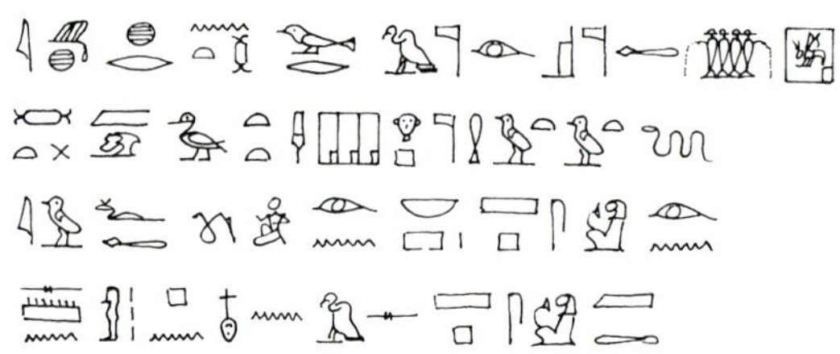

Inscription on the base: "Revered by Neith, the great, the mother of the god, the mother of Osiris, the great, who is in front of the temple of the North, Neitemhat, daughter of the administrator of the temples of Hapi, priest of Utut (?), Iuefaarudj, made by (the daughter of) Shepes. She made this fine monument for her mother Shepes, justified."

NOTES AND COMMENTS

Calouste Gulbenkian acquired this statuette at the sale of the collection of Dr. Eddé, in Alexandria. It was sent on a long-term loan to the Louvre in June 1911, and in September 1911, it underwent a cleaning procedure at the museum that left it in its current condition.

The statuette clearly reveals the somewhat archaic style that was fashionable in the Saite 26th dynasty, although it had already started in the 25th dynasty (of Nubian origin). The rounded forms recall the style that was popular under the Old Kingdom, yet the tightly-fitting robe is in line with the subsequent fashion that continued throughout the Middle Kingdom and the New Kingdom (see the female statuettes from this period in this collection). At first sight, the lady appears to be naked, which is why the sales document from Graat et Madoulé (6 June 1911) recorded the figure as "femme nue en marche", a description that also appears in the Paris catalogue (vol. II, p. 21).

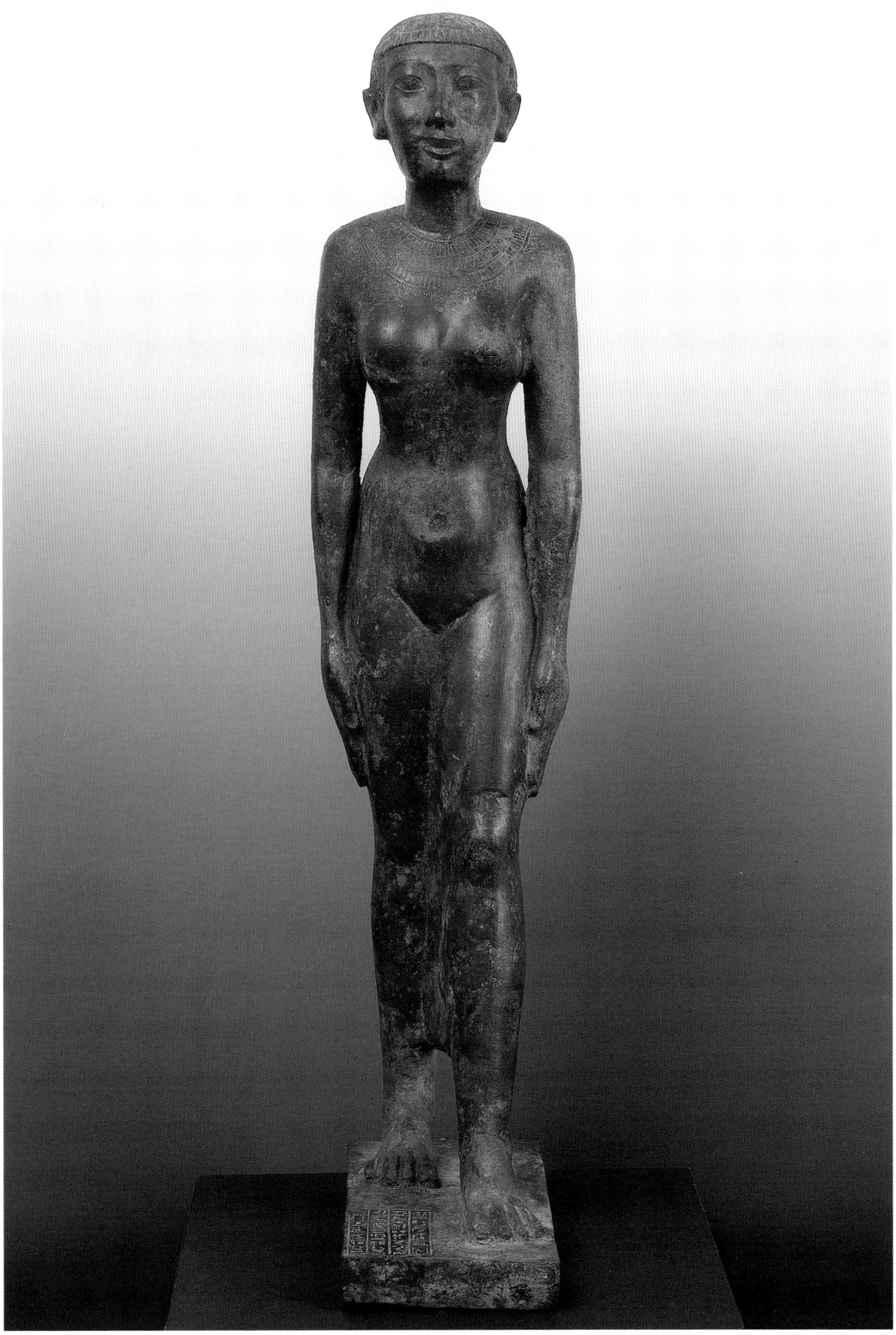

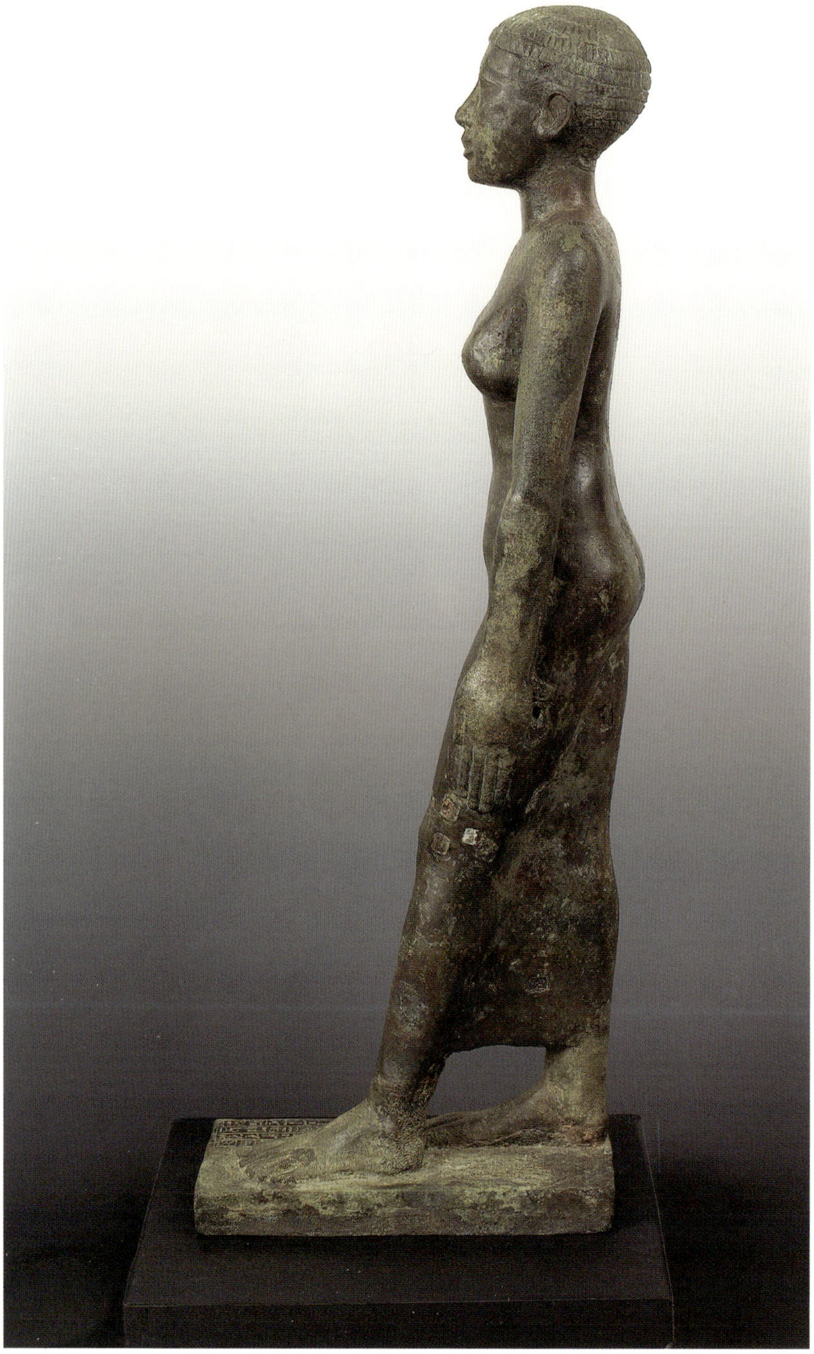

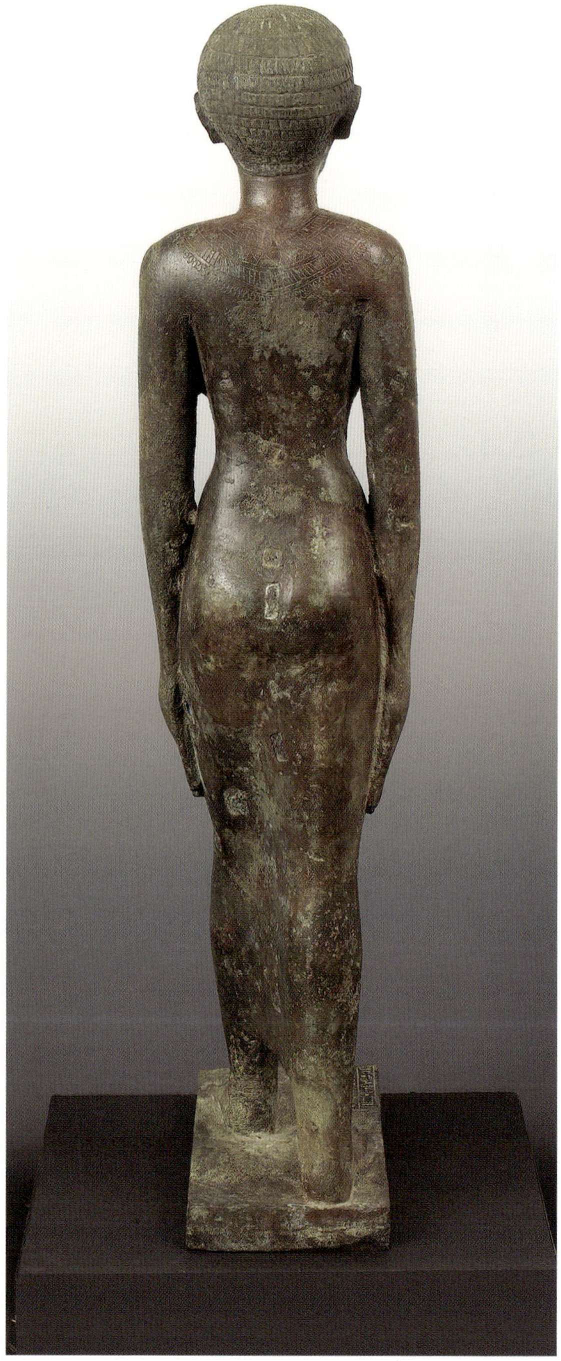

The Christos Bastis Collection includes a bronze statuette of a priestess or princess from the Nubian 25th dynasty (Bothmer, 1988: 36-38). Large numbers of statuettes of deities, kings, private citizens and animals were produced in the Late Period, maintaining a tradition that dated back to the Third Intermediate Period and that record Egypt's increasing closeness to the Mediterranean trade routes, specifically those involving the Greeks and Phoenicians. It was this clear Mediterraneanisation of Egypt that would trigger a backlash and return to an archaic style, first observable under the Nubian 25th dynasty and developed under the Saite 26th dynasty. Some authors believe that the "Saite smile" is a sign of the Greek influence that was then starting to take effect in Egypt (Assam, 1991: 78).

While using the version of the hieroglyph inscription that was published in the catalogue of the temporary exhibition at the British Museum (Smith & Edwards, 1937: 23), my interpretation of some signs is different. The important title *kherep* has been translated as "administrator" (Faulkner, 1962: 196), and a literally translation has been made of the terms *khenti* (who is in front of), and *iret en* (made by). The temple of the North may be the Serapeum in Sais or another shrine in the West Delta region, although doubt remains as to the meaning of Utut. The determiner of the name Iuefaarudj should be 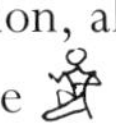 but the sign 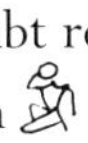 is rather unusual.

EXHIBITIONS

1937 – Ancient Egyptian Sculpture lent by C. S. Gulbenkian, Esq. London, British Museum.

1949 – Egyptian Sculpture from the Gulbenkian Collection. Washington, D. C., National Gallery of Art.

28

**STATUETTE OF THE OFFICIAL BES**

Late Period, early 26th dynasty (660-610 BC)
Compact limestone
H: 32.2 cm; W: 20.9 cm
Provenance: The MacGregor Collection
Date incorporated: 1922
Inv. no. 158

This statuette is made of finely grained limestone that seems like marble. The stone in question is exceptionally good for sculpture, and this certainly helped in the excellent technical execution of this figure. The statuette was broken into three fragments at the neck and waist, and shows a (now restored) long fracture running down to the ankle of his raised left leg. The spaces between the figure's trunk and arms were not open, which further emphasised the compact and cohesive appearance of this statuette, whose subject is shown wearing a simple kilt.

Bes has a well-proportioned head, and his face has gentle, restful features without any wrinkles. His eyebrows and upper eyelids are gracefully arched and his eyes are set at an angle; his nose has been broken, and only part of his left nostril can now be seen; his lips are closed, with the fleshy upper one protruding slightly. As the corners of his mouth are raised, he has a slight smile known as the "Saite smile", a characteristic of many contemporary and later statues. His chin protrudes slightly and his ears are clearly defined. The division between his forehead and bag wig is clearly marked by a raised line, probably showing that this was a wig used over the official's polished bald head.

His trunk starts with a thick neck, and his muscle and bone structures are solidly recreated, with particular detail being paid to his nipples and the surrounding areolas. His right hand rests on his bent right knee and holds the edge of his kilt, while his left hand lies on his raised left knee. The cuticles on his fingernails can be seen.

The pose is a traditional one in Egyptian sculpture, especially for scribes and other officials. However, in this case, the more usual cross-legged pose is discarded in favour of showing his left leg raised and bent at the knee, with his foot on the front left corner of the trapezoid base.

The inscriptions on the base, kilt and rear of the statuette offer information on Bes, a senior court official of King Psamtek I, who founded the 26th dynasty and whose name appears on the figure's right shoulder inside a cartouche, preceded by the title "son of Ra".

Inscription on the shoulder:

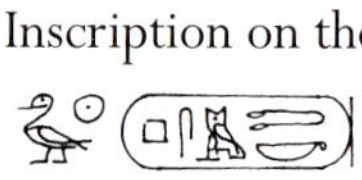

"Son of Ra, Psamtek."

On the kilt:

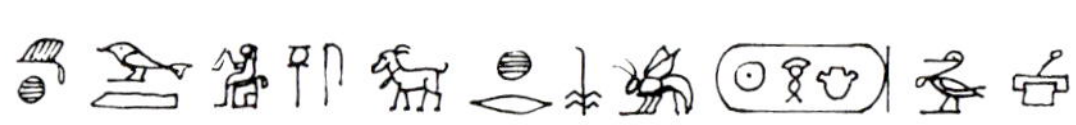

"Oh revered, great, true, noble, companion and dignitary of the king of Upper and Lower Egypt Wahibra, Bes."

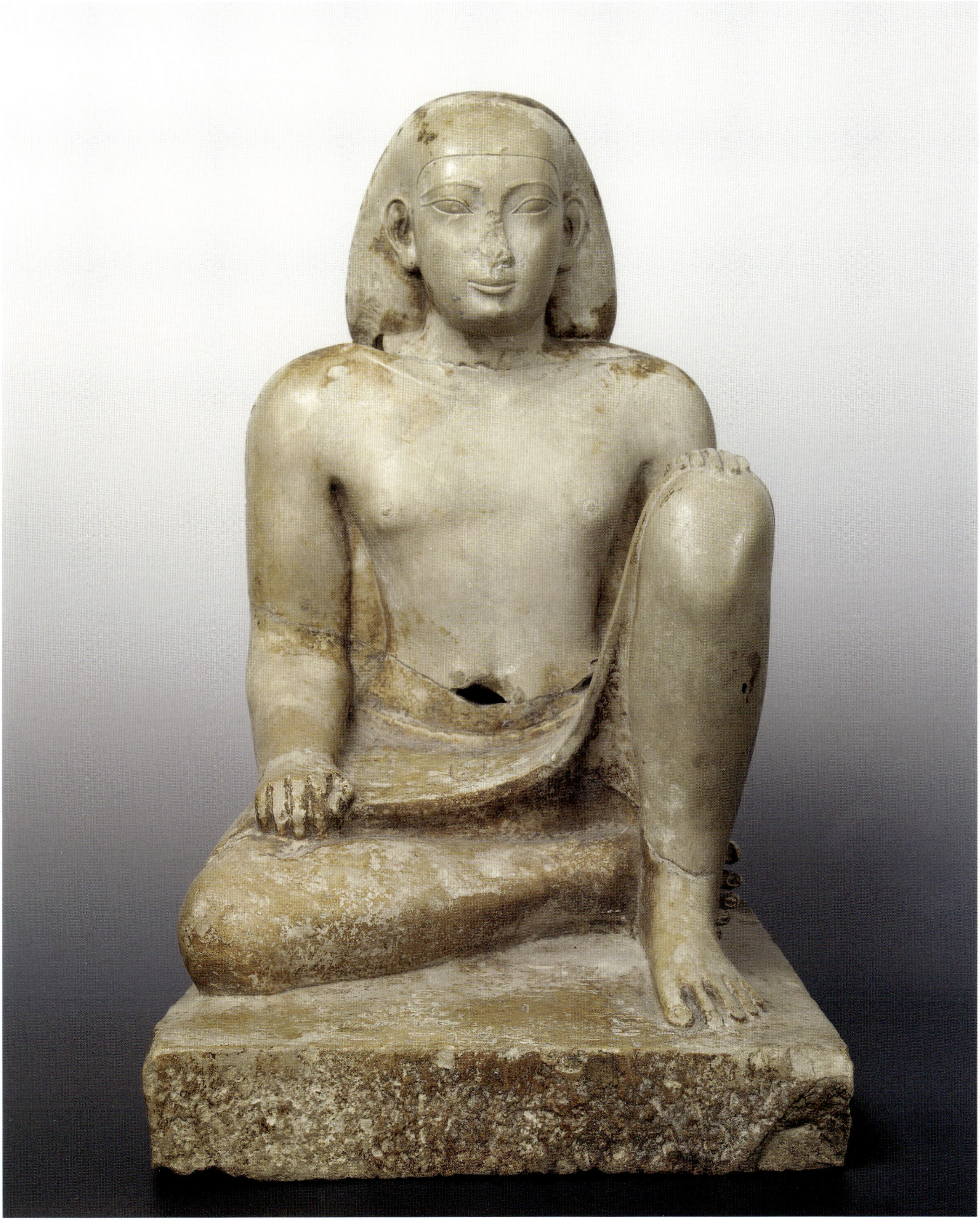

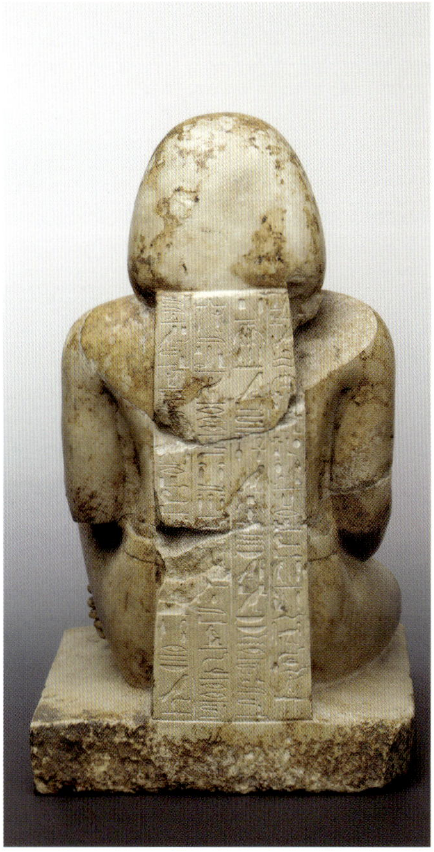

On the left of the pedestal:

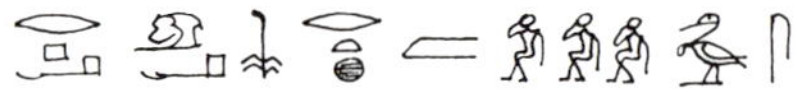

"Oh hereditary noble, governor, known to the king in the chambers of the royal children, Bes."

On the right of the pedestal:

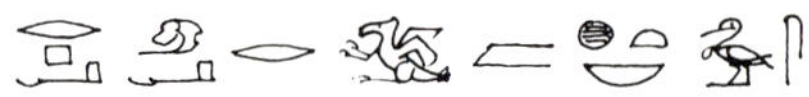

"Oh hereditary noble, governor of the people in all matters, Bes."

On the supporting pillar:

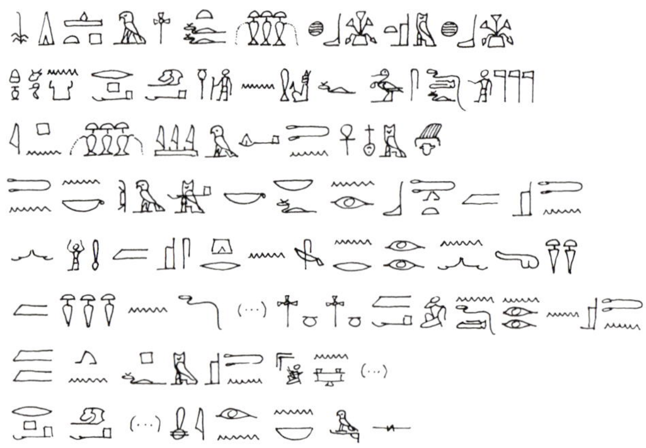

"Offered by the king to Horus, avenger of his father, who is in Akhbit, and Isis, who is in Akhbit, [that they may grant] bread, beer, beef and fowl for the *ka* [of the] hereditary noble, governor, companion of his majesty, Bes. He says: Oh gods who are in the fields of Horus, grant me a good life, with joy, [...] to the follower of Horus. Behold (?), I have not committed any mistake in your place (the temple), nor raised my voice in the place of silence (the temple or necropolis), nor committed bad deeds (?), [...] nor borne [false] witness before the judges of the court [...], nor uttered improprieties in your place [...] the noble, the governor [...]."

At the top of the pedestal: 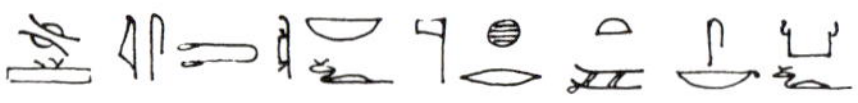 "(?) follows his divine lord, under Atum, who [does not] destroy his *ka*..."

At the bottom of the pedestal: 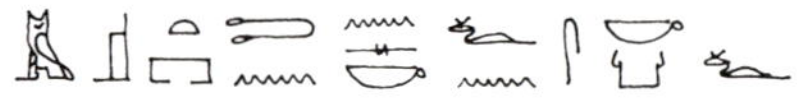 "...in your place. He does not destroy, not destroy his *ka*!"

In the middle of the base, between the deceased man's titles, the request is repeated: 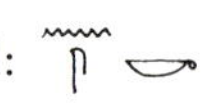 "He does not destroy" (*ne sek.f*).

NOTES AND COMMENTS

This statuette of exceptional artistic quality seems to have been produced at a royal workshop, although excellent production centres did exist at the time independently of the court (Bothmer, 1960: 34-35; Assam, 1991: 80). The precise location where it was produced is not known, although the reference to Akhbit (Khemmis), in the West Delta, may suggest that it came from that area, which had strong links to the cult of Isis and her son Horus, who are both mentioned in the text: Horakhbit and Isitakhbit. According to the mythology, this was the place in the Delta where Isis protected her son Horus from persecution by the deceitful Set.

This is the earliest example of the use of this type of bag wig in the Late Period, although there are similarities to statues from previous periods. The figure's smile is the first known example of this type of expression, which would appear in many images from the Late Period and continue on into the Ptolemaic dynasty (Greco-Roman Period), before declining during the 1st century BC until it became more of a grimace. The form in this case is the so-called "Saite smile", part of the sculptural repertoire of the Late Period and subsequent times. It may be interpreted as a reaction against the Kushite realism of the Nubian 25th dynasty, and perhaps reflect some Greek influence, as is thoroughly documented for the "archaic smile" on statues of the *kouroi* from this era (Bothmer, 1960: 34-35).

The figure's pose is unusual in that it avoids the symmetry of the "law of frontality". However, there are known works from previous periods – even some from as early as the Old Kingdom – that adopt the same position. Pieces of the limestone are now missing from the right shoulder, near the navel and at the back. In the last case, this impedes any reading of the hieroglyphic inscription, which is in itself extremely complex.

The main text, engraved in high-quality hieroglyphic symbols, starts on the rear pedestal in four vertical columns with borders, and ends on the front of the pedestal, where it mixes with other texts that refer to the subject and the subject's various courtly titles. The text is an *apologia* that is very difficult to interpret, as recognised by all the experts who have tried to do so. Such difficulties also seem to be reflected in the fact that only the subject's name and titles, as engraved on the pedestal, appeared in the catalogue of the temporary exhibition at the British Museum (Smith & Edwards, 1937: 23). The translation proposed here – notwithstanding reservations about some sentences – was produced using Raymond Faulkner's dictionary and Sir Alan Gardiner's grammar.

The text starts with the traditional introduction of *hotep-di-nesu* (offering made by the king), as found in other objects from the collection. This is followed by a reference to a major title related to Horus: Hornedjeti, or Horus avenger of his father. Then it mentions a sacred location in the Delta (Akhbit) before the offering formula, which unusually does not include the customary *peret-kheru* (invocations-offerings) before starting the short list of goods for the deceased's *ka*. The *ka* then calls upon the gods in the fields of Horus (Sekhet Hor) and begins the defence of the subject's exemplary life on earth. Among several other doubts, the most significant is the sentence in which Bes says he has not given false witness before the gods of the court: the sentence is correct if one accepts the possible haplological contraction suggested by the sign 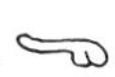, first with the meaning of "witness" (*mtr*) and then as the preposition "before" (*m-b3ḥ*). The reference to the judges and the court is acceptable if the translation of the sign , repeated in the text, is put in the place of 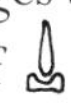, as seems to be the case (Faulkner, 1988: 78, 121, 319). The last sentence (in the bottom left corner of the pillar's fourth column, after the break in the stone) is effectively impossible to interpret, and the text ends on the base of the statue.

EXHIBITIONS

1921 – Ancient Egyptian Art. London, Burlington Fine Arts Club.

1937 – Ancient Egyptian Sculpture lent by C. S. Gulbenkian, Esq. London, British Museum.

1949 – Egyptian Sculpture from the Gulbenkian Collection. Washington, D. C., National Gallery of Art.

1960 – Egyptian Sculpture of the Late Period. Brooklyn, New York, Brooklyn Museum.

1965 – Obras de Arte da Fundação Calouste Gulbenkian. Oeiras, Pombal Palace.

1999 – "Only the Best": Masterpieces of the Calouste Gulbenkian Museum. New York, The Metropolitan Museum of Art.

29

**STATUETTE OF A CAT**

Late Period, 26th dynasty (664-525 BC)
Bronze
H: 14 cm
Provenance: Acquired from Howard Carter
Date incorporated: 1929
Inv. no. 219

This statuette of a seated cat is made in bronze and has a greenish patina. The facial features are moulded with some cursory anatomical details, including ears with diagonal incisions that are not found as traditional feline whiskers. The tail curves around the body and appears at the front on the right, ending near the respective paw. It has pierced ears to hold earrings (now lost) that were evidently made of gold. The left ear has a crack at its base, and the figure is sitting on a non-original base.

NOTES AND COMMENTS

This small statuette was restored at the Conservation Laboratory at the Museu Monográfico de Conímbriga. The respective laboratory report noted that it had a "good green patina with no signs of active corrosion".

There are countless statuettes of cats in many public and private museums. The Egyptian Museum in Cairo alone has many that illustrate the different forms of depicting the animal's fur and the diverse iconography that generally accompanies such bronze images. One of the most interesting and complete cat statuettes is the one at the British Museum, which shows the animal in the traditional seated pose, like the pieces in the Gulbenkian Collection, but which still has the gold earrings and a gold ring in its nose. In addition, it also has a silver collar with the eye of Horus (*udjat*). The rich iconography on the piece in London also includes a three-string incised collar round the neck, with a teardrop-shaped pendant decoration around the collar, a winged scarab (incised onto the chest) that is pushing a silver solar disc and a relief scarab on the animal's head (Quirke & Spencer, 1992: 46; Málek, 1993: 12-13).

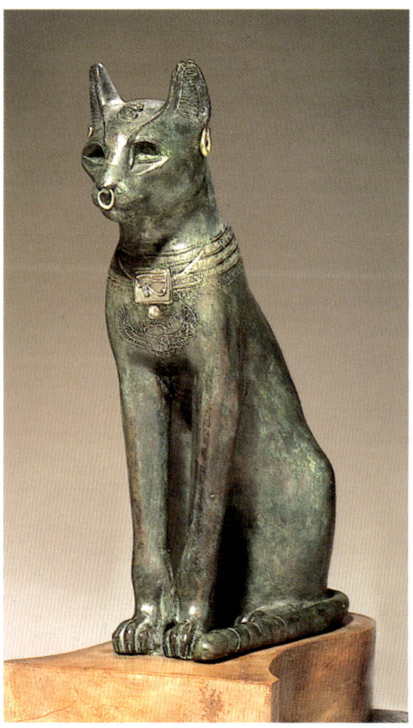

Bronze cat, Late Period, ca. 664-630 BC, H. 42 cm. British Museum, inv. no. EA64391 © Courtesy of the Trustees of the British Museum

The Louvre owns an attractive variation: a bronzed cat with gold adornments and decoration on the front, an incised éguis pectoral and – a rarity in this type of statuette – a hieroglyphic inscription on the base, bearing the names (set in cartouches) of Wahibra Psamtek (King Psamtek I) (Ziegler, 1990: 78). Moreover, the small Egyptian Collection at the Musée Champollion, Figéac, includes a cat whose fur is shown by small incisions in the bronze and a beautifully drawn eye of Horus (*udjat*) on its chest. The animal is shown sitting on a *neb* basket (Dewachter, 1986: 52-53).

Based on his study of a bronzed statuette of a cat with a multiple string collar and an *udjat* eye on its chest, part of the Christos Bastis Collection, Bernard Bothmer believes that the incisions on the ears could suggest the ostrich feather that symbolised Maet, the well-known goddess of truth, justice, balance and order. However, this does not apply either to this statuette or to the others examined here, including the two from the Calouste Gulbenkian Museum (Bothmer, 1988: 54).

The cat was the sacred animal of the feline goddess Bastet, a kindly deity who became very popular in Egypt, especially during the Late Period. She was particularly venerated in the Delta, specifically in

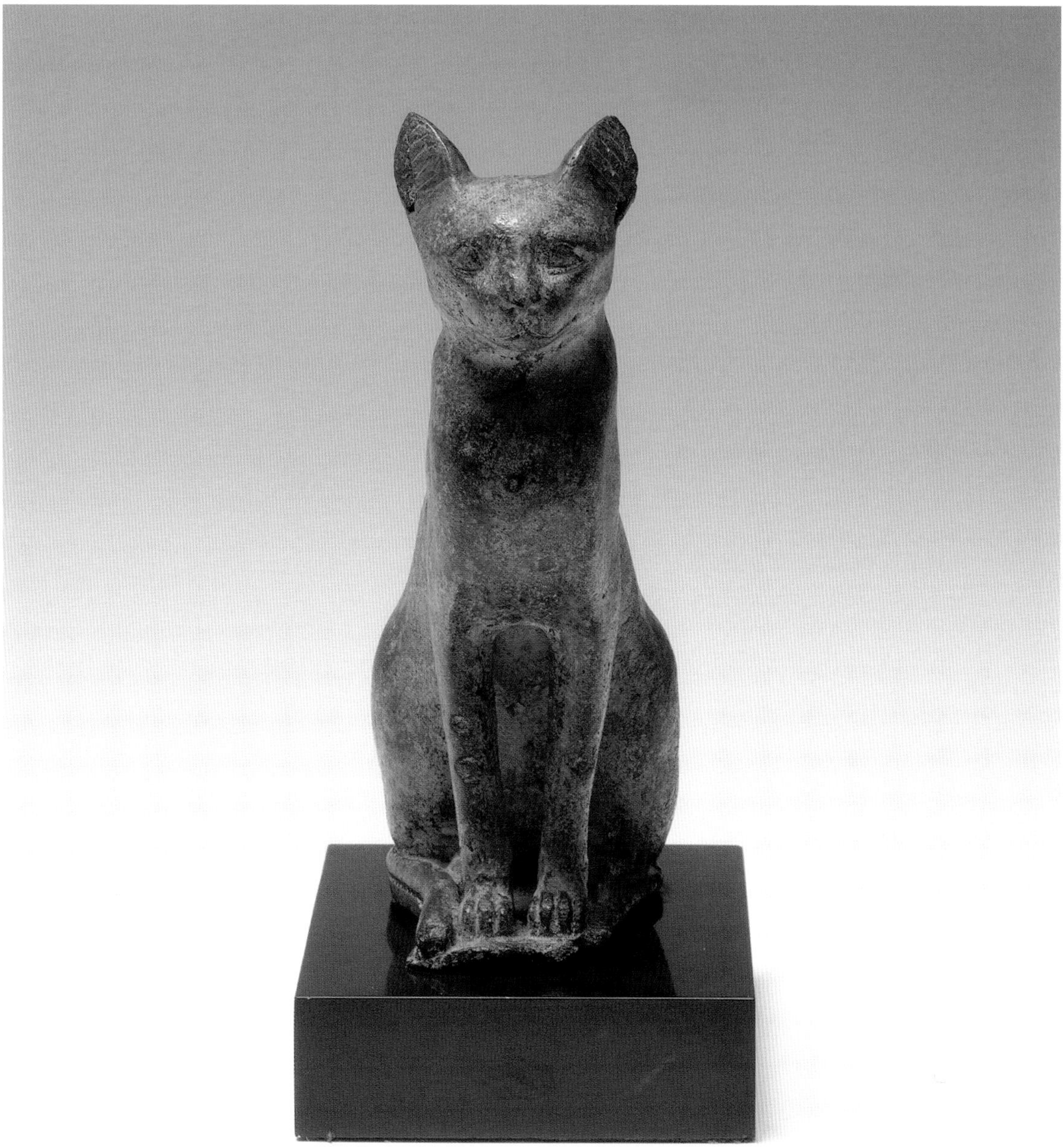

Bubastis and Sais, and enjoyed pharaonic protection as from the 26th dynasty. The goddess was also depicted as a woman with a cat's head, as shown by many bronze statuettes. The Egyptian Collection at the Museu Nacional de Arqueologia, Lisbon, owns one such piece (Araújo, 1993: 351-352), while another in excellent condition can be seen in the Egyptian Collection of the Antiquities Museum in Leiden (Rijksmuseumm van Oudheden), albeit without the earrings (Schneider, 1987: 119). A similar piece in the Christos Bastis Collection is better still, as it still has the gold earrings (Bothmer, 1988: 85-86).

30

**STATUETTE OF A CAT**

Late Period, 26$^{th}$ dynasty
Bronze
H: 19 cm
Provenance: The Carmichael Collection
Date incorporated: 1926
Inv. no. 399

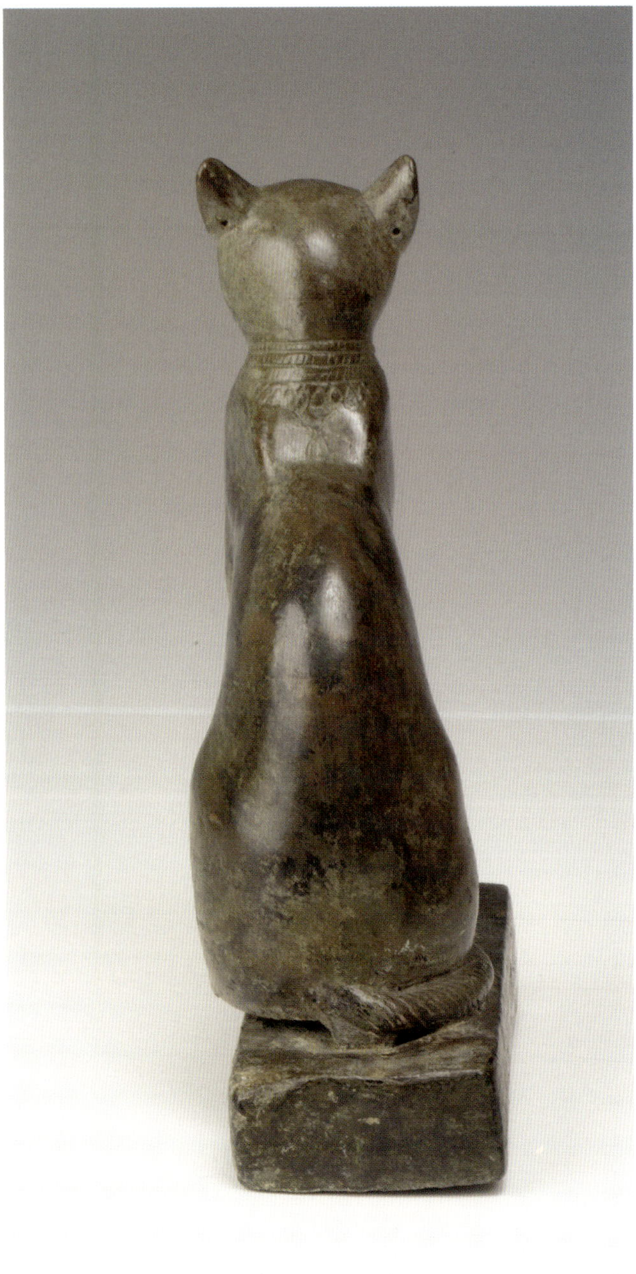

This statuette of a seated cat is made of bronze and has a brownish patina. The facial features are moulded in some detail, showing the incised whiskers and the inside of the ears with diagonal incisions, which are more detailed than in the previous piece. The ears are pierced to hold earrings that have since been lost. The figure has a floral three-string collar ending in a line of teardrop pendants, and what seems to be a sketched eye of Horus (*udjat*) hangs from this line. The cat's tail encircles its body to the right and appears (as is usual) in front of the animal's right paw. The animal is sitting slightly to the left on its original hollow rectangular base, also made of bronze, and the figure was probably designed to contain the remains of a cat.

NOTES AND COMMENTS

This small statuette was affected by the major flooding in November 1967, and was restored at the Conservation Laboratory at the Museu Monográfico de Conímbriga. The piece was acquired via Howard Carter from the Carmichael Collection.

It is sometimes claimed that the small bases under statuettes of cats could have stored the animals' ashes, but there is no proof of this practice. The preferred process was mummification, and the animals' bodies were then stored inside the bases, although some smaller containers may only contain kittens or mummified parts of cats (Málek, 1993: 124-134).

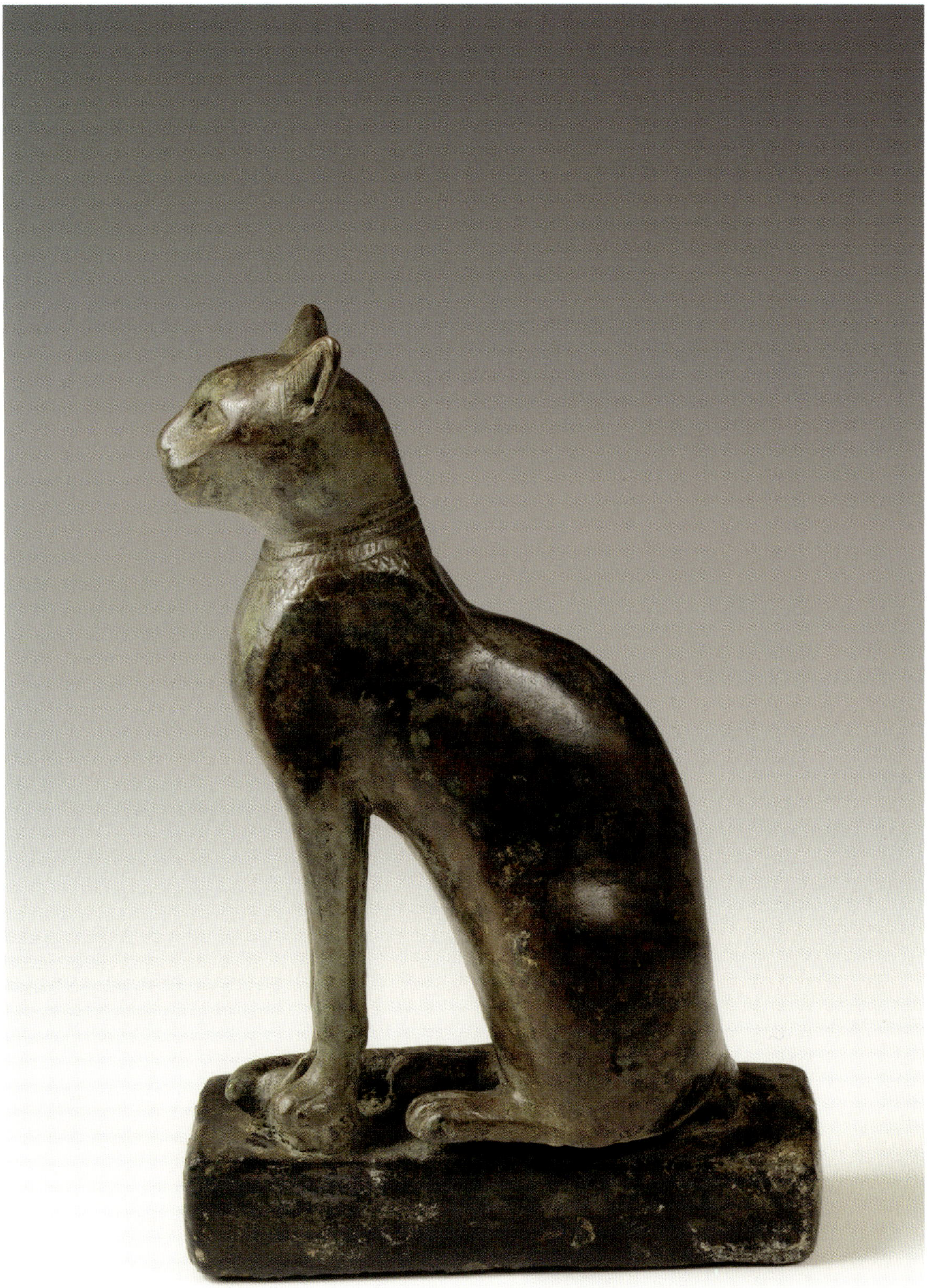

**CAT WITH KITTENS**

Late Period, 26th dynasty
Bronze
H: 25.5 cm; L: 55.3 cm
Provenance: The Durighello Collection
Date incorporated: 1924
Inv. no. 21

This sculpted bronze group with a greenish patina and a brownish tone on some parts shows a reclining cat feeding one of her kittens and holding another between its front paws. The cat has pierced ears for earrings that have been lost and would have been made of gold. The feline features of the face show some anatomical detail, while light incisions create the impression of the animal's fur. The right rear section is finely modelled and the cat's tail falls down beside the hollow rectangular base that held the mummified remains of a cat. The base has a rough surface and a hole on the side where the tail passes.

NOTES AND COMMENTS

The purchase record of this "chatte allaitant ses petits" shows that it was bought via Graat et Madoulé at the sale of objects from the Durighello Collection, held in 1924 at Galerie Georges Petit, Paris. Calouste Gulbenkian kept this exceptional piece in his house in Avenue d'Iéna, Paris, until he sent it to London in 1936 for exhibition at the British Museum. This fine sculpted group clearly stood out from similar groups then exhibited at the museum. While interesting, these somewhat eroded pieces showed cats with several kittens on elongated bases that acted as sarcophagi for the mummified animals (Málek, 1993: 103, 111).

The Egyptian Museum in Cairo has identical objects, such as a cat with kittens that may date from the Late Period (Bongioanni & Croce, 2001: 552). Other museums have similar groups, but one of the best conserved of its kind is undoubtedly at the Antiquities Museum in Leiden (Rijksmuseumm van Oudheden), although this only shows a cat on the sarcophagus base (Seipel, 1989: 321).

EXHIBITIONS

1937 – Ancient Egyptian Sculpture lent by C. S. Gulbenkian, Esq. London, British Museum.

1949 – Egyptian Sculpture from the Gulbenkian Collection. Washington, D. C., National Gallery of Art.

1965 – Obras de Arte da Fundação Calouste Gulbenkian. Oeiras, Pombal Palace.

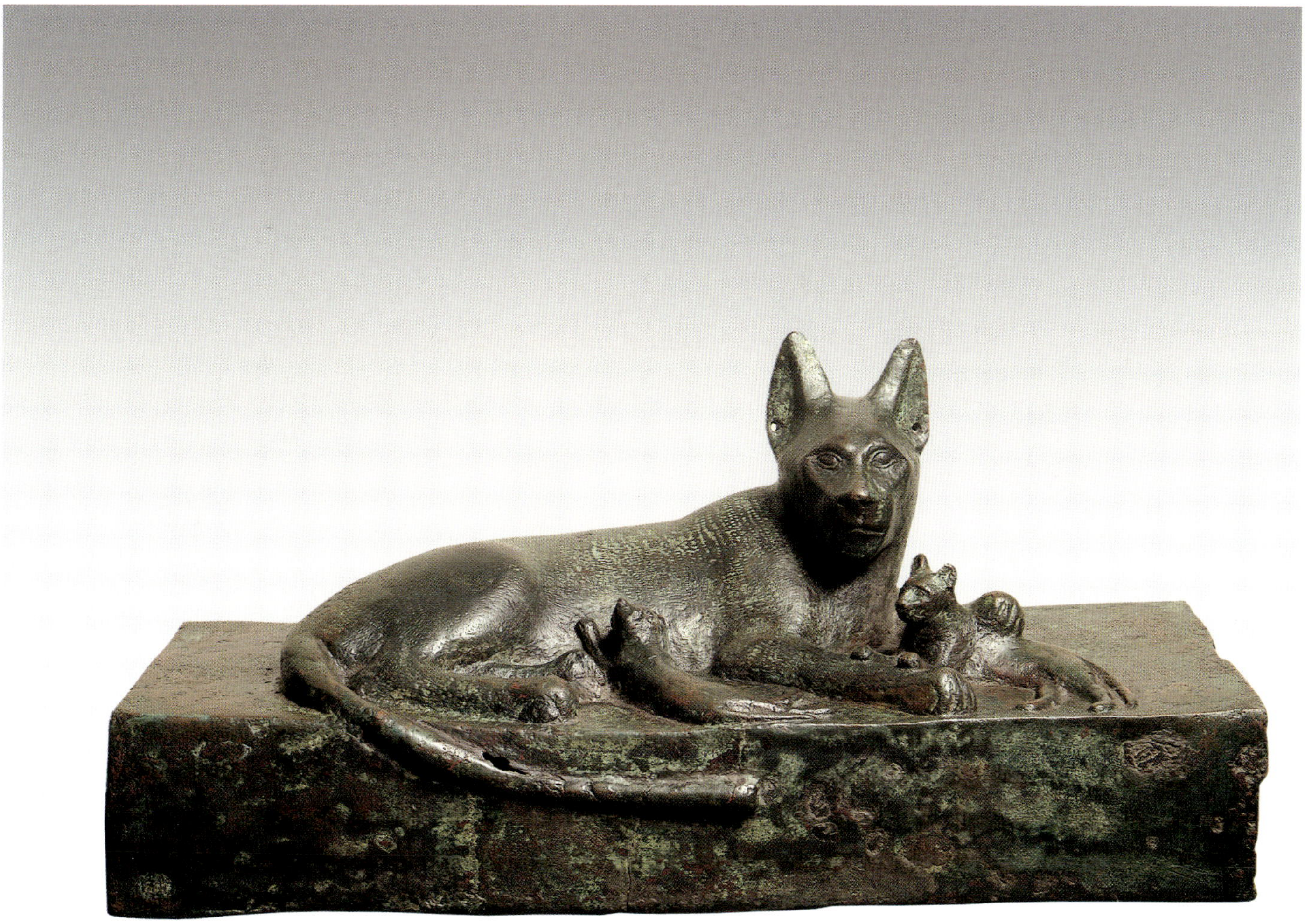

32

**FUNERARY MASK**

Late Period, 30th dynasty (664-525 BC)
Gilded silver
H: 43.5 cm
Provenance: The John Maxwell Collection
Date incorporated: 1928
Inv. no. 62

This gilded silver funerary mask shows the idealised face of the deceased, whose name has been lost. Although the piece has none of the floral decoration or traces of any inscription that are customarily found in this type of funerary equipment, it does feature outstanding detail in its accurate depiction of the face. The figure's eyes run sideways under marked eyebrows, he has a well-proportioned nose with a natural-looking hollow between the nose and the upper lip, while the lower lip is defined by a high relief line. The slightly raised corners of his harmonious mouth help enliven the smile on his face. His hair, created in high relief, starts from the middle of his forehead, runs over his ears and falls onto his chest, surrounding his face, which has gentle features and traces of brownish polychrome on the eyebrows and eyes.

The piece reveals fine technical work on the metal, managing to create a thin surface with a maximum of two millimetres and showing excellent repoussé work. However, attempts to make this even thinner led to the metal becoming pierced near the ears and at the join between the face and the hair.

NOTES AND COMMENTS

This excellent funerary mask was acquired via Howard Carter at the sale of the collection of General John Maxwell, held at Sotheby's in London. It was then kept at Calouste Gulbenkian's Paris home in Avenue d'Iéna until 1936, when it was sent to London for exhibition at the British Museum.

Funerary mask, Ptolemaic Period, ca. 50 AD. Painted and gilded cartonnage, H. 44 cm. British Museum, inv. no. EA29472
© Courtesy of the Trustees of the British Museum

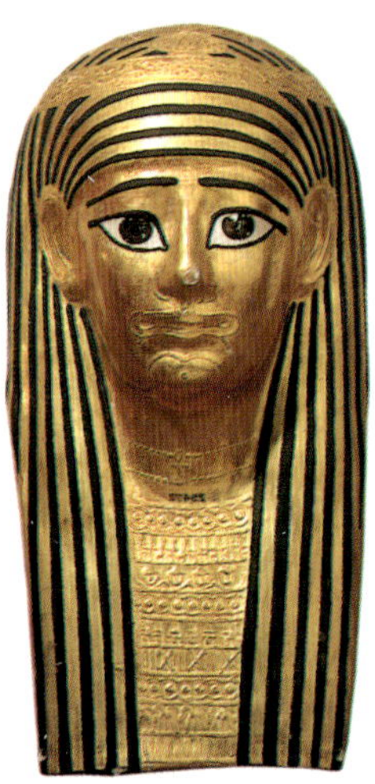

In the sales catalogue for the John Maxwell Collection, published in 1928, Howard Carter noted that only two gold funerary masks were known, both in the Egyptian Museum in Cairo (Tiradritti, 1998: 179, 235). One belonged to Touia, the mother of Queen Ti (the wife of Pharaoh Amenhotep III), and was made of cartonnage coated with gold-leaf; the other belonging to Tutankhamun. However, some ten years later, gold funerary masks of kings from the 21st dynasty (Psusennes I and Amenemope) and of the official Wendjebauendjed (probably a relative of Psusennes I) were found in the royal tombs of Tanis, specifically in the courtyard of the Tanite temple of Amun (*Ibidem*: 315, 324, 326).

Most known funerary masks – as found in several museums in Europe and the USA, as well as in the Egyptian Museum in Cairo – are made of cartonnage, and many were gilded, sometimes also showing blue painted hair, suggesting fine colouring using lapis-lazuli. One of the most expressive examples is at the British Museum, London (Málek, 2003: 351).

Gilded funerary masks on painted cartonnage can be seen in the Egyptian collection of the Museu Nacional de Arqueologia, Lisbon (Araújo, 1993: 305). One of these was recently and excellently restored at the Museu Monográfico de Conímbriga, which has also worked on some pieces from the Gulbenkian Collection. Funerary masks rarely portray the face of the deceased, but instead aimed to create an image with gentle lines and an expressive gaze that demonstrated a good physical and spiritual state of health and an absolute confidence that the deceased would attain eternity.

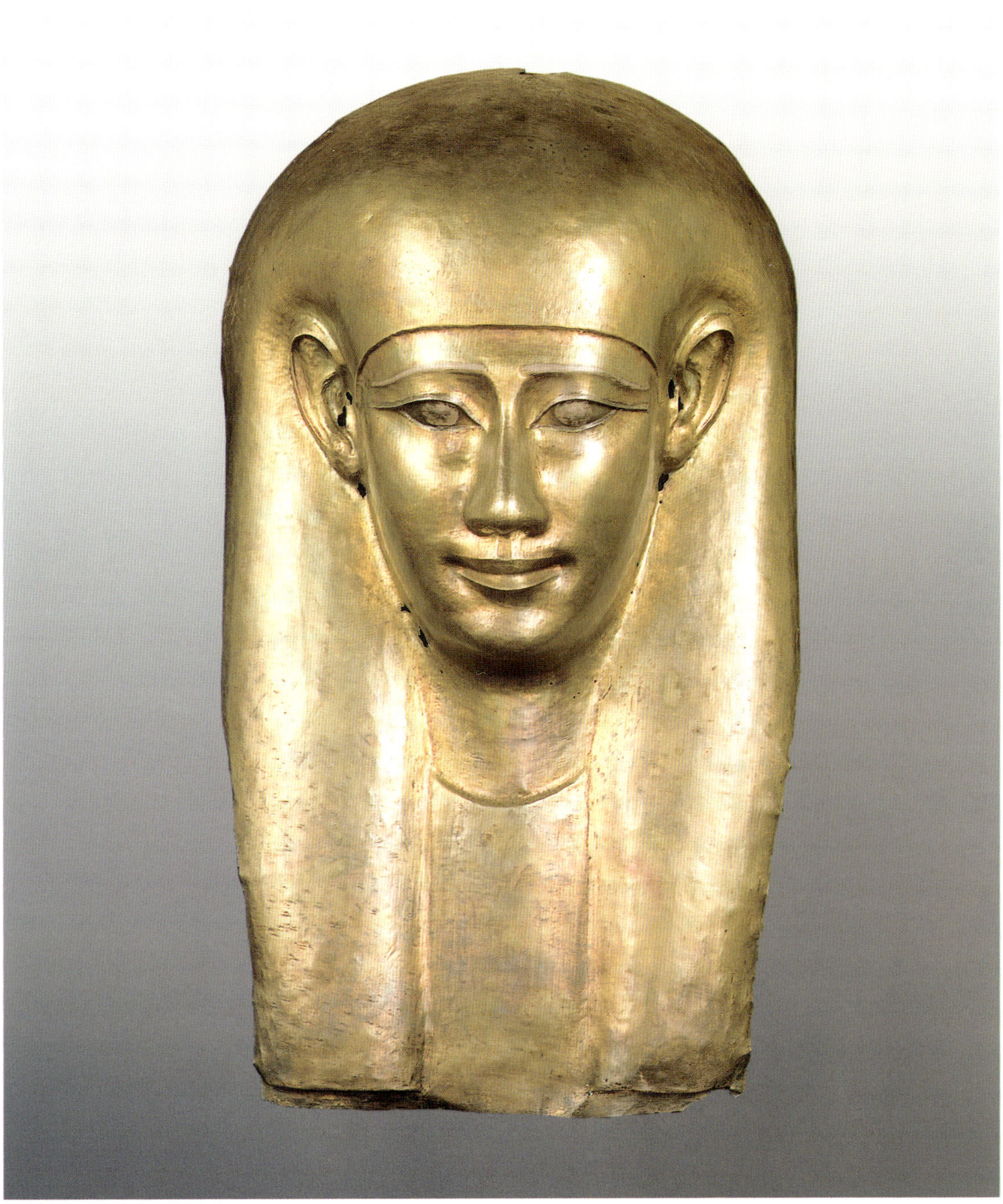

EXHIBITIONS

1937 – Ancient Egyptian Sculpture lent by C. S. Gulbenkian, Esq. London, British Museum.

1949 – Egyptian Sculpture from the Gulbenkian Collection. Washington, D. C., National Gallery of Art.

1965 – Obras de Arte da Fundação Calouste Gulbenkian. Oeiras, Pombal Palace.

33

**SOLAR BARQUE OF DJEDHOR**

Late Period, 26th-30th dynasty (ca. 380-343 BC)
Bronze
H: 31.3 cm; L: 26.3 cm
Provenance: Sotheby's, London
Date incorporated: 1924
Inv. no. 168

This processional insignia is shaped like the earliest barques from the River Nile and is dedicated to Djedhor, as shown by the inscriptions on the hull and the walls of the small shrine in the centre. The latter has images of several deities: Isis and Nephthys flanking the entrance, Horus in falcon form and wearing the crown of Upper and Lower Egypt on the shrine, the falcon-headed Ra-Horakhty inside, and the crocodile-shaped god Sobek supporting the boat and symbolising the River Nile. The boat also holds a standing royal sphinx at the front, crowned with two tall feathers, horns and the sacred serpent, as well as the divine beard; and the helmsman at the stern, clearly representing the deceased. The boat ends in open lotus-flower buds, a stylised image of the appearance of some boats from the Nile. Another lotus bud simultaneously acts as the support for Sobek, and socket for the upper end of the wooden pole held by the priest when the boat was carried in processions.

The central cabin has straight lines forming a shrine form that corresponds to the hieroglyphic sign O 21 (Sir Alan Gardiner's list). The figure of Ra-Horakhty appears inside the shrine, his falcon's head crowned by the solar disc, while the entrance to the shrine has two goddesses who can be recognised by the hieroglyphic signs on their heads, resting on small crowns with serpents. This means that they can be identified as Isis (on the right) and Nephthys (on the left). The top front of the shrine is decorated with a frieze of six solarised sacred serpents, while a Horus falcon crowned with the *pa-sekhemti* (*pchent*) stands on top. The sides of the shrine have two types of decoration: openwork and incisions to open the walls; and incised decoration. The theme in the upper section again shows the goddesses Isis (with solarised lily-shaped horns) and Nephthys (with the hieroglyphs of her name on her head). Their arms are stretched out in different directions, and lead to open wings that support a central tuft of stylised vegetation. The lower section is different on each side: on the left, it shows the deceased before the enthroned god Atum, who is holding the *uase* sceptre (prosperity) and the well-known sign of life (*ankh*); on the right, the god Ra-Horakhty in the same pose appears instead of the solar god Atum. Both these deities are closely associated to the sun, and Atum is seen as a creator of the world.

The decoration on the hull comprises sixteen relief circles that loosely follow the curve of the deck, while the lotus-flowers at the prow and stern have incised images of a boat with a central rear oar sailing on a hieroglyph that is read *ché* (š) and means "lake" (among other interpretations), here suggesting sailing in the solar boat. The crocodile supporting the boat was made with fine details on the head, feet and tail.

Inscription on the hull:

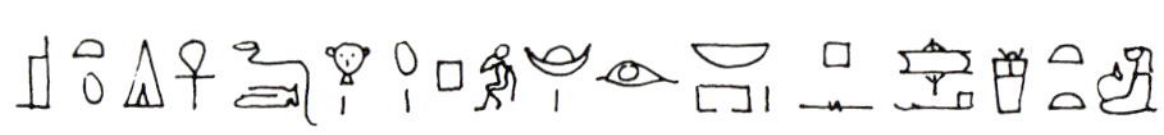

"May Isis grant life to Djedhor, the son of Pa-cheriah, made by (the son of) lady of the house Pasetjauemauibastet."

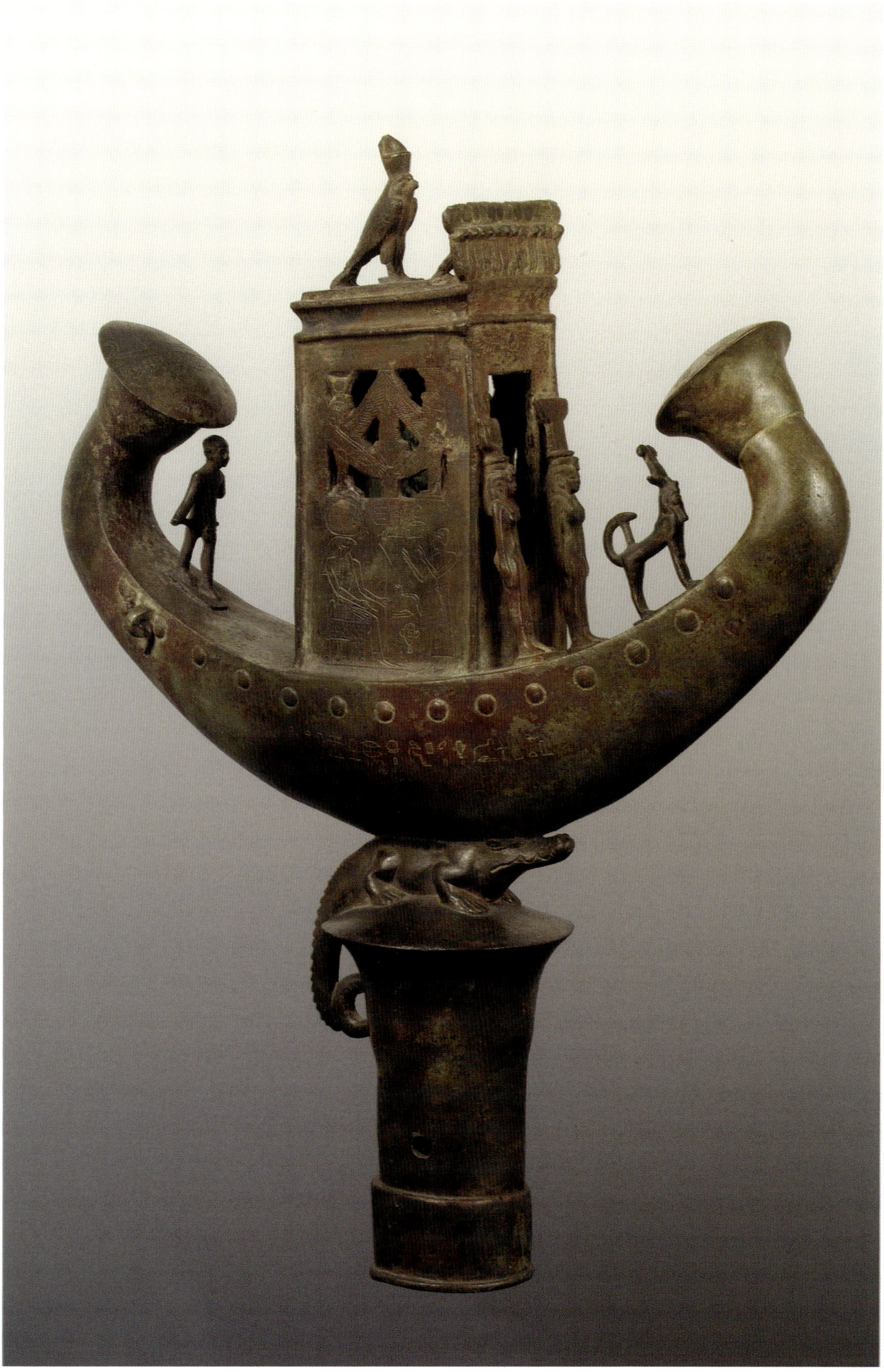

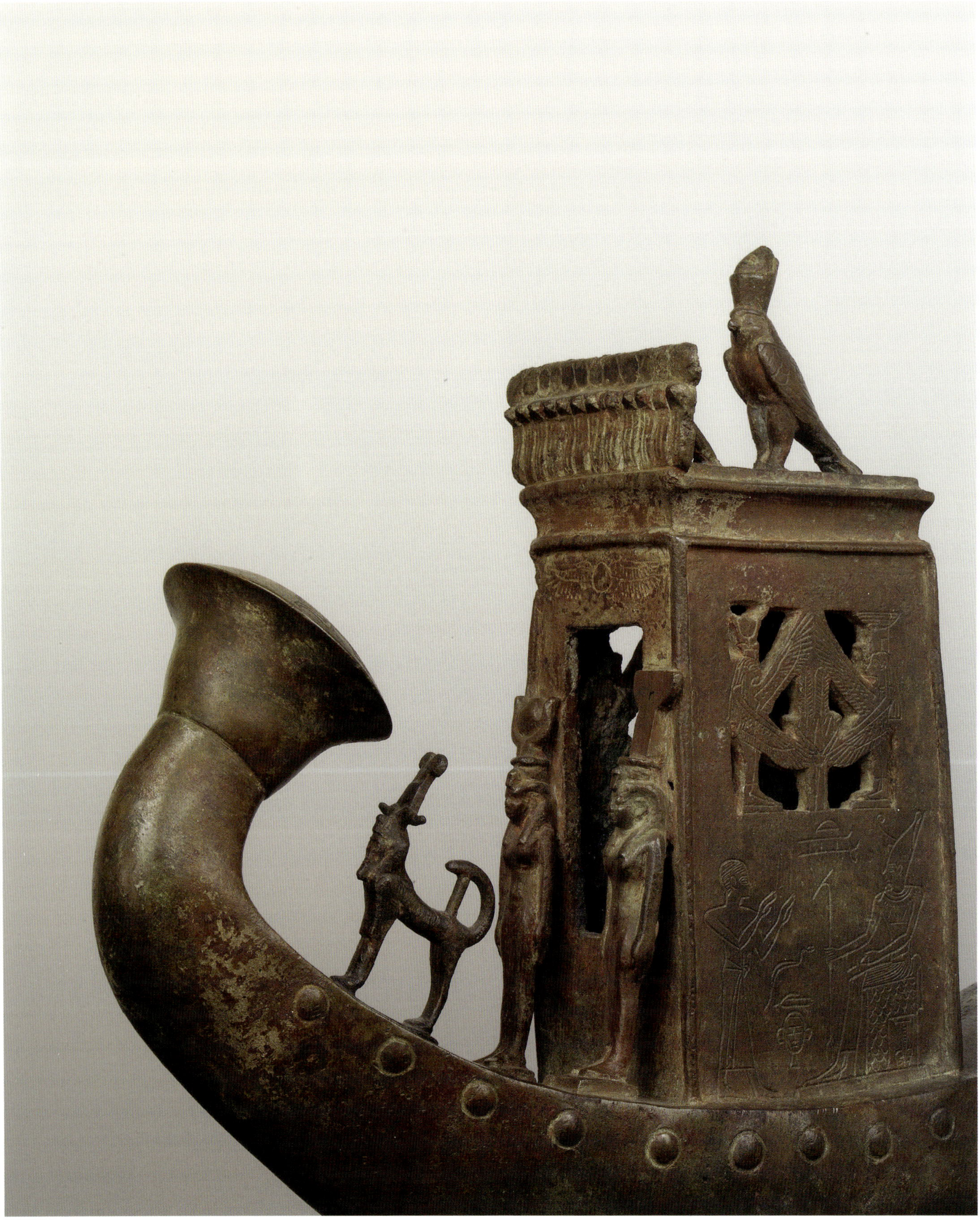

On the left side of the shrine: an image of Atum with the deceased Djedhor, bearing the respective hieroglyph inscriptions.

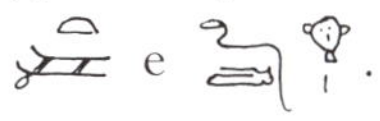

On the right side of the shrine: an image of Ra-Horakhty with the deceased, bearing the respective hieroglyph inscriptions.

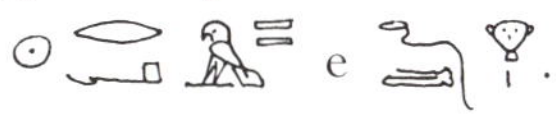

NOTES AND COMMENTS

The bronze figurines were made separately and are attached to the boat by small metal rivets. One of the figures represents the god Ra-Horakhty, although previous studies identify him as Amun-Ra (Smith & Edwards, 1937: 13; Assam, 1991: 90). Small technical details can be seen on the reinforcement and support shafts that hold the sphinx's curving tail and the frieze of sacred serpents on the shrine. The ring between the crocodile's tail and the lotus flower at the top of the pole seems to be designed exclusively to support the animal's hanging tail. The stylised lotus flower has holes so that the now lost wooden pole can be attached.

A very similar piece can be found in the Egyptian collection at the Museum of Antiquities in Leiden (Rijksmuseum van Oudheden), although there is no crocodile on the base and there is a cow with solarised lily-shaped horns between the goddesses Isis and Nephthys at the entrance to the shrine. Like the piece in the Gulbenkian Collection, this holds an image of Ra-Horakhty (Schneider, 1987: 725, plate 161).

I have used the version of the translation from the catalogue for the temporary exhibition at the British Museum (Smith & Edwards, 1937: 26) to translate the hieroglyphic text. The style is similar to the one in the text on the work at the Antiquities Museum in Leiden. The title "lady of the house" (*nebet-per*), attributed here to Pasetjauemauibastet, Djedhor's mother, also appears on the fine statuette of Henut-tauy (cat. no. 14) and the statue of the Lady Shepes, the mother of Neitemhat (cat. no. 27). Finally, the more complex god-related name of Pasetjauemauibastet invokes the well-known goddess Bastet, who was very widely venerated at that time, and means "Her breath is in the hands of Bastet".

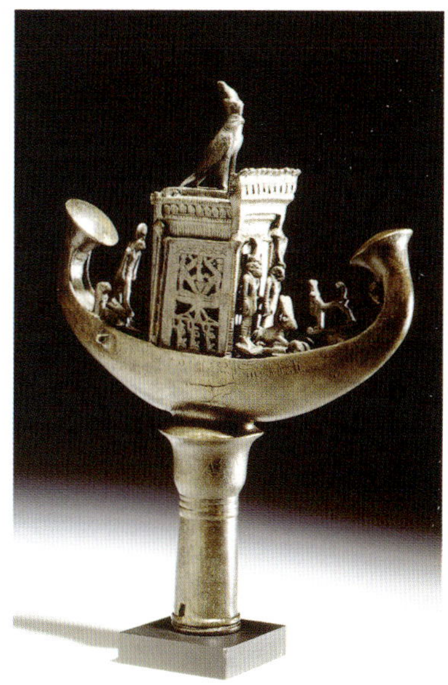

Solar boat, Late Period, ca. 500 BC. Bronze, H. 34 cm. Museum of Antiquities, Leiden, inv. no. AED87

EXHIBITIONS

1937 – Ancient Egyptian Sculpture lent by C. S. Gulbenkian, Esq. London, British Museum.

1949 – Egyptian Sculpture from the Gulbenkian Collection. Washington, D. C., National Gallery of Art.

1965 – Obras de Arte da Fundação Calouste Gulbenkian. Oeiras, Pombal Palace.

34

## STATUE OF DJEDHOR

Greco-Roman Period, early Ptolemaic dynasty (ca. 300-250 BC)
Basalt
H: 54 cm
Provenance: The Hope Collection
Date incorporated: 1917
Inv. no. 403

This unpolished basalt statuette depicts a kneeling figure holding a small shrine with an image of the god Osiris. The figure wears the typical bag wig of the Late Period, and the Ptolemaic Period, he has clearly defined eyes and eyebrows, his nose is fractured and he has the traditional "Saite smile", albeit lacking the expressiveness of similar images. His chest protrudes and he has no sign of any clothing. His hands and feet are slightly stylised, as his toes are in unrealistic positions that recall the same pose found on figures of New Kingdom officials. The image of Osiris inside the shrine, which has two upper rims, is shown in his typical mummified pose, and the god of eternity is wearing the *atef* crown with lateral feathers. His folded hands, which emerge from the funerary shroud, hold the two royal sceptres: the *hekat* in his left hand; the *nekhakha* in his right.

The dorsal pillar has an incised hieroglyphic inscription that is difficult to read. It continues through two lines inscribed on the base (except on the front), recording the name of Djedhor and his titles, the names of relatives and their titles, some of which cannot be easily interpreted.

The text on the dorsal pillar and sides of the pedestal reads as follows:

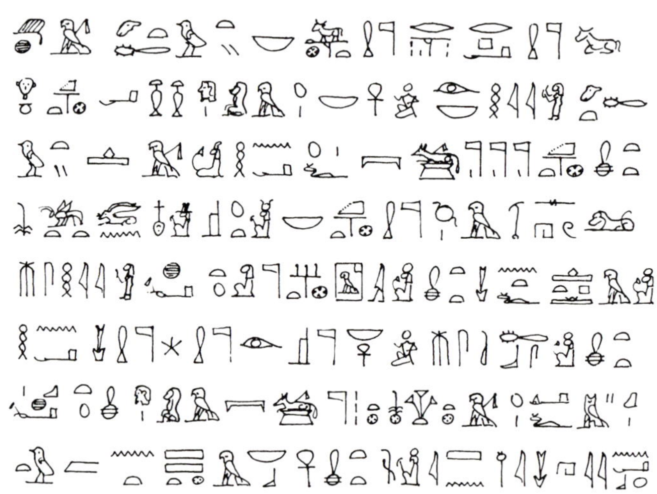

"Venerated by Horus Khenti-kheti (...), lord of Athribis, priest entrusted with the wardrobe, hereditary noble, priest of Kemuer, that is in (the middle of) Athribis, (...) Djedhor, son of Nebankh, made by (the son of) the sistrum-player of Khenti-kheti, Hetep-hor, and her son, guardian of the mysteries of the gods of Athribis and also of the king of Upper and Lower Egypt, Wennefer and Isis, lords of Athribis, the priest of Horus, Wasehul, born of (the son of) sistrum-player of Khuit (...) Hathorii, and his sister Hetephor, and (his) brother, priest of (...) and priest of Osiris, Nebankh, born of Takhebes, and of (...) Djedhor, and the guardian of the mysteries of the gods of Upper and Lower Egypt, Hor, son of (...) Hornebankh, and also companion of Ra (...)."

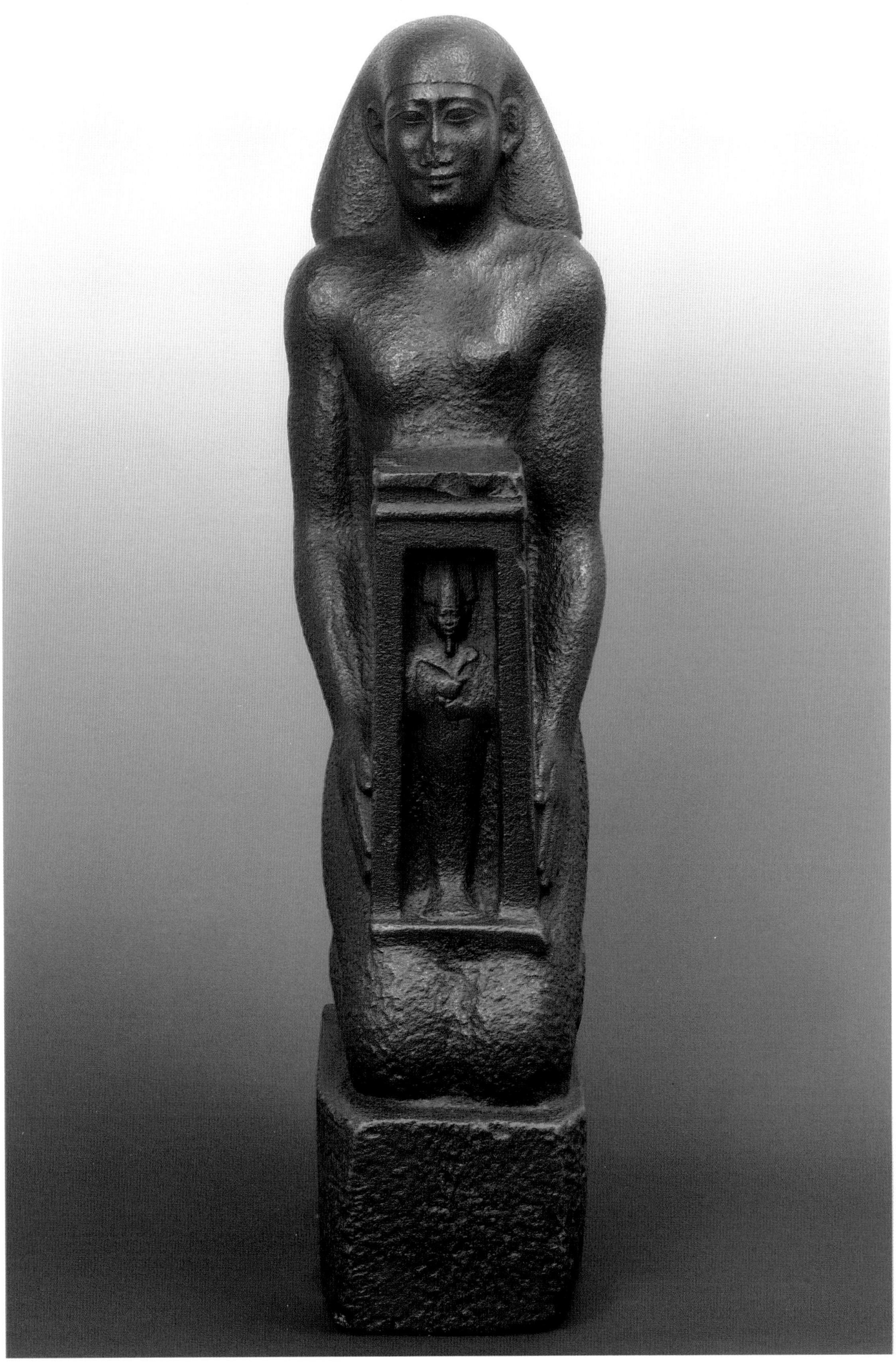

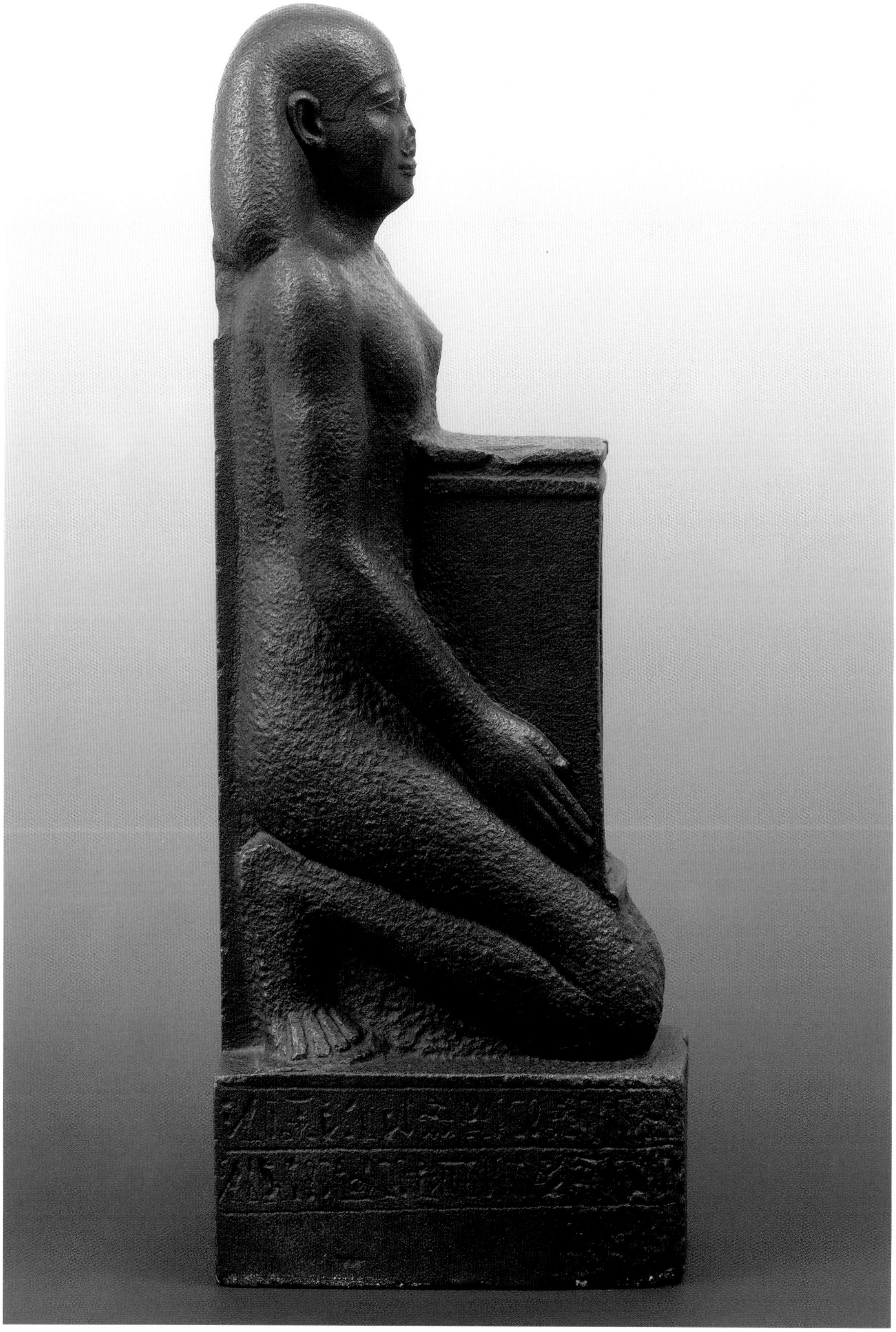

NOTES AND COMMENTS

Although the name of this statuette's owner is apparently identical to that of the person from the previous piece (cat. no. 33), it is merely a homonym, a common occurrence in the Late Period and the Greco-Roman Period. The identities can only be decoded through the presence of the parents' names (in this case, it is the mother's name that establishes the difference). The name Djedhor does not here seem to be complete, as the meaning of the initial sign  still requires clarification. It is, however, known that the mother of the previous Djedhor was Pasetjauemauibastet, and that the mother of this one was the Lady Hetep-hor. It is also clear that Djedhor served in Athribis (the Central Delta), formerly known as Huttaherib, where the main god was Horus and a black bull called Kemuer was venerated. Djedhor claims to be a priest of this god (Baines & Málek, 1980: 171).

The naophorous statue of Djedhor bears clear similarities to the one of Guemenefherbak at the Kunsthistorisches Museum in Vienna, dating from the 30th dynasty or early Ptolemaic Period (Satzinger, n.d.: 61-63, plate 28), although the shrine holds an image of Neith, a goddess who was widely worshipped in the Delta.

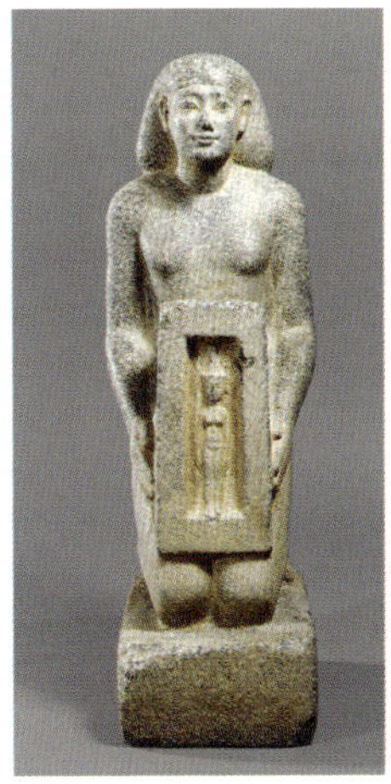

Naophorous statue of Guemenefherbak. Egypt, Late Period, 30th dynasty Granite, H. 51 cm. © Vienna, Kunsthistorisches Museum mit MVK und ÖTM, inv. AEOS 62

The inspiration for the subject's pose – with a shrine containing various different deities – came from the New Kingdom. This is demonstrated by the limestone naophorous statue made for the senior official Raia, at the Museum of Antiquities in Leiden (Rijksmuseum van Oudheden), which holds a beautiful image of the god Ptah (Schneider, 1987: 42-44), and another of the royal scribe Iuni, whose shrine holds an image of Osiris, exhibited at the Metropolitan Museum of Art de New York (Hayes, 1990: II, 351).

I have used the version of the translation from the catalogue for the temporary exhibition at the British Museum (Smith & Edwards, 1937: 23) to translate the hieroglyphic text, despite the many gaps due to difficulties in reading the text. The additions proposed here aim to help an understanding of this dense and sometimes obscure inscription, which has some illegible hieroglyphs.

The complex text offers a vision of the family ties between the various figures, since Djedhor mentions his father (Nebankh), mother (Hetep-hor) and son (Wasehul), as well as a sister (also called Hetep-hor) and a half-brother (also called Nebankh), the son of his father and another lady (Takhebes):

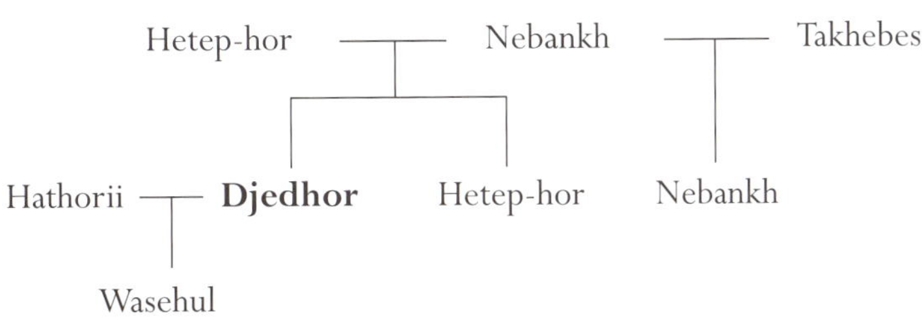


The text also mentions other figures, but their family relationship to Djedhor is not clear. The unusual name of Wasehul seems to be of non-Egyptian origin.

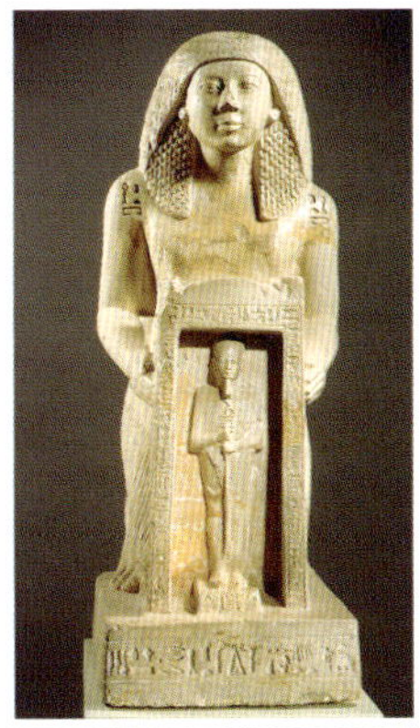

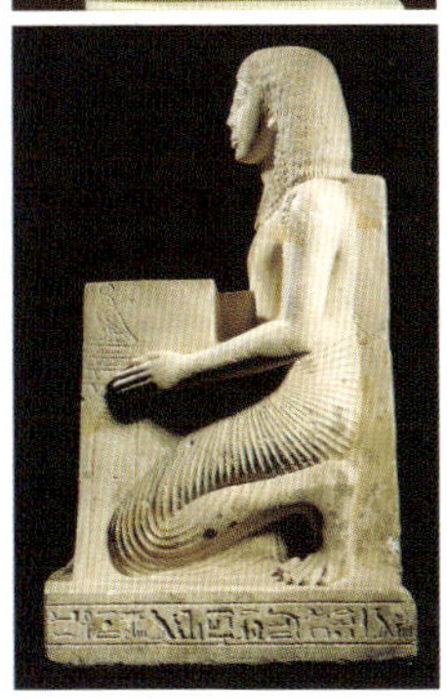

Naophorous statue of Raia (front and side), New Kingdom, 19th dynasty, ca. 1275 BC. Limestone, H. 80 cm. Museum of Antiquities, Leiden, inv. no. AST 11

EXHIBITIONS

1937 – Ancient Egyptian Sculpture lent by C. S. Gulbenkian, Esq. London, British Museum.

1949 – Egyptian Sculpture from the Gulbenkian Collection. Washington, D. C., National Gallery of Art.

1965 – Obras de Arte da Fundação Calouste Gulbenkian. Oeiras, Pombal Palace.

35

**MODEL OF A SPHINX**

Greco-Roman Period, early Ptolemaic dynasty (ca. 300-250 BC)
Limestone
H: 14 cm; L: 27 cm
Provenance: The MacGregor Collection
Date incorporated: 1922
Inv. no. 401

This limestone statuette adopts the typical form of a sphinx: a lion with a human head. This apparently unfinished model shows an elongated and stocky lion's body whose tail rises up the right side. It has a smiling, rounded face, almond-shaped eyes, and a cloth covering on its head with the descending sacred serpent on the front, while a plait lies along its back. There is a suggestion of a collar – without the customary iconography of the *usekh* necklace – starting at the shoulders and descending on the animal's chest, following the curve of its front paws.

The sphinx is lying on a low dais measuring 27 x 9 centimetres that still has traces of the squared lines that acted as the guiding structure for producing the work. There are fractures on the head's covering, the serpent, the nose, the chin, the left front paw and various parts of the base.

NOTES AND COMMENTS

This piece was damaged in the flooding (1967) at the Pombal Palace, Oeiras, and was restored at the Conservation Laboratory in the Museu Monográfico de Conímbriga. As Howard Carter, via whom the piece was acquired, noted in his "Carnet Spécial", it may have been a sculptor's unfinished model.

The iconography suggests it should be dated to the early Ptolemaic Period (Ptolemaic dynasty), although there was a long tradition of portraying the sphinx in Ancient Egypt. The most famous image of this type is unquestionably the Giza Sphinx, dating from the reign of King Khafra (4th dynasty), who built the second largest pyramid in Egypt. Several Middle Kingdom sphinxes are also well known, and some were restored in later periods, when certain monarchs used these powerful figures to enhance their personal imagery, inscribing their names inside cartouches on the statues. The tradition of producing these characteristic images continued throughout the New Kingdom, and sphinxes were sculpted for Amenhotep II (one is still found among the remains of ancient Memphis, in the place now called Mit-Rahina), Hatshepsut and Thutmose III, among other 18th and 19th-dynasty rulers. The Ancient Egyptians called these imposing sculptures *chesep-ankh* or "living images", which the Greeks reinterpreted as sphinx, adding their existing aura of somewhat impenetrable mystery. The Greeks also established that sphinxes were female, a status they had not originally had (Araújo, 2001: 337). Besides sphinxes with human heads, there are also ram-headed sphinxes that evoke the god Amun, whose sacred animal was a ram. A small ram-headed sphinx can be seen in the Egyptian collection at the Museu Nacional de Arqueologia, Lisbon (Araújo, 1993: 178-179).

Many pieces similar to the one in the Gulbenkian Collection and dating from the Greco-Roman Period can be found in Egyptian collections. The small limestone sphinx at the Kunsthistorisches Museum, Vienna, is particularly interesting as it has a hieroglyphic inscription on the base with the name of the official Wahibra (Satzinger, n.d.: 67-69, plate 30).

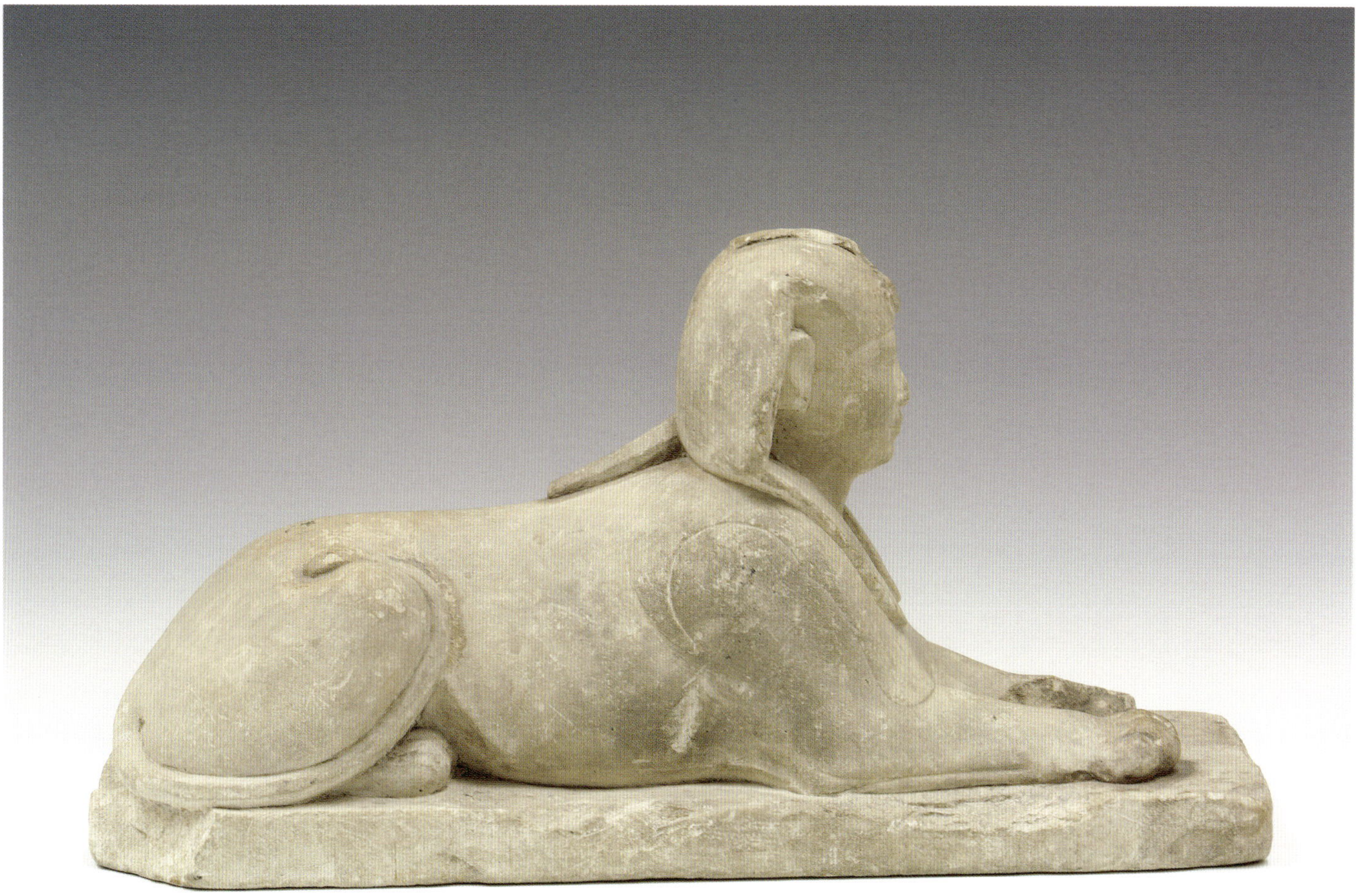

Depicting the king in a lion-like pose, with a human head wearing the royal headdress with the sacred serpent on the front and the divine beard is a variation on very ancient images in which the monarch appears as a falcon or a bull trampling his enemies. The Narmer Palette is a fine example of the latter imagery, dating from the emergence of unified Egypt around 3000 BC).

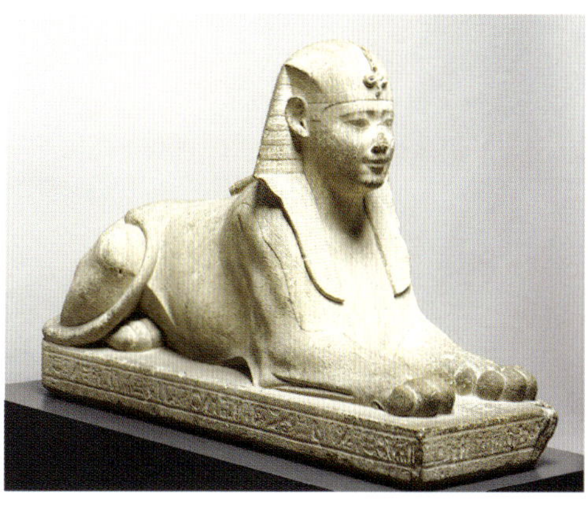

Sphinx of Wahibra,
end of the Late Period –
early Greco-Roman Period,
ca. 350-300 BC. Limestone,
L. 105.5 cm.
©Vienna, Kunsthistorisches
Museum mit MVK und ÖTM,
inv. no. AEOS 76

36

**LOW-RELIEF OF A PHARAOH**

Greco-Roman Period, early Ptolemaic dynasty (ca. 300-250 BC)
Fine limestone
H: 24 cm; W: 18 cm
Provenance: Khawam Brothers, Cairo
Date incorporated: 1926
Inv. no. 167

This fine limestone plaque with high-relief decoration shows the head of a pharaoh and seems to be a study for a portrait. The head, depicted in profile, is wearing the *kheprech* (blue crown), which is covered with small circles and decorated with the descending sacred serpent. The serpent has relief decoration on its swollen neck, showing its dilated scales, while its round eye occupies most of its head. The rear of the crown bears the falcon of the god Horus stretching its open wings, a typical iconographic image of protection that dates back at least as far as the Old Kingdom. The falcon, with the solar disco on its head, holds the protective sign *chen* in its talons.

The delicate details on the pharaoh's face were created with great care. His eyebrows and the outlines of his eyes are clearly defined in gentle relief; he has a well-proportioned nose and lips defined by an outline above and below, followed by a small rounded chin. His relief sculpted ear emerges from the curve of the crown. The formal, floral, four-string necklace, known as the *usekh*, is also carved in great detail, with a variety of decorations: two rows of pearls above, then four rows with a range of themes including stylised flowers, ending in a row of drop-shaped pendants.

The plaque has a crack in the upper right corner and incrustations of earth on the surface, while the part of the necklace by the left shoulder is worn.

NOTES AND COMMENTS

Calouste Gulbenkian acquired this fine limestone plaque with a well-sculpted image of a pharaoh thanks to Howard Carter's contacts with the sellers (Khawam Brothers, Cairo).

The image was evidently based on royal portraits from the New Kingdom. In this case, the face recalls the youthful features of Amenhotep III, with his sloping almond-shaped eyes. It also follows the style of more recent depictions, as can be seen from a limestone plaque from the 30th dynasty which has low-reliefs on both sides, probably showing Nectanebo II, the last native Egyptian pharaoh (Bothmer, 1988: 76-77).

Plaque of King Nectanebo II (?), Late Period, 30th dynasty. Limestone. Leigh Keno Collection, New York © Sotheby's

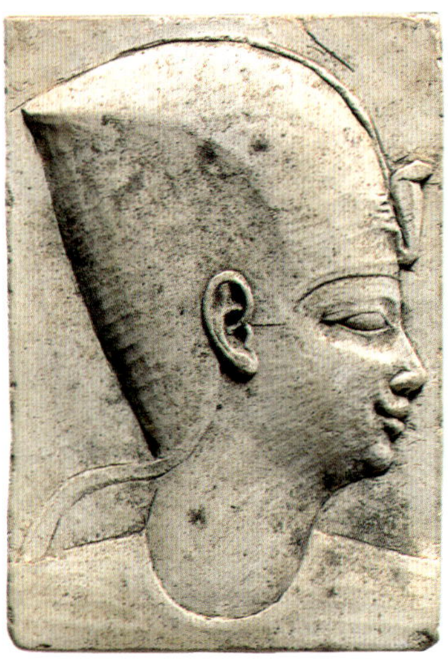

The Ptolemaic dynasty maintained the tradition of portraying the smiling heads of kings and gods in gentle low-reliefs, as can be seen from a plaque with a female head – possibly the goddess Isis or a queen from the middle of the dynasty (ca. 150 BC) – now at the Ashmolean Museum, Oxford (Málek, 2003: 331). There are several hypotheses regarding the purpose of such plaques, some of which are sculpted on both sides and bear inscriptions: the female image in Oxford and the piece in the Gulbenkian Collection may both be studies for a final sculpture, models to act as sources for the new sculptors admitted to the royal workshops, or even votive plaques in tribute to kings or deities.

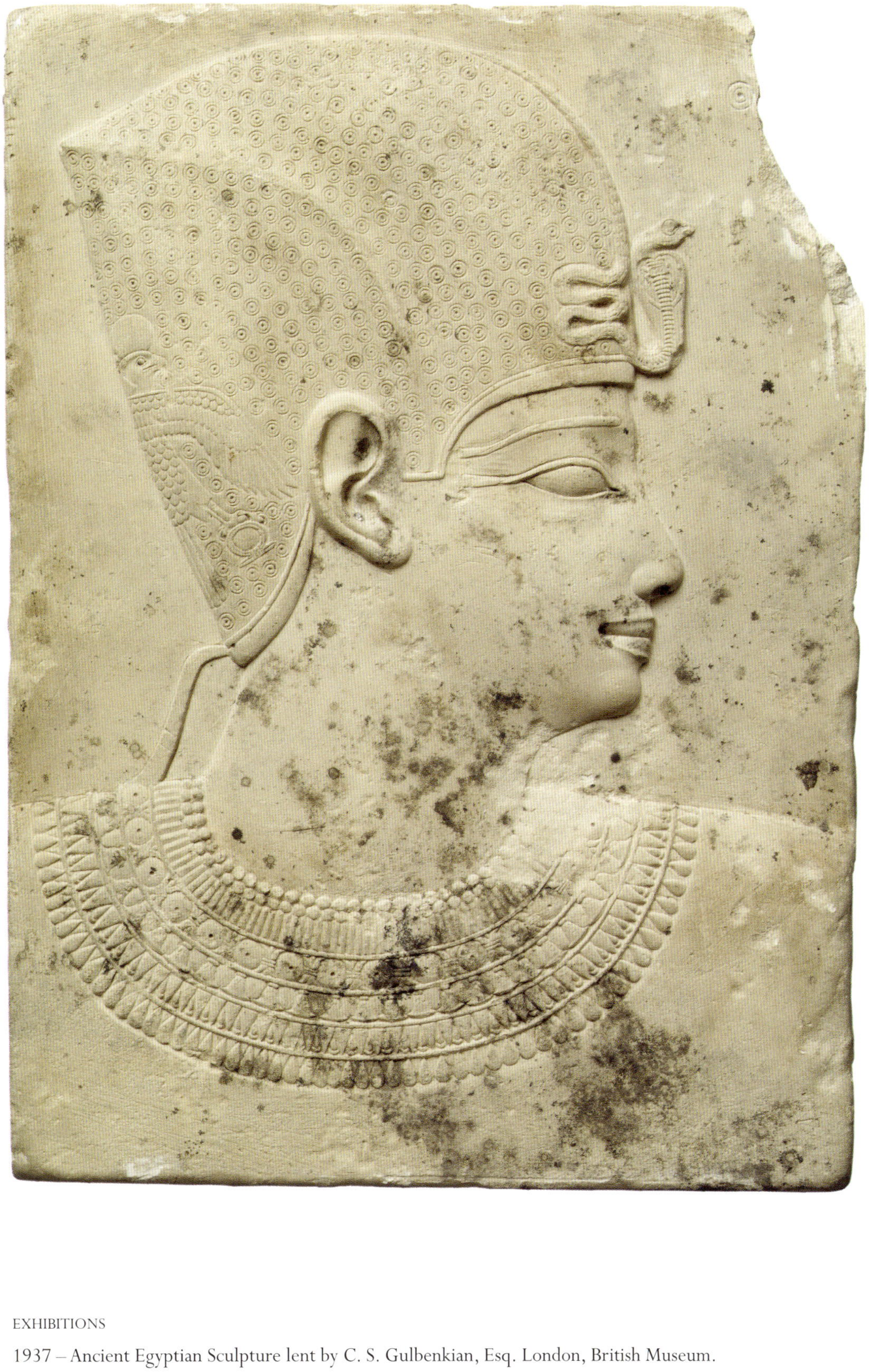

EXHIBITIONS

1937 – Ancient Egyptian Sculpture lent by C. S. Gulbenkian, Esq. London, British Museum.

1949 – Egyptian Sculpture from the Gulbenkian Collection. Washington, D. C., National Gallery of Art.

1965 – Obras de Arte da Fundação Calouste Gulbenkian. Oeiras, Pombal Palace.

37

## STATUETTE OF THE GOD HARPOCRATES

Greco-Roman Period, early Ptolemaic dynasty (ca. 300-250 BC)
Silver
H: 8.5 cm
Provenance: The MacGregor Collection
Date incorporated: 1922
Inv. no. 161

Small silver figure depicting a naked deity with the symbols of infancy: his right forefinger in his mouth and a strand of hair emerging from under the base of the crown and falling in a spiral that ends in front of his right shoulder. The image portrays the Horus the child god or Harpocrates (Horpakhered in the original Egyptian form). He is wearing the double crown of Upper and Lower Egypt with the (severely eroded) sacred serpent on the front. The facial features are not very clear, but the plaited strand of hair is still visible. This small piece would have been used as an amulet, which explains the suspension ring at the back.

NOTES AND COMMENTS

This small statuette was acquired via Howard Carter, and brought an added value to Calouste Gulbenkian's collection of Egyptian goods as it is made of silver, a metal that was even rarer in Ancient Egypt than gold. The childlike pose in identical figures of Horus the child god reproduces the typical hieroglyphic iconography of infancy.

Horus the child (Harpocrates or Horpakhered) is widely portrayed in bronze statuettes now found in almost every collection of ancient Egyptian pieces. This applies to several collections in Portugal, where he appears either sitting on his mother's lap while she (Isis) breastfeeds him, or alone as if enthroned. Both these forms can be seen in the collection of the Museu Nacional de Arqueologia, Lisbon. Some such figures are crowned (Araújo, 1993: 348-351).

The cult of Harpocrates, which expanded enormously under the Ptolemaic dynasty, continued under Roman rule and then spread throughout the empire, although without the same success achieved by the cult of his mother, Isis.

EXHIBITIONS

1921 – Ancient Egyptian Art. London, Burlington Fine Arts Club.
1937 – Ancient Egyptian Sculpture lent by C. S. Gulbenkian, Esq. London, British Museum.
1949 – Egyptian Sculpture from the Gulbenkian Collection. Washington, D. C., National Gallery of Art.
1980 – A Criança e a Colecção Calouste Gulbenkian. Lisbon, Calouste Gulbenkian Museum.

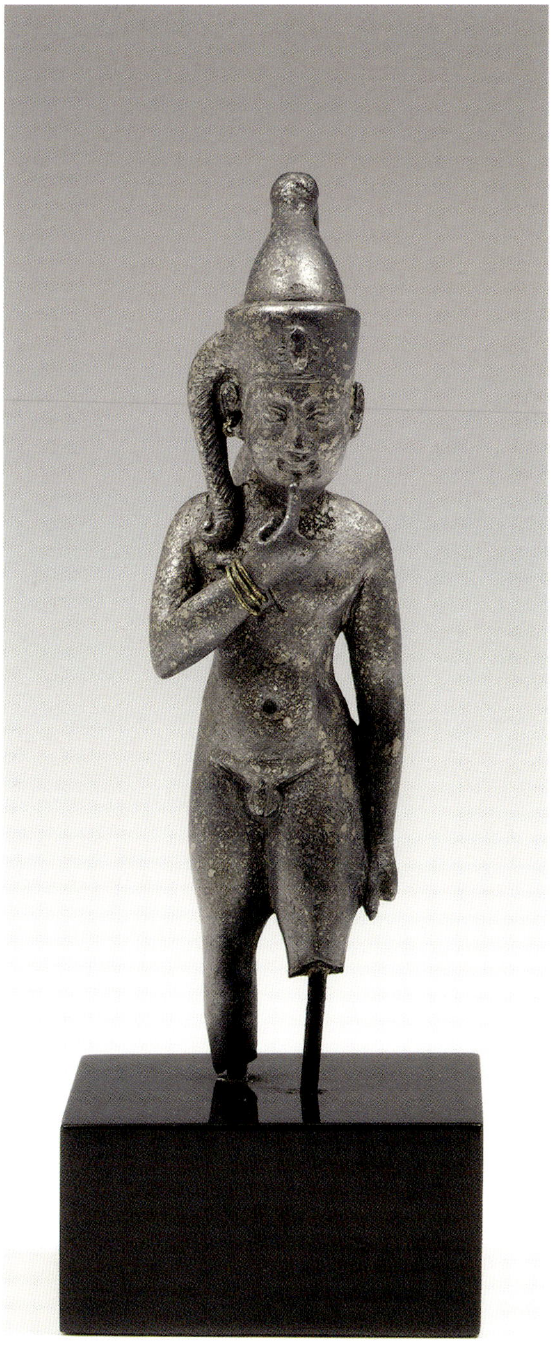 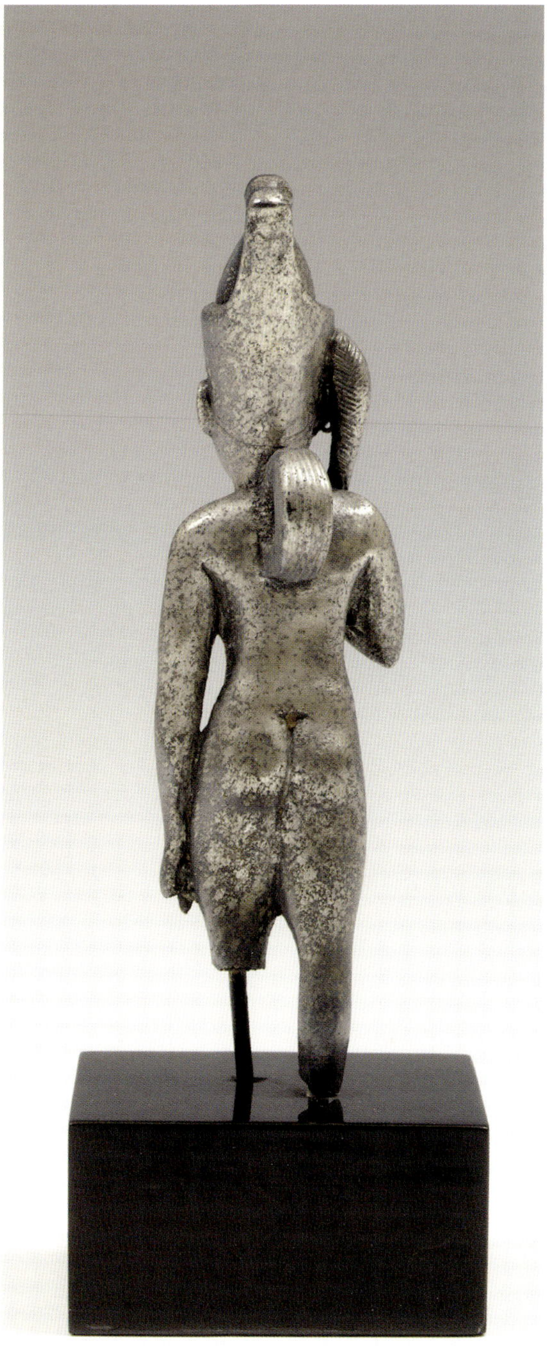

38

**BOWL**

Greco-Roman Period, Ptolemaic dynasty (305-30 BC)
Breccia
H: 10 cm; Diameter: 15.5 cm
Provenance: Christie's, London
Date incorporated: 1907
Inv. no. 1064

The colours of this breccia bowl are black mixed with yellowish white. The material is a volcanic rock that had been used since the Predynastic Period and was difficult to sculpt, which makes the fluting on the outside particularly noteworthy, even though it is not easy to detect at first sight. The vertical fluting does not extend up to the rim, nor is it found on the small base.

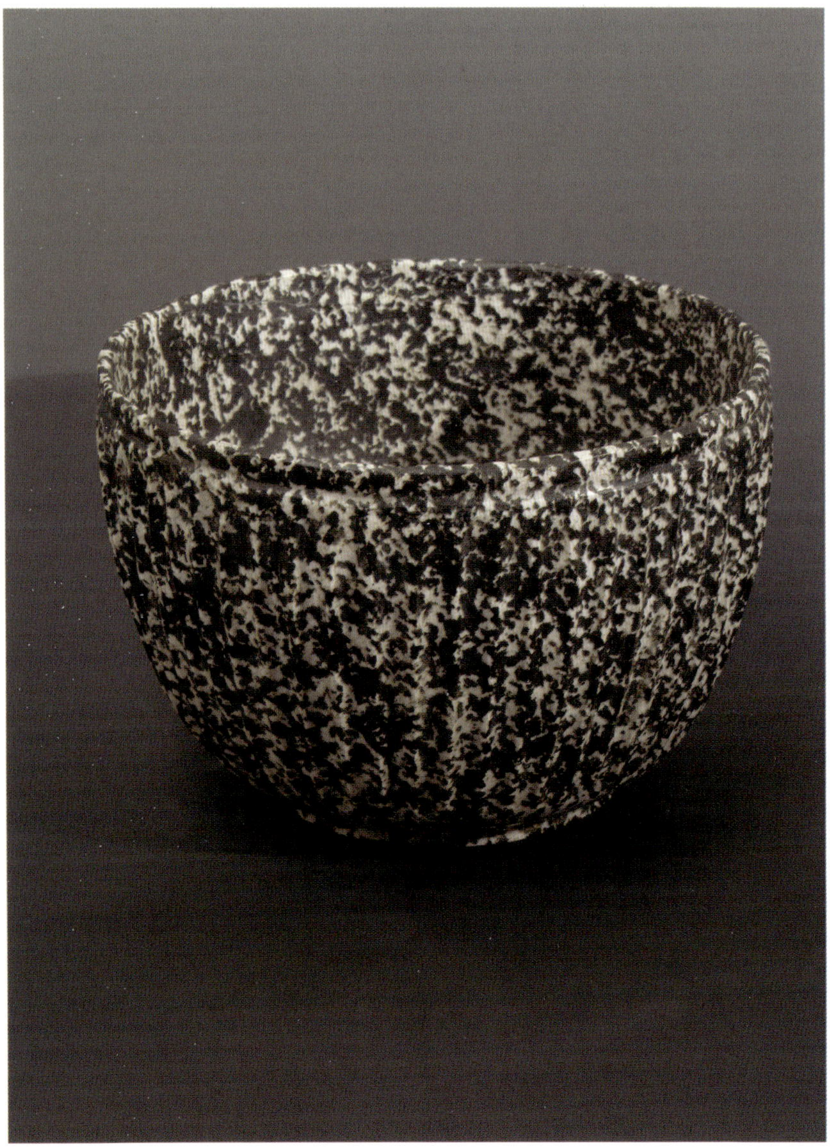

NOTES AND COMMENTS

According to the dates on the documents recording Gulbenkian's acquisitions, this bowl was the first piece in the Egyptian section, having been purchased in 1907. The relief decoration on the outside seems to have been influenced by identical work in metal (Smith & Edwards, 1937: 23; Tiradritti, 1998: 264, 307). On the other hand, this work (in a stone that is hard to carve) is a fine illustration of the continuing long tradition in making and decorating vessels in hard stones, which dated back to the Predynastic Period, and which produced fine containers in the Early Dynastic Period and the Old Kingdom, as can be seen from the interesting pieces at the Museu da Farmácia, Lisbon.

EXHIBITIONS

1937 – Ancient Egyptian Sculpture lent by C. S. Gulbenkian, Esq. London, British Museum.

1949 – Egyptian Sculpture from the Gulbenkian Collection. Washington, D. C., National Gallery of Art.

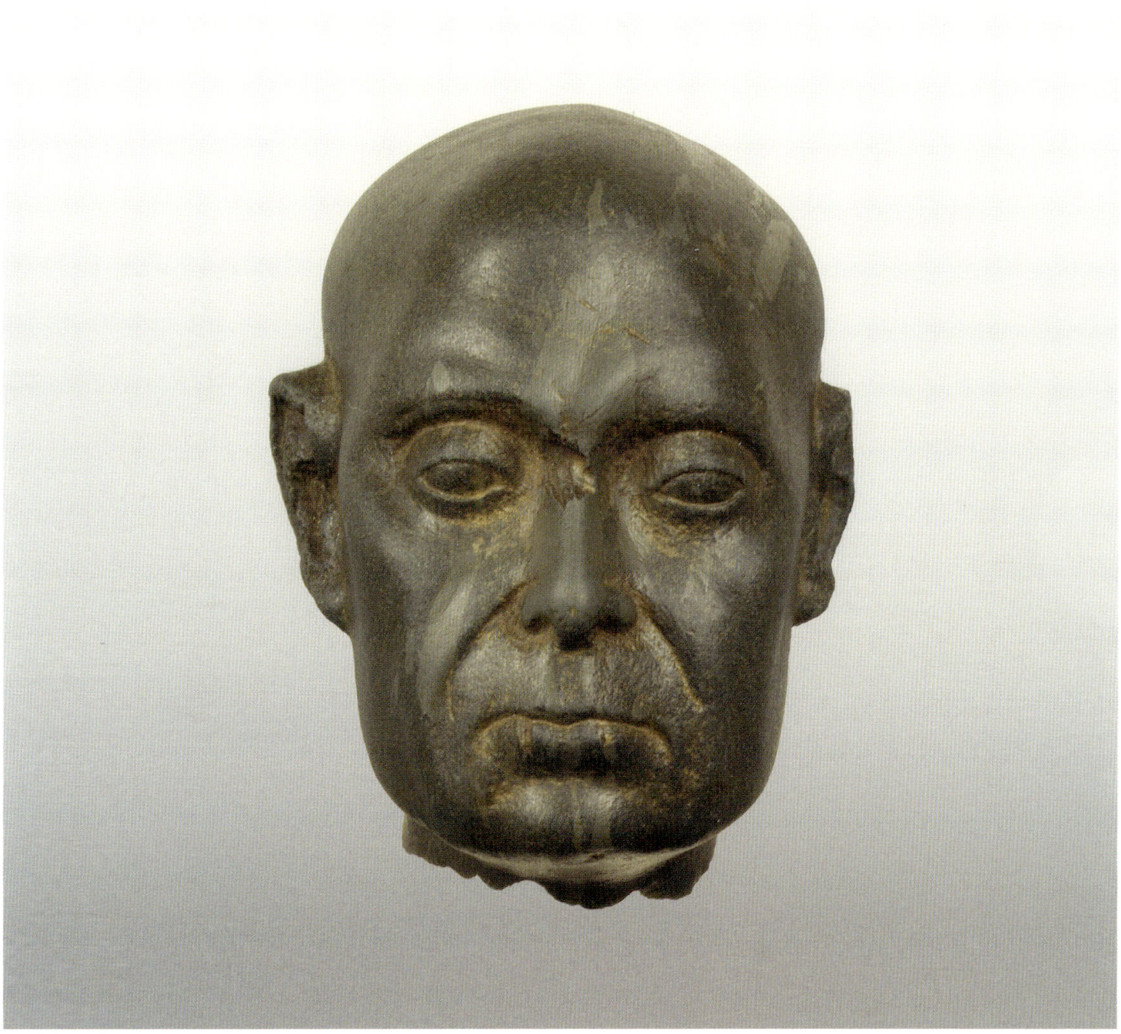

39

**HEAD OF AN OFFICIAL**

Greco-Roman Period, middle of the Ptolemaic dynasty (ca. 200 BC)
Green schist
H: 9.5 cm
Provenance: The Dr. Fouquet Collection, Cairo
Date incorporated: 1922
Inv. no. 46

This superbly modelled green schist head depicts an elderly man who may have been a priest or a senior official in the administration. His clearly defined facial features, polished bald head and very expressive gaze all reveal an educated man with considerable experience of life. Indeed, the intention of the artist who used his mastery to produce this work was to transmit that very image of a person with a respectable and wise appearance, and the resulting work is an exceptional record of the art of psychological

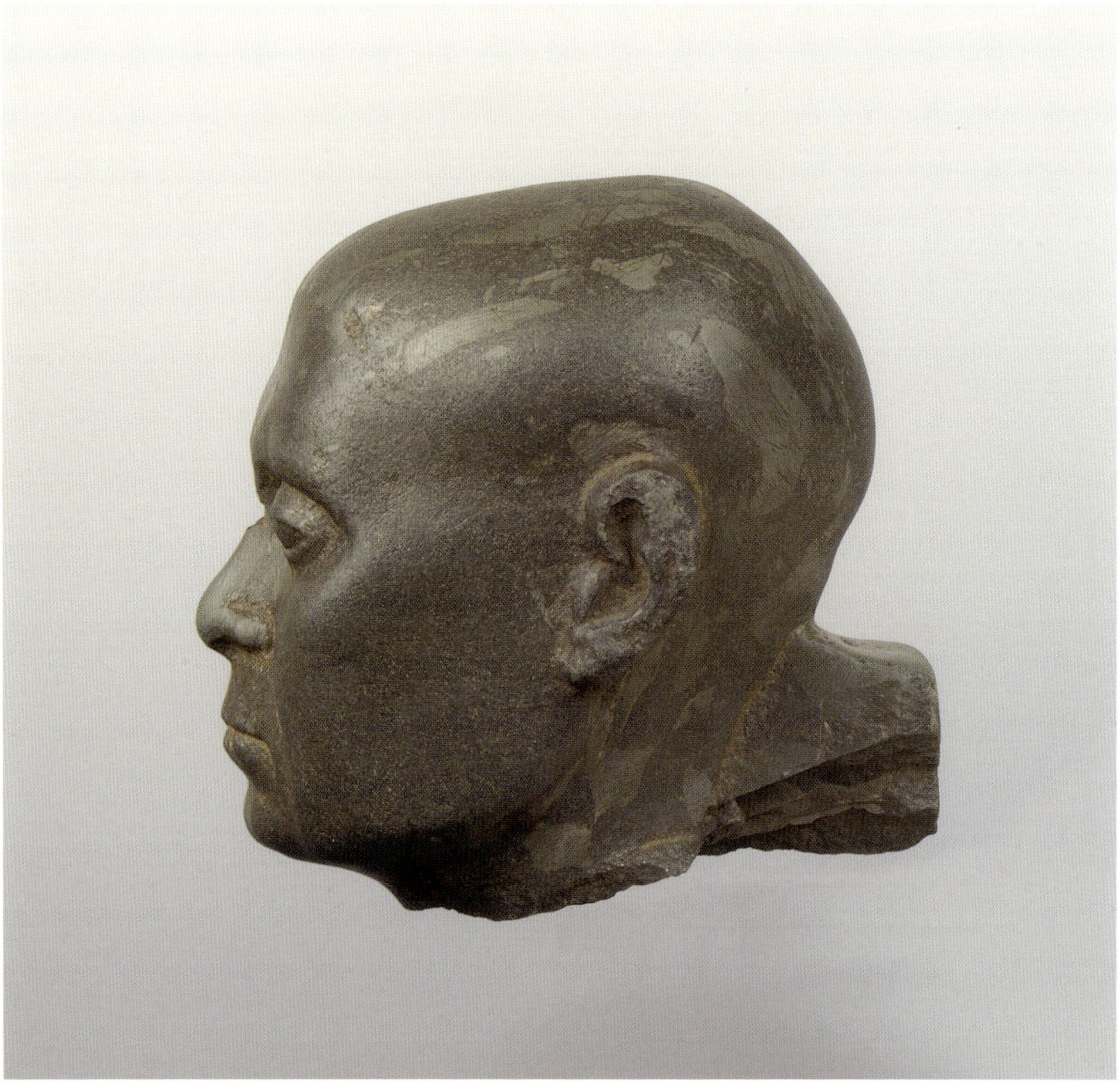

portraiture from the Ptolemaic Period. This comes in striking contrast to other portraits from the same period, which preferred to show officials with a younger and healthier appearance.

The shape of the subject's skull suggests close anatomical observation: his eyes have heavy lids, although there is no sign of an iris, his cheekbones protrude slightly and emphasis is given to two lines running down to the corners of his mouth. In turn, his mouth has fine, closed lips, suggesting a somewhat disdainful air that is reinforced by a slight facial asymmetry visible in the aforementioned two lines. The lines between his nose and mouth differ from one another, adding a conventional aspect to the image. There are small fractures on the nose and ears, produced without any great anatomical detail, and there are signs of a dorsal pillar at the back.

NOTES AND COMMENTS

Although the catalogue drawn up for the sale of the Fouquet Collection, of which this head formed part, refers to a face "tourmentée par la souffrance", the outstanding feature is the subject's dignity and his profound wisdom and experience of life.

This magnificent and anatomically highly accurate piece has been identified as the head of a priest (Assam, 1991: 100), of an old man (Lisbon, 2002: 22), and of a sage (Bothmer, 1960: 136). The option taken here to identify it as the head of an official seems sociologically closer to the definition used in Ancient Egypt for a person who could read and write and who exercised some authority. Moreover, the term is broad enough to embrace a wide range of people (priests, scribes, governors, supervisors, stewards, military leaders, architects, etc) all civilised and educated people whose activities would result in the smooth-running of a controlled and hard-working society.

The artistic treatment of this head bears all the hallmarks of the art of accurate portrayal (Bothmer, 1960: 136), achieving a strongly realistic expression of a specific person. Apparently, it was the client's choice whether he was represented in a more dynamic (even youthful) pose or as a mature man whose older appearance transmitted the image of a civilised, educated and experienced official, depicted with impressive realism. This physiological realism dates from an earlier age, as traces of this style can be found during the Nubian 25th dynasty. In fact, the taste for more mature features came from that dynasty, as superbly exemplified by the deeply marked face carved in a granite statue made for a priest of Amun called Mentuemhat (Tiradritti, 1998: 250). This taste would continue throughout the Late Period, as shown by several heads, especially a 27th-dynasty piece from the Christos Bastis Collection, whose bag wig surrounds a face that features deep-set eyes, protruding upper eye-sockets, a mouth with closed fine lips and deep wrinkles (Bothmer, 1988: 60-63). Interestingly, these heads of elderly men often appeared alongside other younger and more idealised images, exemplified by another head from the same collection and the same dynasty (*Ibidem*: 65-66).

There was evidently an ongoing wish to be depicted as an older man, which in some cases joined the art of accurate portrayal. Several museums contain pieces that confirm this form, which reached its peak during the Ptolemaic Period, as shown by the male head in schist at the Museum of Fine Arts, Boston (Simpson, 1987: 66) and the famous "green head" at the Egyptian Museum in Berlin (Wildung, 1999: 50; Málek, 2003: 347).

"Green head", Late Period, ca. 400-300 BC. Green schist. Egyptian Museum, Berlin

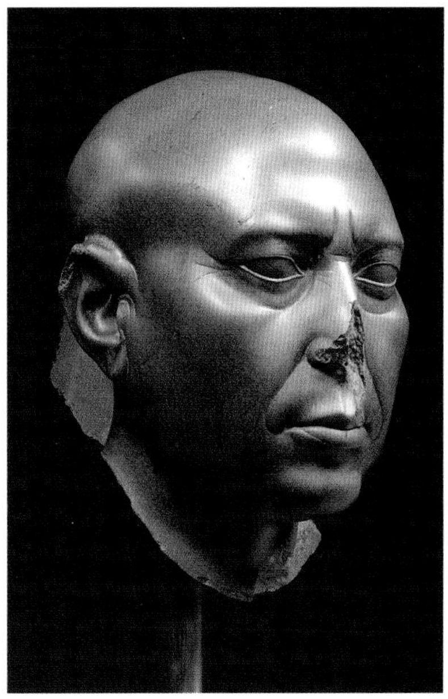

The head at the Kunsthistorisches Museum, Vienna, from approximately the same period (Satzinger, n.d.: 69-70, plate 31), has a very similar face, revealing a strongly marked personality. In turn, the British Museum has a naophorous statue from a slightly later date, possibly the Roman Period. The piece in question belonged to the bearer of a shrine dedicated to Atum, and shows highly realistic features (Quirke & Spencer, 1992: 57). The Egyptian collection at the Museo Civico Archeologico, Bologna (Pernigotti, 1994: 108), includes a head whose features emphasise the individual's maturity and that also deserves mention in this "rhetoric of old age", although the same collection also has another head from approximately the same period where the dominant feature is the face's youthful idealisation (*Ibidem*: 106).

EXHIBITIONS

1937 – Ancient Egyptian Sculpture lent by C. S. Gulbenkian, Esq. London, British Museum.

1949 – Egyptian Sculpture from the Gulbenkian Collection. Washington, D. C., National Gallery of Art.

1960 – Egyptian Sculpture of the Late Period. Brooklyn, New York, Brooklyn Museum.

1965 – Obras de Arte da Fundação Calouste Gulbenkian. Oeiras, Pombal Palace.

1999 – "Only the Best": Masterpieces of the Calouste Gulbenkian Museum. New York, The Metropolitan Museum of Art.

40

## TORSO OF THE GODDESS VENUS ANADIOMENE

Greco-Roman Period, Roman Period (30 BC-300 AD)
Faience
H: 12 cm
Provenance: The MacGregor Collection
Date incorporated: 1922
Inv. no. 163

This varnished terracotta torso depicts the goddess Venus, from the Greek pantheon. She is shown emerging from the waters, identifying her specifically as Venus Anadiomene. The figure has a three-string necklace, is leaning slightly to the left and resting against a column in a pose that falls outside the normal conventions of Egyptian art, reflecting Greco-Roman influences. She has well rounded outlines and firm breasts with protruding nipples, and also has a deep-set navel. The remains of her left arm have traces of an armband with corded decoration. The division near the neck reveals that the piece is hollow, suggesting that it may have been an anthropomorphic vessel that was evidently used in ritual ceremonies.

NOTES AND COMMENTS

This fragmented statuette with crackled glazing on several parts of the surface was made in two moulds. It was acquired via Howard Carter, whose notes suggest that it may have come from the Faiyum region in Middle Egypt.

The rear has signs of a pillar reaching the end of the buttocks, and the inside is coated with a pale blue varnished surface.

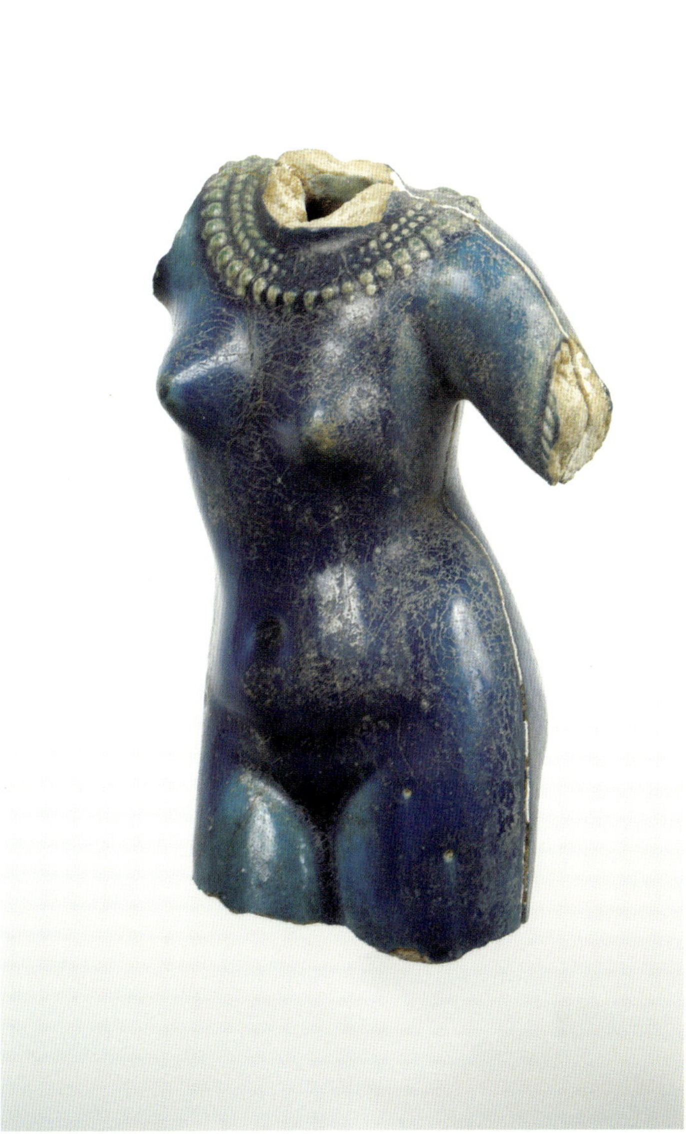

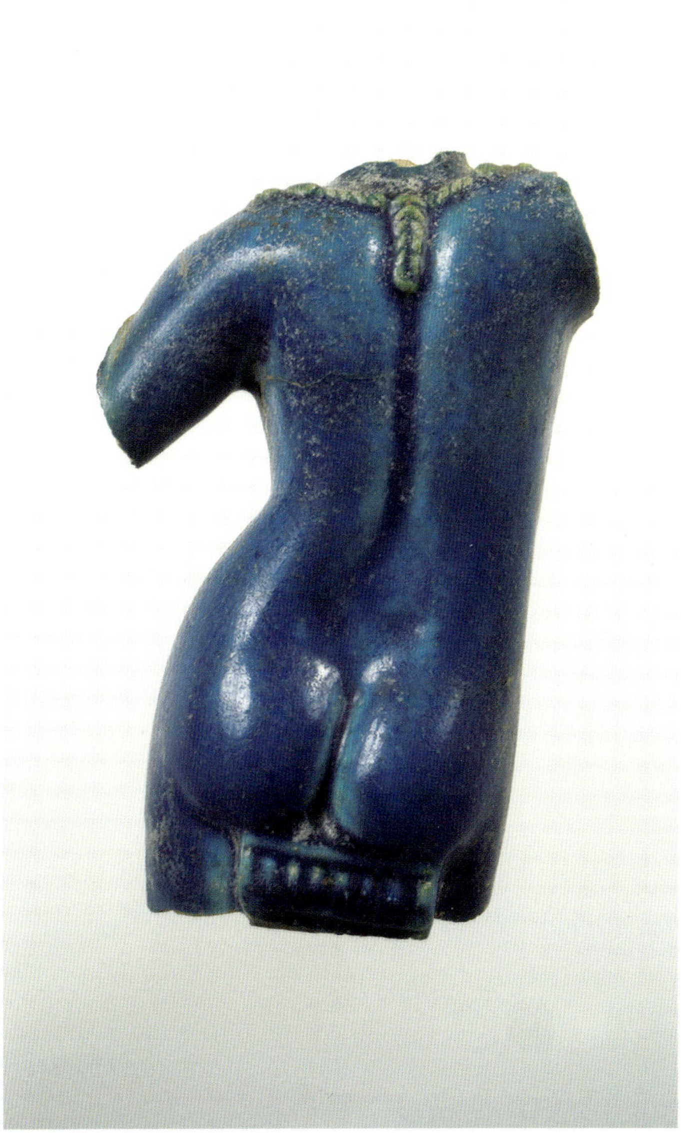

# STORAGE

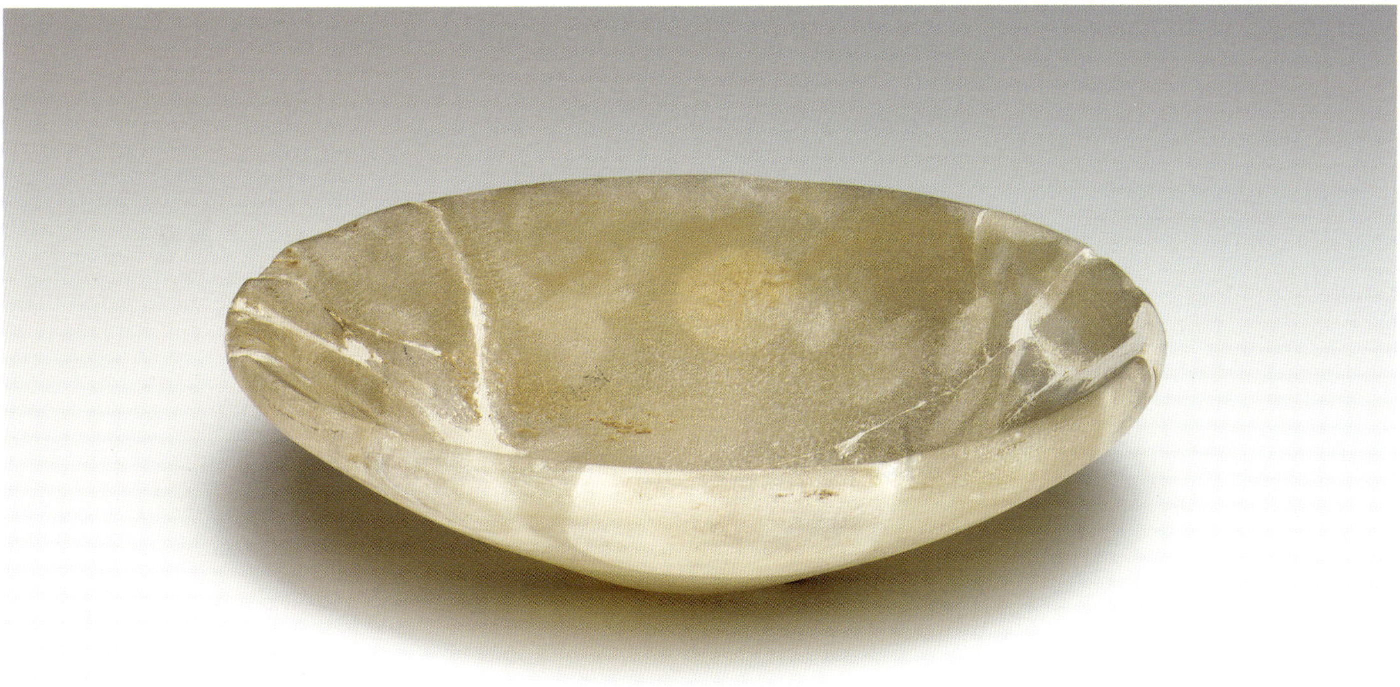

41

**BOWL**

Old Kingdom (?), 3rd dynasty (?) (ca. 2700-2600 BC)
Alabaster
H: 3.8 cm; Diameter: 5 cm
Provenance: The MacGregor Collection
Date incorporated: 1922
Inv. no. 409 B

This severely fractured and restored vessel has straight walls that narrow towards the flat bottom.

NOTES AND COMMENTS

The Collection records indicate that this bowl was part of a set that included an alabaster cup (cat. no. 1). However, observation of the two pieces reveals that this is not possible. First, the bowl lacks the translucent quality and delicacy of the fine work on the cup; secondly, no such two-piece combinations are known in this type of Old Kingdom service. The style of this bowl is commonly found among various Old Kingdom objects, and frequently in tomb goods with different shapes, exemplified by a group of alabaster objects at the Kunsthistorisches Museum, Vienna (Seipel, 1989: 75).

Table service, Thebes, Old Kingdom. Table: H. 8.5 cm; diameter. 24 cm. Service: alabaster, H. ca. 4-7 cm.  inv. AEOS 5952

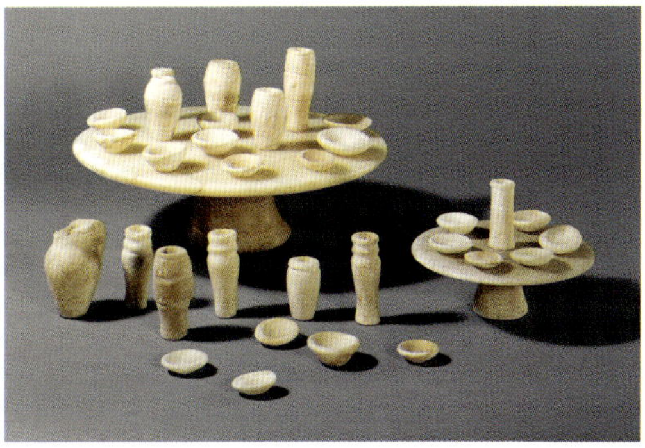

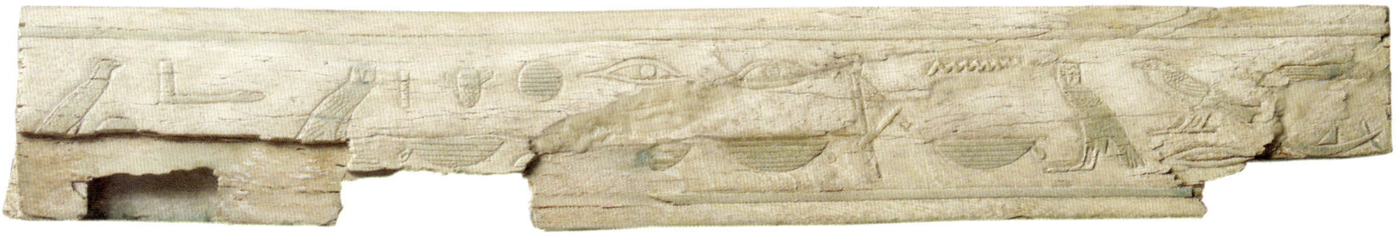

42

**PANEL FROM A CASKET**

Late Period, 26th dynasty (?)
Ivory
H: 2.7 cm; L: 18.7 cm
Provenance: The MacGregor Collection
Date incorporated: 1922 (C)
Inv. no. 164 (C)

Carved in fine low-relief, this panel (like others from the same small casket) is considered to be among the most beautiful Egyptian works in ivory. The panels decorated a casket or jewel-box, yet this fragment differs from the others as it is not only horizontal (in contrast to the other vertical ones), but also bears a hieroglyphic inscription. The text was engraved with fine hieroglyphs that – judging from the traces of colour found on the other fragments – were painted green. The short text, which is divided into two parts, has two low-relief lines above and below. The text, which has no dividing line between these two parts, is separated by the expression 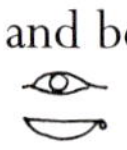 *ir.k* (second person singular of the verb "to make"). One part runs from left to right, the other from right to left, starting from the form *ir.k*, which is repeated in the middle.

Text from right to left: 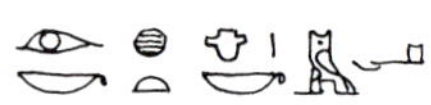 "Do what your heart wishes..."

Text from left to right: 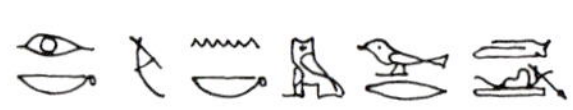 "Do what you wish and do not worry"

NOTES AND COMMENTS

The short double text on this small plaque calls on man to enjoy the pleasures of life according to his heart's desires, with particular reference to love and fully enjoying the pleasure of the company of the woman he loves. This recalls the encouragement of the "songs of the harpist" that praise life and lament the coming of death (Carreira, 2005: 125). The message was that most important thing was to enjoy life on earth to its fullest extent, as the song clearly says:

"Follow your heart
All the time you are alive!
Put myrrh on your head,
Dress yourself in fine linen,
Anoint yourself with oils fit for a god.
Pile up your joys,

Let not your heart fall!
Follow your heart and your happiness,
Deal with your business to the tune of your heart."

Objects used when preparing for love fell within this idyllic environment with erotic overtones, which explains the large-scale production of adornments and dressing-table objects such as 'spoons' for cosmetics, exemplified by the one in this Collection (cat. no. 9). The respective small casket or jewel-box held such objects, which would help create an appealing and seductive appearance. Thus, in this context, the exhortation in the text on this plaque could not be more appropriate: "Do what your heart wishes!" This enticing invitation on the casket matches the appeal made in the song: "Follow your heart."

The translation of the text on the ivory panel, which is 18.7 centimetres long and 2.7 tall, uses the version in the catalogue for the temporary exhibition at the British Museum (Smith & Edwards, 1937: 23). In this case, the negative form adopts the imperative *m.* The final word *ured* does not appear in the dictionary by Raymond Faulkner. The closest word is the term *wrdw,* which means "boredom". The use of the boat as the sole determinant at the end of the word *wrd* may suggest the monotony or profound boredom induced by certain sea crossings (Faulkner, 1988: 65).

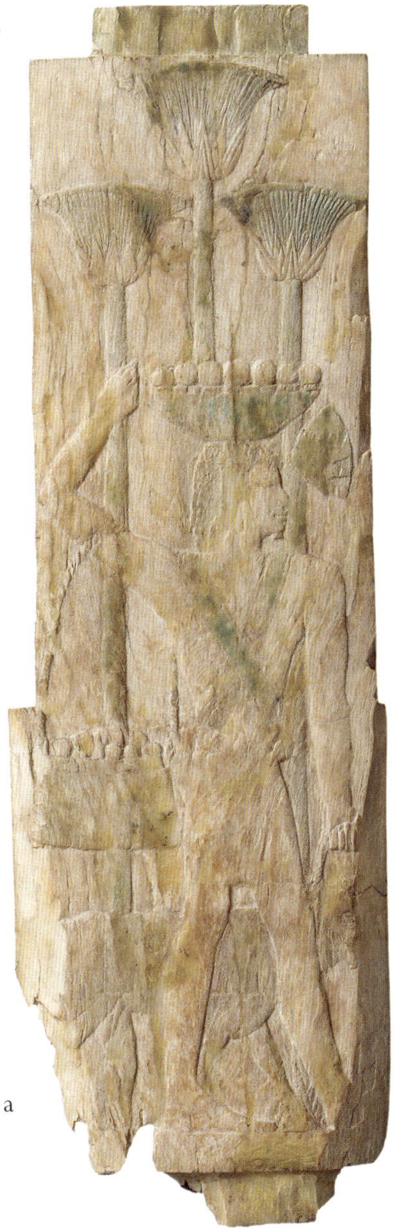

---

**PANEL FROM A CASKET**

43 Late Period, 26th dynasty (?)
Ivory
H: 16.7 cm; W: 5.3 cm
Provenance: The MacGregor Collection
Date incorporated: 1922
Inv. no. 164 (D)

Carved in fine low-relief, this panel (like others from the same small casket) is considered to be among the most beautiful Egyptian works in ivory, particularly the panels in exhibition at the Calouste Gulbenkian Museum (cat. nos. 17 and 18). The panels decorated a casket or jewel-box, and still have traces of green polychrome. The scene depicted shows a procession of people bearing offerings, specifically in this piece, a man with a short beard and two green bands starting from his shoulders and crossing on his chest. On his head, there is a green-painted basket full of fruit that he is holding with his open right hand. The fruit is shown by seven small circles, while the basket is crowned by a lotus flower. A rectangular basket with fruit hangs from a rope that (in turn) hangs from his left arm, while his left hand grasps a rope holding a small cow.

NOTES AND COMMENTS

See the notes and comments on cat. nos. 17 and 18.

44

**PANEL FROM A CASKET**

Late Period, 26th dynasty (?)
Ivory
H: 16.5 cm; W: 3 cm
Provenance: The MacGregor Collection
Date incorporated: 1922
Inv. no. 164 (E)

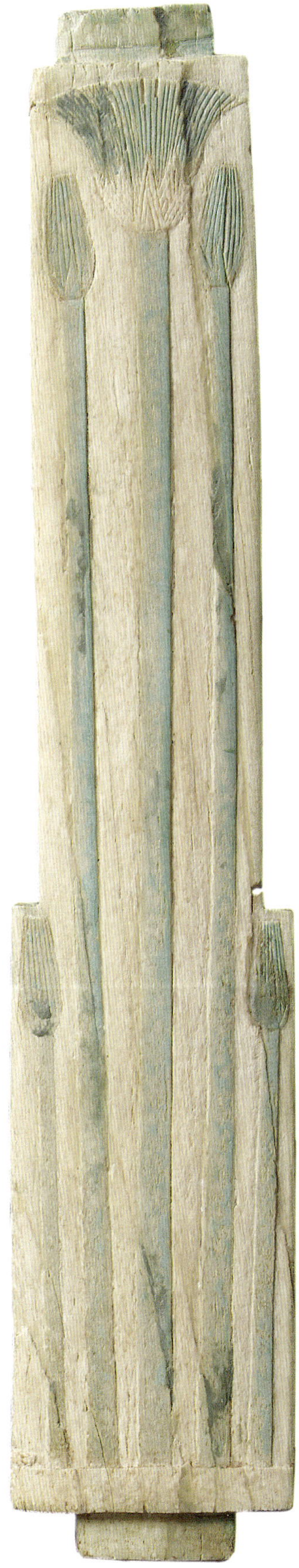

Carved in fine low-relief, this panel (like others from the same small casket) is considered to be among the most beautiful Egyptian works in ivory, particularly the panels in exhibition at the Calouste Gulbenkian Museum (cat. nos. 17 and 18). The panels decorated a casket or jewel-box, and still have traces of green polychrome. The scene depicted shows a procession of people bearing offerings, although they cannot be seen on this fragment. The background has a papyrus decoration, and the central motif is a tall papyrus flower drawn in great detail and painted green except for the base of the corolla where the tufts sprout from. This is flanked by a total of four closed papyrus buds (two larger and two smaller ones on each side).

NOTES AND COMMENTS

See the notes and comments on cat. nos. 17 and 18.

45

**PANEL FROM A CASKET**

Late Period, 26th dynasty (?)
Ivory
H: 9.5 cm; W: 2 cm
Provenance: The MacGregor Collection
Date incorporated: 1922
Inv. no. 164 (F)

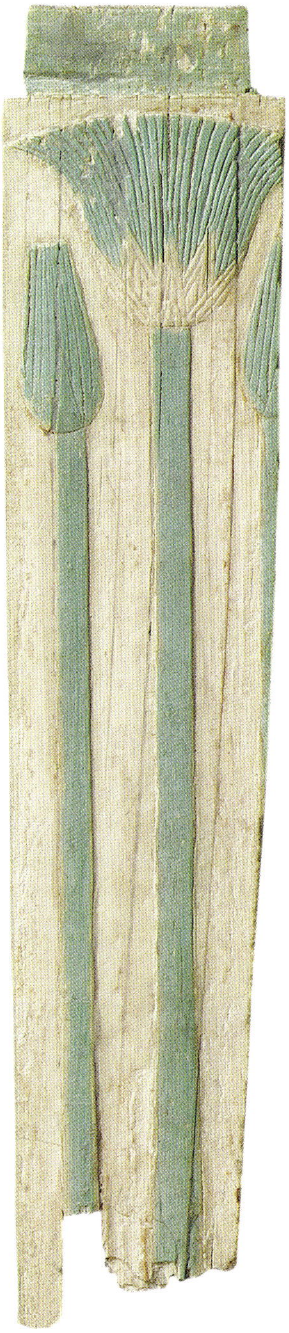

Carved in fine low-relief, this panel (like others from the same small casket) is considered to be among the most beautiful Egyptian works in ivory, particularly the panels in exhibition at the Calouste Gulbenkian Museum (cat. nos. 17 and 18). The panels decorated a casket or jewel-box, and still have traces of green polychrome. The scene depicted shows a procession of people bearing offerings, although they cannot be seen here. The background has a papyrus decoration, and the fragment has a tall papyrus flower that (as in the previous fragment) should be flanked by two papyrus buds. However, the one on the right has been lost. The papyrus flower has traces of green paint, except for the corolla where the tufts sprout from.

NOTES AND COMMENTS

See the notes and comments on cat. nos. 17 and 18.

46

**PANEL FROM A CASKET**

Late Period, 26th dynasty (?)
Ivory
H: 8 cm; W: 4.5 cm
Provenance: The MacGregor Collection
Date incorporated: 1922
Inv. no. 164 (G)

Carved in fine low-relief, this panel (like others from the same small casket) is considered to be among the most beautiful Egyptian works in ivory, particularly the panels in exhibition at the Calouste Gulbenkian Museum (cat. nos. 17 and 18). The panels decorated a casket or jewel-box, and still have traces of green polychrome. The scene depicted shows a procession of people bearing offerings, although they cannot be seen here, and the background has a papyrus decoration. The fragment is broken approximately in the middle, and the upper part is missing, although the ends of the three papyrus stems can be seen. A male figure is delicately holding a small basket at waist level. His other (lost) hand would have been holding a basket on his head. Like the other fragments, the image would end in the corollas of the open papyruses.

NOTES AND COMMENTS

See the notes and comments on cat. nos. 17 and 18.

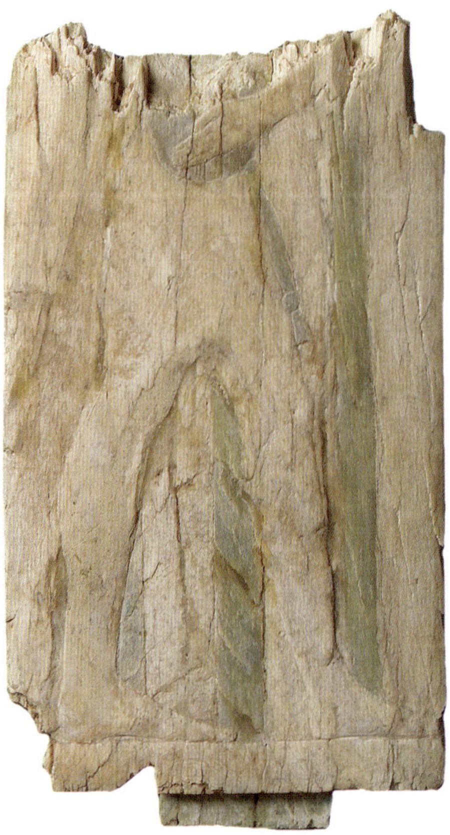

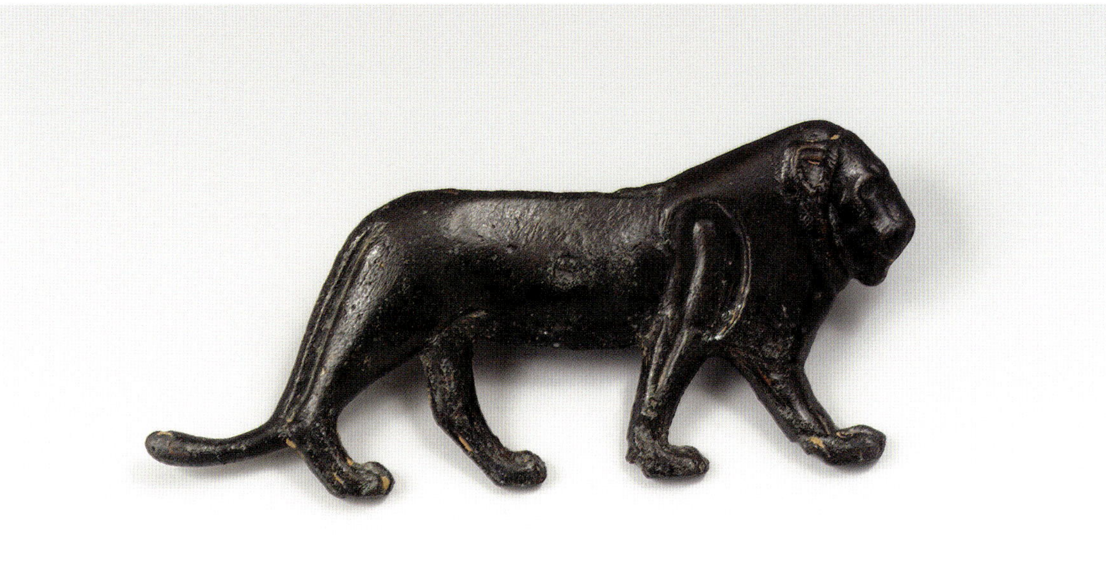

47

**LION**

Greco-Roman Period, early Ptolemaic dynasty (ca. 300-250 BC)
Bronze
H: 5.4 cm; L: 12.5 cm
Provenance: The MacGregor Collection
Date incorporated: 1922
Inv. no. 49

This image shows a walking lion whose paws and ears are cursorily drawn, while the anatomy of the head reveals some accuracy. The muscles on the front paw, which rises to join the animal's thick mane, merit some emphasis. Part of the animal's fur is indicated by incisions. Behind the figure, there is a piece used to attach the plaque, which could have decorated a piece of furniture.

NOTES AND COMMENTS

This bronze figure was acquired via Graat et Madoulé at the sale of the collection of Dr. Fouquet in Cairo, where it was part of a lot of pieces found at excavations in the area of Tell el-Muqdam, formerly Leontopolis, the capital of Egypt under the 23rd dynasty, founded by King Pedubast (see cat. no. 16). Other bronze works depicting lions were sold at the same auction, and some would be incorporated into the Egyptian Collection of the Brooklyn Museum, New York. One of these figures, dating from the early Ptolemaic Period, appears in the *Atlas* by John Baines and Jaromír Málek as part of the entry on Leontopolis, where the lion-god Mahes, which can be translated as "furious lion", was worshipped (Baines & Málek, 1981: 172). The Greeks reinterpreted the Egyptian name as Miysis or Mihos.

This piece was kept at Calouste Gulbenkian's Paris house in Avenue d'Iéna until it was moved to Portugal in 1958. It previously had a limestone base that Howard Carter removed to make it easier to exhibit in a display-case in the so-called "Assyrian Room" at Gulbenkian's house.

## 48

**SCARAB**

Late Period, 26$^{th}$ dynasty (?)
Faience
W: 2.5 cm; L: 3.5 cm
Provenance: Acquired from Howard Carter
Date incorporated: 1925
Inv. no. 412

This turquoise faience scarab has cursory clypea, a flat prothorax, elytrons that are clearly separated by a cut and marked by incisions. Its feet rest on the oval base that has no inscription but has six holes (two on the left, two on the right, one at the front and one at the back) around it so that the object can be sewn onto the linen bands wrapped around the mummy or other funerary materials.

NOTES AND COMMENTS

The surviving receipt shows that Calouste Gulbenkian acquired this attractive piece directly from Howard Carter. The piece was kept in a display-case in the so-called "Assyrian Room" at the collector's Paris house in Avenue d'Iéna until it was moved to Portugal in 1958. It was put directly in the storeroom and has never been exhibited.

This scarab is similar to one at the Liebieghaus in Frankfurt (Gessler-Löhr, 1981: 48), among countless others now in collections in many museums worldwide. This includes Portugal, whose public and private collections have scarabs in all different sizes and forms. For the iconographic and ideological significance of the scarab as a much sought-after amulet, see the notes and comments on the winged scarab in exhibition (cat. no. 19).

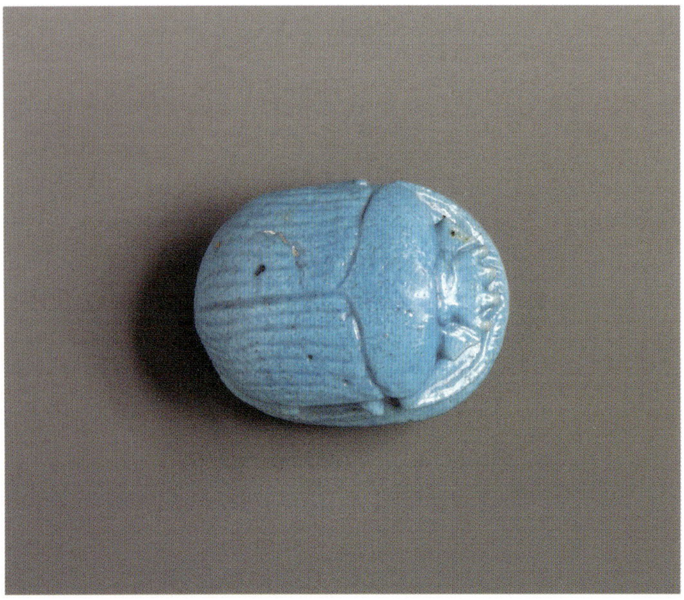

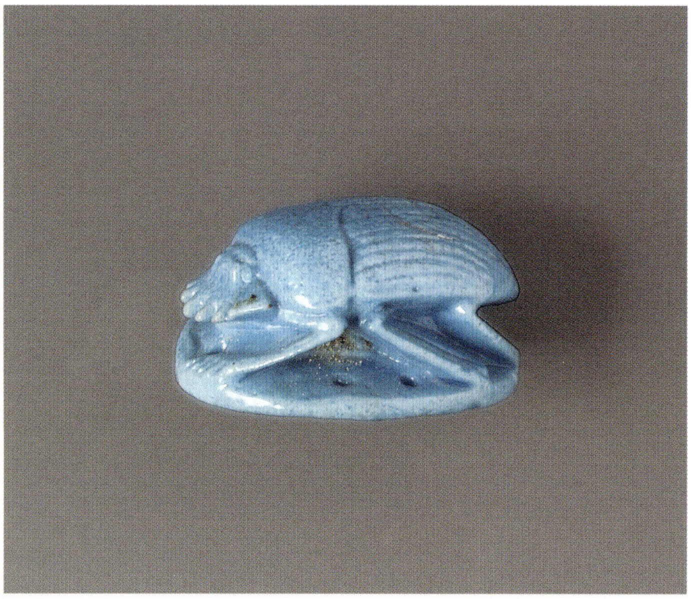

49

## FUNERARY STATUETTE

Late Period, 26th dynasty (?)
Blue faience
H: 14.5 cm; W: 4.2 cm
Provenance: Unknown
Date incorporated: Unknown
Inv. no. 1048

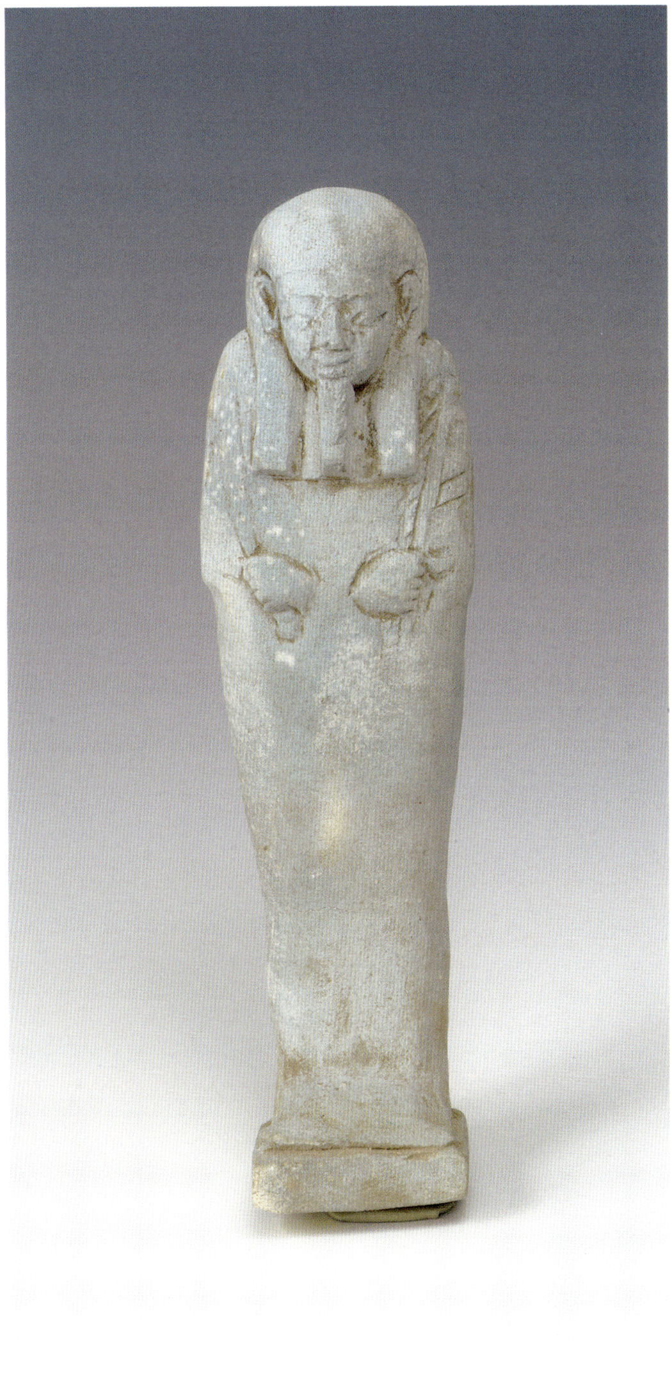

This funerary statuette, called an *shabti*, is made in blue faience, does not have the typical glaze, and stands on a small base measuring 3.5 x 3.2 centimetres. The facial features are crudely modelled, creating a grimace that is unusual in this type of imagery. The round face has protruding ears emerging from its surrounding three-part wig. Two sections of the hair hang over the chest, flanking the plaited beard. Two crossed hands emerge from the shroud, holding the customary farming tools: his right hand holds a pickaxe and a rope securing a bag of seeds slung over his shoulder and hanging down over his back; his left has a small hoe. The back of his hair is flat and there is a small bag on his left shoulder. Behind the figure, there is a dorsal pillar bearing a hieroglyphic inscription with clumsy signs (some are some illegible) in two vertical columns separated by a central incision.

Inscription on the dorsal pillar:

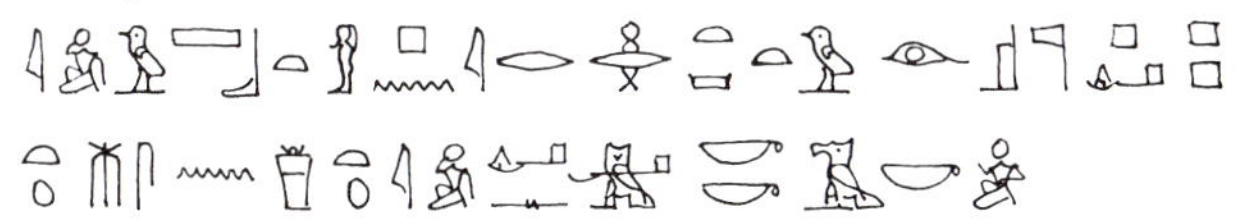

"Oh *ushabti* (this one), if the Osiris Padipepet, daughter of Bastetirdis is called. Note well, I am here!

NOTES AND COMMENTS

The Collection archives do not have any documents revealing how this funerary statuette was acquired. However, it is mentioned in the Paris catalogue, vol. II, p. 31 B. In fact, some auction houses gave small objects to people who purchased significant and expensive pieces as a sort of gesture of appreciation. This may have been the case with this statuette and the following one (no. 50), for which there is no copy of an invoice or receipt.

This type of statuette is part of the group of the *ushabtis* with inscriptions on the dorsal pillar, superbly exemplified by the funerary statuettes made for the senior official Hekaemsaf, admi-

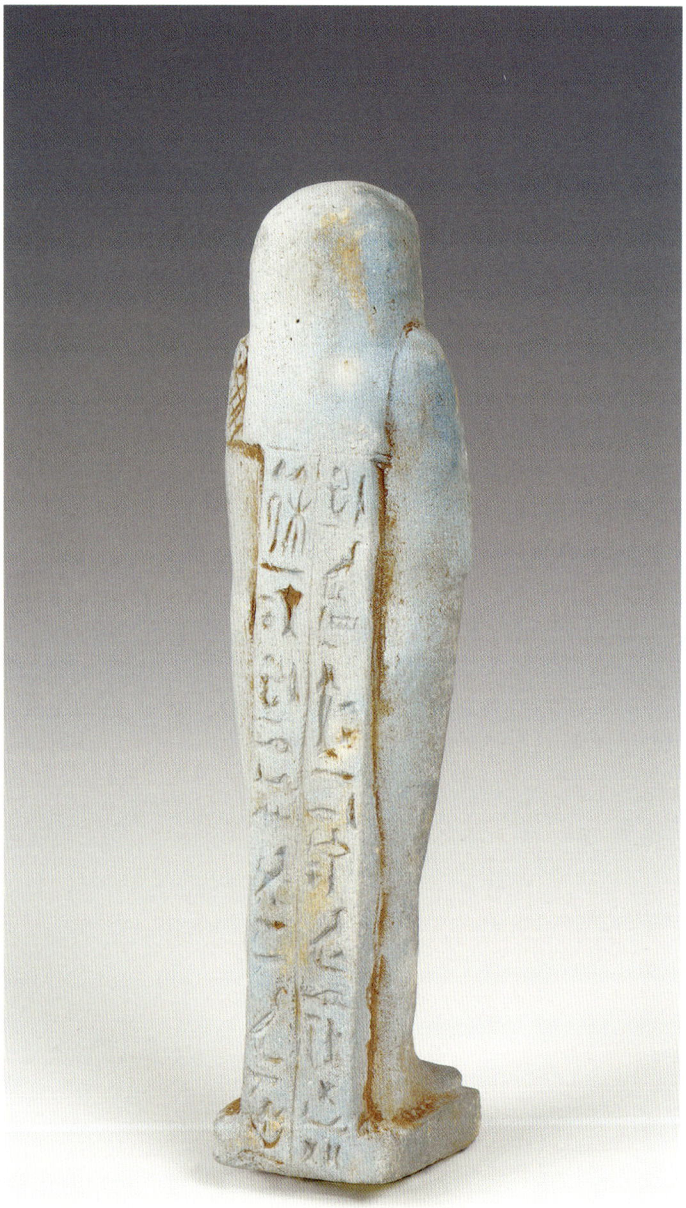

ral of the royal navy in the 26th dynasty (Björkman, 1971: 34-35, fig. 7), or – albeit with the text on the front – three figures at the Kunsthistorisches Museum, Vienna (Seipel, 1989: 221).

The terms *shabti* and *ushabti*, used for funerary statuettes, are related to the period in which they were produced. Intensive production of such pieces began in the Middle Kingdom and continued for the next two thousand years. Until the 21st dynasty, they were called *shabtis*, a name that derives from *chauab*, the wood of the persea tree from which they were originally made; but they then started being called *ushabtis*, a name that derives from the verb *ucheb*, "to respond", since it was believed that these statuettes would respond in the next world – instead of the deceased – when they were summoned to work the land (Araújo, 2003: 108-114).

The text on this statuette is a short excerpt summarising the beginning and end of Chapter 6 of the "Book of the Dead". The centre has a strange graphic format created by the hieroglyphs 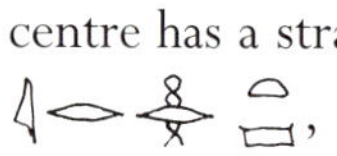, which presumably replaces the customary passive conditional formula 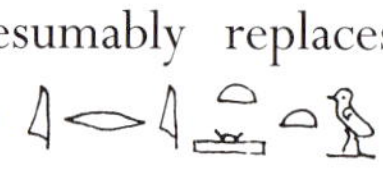 *ir ip.tw,* "if called" (*ir ipetu*).

50

**FUNERARY STATUETTE**

Late Period or Greco-Roman Period
Blue faience
H: 12 cm; W: 3.7 cm
Provenance: Unknown
Date incorporated: Unknown
Inv. no. 1049

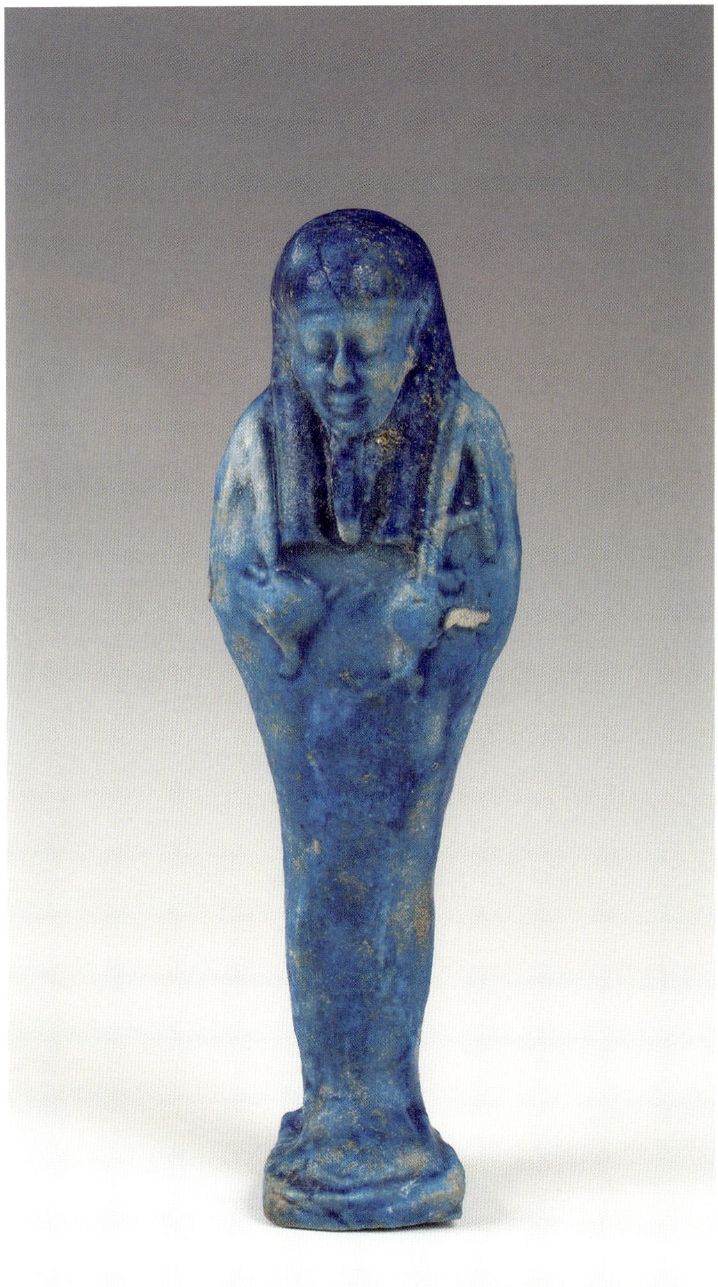

The hair on this funerary statuette is darker than the covering, which was intended to have the colour of lapis-lazuli. This *shabti*, with no inscription, stands on a trapezoidal base measuring 3 x 2.4 centimetres. The facial features are drawn in some detail, showing the divine beard and the hands crossed on his chest. His right hand is holding a pickaxe and a rope hanging over his shoulder and securing a bag of seeds that hangs over his back, while his left holds a hoe. There is a dorsal pillar that adapts to the figure's body, but bears no inscription.

NOTES AND COMMENTS

The Collection archives do not have any documents revealing how this funerary statuette was acquired. Like the previous piece, it is mentioned in the Paris catalogue, vol. II, p. 31 B, where it is described as a "statuette d'un personnage".

51

**STATUETTE OF THE GOD OSIRIS**

Late Period (?)

Bronze

H: 15.6 cm; W: 4.2 cm

Provenance: Unknown

Date incorporated: Unknown

Inv. no. 1050

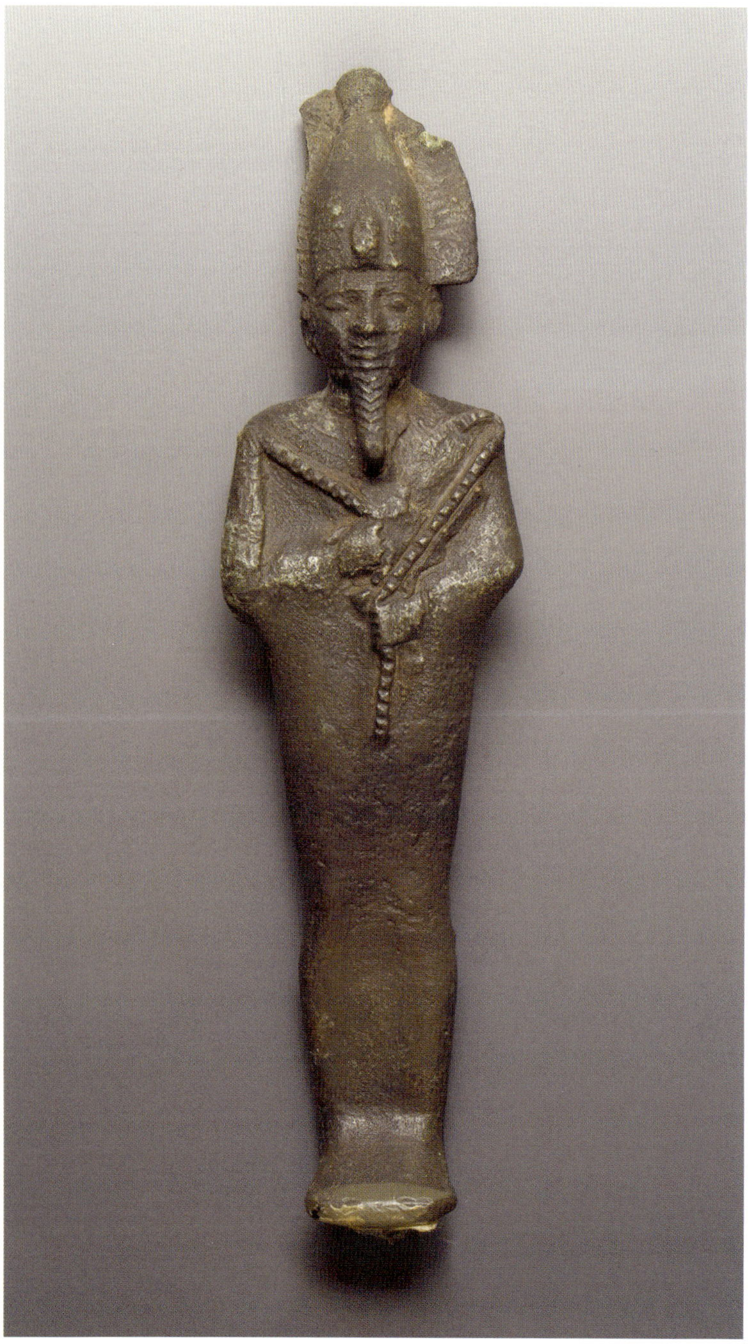

This bronze statuette shows the god Osiris, wearing the *atef* crown with the sacred serpent *uraeus* (*iaret*) flanked by feathers. The feather on the left is fractured at the top and the one on the right has been almost completely lost. The facial features are sculpted in some detail and the divine beard is plaited. The god's hands emerge from the front of the shroud, holding sceptres. His right hand (positioned over the left) holds the *nekhakha* sceptre (northern royalty), while his left hand (underneath) holds the *hekat* sceptre (southern royalty). Both sceptres have regularly spaced incisions. The base has a small spike so that it could be fixed onto another base (now lost).

NOTES AND COMMENTS

The Collection archives do not have any documents revealing how this funerary statuette was acquired. The Paris catalogue, vol. II, p. 31 B, describes it as a "statuette d'un personnage à barbiche".

See the comments on cat. no. 26.

52

**STATUETTE OF THE GOD HARPOCRATES**

Late Period (?)
Bronze
H: 11 cm; W: 2.8 cm
Provenance: Unknown
Date incorporated: Unknown
Inv. no. 1047

Statuette portraying Harpocrates or Horus the child god, using the typical iconography from such images: the dual crown of Upper and Lower Egypt, with a plaited and spiralling strand of hair falling over his right shoulder. Although the facial features are partly eroded, some anatomical details can still be seen. As is usual, the body is naked, with his left arm hanging alongside his body and a space between his forearm and trunk, while his bent right arm brings his hand close to his mouth and his forefinger points up towards his lips. His left leg is pushed forward on the small base.

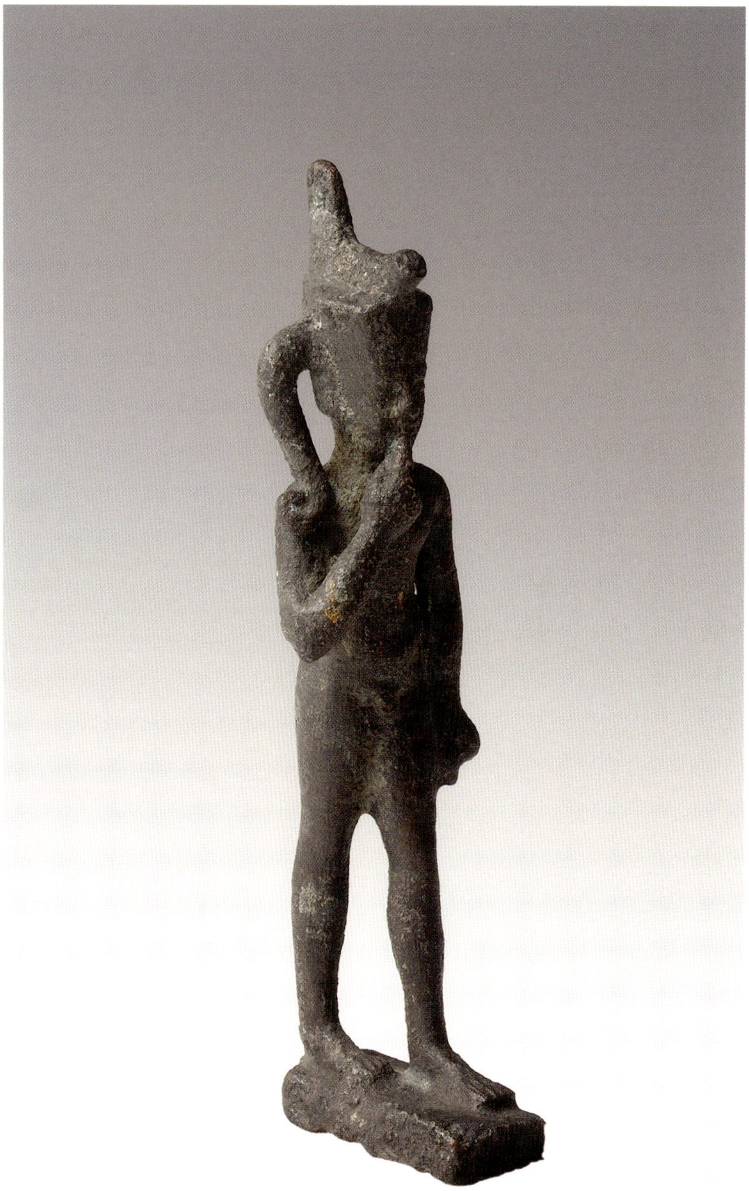

NOTES AND COMMENTS

The Collection archives do not have any documents revealing how this funerary statuette was acquired. The Paris catalogue, vol. II, p. 31 B, describes it as a "statuette d'un personnage en marche".

See the comments on cat. no. 26.

53

## STATUETTE OF AN OFFICIAL

Old Kingdom, 6th dynasty (?)
Limestone
H: 46.5 cm; W: 13.5 cm
Provenance: The Viscount Rothermere Collection
Date incorporated: 1942
Inv. no. 2366

The statuette of a walking man shows him with his left leg forward, standing on a plinth 4.5 centimetres high. The figure has accurate anatomical proportions and the body is painted in a reddish tone. His hair has a centre parting and falls in a fan-pattern over his shoulders and the pillar behind the figure. The facial features are well defined: his eyes and eyebrows are painted black and he has a small moustache. There are traces of a painted necklace. His arms hang alongside his body, and his hands hold two cylinders, suggesting the symbols of authority which – as is usual – are never completely shown so as to avoid protrusions on the sculpture. The white kilt is superbly produced, revealing the folds in the fabric, crossed at the front, and with the clasp and belt painted yellow. There is a narrow, decentred pillar behind the figure.

NOTES AND COMMENTS

The statuette was acquired at Sotheby's, London, at the auction of the Egyptian collection of Viscount Rothermere (no. 66 in the catalogue). In 1948, the work's authenticity was challenged by William Smith, an Egyptologist from the Boston Museum and professor of Egyptian Art at the University of Harvard. Nonetheless, the statuette was still exhibited, alongside another from the same era (cat. no. 54), at the National Gallery of Art, Washington, between 1949 and 1960, when it returned to Lisbon. In 1963, the Brooklyn Museum, New York, asked the Calouste Gulbenkian Foundation to loan the statuette for an exhibition of fake objects. The Foundation declined, claiming that there is no proof that it is false.

When Calouste Gulbenkian acquired the statuette in 1942, Egyptologists such as Howard Carter (prior to his death in 1939) and Stephen Glanville believed it to be genuine. Although Christiane Desroches-Noblecourt, does not state it clearly, she expressed doubts as to its authenticity in a letter to the Museum dated May 1969.

The question can be summarised as follows: William Smith had doubts about the statuette because the hair was not the correct colour, the lips were painted, and the piece had some stains that seemed to be made by acid, a technique often used to make objects seem ancient. Christiane Desroches-Noblecourt added other concerns that she had not expected: the marked softness of the face, the form of the eyebrows, the pursed lips, the insipid gaze, the swollen cheeks, the hooked nose, the smoothness of the hair, the body's pose and the connection between the arms and the trunk, the inappropriately advanced left leg and the position of the hands.

It is strange that none of these Egyptologists mentioned the decentred dorsal pillar. This feature appeared in the late 4th dynasty, but its initial purpose was not to bear inscriptions, a later development.

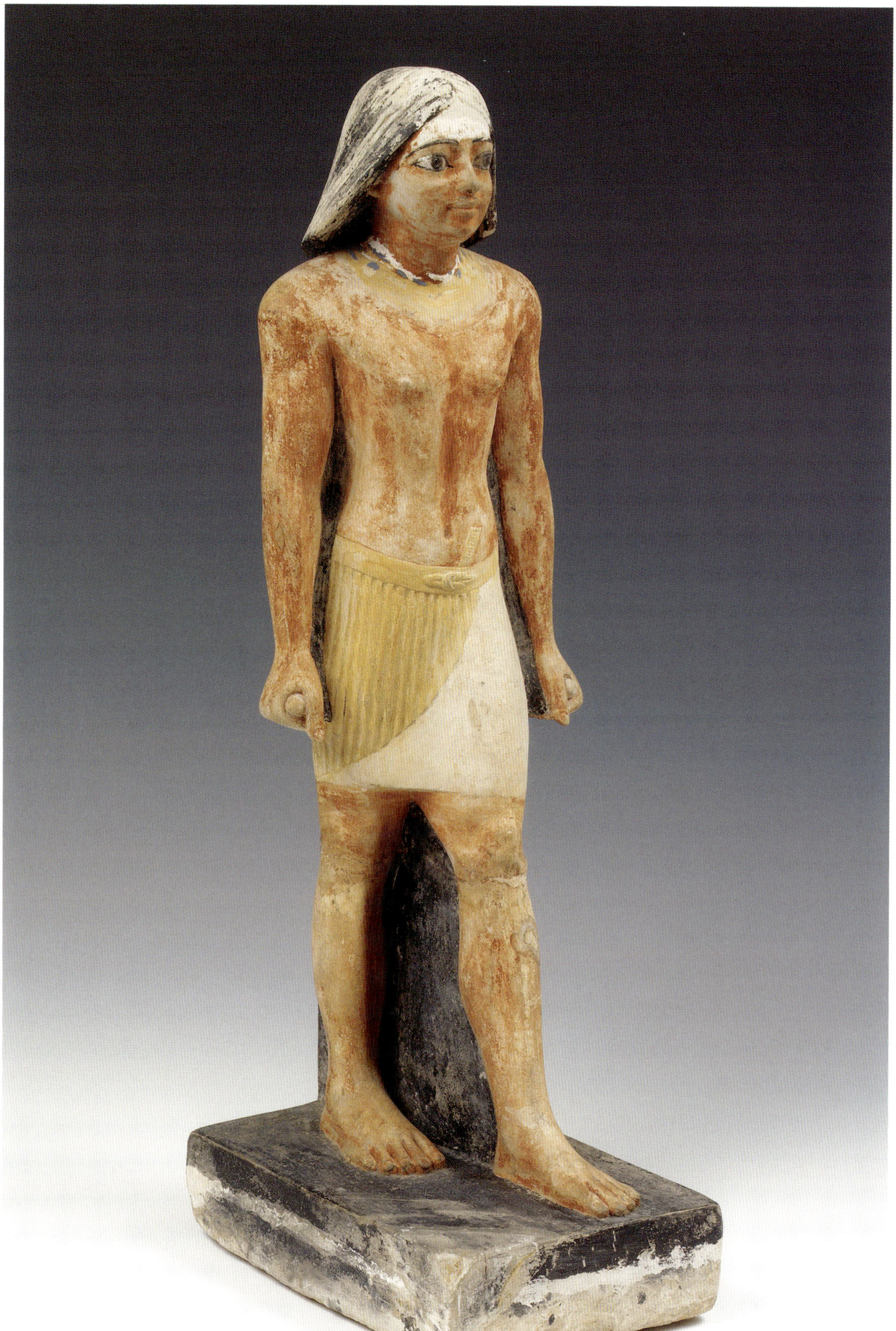

54

## STATUE OF AN OFFICIAL

Old Kingdom, 6th dynasty (?)
Limestone
H: 54 cm; W: 14.5 cm
Provenance: The Viscount Rothermere Collection
Date incorporated: 1942
Inv. no. 2365

The statue of a walking man shows him with his left leg forward, standing on a plinth seven centimetres high. The figure has accurate anatomical proportions and the body is painted in a reddish tone. He has short, curly hair (painted a colour that now seems purple) covering his ears. His facial features are clearly defined, and his eyes and eyebrows are painted black. His arms hang alongside his body, and his hands hold two cylinders, suggesting the symbols of authority which – as is usual – are never completely shown so as to avoid protrusions on the sculpture. The white kilt is superbly produced, revealing the folds in the fabric, crossed at the front, and with the clasp and belt painted yellow. There is a narrow, decentred pillar behind the figure.

NOTES AND COMMENTS

The piece was acquired at Sotheby's, London, at the auction of the Egyptian collection of Viscount Rothermere (no. 65 in the catalogue). See the notes and comments on the previous piece.

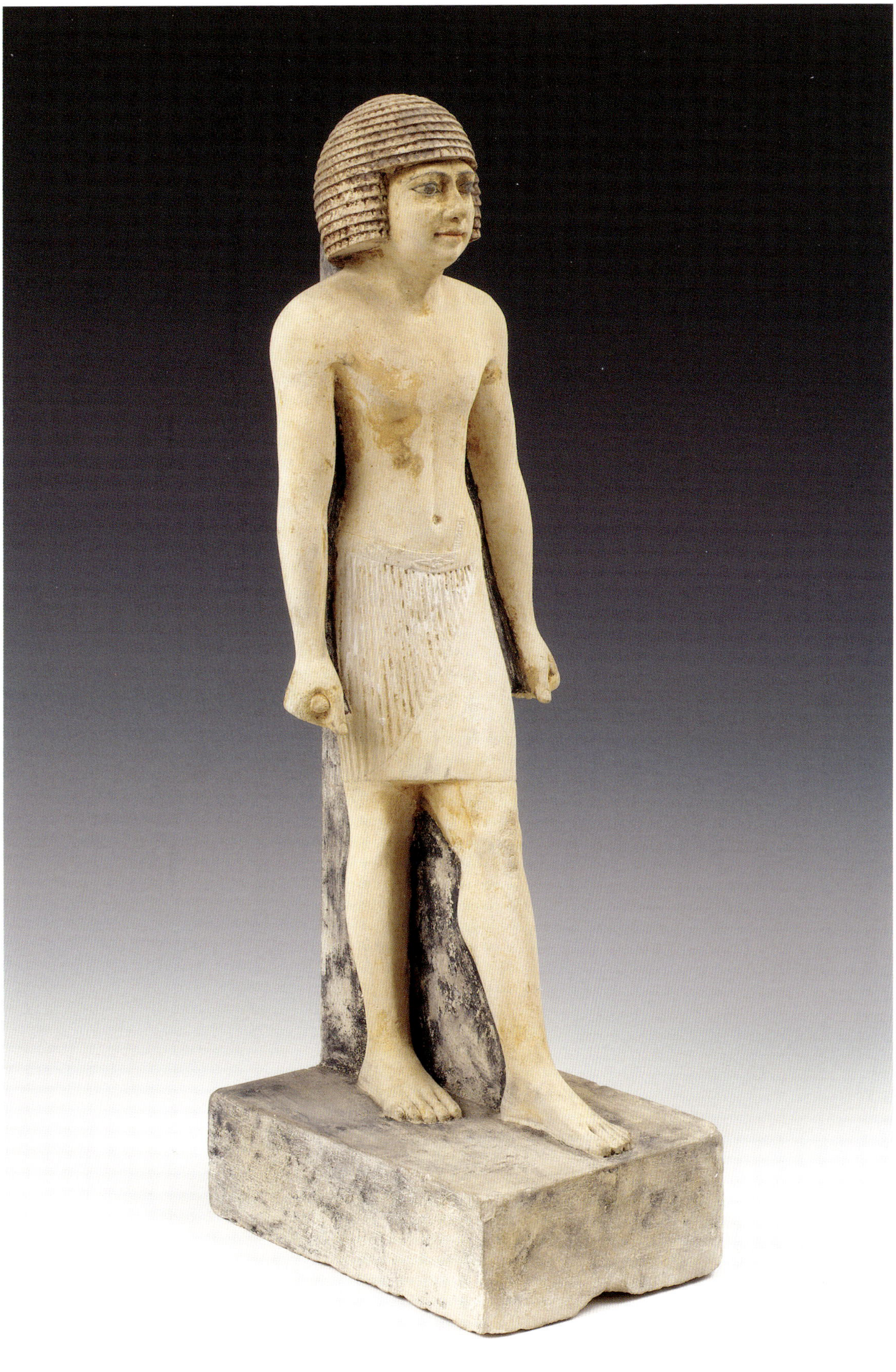

# DOCUMENTS

## SUNDRY CORRESPONDENCE RELATING TO THE ACQUISITION OF EGYPTIAN PIECES FOR THE GULBENKIAN COLLECTION

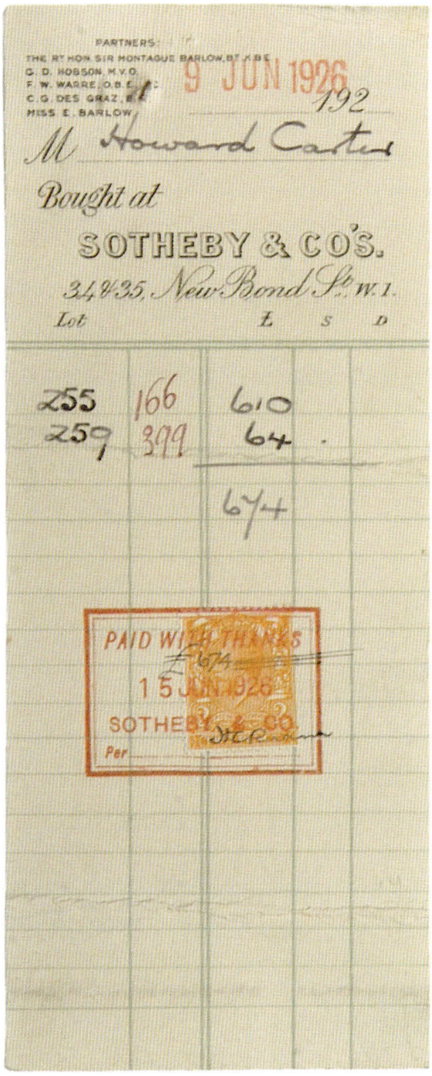

PARTNERS:
THE RT HON. SIR MONTAGUE BARLOW, BT K.B.E.
G. D. HOBSON, M.V.O.
F. W. WARRE, O.B.E.
C. G. DES GRAZ, E.
MISS E. BARLOW

9 JUN 1926

M Howard Carter

Bought at

SOTHEBY & CO'S.

34 & 35, New Bond St. W. 1.

| Lot | | £ | S | D |
|---|---|---|---|---|
| 255 | 166 | 6 | 10 | |
| 259 | 399 | 6 | 4 | |
| | | 6 | 74 | |

PAID WITH THANKS
£6.7.4
15 JUN 1926
SOTHEBY & CO.
Per

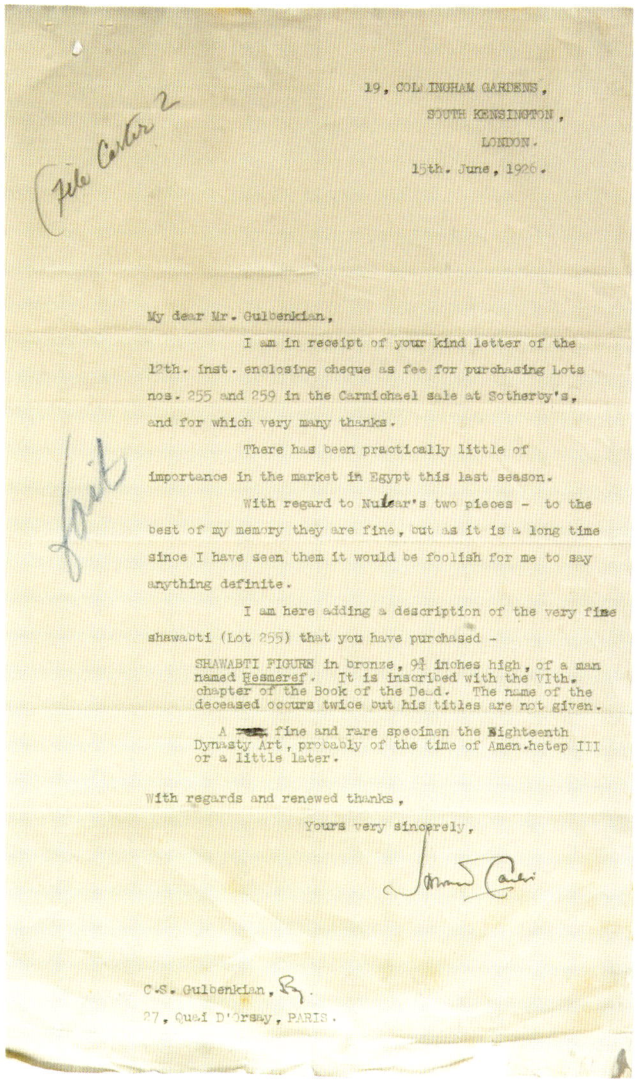

19, COLLINGHAM GARDENS,
SOUTH KENSINGTON,
LONDON.
15th. June, 1926.

File Carter 2

My dear Mr. Gulbenkian,

I am in receipt of your kind letter of the 12th. inst. enclosing cheque as fee for purchasing Lots nos. 255 and 259 in the Carmichael sale at Sotherby's, and for which very many thanks.

There has been practically little of importance in the market in Egypt this last season.

With regard to Nubar's two pieces - to the best of my memory they are fine, but as it is a long time since I have seen them it would be foolish for me to say anything definite.

I am here adding a description of the very fine shawabti (Lot 255) that you have purchased -

SHAWABTI FIGURE in bronze, 9¼ inches high, of a man named Hesmeref. It is inscribed with the VIth. chapter of the Book of the Dead. The name of the deceased occurs twice but his titles are not given.

A fine and rare specimen the Eighteenth Dynasty Art, probably of the time of Amen.hetep III or a little later.

With regards and renewed thanks,

Yours very sincerely,

Howard Carter

C.S. Gulbenkian, Esq.
27, Quai D'Orsay, PARIS.

Receipt for the funerary statuette of Hesmeref, no. 255 (cat. no. 11) and a bronze no. 259 (cat. no. 29).
Calouste Gulbenkian Archives

Letter from Howard Carter to Calouste Gulbenkian on the funerary statuette of Hesmeref (cat. no. 11).
Calouste Gulbenkian Archives

Letter from Howard Carter to Calouste Gulbenkian informing him about the acquisition of pieces from the McGregor Collection.
Calouste Gulbenkian Archives

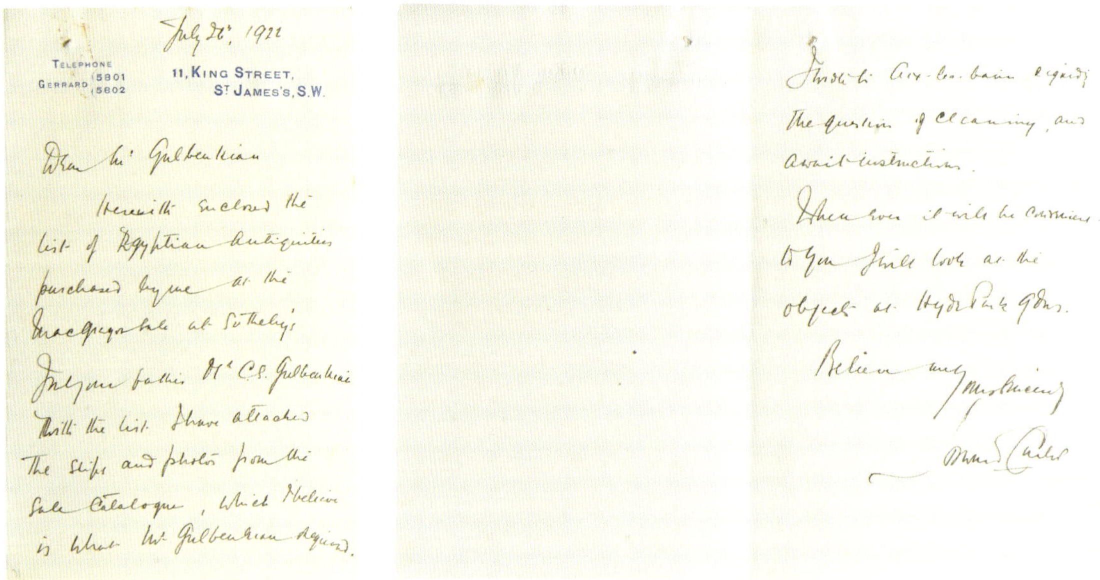

July 20th 1922

TELEPHONE GERRARD 5801 5802

11, KING STREET, ST JAMES'S, S.W.

Dear Mr Gulbenkian

Herewith enclosed the list of Egyptian Antiquities purchased by me at the MacGregor Sale at Sotheby's for your father Mr C.S. Gulbenkian. With the list I have attached the slips and photos from the Sale Catalogue, which I believe is what Mr Gulbenkian required.

I write to [illegible] regarding the question of cleaning, and await instructions.

Whenever it will be convenient to you I will look at the objects at Hyde Park Gdns.

Believe me, Yrs sincerely

Howard Carter

Letter from Howard Carter to Calouste Gulbenkian on the acquisition of the "head of Amenemhat III" (Senwosret III, cat. no. 4).
Calouste Gulbenkian Archives

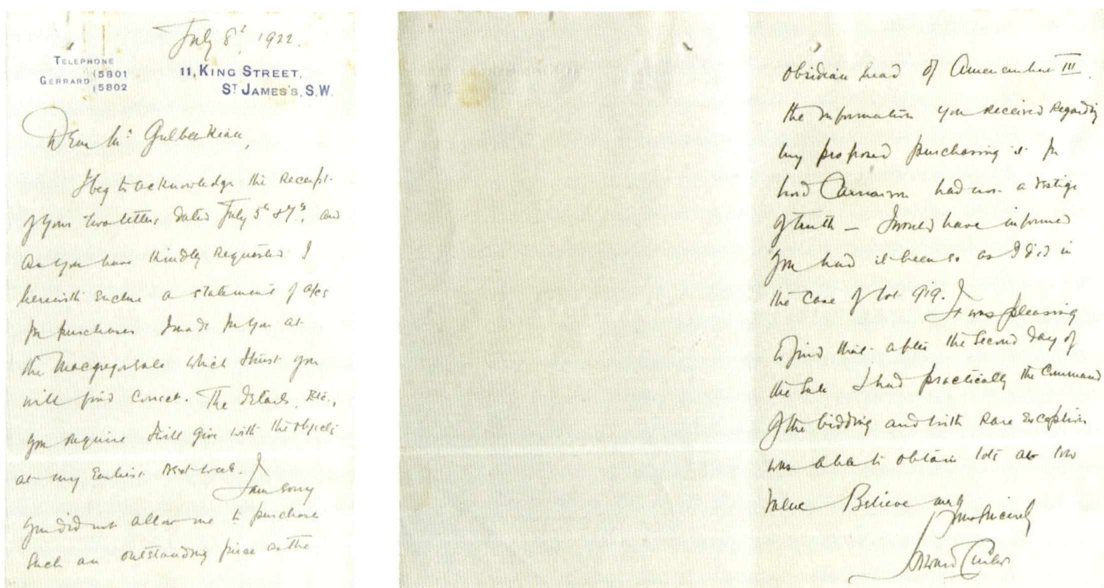

July 8th 1922

TELEPHONE GERRARD 5801 5802

11, KING STREET, ST JAMES'S, S.W.

Dear Mr Gulbenkian,

I beg to acknowledge the receipt of your two letters dated July 5th & 7th, and as you have kindly requested I herewith enclose a statement of a/cs for purchases made for you at the MacGregor Sale which I trust you will find correct. The details etc., you require I will give with the objects at my earliest [illegible].

I am sorry you did not allow me to purchase such an outstanding piece as the obsidian head of Amenemhat III. The information you received regarding my proposed purchasing is [illegible] had not a vestige of truth – I would have informed you had it been so as I did in the case of lot 919.

It was pleasing to find that after the second day of the sale I had practically the command of the bidding and with rare exceptions was able to obtain lots at low value. Believe me, Yrs sincerely

Howard Carter

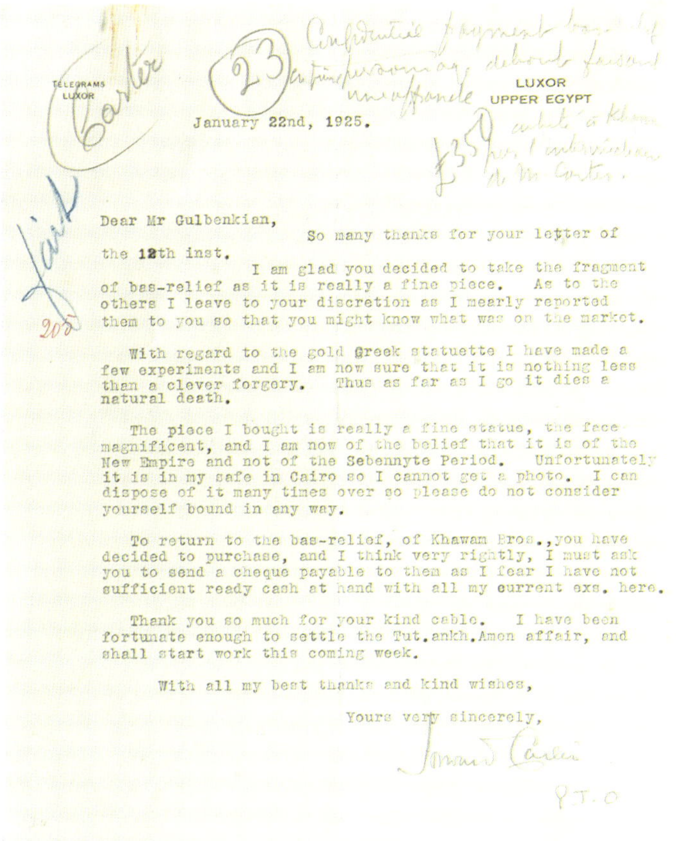

TELEGRAMS LUXOR

LUXOR UPPER EGYPT

January 22nd, 1925.

Dear Mr Gulbenkian,

So many thanks for your letter of the 12th inst.

I am glad you decided to take the fragment of bas-relief as it is really a fine piece. As to the others I leave to your discretion as I mearly reported them to you so that you might know what was on the market.

With regard to the gold Greek statuette I have made a few experiments and I am now sure that it is nothing less than a clever forgery. Thus as far as I go it dies a natural death.

The piece I bought is really a fine statue, the face magnificent, and I am now of the belief that it is of the New Empire and not of the Sebennyte Period. Unfortunately it is in my safe in Cairo so I cannot get a photo. I can dispose of it many times over so please do not consider yourself bound in any way.

To return to the bas-relief, of Khawam Bros.,you have decided to purchase, and I think very rightly, I must ask you to send a cheque payable to them as I fear I have not sufficient ready cash at hand with all my current exs. here.

Thank you so much for your kind cable. I have been fortunate enough to settle the Tut.ankh.Amon affair, and shall start work this coming week.

With all my best thanks and kind wishes,

Yours very sincerely,

Howard Carter

P.T.O

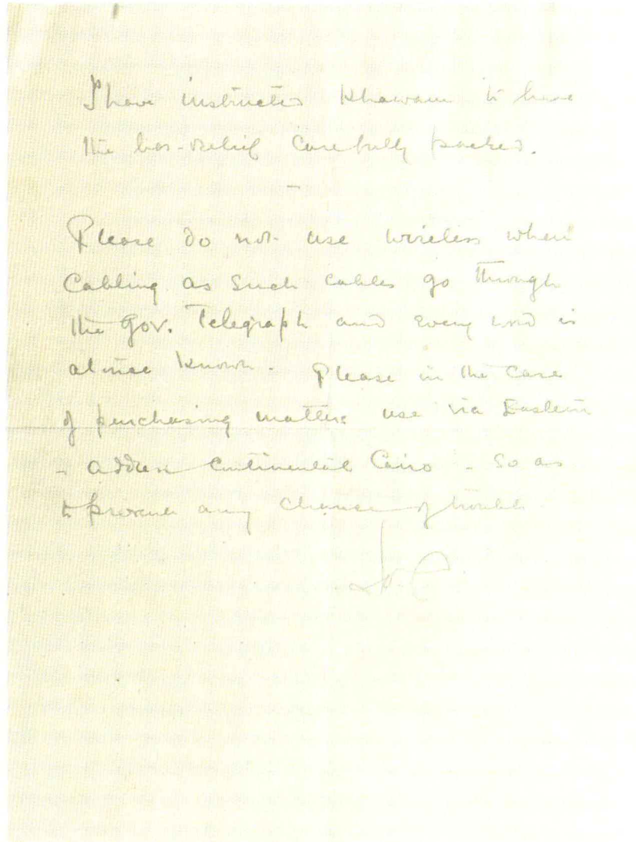

I have instructed Khawam to have the bas-relief carefully packed.

Please do not use wireless when cabling as such cables go through the Gov. Telegraph and every word is at once known. Please in the case of purchasing matters use via Eastern - address Continental Cairo - so as to prevent any chance of trouble.

H.C.

Letter from Howard Carter to Calouste Gulbenkian on the acquisition of the low-relief of Ameneminet (cat. no. 15).
Calouste Gulbenkian Archives

Note from Howard Carter on packaging and shipping the low-relief of Ameneminet (cat. no. 15).
Calouste Gulbenkian Archives

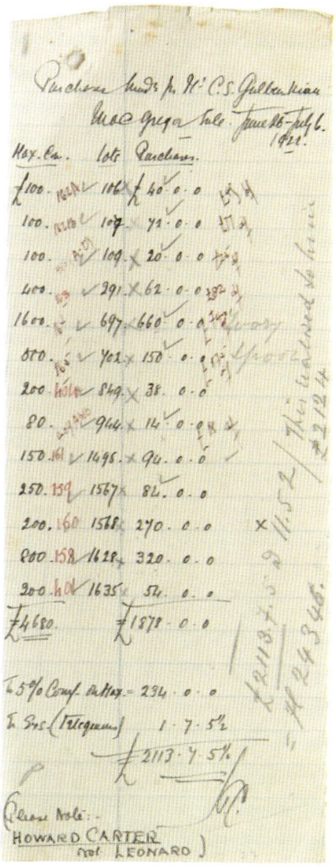

Purchases made for Mr C.S. Gulbenkian MacGregor Sale June 26-July 6. 1922.

| Max. Ex. | Lots | Purchases |
|---|---|---|
| £100. | 106 | £40.0.0 |
| 100. | 107 | 71.0.0 |
| 100. | 109 | 20.0.0 |
| 400. | 291 | 62.0.0 |
| 1600. | 697 | 660.0.0 |
| 800. | 702 | 150.0.0 |
| 200. | 849 | 38.0.0 |
| 80. | 944 | 14.0.0 |
| 150. | 1498 | 94.0.0 |
| 250. | 1567 | 84.0.0 |
| 200. | 1568 | 270.0.0 |
| 800. | 1628 | 320.0.0 |
| 200. | 1635 | 52.0.0 |
| £4680. | | £1878.0.0 |

+ 5% Comp. on Max. = 234.0.0

Exs (Telegrams) 1.7.5½

£2113.7.5½

Please Note:- HOWARD CARTER not LEONARD

List of the lots acquired by Calouste Gulbenkian at the McGregor sale in June-July 1922:
106 – cat. no. 19;
107 – cat. no. 25;
109 – cat. nos. 21-24;
291 – cat. no. 40;
697 – cat. nos. 17-18, 42-46;
702 – cat. no. 9;
849 – cat. no. 26;
944 – cat. no. 1;
1498 – cat. no. 37;
1567 – cat. no. 2;
1568 – cat. no. 10;
1628 – cat. no. 28;
1635 – cat. no. 35.
Calouste Gulbenkian Archives

# GLOSSARY

**ABU SIMBEL**
Place in Nubia famous for two rock temples that were built by order of Rameses II for him and his favourite wife, Queen Nefertari. The temples were moved from their original site due to the construction of the Aswan dam.

**ABYDOS**
Place in Upper Egypt where the god Osiris was worshipped. This site is very rich in archaeological remains from various eras of Egyptian history. The most important monuments are the temples built there by Sety I and Rameses II.

**ADOBE**
Clayey earth mixed with water and strengthened with straw or chips of wood, then set in wooden brick-shaped moulds and left to dry in the sun. It was widely used in construction. The first Egyptian tombs were made of adobe bricks, a tradition that continued in the following eras.

**AHMOSE**
He expelled the Hyksos from Egypt around 1550 BC by destroying their city of Sharuhen in Palestine, founding the 18th dynasty of the New Kingdom. His name means "Son of the Moon" and the Greek version of his name is Ahmosis. His image can be seen on a stele in the Gulbenkian Collection.

**AKH**
The psychic component of the human after successfully passing through the court of Osiris, reaching the next world and being transformed into a luminous being. The term can be translated as brilliance or clarity, invoking light and glory, magnificence and efficacy, joining the *ka* and *ba* to strengthen the human body.

**AKHENATEN**
Name that means "He who is useful to Aten", or alternatively "the brilliance of Aten", adopted by Pharaoh Amenhotep IV, who spurned the cult of the god Amun (part of his former name of Amenhotep ("Amun is satisfied"). The cult of Aten that the king tried to establish was not monotheistic, but an extreme form of henotheism.

**AKHETATEN**
City founded in Middle Egypt by Akhenaten, who abandoned Thebes and spurned the cult of Amun. The city's name can be translated as the "Horizon of Aten", a reference to the god Aten, who the king fervently worshipped as the "sole" god.

**ALABASTER**
Type of white, translucent, soft marble. The finest alabaster came from the Hatnub region in Middle Egypt. Alabaster became the customary term used when describing stone, although calcite is more accurate.

**AMENEMHAT I**
His name means "Amun is in control". This former vizier, the highest position in the administration, later became king and founded the 12th dynasty in Thebes-Waset. He moved the capital to the Faiyum region.

**AMENEMHAT III**
12th-dynasty king, the son of Senwosret III. He reaped the benefits of his father's prosperous reign, when Egypt reached an exceptional economic, artistic and cultural peak. He had two pyramids built in Hawara and Dahshur.

**AMENHOTEP III**
18th-dynasty king whose name means "Amun is satisfied". His reign was a highpoint in Egyptian history, defined by peace with the neighbouring countries and high quality art. Some experts consider this to be the golden age of Ancient Egypt.

**AMENHOTEP IV**
18th-dynasty king, the son of Amenhotep III. Owing to his intransigent struggle with the clergy of Amun, he changed his name to Akhenaten and devoted himself to worshipping his "sole" god Aten, based in his capital of Akhetaten and showed some religious intolerance.

**AMULET**
Magical and protective object that kept its owner safe from disease, misfortune or the evil eye. These amulets were worn by the living and the dead alike, as they were placed among the bands enveloping the mummies.

**AMUN**
God who was worshipped in the region of Thebes and who gained enormous importance in the New Kingdom, when he was called the "king of the gods". He had universal, solar characteristics. Massive temples were built for him.

**ANUBIS**
God of mummification and death, protector of the dead, depicted with the body of a man and the head of a wild dog. It was Anubis who taught Isis how to mummify Osiris after he had been slain by Set.

**ATEN**
Deity represented by a solar disc whose rays ended in hands, some of which are bestowing the gift of the sign of life (*ankh*). This god was worshipped by Akhenaten, Nefertiti and their followers in Amarna-Akhetaten.

**ATUM**
The god of Heliopolis who appeared on the primordial hill on the initial Nun (the still waters of chaos). He masturbated and swallowed his own semen, thereby creating two gods (Shu and Tefnut) as well as the universe and life itself.

**AXIS**
Rigid central line in architecture and sculpture that kept the forms symmetrically divided in the middle. The axis in sculpture is the basis of the "law of frontality" that kept the figure upright.

**BA**
One of the three spiritual principles linked to the human being, forming man's harmonious whole (in conjunction with the *ka* and the *akh*) that makes it possible for man to move. He is gen-

erally depicted as a long-legged bird – the stork – but is sometimes shown as a falcon.

**BARQUE ROOM**
This came after the temple's hypostyle hall, before the shrine holding the statue of the god. This statue was carried on processions on a barque that was kept on a stone plinth in the room of the same name.

**BASTET**
Goddess portrayed as a woman with a cat's head. She had the gentle characteristics of maternal protection. She was particularly revered in Bubastis and Sais, in the Delta. Her sacred animal was the cat, as can be seen from pieces in the Gulbenkian Collection.

**BEARD**
The Ancient Egyptians normally had either well-tended beards or were clean shaven. The gods were often shown with an extended goatee beard, and the pharaoh would wear a wavy or plaited false beard held to the chin by a string. This is how such figures were portrayed in works of art, as can be seen from pieces in the Gulbenkian Collection.

**BLACK LAND**
The fertile land deposited by the Nile flooding its banks. The Egyptians called this land Kemet and considered it to be the true Egypt – life. The rest was Desheret, the red land, the desert – death.

**BOATS**
Egyptian boats, with oars or sails, guaranteed proper means of communication and enabled people and goods to be transported. Other boats, such as the bronze solar barque of Djedhor in the Gulbenkian Collection, were used in religious ceremonies.

**"BOOK OF THE DEAD"**
Set of religious texts that had a magical nature, written on a papyrus placed in the tomb so that the deceased could reach the next world. They were written as from the New Kingdom, based on previous texts.

**BRONZE**
Alloy of copper and tin that was mainly used in the Third Intermediate Period and the Late Period. Some pieces in the Collection are made of bronze, including a funerary statuette from the New Kingdom.

**CANALS**
Extremely useful in farming, they were mostly built during the Middle Kingdom to take water from the Nile to Lake Faiyum during the flooding. When the flood season was over, the canals were closed and the water trapped in the lake. Many canals were made all along the Nile to transport water to places far away from the river.

**CARTOUCHE**
Name given to the oval vignette that holds the name of a king or a queen. The king's titles were set inside two cartouches, one for his throne name and the other for his birth name. Cartouches can be found on several objects in the Collection, with the names of Khufu, Ahmose, Pedubast, Menkheperra and Psamtek.

**"COFFIN TEXTS"**
Magical funerary texts that first started being inscribed on sarcophagi as from the First Intermediate Period. They were an adaptation of the earlier "Pyramid Texts".

**COPPER**
Metal used in Egypt from a very early stage, possibly in the fifth millennium BC, mainly to make farming and building tools, and for weapons and adornments. The need for greater quantities of copper led to imports from Cyprus and the Sinai.

**COPTS**
Name given to Egyptian Christians, who started becoming a minority in the country following the Arab conquest in the seventh century. They created their own type of script and produced modest artistic work.

**CRAFTSMAN**
This name, *hemu* in Egyptian, was used for carpenters, painters, drawers, jewellers, gardeners and sculptors, among others. This mixed those who created works of art with those who produced utilitarian objects. All the above produced pieces of work (*kat*).

**CROPS**
The peasants of Ancient Egypt grew cereals – mainly wheat and barley – as well as flax and fruit and vegetables (onions, garlic, leeks, beans, lentils, peas, chickpeas, lettuce, cucumber, watermelon, melon, etc.), as well as tending vines.

**CRYPT**
Inaccessible part of a tomb, normally underground, where the body was placed, sometimes alongside the deceased's goods and foodstuffs for use in the next world. In the ancient *mastabas*, access was via a large vertical shaft.

**DEMOTIC SCRIPT**
Simplified cursive script derived from hieratic script. It was created as from the 7th century BC, and mainly used to record administrative, legal and even literary texts on papyruses. Very rarely used on monuments.

**DENDERA**
Place in Upper Egypt with ruins from various periods. The most significant is the temple dedicated to Hathor, who was worshipped in that area. It is on the trade route leading to the Red Sea, and had a sanatorium during the Greco-Roman Period.

**DJOSER**

3rd-dynasty king who built the great funerary complex in the Saqqara region. The outstanding feature of this is his stone, six-step pyramid. During his reign, art developed enormously, especially the production of large stone vessels.

**DUAMUTEF**

One of the four sons of Horus. He had the dark coloured head of a wild dog and protected the deceased's stomach, covering the canopic jar that held the organ. The Museum's Collection includes a figurine of Duamutef.

**EDFU**

City in Upper Egypt with a large temple dedicated to Horus. This temple, one of the best preserved in Egypt, dates from the Greco-Roman Period. The Egyptian name was Behedet.

**ENNEAD**

Group of nine gods from Heliopolis, comprising Atum, Shu (the air) and Tefnut (moisture), Geb (the earth) and Nut (the sky), Osiris, Isis, Set and Nephthys. There were other enneads in Ancient Egypt, but the Heliopolis Ennead is the most famous.

**FAIYUM**

Region in Middle Egypt formed by a major geographical depression holding a lake (now smaller than in pharaonic times). It contains traces from all ages, but especially from the Middle Kingdom.

**FLOODING**

Annual phenomenon that started in mid-July when the waters of the Nile began to rise and broke the banks, fertilising the surrounding land. The flooding season, called Akhet in Egyptian, lasted four months, from the middle of July to the middle of November.

**FOREMEN**

Officials entrusted with managing agriculture and the various construction projects. They are generally shown with raised whips or staffs. Some funerary statuettes show foremen controlling the work done in the next world.

**GEB**

God of the earth, the son of Shu (the air) and Tefnut (moisture), and the husband of Nut. He was one of the Heliopolis Ennead, and is considered to be the father of Osiris, Isis, Set and Nephthys. His sacred animal (and hieroglyphic symbol) was the goose.

**GIZA**

Plain a few kilometres west of what is now Cairo. Massive pyramids were built there for Khufu, Khafra and Menkaura, 4th-dynasty kings, and the site also houses the famous colossal statue of the sphinx.

**GOD**

In Ancient Egypt, the king was believed to be a living god (living Horus) and the son of the gods (the son of Ra, but also other deities). The Egyptian king's divinity should be understood from the basis of African divine royalty rather than from the Judaeo-Christian point of view (as is sometimes the case). The Egyptian religion had many gods.

**GOLD**

Egypt was a land of gold (in Egyptian, *nebu*) that was extracted in the Predynastic Period and in the Middle Kingdom. Under the New Kingdom, the eastern countries that Egypt conquered and subjugated paid tribute in gold, increasing the pharaohs' treasure.

**HAIRPIECE**

There are short, smooth wigs, as worn in the Old Kingdom, or long, complex ones, as worn in the New Kingdom. They helped establish their wearers as people of distinction. Important people would normally shave their heads.

**HAPY**

One of the four sons of Horus who were entrusted with protecting the viscera of the dead. Hapy had a baboon's head and protected the lungs. The Museum's Collection has two figurines of Hapy, whose name was also applied to the deified River Nile.

**HARPOCRATES**

Name of Greek origin that refers to Horus the child god, in turn corresponding to the Egyptian form Horpakhered. He was a god of good deeds who was widely worshipped in the Greco-Roman Period. The Egyptian Collection includes a silver figurine of Harpocrates on display.

**HATHOR**

Goddess whose name means "House of Horus" and who was associated to joy, love, eroticism, maternity and death, as the protector of the dead. Some myths consider her to be Horus' mother. The Collection has a head of Hathor, part of a votive sistrum, on display.

**HATSHEPSUT**

Queen who was in power between *circa* 1490 and 1468 BC. She came to the throne because her stepson Thutmose III was a minor. However, instead of abdicating when the time came, she proclaimed herself pharaoh. Thutmose III was only able to reign when she died.

**HELIOPOLIS**

Historic location north of what is now Cairo, where the sun god Ra was worshipped. Nothing remains of the large temple of Ra and other constructions in Heliopolis except for an obelisk of Senwosret I.

**HERAKLEOPOLIS**

City located south of Faiyum, with necropolises from various eras. The Egyptian name was Neninesut or "city of the royal child", and a little-known god called Herishef was worshipped there.

**HIERAKONOPOLIS**

Greek name for Nekhen, in Upper Egypt, where Horus was worshipped and where several historical documents were found, including the Narmer Palette. It is now called Kom el-Ahmar.

**HIERATIC SCRIPT**
Simplified cursive form of hieroglyphic script. It was more practical and faster to use on papyrus, and was used to record important historical, military, medical and administrative information, etc.

**HIEROGLYPHIC SCRIPT**
A form of script that was created when the pharaonic monarchy emerged, although some signs are known from Egypt's proto-history. Its proper use required good drawing skills and a fine concept of graphic aesthetics. It was made up of ideograms and phonograms.

**HIEROGLYPHS**
Signs used in hieroglyphic script. They can be written from left to right or vice versa, and from top to bottom. When well drawn, animals, plants, human and divine figures, tools etc. are easily recognisable. In the Greco-Roman Period, there were over 3,000 signs, some of which have a cryptographic meaning.

**HIGH PRIEST**
Title of the man who led the priests that served in a temple, worshipping a specific deity. The most important high priest led the clergy of Amun.

**HOREMHEB**
18th-dynasty king who started as a scribe in the army, became a military commander of the forces stationed on the eastern front and then a senior official under Tutankhamun and Kheperkheperura Ay. His reign was peaceful and saw several constructions.

**HORUS**
Falcon-shaped god and protector of royalty whose name means "The Distant One", and can be seen on the shrine on the solar barque of Djedhor. He was part of the Heliopolis Ennead, where he was considered to be the son of Osiris and Isis. The pharaoh was seen as a living Horus ruling on earth.

**HYKSOS**
Collection of peoples from Syria-Palestine who gradually penetrated into the Delta in the late 18th century BC and ultimately seized power, forming the 15th and 16th dynasties. They were expelled in the middle of the 16th century BC. The name is derived from the Egyptian form Hekau-khasut, which means "Rulers of foreign countries".

**HYPOGEUMS**
Tombs cut into the rock, mostly dating from after the 4th dynasty. During the Middle Kingdom, they had monumental façades, but their entrances were later disguised to prevent robberies.

**HYPOSTYLE COURTYARD**
Courtyard after the pylon at the entrance to a temple. It was surrounded by several decorated columns and sometimes with statues of the gods or of the king who had built the temple. This courtyard was followed by the hypostyle hall.

**HYPOSTYLE HALL**
This hall, whose ceiling was supported on columns, came after the temple's pylon and hypostyle courtyard. The number and height of these columns varied according to the size of the hall itself.

**IMHOTEP**
Important figure who was praised in the sacred texts from the Late Period for his wisdom, and was considered to be the god of wisdom, of writing and of medicine. He was responsible for the significant funerary complex of Saqqara, built for Horus Djoser.

**IMSETY**
One of the four sons of Horus, as shown on one of the lids on the four canopic jars. He had a human head and protected the deceased's liver. The Collection includes a figurine of Imsety with a pale face, suggesting his hermaphrodite nature.

**ISIS**
Goddess who enjoyed great fame for her magical arts associated to maternity. She was the sister and wife of Osiris and the mother of Horus. According to the myths, she searched for the cut-up pieces of her brother and husband and made him into the first mummy, and later resuscitated him. She appears in the Collection on a funerary adornment and the solar barque of Djedhor.

**IVORY**
Bone-like substance that forms the teeth of some animals, particularly the elephant and the hippopotamus. The finest ivory came from Nubia. It was used to produce exceptional works of art and adornments, such as the "spoon" belonging to the Collection.

**KA**
The immaterial, invisible and magical principle that formed part of the human body, acting as the vital and sexual force that was maintained even in eternity. As exemplified by the wooden statues in the Collection, statues were containers for the *ka*.

**KARNAK**
Name of the largest temple from Ancient Egypt, dedicated to Amun-Ra, located in Thebes-Waset. It was built during a period lasting over a thousand years by several pharaohs. Although now severely damaged, it still maintains some of its grandeur.

**KEBEHSENUEF**
One of the four sons of Horus who appear on the lids of canopic jars. He had a falcon's head and protected the deceased's intestines. The Collection does not include a figurine of Kebehsenuef.

**KHAFRA**
The son of Khufu, he built a pyramid on the Giza plain. Exceptional works of sculpture were produced during his reign. His

Greek name was Chefren, but the Egyptian form – meaning "Shines like Ra" – is increasingly used.

**KHEPRECH**
This exclusively pharaonic crown was blue and could be decorated with small metal discs. The front showed the sacred serpent with its raised head, and it was sometimes considered to be the "war crown", although it had a wide range of functions. It appeared at the start of the New Kingdom, and can be seen on several pieces in the Collection.

**KHEPRI**
Young solar god who was identified with the morning sun and depicted with a scarab. His name means "That which comes into existence". He can be depicted with a human body and the head of a scarab.

**KHNUM**
God worshipped in Elephantine (Aswan), where he is regarded as the "Lord of the cataract" and the god responsible for the waters of the Nile rising. He was also seen as a god who had created living beings by shaping the clay of the earth.

**KHUFU**
The second king in the 4th dynasty and the son of Sneferu. The largest pyramid on Giza was built for him. In Greek, his name was Cheops, a form that is less and less used. His Egyptian name can be read on the low-relief of Merytites in the Collection.

**LAW OF FRONTALITY**
Firmly established rule followed by Egyptian artists where they were guided by a previously designed line that divided an image in half from top to bottom, staying upright on its vertical axis.

**LOTUS**
The lotus could be white or blue. It was the symbol of the Nile and fertile land, and the specific heraldic symbol of the south. It was also the symbol of eternity, and was consequently carried by the deceased, as shown on statuettes and funerary steles.

**LOW-RELIEF**
Sculpture carved on practically the same level as the surface. It could be slightly cut into the surface or raised, as seen on some pieces in the Gulbenkian Collection. Once carved, low-reliefs were normally painted.

**MAET**
Goddess of goodness, truth, justice, decency, balance, harmony, and cosmic and universal order. She was believed to be the daughter of Ra and sometimes of Amun. The concept of *maet* lies at the heart of the orderly operation (with solidarity) of pharaonic society, and it also explains the survival of Egyptian civilisation as we know it for such a long time.

**MAHES**
Lion-like deity who was mainly worshipped in Leontopolis, in the Central Delta (now Tell el-Muqdam), which was the capital of the 23rd dynasty, founded by Pedubast I. His name means "furious lion", and he was considered to be the son of the goddess Bastet.

**MASTABA**
Arabic word meaning "bench" used for a type of tomb with several rooms and a crypt that was typical of the Old Kingdom and used for officials and courtiers. There are individual and family *mastabas*, and they can be made of brick or stone.

**MATHEMATICS**
Amongst other purposes, mathematics was useful when calculating how to divide the fields for constructions and to record the products stored and distributed. The number zero was not known at that time.

**MEDITERRANEAN**
The Ancient Egyptian called the Mediterranean "The Great Green", fearing it and preferring to sail on the Nile or to travel overland to Syria-Palestine. Unlike other nations, Egypt was never interested in creating a powerful navy.

**MEMPHIS**
City founded by Narmer near the point where Upper and Lower Egypt meet and where the Nile branches out to form the Delta. The city was the political capital of the Old Kingdom and the main god worshipped there was Ptah. Even when it stopped being the capital, it never lost its political and cultural significance. Its Egyptian name is Ineb-hedj.

**MENES**
Greek version of the Egyptian name Meni, who appears in king-lists as the first king of unified Egypt. Some people identify Menes with Narmer, who unified the Two Lands, while others believe Menes is the Horus Aha.

**MENKAURA**
4th-dynasty king with the smallest of the three pyramids on the Giza plain. His funerary temple included beautiful statues showing him with his wife and deities. The Greek form of his name is Mykerinos.

**MERENPTAH**
Thirteenth son of Rameses II, he came to the throne at a late age due to the exceptional length of his father's reign. He repelled the foreign invasion of the Delta. From his reign onwards, Egypt went through serious social and political problems.

**MIDDLE KINGDOM**
Historical period dating from *circa* 2040 until 1780 BC. It featured great political and economic stability under the 11th and 12th dynasties, which brought exceptional quality in the arts and literature. The kings from this period implemented the principles of *maet*.

**MIN**
God of fecundity and fertility, protector of the desert and foreign lands. He is generally shown with an erect phallus and was

particularly worshipped in Coptos and Akhmim. He was also worshipped in the syncretic form of Amun-Min.

### MUMMIFICATION
Long process of treatment for the body of the deceased so as to guarantee it would be preserved for all eternity. Mummification involved the use of natron (sodium carbonate), followed by embalming and wrapping strips of linen around the body.

### NARMER
Name of the king credited with unifying Upper and Lower Egypt around 3000 BC. He left Thinis in the south and conquered the Delta. He is sometimes identified with Menes, the mythical founder of Egypt.

### NARMER PALETTE
Schist plaque with engravings and inscriptions on both sides, found in Hierakonopolis. This palette is of enormous historic importance as it records the unification of Upper and Lower Egypt by the Horus Narmer around 3000 BC. This exceptional piece also reveals some of the fundamental conventions of Egyptian art.

### NATRON
Chemical used in the process of mummifying bodies. It consists of crystallised sodium carbonate that was mainly obtained from Wadi Natrun. It removes all the humidity in the deceased's body, thereby mummifying them.

### NEFERTITI
Name that means "the beautiful woman that has come". Some believe she was of Mitannian origin. She was the wife of Pharaoh Akhenaten, had six daughters by him and went through the unique and heretical experience of Amarna-Akhetaten with him. The elegant bust at the Egyptian Museum in Berlin is world-famous.

### NEITH
Goddess who was worshipped in Sais and who had an enormous cult in the Late Period, since the 26$^{th}$ dynasty came from that city. The Collection includes a statuette of the Lady Shepes, dedicated to her by her daughter Neitemhat, a name that suggests Neith.

### NEPHTHYS
Goddess and sister of Isis and Osiris, also sister and wife of Set, and mother of Anubis. She is invoked as the protector of the dead. She was part of the Heliopolis Ennead. According to the myths, she helped Isis to protect the young god Horus, who was being pursued by her evil husband Set.

### NEW KINGDOM
Historical period dating from *circa* 1550 until 1070 BC (18$^{th}$, 19$^{th}$ and 20$^{th}$ dynasties), whose golden age came under Amenhotep III. This was a period of conquests and of a well-being that was reflected in art and literature.

### NUBIA
Region to the south of Egypt, after Aswan, divided into Wawat or Lower Nubia, and Kush or Upper Nubia. The Egyptians brought gold, hides, ivory, exotic woods, ostrich feathers and labour (among other resources) from this region.

### NUBIANS
Generic name given to the inhabitants of Nubia, the region to the south of Aswan. In Egyptian, these people were called *Nehesiu* (blacks), and according to the era in question, variously despised or well received. The Collection includes the head of a Nubian in black granite.

### NUN
Cosmic deity that represented the initial chaos, comprising an amorphous, watery mass, before the world was created. A lotus-flower then emerged, containing the Sun. A different myth claims that this shapeless mass emerged from a hill where the god Atum was sitting.

### NUT
Goddess of the sky, the daughter of Shu (the air) and Tefnut (moisture), and wife of Shu. She was one of the Heliopolis Ennead, and is sometimes depicted as the sky that gives birth to the Sun every day.

### OBELISKS
Elegant, narrow stone monuments, sometimes bearing inscriptions and with a pyramidal shape covered in metal at the top. They were symbols of the sun and were built at the entrances to temples, normally in pairs.

### OFFERING TABLE
Tables shown on mural reliefs or sculptures with the foodstuffs that were symbolically offered to the gods drawn onto the surface. These foodstuffs could be solid food, such as bread, cakes, grains of cereals, fruit, vegetables, fowl or beef, and sometimes fish; or liquid, symbolised by vessels containing water, wine or beer.

### OFFICIALS
General term applied to all those who could read and write and who held positions of authority in Ancient Egypt. Priests and scribes were officials. Some senior officials even became pharaohs in certain ages.

### OINTMENTS
Fatty perfumed substance used on skin. Normally kept in special containers, many of which were placed in tombs. Several ointments were used when embalming bodies.

### OLD KINGDOM
The period called the Old Kingdom lasted from approximately 2660 until 2180 BC. This was the period when the great pyramids were built and was a time of intense trade with Nubia and Syria-Palestine. Major royal and private works of sculpture date from this period.

**OSIRIS**
God who ruled in the other world as the protector of the dead. He was also associated to agriculture. He was the brother and husband of Isis and the father of Horus. He was killed by his jealous and evil brother Set. Osiris was part of the Heliopolis Ennead. The Collection has several images of Osiris, the most significant of which is a fine schist statuette.

**PALETTE**
Name given to schist or amphibolite plaques used as the bases where cosmetics such as galena and malachite were ground. They were widely used in the Predynastic Period, but later disappeared or took other forms.

**PAPYRUS**
Plant used as the emblem of the Delta or Lower Egypt. It also provided the sheets used for writing, while being exclusively reserved for important religious and administrative texts. Ostraca (potsherds) were used for other texts.

**PATINA**
Normally greenish layer of copper carbonate that forms over time due to oxidation on the surface of copper and bronze objects. It also defines the earthy coat that forms on the surface of marble and other stones.

**PEASANTS**
The peasantry, *sekhtiu* in Egyptian, were the men and women who tended the fields and were responsible for the crops that grew thanks to the fertility of the Nile. They accounted for approximately 90% of the people in Ancient Egypt.

**PEDUBAST**
Founder of the 23rd dynasty, whose capital was in Leontopolis. He came to the crown due to rivalry with the Thanis-based royalty of the 22nd dynasty. The Collection includes a bronze torso of the monarch, who was of Libyan origin despite his clearly Egyptian name.

**PHARAOH**
Name of Hebrew origin given to the king of Ancient Egypt. The word comes from *per-aá* ("large house", or palace), a way for the Egyptians to make indirect and respectful reference to their king.

**PRIESTS**
Officials who served a deity in the respective temple. The most influential and important from the New Kingdom onwards were the priests of Amun. There were also funerary priests, such as Ameneminet (for Thutmose III), as shown by a stone fragment in the Collection.

**PSAMTEK I**
The first pharaoh of the 26th dynasty. He freed Egypt from the Assyrians and ruled between 664 and 610 BC, using the support of Greek mercenaries. He adopted Wahibra as his throne name, the form that appears on the statuette of official Bes in the Collection.

**PYLON**
Trapezoidal stone towers located on either side of the entrance to a temple. The pylon was decorated with reliefs and could include tall masts with banners. It was sometimes preceded by statues and obelisks. Sometimes an avenue of sphinxes would lead to the pylon.

**PYRAMIDS**
Pyramid-shaped tombs made for kings and some queens from the Old Kingdom and the Middle Kingdom. The most famous are the three pyramids in Giza, built by the 4th-dynasty monarchs Khufu, Khafra and Menkaura on a plain north of Saqqara. These are considered to be one of the seven wonders of the world.

**"PYRAMID TEXTS"**
Magical funerary texts that appeared at the end of the 5th dynasty, renewing ancient traditions. Pharaoh Unas had them engraved on the inner walls of his pyramid (funerary chamber and access corridors). The "Sarcophagus Texts" derived from these texts.

**RA**
Sun-god of Heliopolis and one of the deities that protected the pharaohs, who called themselves the sons of Ra in the fifth name of their titulary. He was associated to other deities such as Atum-Ra, Sobek-Ra, Ra-Horakhty, Amun-Ra, etc.

**RA-HORAKHTY**
Syncretic god derived from the combination of two sun-gods: Ra and Horakhty, i.e. Horus of the Horizon. He was mainly worshipped in the Heliopolis region and Giza.

**RAMESES II**
One of the most famous pharaohs, he reigned for a long period (ca. 1290-1224 BC), was a major builder, an active warrior and an exceptional patron of the arts. His name means "The god Ra created him" (in Egyptian, Ramessu). He boasted of having won the Battle of Kadesh, although such a victory is highly dubious.

**RAMESES III**
20th-dynasty pharaoh who is considered to be the last great king of Egypt. He defeated an invasion by Egypt's enemies and had major construction work done. After his reign, Egypt entered a phase of slow decline.

**ROSETTA STONE**
A type of headstone found at Rosetta (Rachid) with the same inscription in hieroglyphic, demotic and Greek characters in 196 BC. The inscription enabled Jean-François Champollion to decipher hieroglyphic script in 1822.

**SACRED LAKE**
Many temples had tanks or sacred lakes where the priests could bathe to purify themselves before worshipping the local god. Temple lakes generally used underground water from the Nile.

**SAQQARA**
Vast area of tombs located west of Memphis. It has tombs from all periods, from proto-history through to the Coptic Period. The most important monument is the "step pyramid" of Horus Netjerirkhet Djoser.

**SCARAB**
The winged scarab was an image of Khepri, the god of creation, of the movement of the Sun and of resurrection. Most scarabs are shown without wings, and some were placed over the hearts of mummies. The Collection has a winged scarab and another without wings in the storeroom.

**SCRIBES**
Officials who knew how to read, write and count, which enabled them to occupy positions in the central and regional administration. Studying was hard, but they were subsequently exempt from paying taxes.

**SENWOSRET III**
12th-dynasty king who implemented a firm policy of centralising power. His reign saw a period of great internal prosperity and expansion into Nubia, where he built imposing fortresses. His Greek name is Sesostris, although this is less and less used. The Collection has a fine obsidian head of this king.

**SET**
God of the deserts. From the Late Period onwards, he was cursed and seen as evil and jealous. He was attributed with the murder of Osiris so that he could rule Egypt. He was part of the Heliopolis Ennead.

**SETY I**
19th-dynasty pharaoh. The main features of his brief reign were military actions in Syria-Palestine and major construction work in Karnak and Abydos. He was the father of Rameses II, and his name meant "He of Set", demonstrating how that god was worshipped at the time.

**SHRINE**
The most hidden and reserved part of the temple, which held the statue of the god that was worshipped there. There could sometimes be other statues of gods related to the local deity, making part of the family. Small, chapel-like religious constructions are also called shrines.

**SHU**
God of the air, the son of Atum and husband of Tefnut. He was one of the nine gods of Heliopolis (Ennead). His traditional symbol was a feather, like that of the goddess Maet, and he sometimes appears supporting the celestial vault and thereby justifying his name: "He who raises".

**SILVER**
Metal that did not exist in Egypt and consequently had to be imported. Given its rarity, it was more valuable than gold. One of the 21st-dynasty pharaohs buried in Tanis had a silver sarcophagus. The Collection includes a silver statuette of Harpocrates, or the child Horus.

**SISTRUM**
Metal musical instrument whose sound was like that of a rattle or tambourine. It was associated to worship of Hathor and the funerary cult. It was used by women, priestesses or princesses. The votive Hathor sistrum in the Museum is a faience imitation of the metal instruments used in religious ceremonies.

**SNEFERU**
King who founded the 4th dynasty. This great builder ordered at least two of the pyramids in the Dahshur region to be built: one was the first perfect pyramidal form known in Egypt. His architects continued to work for his son, Pharaoh Khufu.

**SOBEK**
God shown as a crocodile or as a man with a crocodile head, related to the Nile and its abundance, and particularly worshipped in Faiyum and Kom Ombo. An image of a crocodile appears on the base of the Collection's solar barque of Djedhor.

**SONS OF HORUS**
There are four sons of Horus, linked to the funerary cult and responsible for the viscera. This explains why the canopic jars sometimes had lids showing the four deities: Imsety, Hapy, Duamutef and Kebehsenuef.

**STELE**
Memorial or invocative stone, often of a funerary nature. It could be rectangular or have a rounded top. It could include (or not) a text, but always had engraved or painted images. The stele of the scribe Iri, part of the Collection, has a rounded top, as well as text and images.

**TEFNUT**
Goddess of moisture, the daughter of Atum and wife of Shu, and one of the nine gods in the Heliopolis Ennead. She is sometimes shown with a woman's body and a lion's head.

**THEBES**
Greek name for a city in Upper Egypt whose Egyptian name is Waset. This is the location of large temples, such as those of Karnak and Luxor, built to honour Amun-Ra. It was also the site of temples dedicated to Mut, Khonsu, Montu and Osiris. Nowadays the city is known as Luxor.

**THUTMOSE III**
He ruled between 1504 and 1450 BC. As a minor when his father died, his aunt and stepmother Hatshepsut became regent. His name means "Born of Tot" and his forename of Menkheperra means "The form of Ra is stable". He was a great conqueror.

**TITULARY**
Set of five royal names that started being used in the Middle Kingdom, when pharaohs presented themselves with the following names: the Horus name, the name of the Two Ladies, the Horus of Gold name, the name of the king of Upper and Lower Egypt, and the name of the son of Ra (normally the birth-name).

**TOT**
God of wisdom and the creator of writing, protector of scribes and judges. In judgement scenes, he appears next to the scales weighing the heart of the deceased. His Egyptian name was Djehuti.

**TUTANKHAMUN**
18th-dynasty pharaoh, considered to be the son of Amenhotep IV. He changed his name from Tutankhaten to Tutankhamun and abandoned the cult of Aten. His tomb was discovered almost intact in 1922.

**TWO LANDS**
The Two Lands were Lower Egypt – from north of Memphis to the Mediterranean, or the region of the Delta with its broad fertile area and the seven main branches of the Nile (now only two) – and Upper Egypt, stretching south from Memphis to Aswan (Elephantine). In Egyptian, this division was called Taui.

**UDJAT**
Name of the magical eye of the god Horus. This had a great magical and protective value that was associated to rebirth. According to the myths, it was torn out by the jealous god Set, but Tot put it back in place. It often appears in iconography.

**URAEUS**
Serpent-shaped decoration that appears on the front of crowns of royalty and of some gods as a symbol of divine power. The name *uraeus* is of Greek origin, and corresponds to the Egyptian *iaret,* the sacred serpent.

**WIG**
The Ancient Egyptians often used wigs on special occasions, such as banquets and receptions. These wigs could be made of real hair or include entwined plant fibres.

**WRITING INSTRUMENTS**
These comprised a palette with two holes (one for black ink, the other for red), a small container, a papyrus-smoother and a case for styluses or brushes.

**YEAR**
The Egyptian year had 365 days divided into three seasons. Each season had four months, and each month had thirty days. The seasons were called Akhet (Flood, July to October), Peret (Winter, November to February) and Shemu (Summer, March to June). Five days were added at the end to make up the 365 days.

# BIBLIOGRAPHY

## SPECIALISED BIBLIOGRAPHY

**Assam, 1991**
Maria Helena Assam, *Arte Egípcia,* Colecção Calouste Gulbenkian, Lisbon: Museu Calouste Gulbenkian, 1991

**Baetjer & Draper, 1999**
Katharine Baetjer & James David Draper (eds.), *"Only the Best": Masterpieces of the Calouste Gulbenkian Museum, Lisbon,* exhibition catalogue, New York: The Metropolitan Museum of Art, 1999

**Bénédite, 1924**
Georges Bénédite, "Vraie ou fausse?: Au sujet d'une statuette égyptienne", in *La Revue de l'Art,* XIV, Paris: January-May 1924

**Gardiner, 1920**
Alan Gardiner, "A stele in the MacGregor collection", in *Journal of Egyptian Archaeology,* IV, London, 1920, pp. 188-189

**Goofen, 1982**
Rona Goofen, *Museums Discovered: The Calouste Gulbenkian Museum,* Florida: Woodbine Books, 1982 (Portuguese edition, 1984)

**Lisbon, 1969**
*Museu Calouste Gulbenkian: Roteiro 1,* Lisbon: Fundação Calouste Gulbenkian, 1969

**Lisbon, 1975**
*Museu Calouste Gulbenkian: Roteiro,* Lisbon: Fundação Calouste Gulbenkian, 1975

**Lisbon, 1982**
*Calouste Gulbenkian Museum: Catalogue,* Lisbon: Calouste Gulbenkian Foundation, 1982

**Lisbon, 2002**
*Calouste Gulbenkian Museum,* 2nd edition, revised and updated, Lisbon: Calouste Gulbenkian Foundation, 2002

**Oeiras, 1965**
*Obras de Arte da Colecção Calouste Gulbenkian,* Palácio Pombal, exhibition catalogue, Oeiras: Fundação Calouste Gulbenkian, 1965

**Perdigão, 1969**
José de Azeredo Perdigão, *Calouste Gulbenkian Collector,* Lisbon: Calouste Gulbenkian Foundation, 1969 (3rd edition, revised, 2006)

**Smith & Edwards, 1937**
Sidney Smith & I. E. S. Edwards, *Ancient Egyptian Sculpture Lent by C. S. Gulbenkian, Esq.,* exhibition catalogue, London: British Museum, 1937

**Walker & Edwards, 1949**
John Walker & I. E. S. Edwards, *Egyptian Sculpture from the Gulbenkian Collection,* exhibition catalogue, Washington: National Gallery of Art, 1949

## CATALOGUES AND COLLECTIONS

**Affholder-Gérard & Cornic, 1990**
Brigitte Affholder-Gérard & Marie-Jeanne Cornic, *Angers, Musée Pincé. Collections Égyptiennes,* Paris: Angers, Éditions de la Réunion des Musées Nationaux, Musées d'Angers, 1990

**Araújo, 1993**
Luís Manuel de Araújo, *Antiguidades Egípcias,* I, Museu Nacional de Arqueologia, Lisbon: Instituto Português de Museus, 1993

**Araújo, 1994-1995**
Luís Manuel de Araújo, "O núcleo egípcio da colecção Assis Ferreira", in *Cadmo,* 4/5, Instituto Oriental da Faculdade de Letras de Lisboa, Lisbon: Edições Colibri, 1994-1995, pp. 75-94

**Araújo, 1998-1999**
Luís Manuel de Araújo, "O núcleo egípcio da colecção Miguel Barbosa", in *Cadmo,* 8/9, Instituto Oriental da Faculdade de Letras de Lisboa, Lisbon, 1998-1999, pp. 89-106

**Araújo, 1999**
Luís Manuel de Araújo, "O núcleo egípcio da colecção Luís Teixeira da Mota", in *Carlos Alberto Ferreira de Almeida, In Memoriam,* I, Faculdade de Letras da Universidade do Porto, 1999, pp. 117-124

**Araújo, 1999a**
Luís Manuel de Araújo, "O núcleo egípcio da colecção Fernando Freitas Simões", in *Clio,* 4, journal of the Centro de História da Universidade de Lisboa, Lisbon, 1999, pp. 7-25

**Araújo, 1999b**
Luís Manuel de Araújo, "Collections égyptiennes au Portugal", in *Nilus,* 8, Barcelona: Societat Catalana d'Egiptologia, 1999, pp. 3-5

**Araújo, 2001**
Luís Manuel de Araújo, "A colecção egípcia do Museu do Caramulo", in *Cadmo,* 11, Instituto Oriental da Faculdade de Letras de Lisboa, Lisbon, 2001, pp. 55-63

**Araújo, 2002**
Luís Manuel de Araújo, "O núcleo egípcio da colecção Sam Levy", in *Artis,* 1, Instituto de História da Arte da Faculdade de Letras de Lisboa, Lisbon, 2002, pp. 31-56

**Berman, 1999**
Lawrence M. Berman, *Catalogue of Egyptian Art,* Cleveland: The Cleveland Museum of Art, 1999

**Björkman, 1971**
Gun Björkman, *A Selection of the Objects in the Smith Collection of Egyptian Antiquities at the Linköping Museum, Sweden,* Bibliotheca Ekmaniana, 65, Stockholm: Almqvist & Wiksell, 1971

**Bongioanni & Croce, 2001**
Alessandro Bongioanni & Maria Sole Croce (eds.), *The Illustrated Guide to the Egyptian Museum in Cairo,* Cairo: The American University in Cairo Press, 2001

**Bothmer, 1960**
Bernard v. Bothmer, *Egyptian Sculpture of the Late Period,* exhibition catalogue, Brooklyn, New York: The Brooklyn Museum, 1960

**Bothmer, 1988**
Bernard v. Bothmer, "Egyptian Antiquities", in *Antiquities from the Collection of Christos G. Bastis,* Mainz am Rhein, New York: Verlag Philipp von Zabern, 1988, pp. 1-106

**Cairo, 1979**
*The Luxor Museum of Ancient Egyptian Art, Catalogue,* Cairo: American Research Center in Egypt, 1979

**Donadoni, 1981**
Sergio Donadoni, *L'Egitto,* Turin: Unione Tipografico-Editrice Torinese, 1981

**Donadoni Roveri, 1988**
Anna Maria Donadoni Roveri (dir.), *La Civilisation des Égyptiens, 1: La vie quotidienne*; *La civilisation des Égyptiens, 2: Les croyances religieuses,* Musée Égyptien de Turin, Turin: Istituto Bancario San Paolo di Torino, 1988 (translation of the Italian original)

**Donadoni Roveri, 1989**
Anna Maria Donadoni Roveri (dir.), *La Civilisation des Égyptiens, 3: Les arts de la célébration,* Musée Égyptien de Turin, Turin: Istituto Bancario San Paolo di Torino, 1989 (translation of the Italian original)

**Fazzini, 1975**
Richard Fazzini, *Images for Eternity. Egyptian Art from Berkeley and Brooklyn,* New York: The Brooklyn Museum, 1975

**Gasse, 1991**
Annie Gasse, *Guide des Collections Égyptiennes,* Besançon: Musée des Beaux-Arts et d'Archéologie de Besançon, 1991

**Gessler-Löhr, 1981**
Beatrix Gessler-Löhr, *Ägyptische Kunst in Liebieghaus, Museum Alter Plastik,* Frankfurt am Main: Herbert Beck und Peter C. Bol, 1981

**Hayes, 1990**
William C. Hayes, *The Scepter of Egypt. A background for the study of the Egyptian Antiquities in the Metropolitan Museum of Art,* Part I: From the earliest times to the end of the Middle Kingdom; Part II: The Hyksos Period and the New Kingdom (1675-1080 B.C.), New York: The Metropolitan Museum of Art, 1990

**Hosang, 1989**
F. J. E. Boddens Hosang, *De Egyptische Verzameling van Baron van Westreenen,* The Hague: Rijksmuseum Meermanno--Westreenianum, 1989

**London, 1922**
*Illustrated Catalogue of Ancient Egyptian Art,* exhibition catalogue, London: Burlington Fine Arts Club, 1922

**Moorey, 1992**
Roger S. Moorey, *Ancient Egypt,* 2nd edition, revised, Oxford: Ashmolean Museum, 1992

**Pernigotti, 1994**
Sergio Pernigotti (dir.), *La Collezione Egiziana,* Museo Civico Archeologico di Bologna, Bologna: Leonardo Arte, 1994

**Satzinger, n. d.**
Helmut Satzinger, *Ägyptische Kunst in Wien,* Vienna: MBV, n. d.

**Schlick-Nolte, 1986**
Birgit Schlick-Nolte, *Die Ägyptische Sammlung am Museum Wiesbaden, aus der Sammlung Nassauischer Altertümer,* Wiesbaden: Rolf Felde, 1986

**Schneider, 1987**
Hans D. Schneider, *Art from Ancient Egypt chosen from the Collections of the National Museum of Antiquities at Leiden,* Leiden, Tokyo: Rijksmuseum van Oudheden, The Tokyo Shimbun, 1987

**Schoske & Wildung, 1985**
Sylvia Schoske & Dietrich Wildung, *Ägyptische Kunst München. Katalog Handbuch zur Staatlichen Sammlung Ägyptischer Kunst München,* Munich: Karl M. Lipp Verlag, 1985

**Scott III, 1986**
Gerry D. Scott III, *Ancient Egyptian Art at Yale,* New Haven: Yale University Art Gallery, 1986

**Seipel, 1989**
Wilfried Seipel, *Ägypten, Götter, Gräber und die Kunst. 4000 Jahre Jenseitsglaube,* I, Katalog zur Ausstellung, Schlossmuseum Linz, Linz: OÖ. Landsmuseum Linz, 1989

**Settgast, 1991**
Jürgen Settgast, *Musée Égyptien, Berlin,* 4th edition, Verein zur Förderung des Ägyptischen Museums in Berlin-Charlottenburg, Mainz am Rhein: Philipp von Zabern, 1991 (translation of the German original)

**Simpson, 1987**
William Kelly Simpson, *A Table of Offerings. 17 Years of Acquisitions of Egyptian and Ancient Eastern Art,* Boston: Museum of Fine Arts, 1987

**Smith, 1960**
William S. Smith, *Ancient Egypt as represented in the Museum of Fine Arts,* 6th edition, revised, Boston: Museum of Fine Arts, 1960

**Tiradritti, 1998**
Francesco Tiradritti (dir.), *Les Trésors du Musée Égyptien,* Vercelli: White Star, 1998

**Varga, 1985**
Edith Varga, *Museum of Fine Arts. Egyptian Collection,* Exhibition of Egyptian Antiquities, Budapest: Miklós Szabó, 1985

**Wildung, 1999**
Dietrich Wildung, *Egyptian Art in Berlin. Masterpieces in the Bodemuseum and in Charlottenburg,* Ägyptisches Museum und Papyrussammmlung, Staaliche Museen zu Berlin, Mainz am Rhein: Verlag Philipp von Zabern, 1999 (translation of the German original)

**Wildung, 2000**
Dietrich Wildung, *Ägypten, 2000 v. Chr.* Die Geburt des Individuums, exhibition catalogue, Munich: Hirmer Verlag, 2000

**Ziegler, 1990**
Christiane Ziegler, *The Louvre: Egyptian Antiquities,* Paris: Éditions Scala, Réunion des Musées Nationaux, 1990

## GENERAL BIBLIOGRAPHY

**Aldred, 1972**
Cyril Aldred, *Tutankhamun's Egypt,* London: British Broadcasting Corporation, 1972

**Aldred, 1978**
Cyril Aldred, *Jewels of the Pharaohs. Egyptian Jewelry of the Dynastic Period,* London: Thames & Hudson, 1978

**Aldred, 1980**
Cyril Aldred, *Egyptian Art in the Days of the Pharaohs,* London: Thames & Hudson, 1980

**Aldred, 1987**
Cyril Aldred, *The Egyptians,* revised and expanded edition, Col. Ancient Peoples and Places, London: Thames & Hudson, 1987

**Allen, 1974**
Thomas G. Allen, *The Book of the Dead or Going Forth by Day,* Chicago: The Oriental Institute of the University of Chicago, 1974

**Araújo, 1988**
Luís Manuel de Araújo, *Eça de Queirós e o Egipto Faraónico,* Lisbon: Editorial Comunicação, 1988

**Araújo, 1995**
Luís Manuel de Araújo, *Estudos sobre Erotismo no Antigo Egipto,* Col. Temas Pré-Clássicos, Lisbon: Edições Colibri, 1995

**Araújo, 1999**
Luís Manuel de Araújo, *O Clero do Deus Amon no Antigo Egipto,* Col. Orientalia Lusitana, 2, Lisbon: Edições Cosmos, 1999

**Araújo, 2001a**
Luís Manuel de Araújo (dir.), *Dicionário do Antigo Egipto,* Lisbon: Editorial Caminho, 2001

**Araújo, 2003**
Luís Manuel de Araújo, *Estatuetas Funerárias Egípcias da XXI Dinastia,* Lisbon: Fundação Calouste Gulbenkian & Fundação para a Ciência e a Tecnologia, 2003

**Araújo, 2004**
Luís Manuel de Araújo, *Egipto: As Pirâmides do Império Antigo,* 2nd edition, revised and expanded, Col. Temas Pré-Clássicos, Lisbon: Edições Colibri, 2004

**Araújo, 2005**
Luís Manuel de Araújo, *Mitos e Lendas do Antigo Egipto,* Lisbon: Centralivros, 2005

**Assmann, 1983**
Jan Assmann, *Re und Amun. Die Krise des polytheistischen Weltbilds im Ägypten der 18.-20. Dynastie,* Orbis Biblicus et Orientalis, 51, Universitätsverlag Freiburg, Göttingen: Vandenhoeck & Ruprecht, 1983

**Assmann, 1989**
Jan Assmann, *Maât. L'Égypte pharaonique et l'idée de justice sociale,* Collège de France, Paris: Éditions Julliard, 1989

**Baines & Málek, 1981**
John Baines & Jaromír Málek, *Atlas of Ancient Egypt,* Oxford: Phaidon Press, 1981

**Barbotin, 2005**
Christophe Barbotin, "Un intercesseur dynastique à l'aube du Nouvel Empire", in *La Revue des Musées de France. Musée du Louvre,* 4, Paris, 2005, pp. 19-28

**Bard, 2000**
Kathryn A. Bard, "The Emergence of the Egyptian State (*c.* 3200-2686 BC)", *in* Ian Shaw (ed.), *The Oxford History of Ancient Egypt,* Oxford: Oxford University Press, 2000, pp. 61-88

**Barguet, 1968**
Paul Barguet, *Le Livre des Morts des Anciens Égyptiens,* Littératures Anciennes du Proche-Orient, 1, Paris: Les Éditions du Cerf, 1968

**Barguet, 1986**
Paul Barguet, *Les Textes des Sarcophages Égyptiens du Moyen Empire,* Littératures Anciennes du Proche-Orient, 12, Paris: Les Éditions du Cerf, 1986

**Barocas, 1987**
Claudio Barocas, *L'Antico Egitto,* 3rd edition, Rome: Newton Compton Editori, 1987

**Baud, 1978**
Marcelle Baud, *Le Caractère du Dessin en Égypte Ancienne,* Paris: Librairie d'Amérique et d'Orient Adrien-Maisonneuve, 1978

**Beckerath, 1951**
Jürgen von Beckerath, *Tanis und Theben,* Ägyptische Forchungen, 16, Glückstadt, 1951

**Beckerath, 1984**
Jürgen von Beckerath, *Handbuch der ägyptischen Königsnamen,* Munich, Berlin: Deutscher Kunstverlag, 1984

**Blackman, 1996**
Aylward M. Blackman (ed.), *Gods, Priests and Men. Studies in the Religion of Pharaonic Egypt,* Studies in Egyptology Series, London: Kegan Paul International, 1996

**Bonhême & Forgeau, 1988**
Marie-Ange Bonhême & Annie Forgeau, *Pharaon, les secrets du pouvoir,* Paris: Ed. Armand Colin, 1988

**Bothmer, 1988**
Bernard v. Bothmer, "Egyptian antecedents of Roman republican verism", in *Quaderni de la Ricerca Scientifica,* Rome: CNR, 1988, pp. 17-19

**Bourguet, 1973**
Pierre du Bourguet, *L'Art Égyptien,* Paris: Desclée de Brouwer, 1973

**Bourriau, 2000**
Janine Bourriau, "The Second Intermediate Period (c. 1650-1550 BC)", *in* Ian Shaw (ed.), *The Oxford History of Ancient Egypt,* Oxford: Oxford University Press, 2000, pp. 184-217

**Bryan, 2000**
Betsy M. Bryan, "The 18th Dynasty before the Amarna Period (c. 1550-1352 BC)", *in* Ian Shaw (ed.), *The Oxford History of Ancient Egypt,* Oxford: Oxford University Press, 2000, pp. 218-271

**Bulté, 1991**
Jeanne Bulté, *Talismans égyptiens d'heureuse maternité. "Faïence" bleu vert à pois foncé,* Paris: Éditions du Centre National de Recherche Scientifique, 1991

**Callender, 2000**
Gae Callender, "The Middle Kingdom Renaissance (c. 2055-1650 BC)", *in* Ian Shaw (ed.), *The Oxford History of Ancient Egypt,* Oxford: Oxford University Press, 2000, pp. 148-183

**Carreira, 1994**
José Nunes Carreira, *Filosofia antes dos Gregos,* Biblioteca Universitária, Mem Martins: Publicações Europa-América, 1994

**Carreira, 2001**
José Nunes Carreira, "Mulher", *in* Luís Manuel de Araújo (dir.), *Dicionário do Antigo Egipto,* Lisbon: Editorial Caminho, 2001, pp. 585-592

**Carreira, 2005**
José Nunes Carreira, *Literatura do Egipto Antigo,* Biblioteca Universitária, Mem Martins: Publicações Europa-América, 2005

**Cervelló Autuori, 2001**
Josep Cervelló Autuori, "Monarchie pharaonique et royautés divines africaines", in *Cahiers Caribéens d'Égyptologie,* 2, Martinica: February-March 2001, pp. 27-52

**Clayton, 1994**
Peter A. Clayton, *Chronicle of the Pharaohs: The complete reign by reign record of the rulers and dynasties of Ancient Egypt,* London: Thames & Hudson, 1994

**Daumas, 1982**
François Daumas, *Les Dieux de l'Égypte,* Col. Que sais-je?, 2nd edition, Paris: Presses Universitaires de France, 1982

**Daumas, 1987**
François Daumas, *La Civilisation de l'Égypte Pharaonique,* Col. Les Grandes Civilisations, Paris: Ed. B. Arthaud, 1987

**David, 1982**
Rosalie David, *The Ancient Egyptians. Religious beliefs and practices,* London, New York: Routledge & Kegan Paul, 1982

**Dawson & Uphill, 1995**
Warren R. Dawson & Eric P. Uphill, *Who Was Who in Egyptology,* 3rd revised edition by Morris Bierbrier, London: The Egypt Exploration Society, 1995

**Desroches-Noblecourt, 1962**
Christiane Desroches-Noblecourt, *L'Art Égyptien,* Paris: Presses Universitaires de France, 1962

**Desroches-Noblecourt, 1986**
Christiane Desroches-Noblecourt, *La Femme au Temps des Pharaons,* Le Livre de Poche, Paris: Éditions Stock/Laurence Pernoud, 1986

**Dijk, 2000**
Jacobis van Dijk, "The Amarna Period and the Later New Kingdom (c. 1352-1069 BC", *in* Ian Shaw (ed.), *The Oxford History of Ancient Egypt,* Oxford: Oxford University Press, 2000, pp. 272-313

**Dodson, 1995**
Aidan Dodson, *Monarchs of the Nile,* New York, London: Rubicon Press, 1995

**Donadoni, Curto & Donadoni Roveri, 1990**
Sergio Donadoni, Silvio Curto & Anna Maria Donadoni Roveri, *L'Égypte du Mythe à l'Égyptologie,* Milan, Turin: Istituto Bancario San Paolo di Torino, Fabri Editori, 1990 (translation of the Italian original)

**El-Mallakh & Brackman, 1978**
Kamal el-Mallakh & Arnold Brackman, *The Gold of Tutankhamen,* New York: Newsweek Books, 1978

**Emery, 1972**
Walter B. Emery, *Archaic Egypt. Culture and Civilization in Egypt Five Thousand Years Ago,* Harmondsworth: Penguin Books, 1972

**Faulkner, 1988**
Raymond O. Faulkner, *A Concise Dictionary of Middle Egyptian,* Griffith Institute, revised edition, Oxford: Oxford University Press, 1988

**Fay, 2004**
Biri Fay, "The wooden statue of Nebetia from Kom Medinet Gurab", in *Mitteihungen das Deutschen Archäeologischen Instituts Abteilung Kairo,* Mainz am Rhein: Verlag Philipp von Zabern, 2004, pp. 41-45

**Fischer, 1981**
Henry George Fischer, *L'Écriture et l'Art de l'Égypte Ancienne,* Collège de France, Essais et Conférences, Paris: Presses Universitaires de France, 1981

**Gardiner, 1957**
Sir Alan Gardiner, *Egyptian Grammar, being an Introduction to the Study of Hieroglyphs,* 3rd edition, revised, Griffith Institute, Oxford: Ashmolean Museum, 1957

**Gardiner, 1961**
Sir Alan Gardiner, *Egypt of the Pharaohs. An Introduction,* London, Oxford, New York: Oxford University Press, 1961

**Goyon, 1972**
Jean-Claude Goyon, *Rituels Funéraires de l'Égypte Ancienne,* Col. Littératures Anciennes du Proche-Orient, 4, Paris: Les Éditions du Cerf, 1972

**Grimal, 1988**
Nicolas Grimal, *Histoire de l'Égypte Ancienne,* Paris: Librairie Arthème Fayard, 1988

**Grimm, Schoske & Wildung, 1997**
Alfred Grimm, Sylvia Schoske & Dietrich Wildung, *Pharao. Kunst und Herrschaft im alten Ägypten,* Munich: Kinckhardt und Biermann, 1997

**Hart, 1986**
George Hart, *A Dictionary of Egyptian Gods and Goddesses,* London, New York: Routledge & Kegan Paul, 1986

**Hill & Schorsch, 2005**
Marsha Hill & Deborah Schorsch, "The Gulbenkian torso of King Pedubast: Investigations into Egyptian Large Bronze Statuary", in *Metropolitan Museum Journal*, 40, New York: 2005, pp. 163-195

**Hobson, 1987**
Christine Hobson, *Exploring the World of the Pharaohs. A Complete Guide to Ancient Egypt,* London: Thames & Hudson, 1987

**Hodel-Hoebes, 1991**
Sigfried Hodel-Hoebes, *Leben und Tod im Alten Ägypten. Thebanische Privatsgräber,* Darmstadt: Wissenschaftliche Buchgesellschaft, 1991

**Hornung, 1983**
Eric Hornung, *Conceptions of God in Ancient Egypt. The One and the Many,* London, Melbourne: Routledge & Kegan Paul, 1983 (translation of the German original)

**Husson & Valbelle, 1992**
Geneviève Husson & Dominique Valbelle, *L'État et les Institutions en Égypte des Premiers Pharaons aux Empereurs Romains,* Col. Histoire Ancienne, Paris: Éditions Armand Colin, 1992

**Ions, 1983**
Veronica Ions, *Egyptian Mythology,* Library of the World's Myths and Legends, London, New York: The Hamlyn Publishing Group, 1983

**Jacq, 1993**
Christian Jacq, *Recherches sur les Paradis de l'Autre-monde d'après les Textes des Pyramides et les Textes des Sarcophages,* Paris: Institut Ramsès, 1993

**Johnson, 1978**
Paul Johnson, *The Civilisation of Ancient Egypt,* New York: Atheneum, 1978

**Kaczmarczyk & Hedges, 1983**
Alexander Kaczmarczyk & Robert E. Hedges, *Ancient Egyptian Faience. An Analytical Survey of Egyptian Faience from Predynastic to Roman Times,* Warminster: Aris & Phillips Ltd, 1983

**Kees, 1953-1958**
Hermann Kees, *Das Priestertum im Ägyptischen Staat vom Neuen Reich bis zur Spätzeit,* 2 vols., Probleme der Ägyptologie, 20, Cologne, Leiden: E. J. Brill, 1953-1958

**Kees, 1964**
Hermann Kees, *Die Hohenpriester des Amun von Karnak von Herihor bis zum Ende der Äthiopenzeit,* Probleme der Ägyptologie, Leiden: E. J. Brill, 1964

**Kees, 1977**
Hermann Kees, *Ancient Egypt. A Cultural Topography,* Chicago, London, Phoenix: University of Chicago Press, 1977 (translation of the German original)

**Kemp, 1989**
Barry J. Kemp, *Ancient Egypt. Anatomy of a Civilization,* London, New York: Routledge, 1989

**Kitchen, 1986**
Kenneth Kitchen, *The Third Intermediate Period in Egypt (1100-650 BC),* 2nd edition, revised and with a supplement, Warminster: Aris & Phillips Ltd, 1986

**Lalouette, 1984**
Claire Lalouette, *Textes Sacrés et Textes Profanes de l'Ancienne Égypte. Des Pharaons et des Hommes,* Paris: Gallimard, 1984

**Lalouette, 1986**
Claire Lalouette, *Thébes, ou la Naissance d'un Empire,* série Pharaons, 2, Paris: Librairie Arthème Fayard, 1986

**Lalouette, 1996**
Claire Lalouette, *L'Art Figuratif dans l'Égypte Pharaonique,* Paris: Flammarion, 1996

**Lange & Hirmer, 1968**
Kurt Lange & Max Hirmer, *Egypt: Architecture, Sculpture, Painting,* London: Phaidon, 1968 (translation of the German original)

**Leclant, 1978**
Jean Leclant (dir.), *Les Pharaons, 1: Le Temps des Pyramides,* série Le Monde Égyptien, Paris: Éditions Gallimard, 1978

**Leclant, 1979**
Jean Leclant (dir.), *Les Pharaons, 2: L'Empire des Conquérants,* série Le Monde Égyptien, Paris: Éditions Gallimard, 1979

**Leclant, 1980**
Jean Leclant (dir.), *Les Pharaons, 3: L'Égypte du Crépuscule, de Tanis à Méroé,* série Le Monde Égyptien, Paris: Éditions Gallimard, 1980

**Lehner, 1997**
Mark Lehner, *The Complete Pyramids,* London: Thames & Hudson, 1997

**Lloyd, 2000**
Alan B. Lloyd, "The Late Period (c. 664-332 BC)", *in* Ian Shaw (ed.), *The Oxford History of Ancient Egypt,* Oxford: Oxford University Press, 2000, pp. 369-394

**Lucas & Harris, 1962**
Alfred Lucas & J. R. Harris, *Ancient Egyptian Materials and Industries,* 4th edition, London: Edward Arnold Ltd, 1962

**Lurker, 1980**
Manfred Lurker, *The Gods and Symbols of Ancient Egypt. An Illustrated Dictionary,* London: Thames & Hudson, 1980

**Málek, 1986**
Jaromír Málek, *In the Shadow of the Pyramids. Egypt during the Old Kingdom,* London: Orbis, 1986

**Málek, 1993**
Jaromír Málek, *The Cat in Ancient Egypt,* London: British Museum Press, 1993

**Málek, 1999**
Jaromír Málek, *Egyptian Art,* London: Phaidon Press, 1999

**Málek, 2003**
Jaromír Málek, *Egypt, 4000 Years of Art,* London: Phaidon Press, 2003

**Malheiro, 2001**
Pedro de Abreu Malheiro, "Jóias", *in* Luís Manuel de Araújo (dir.), *Dicionário do Antigo Egipto,* Lisbon: Editorial Caminho, 2001, pp. 459-461

**Manley, 1996**
Bill Manley, *The Penguin Historical Atlas of Ancient Egypt,* Harmondsworth: Penguin Books, 1996

**Mekhitarian, 1978**
Arpag Mekhitarian, *La Peinture Égyptienne,* 2nd edition, Geneva, Paris, New York: Éditions Skira, 1978

**Michalowski, 1968**
Kazimiers Michalowski, *L'Art de l'Ancienne Égypte,* Paris: Mazenod, 1968

**Montpetit, 1992**
Raymond Montpetit, "Les musées à l'âge médiatique: tout exposer pour tous", in *Forces,* 98, Montreal, Summer 1992, pp. 84-87

**Mysliwiec, 2004**
Karol Mysliwiec, *Eros on the Nile,* London: Gerald Duckworth, 2004 (translation of the Polish original)

**Newby, 1980**
P. H. Newby, *Warrior Pharaohs. The Rise and Fall of the Egyptian Empire,* London: Boston, Faber & Faber, 1980

**Nibbi, 1981**
Alessandra Nibbi, *Ancient Egypt and some Eastern Neighbours,* Park Ridge: Noyes Press, 1981

**Nicholson, 1993**
Paul T. Nicholson, *Egyptian Faience and Glass,* Shire Egyptology, 18, Princes Risborough: Shire Publications, 1993

**Padró, 1996**
Joseph Padró, *Historia del Egipto Faraónico,* Alianza Universidad, Madrid: Alianza Editorial, 1996

**Padró i Parcerisa, 1995**
Josep Padró i Parcerisa, *New Egyptian-type Documents from the Mediterranean Littoral of the Iberian Peninsula before the Roman conquest,* Orientalia Monspeliensia, VIII, Montpellier: Université Paul Valéry, 1995

**Paris, 1998**
*Dictionnaire de l'Égypte Ancienne,* Encyclopaedia Universalis, Paris: Albin Michel, 1998

**Payne, 1965**
Blanche Payne, *History of Costume,* New York: Harper & Row, 1965

**Petrie, 1920**
Flinders Petrie, *Ancient Egypt,* London, New York: Macmillan, 1920

**Pinch, 1994**
Geraldine Pinch, *Magic in Ancient Egypt,* London: British Museum Press, 1994

**Portes, 1996**
Elisabeth des Portes, "Collecter: collecte et déontologie", in *Nouvelles de l'ICOM,* Bulletin du Conseil International des Musées, 49, 2, Paris, 1996, pp. 5-7

**Posener, 1970**
Georges Posener (dir.), *Dictionnaire de la Civilisation Égyptienne,* Paris: Fernand Hazan, 1970

**Quirke & Spencer, 1992**
Stephen Quirke & Jeffrey Spencer, *The British Museum Book of Ancient Egypt,* London: British Museum Press, 1992

**Ranke, 1935**
Hermann Ranke, *Die Ägyptischen Personennamen,* I, Glückstadt: Verlag J. J. Augustin, 1935

**Redford, 1992**
Donald B. Redford, *Egypt, Canaan and Israel in Ancient Times,* Ancient History and Archaeology, Princeton: Princeton University Press, 1992

**Robins, 1993**
Gay Robins, *Women in Ancient Egypt,* London: British Museum Press, 1993

**Sadek, 1987**
Ashraf Iskander Sadek, *Popular Religion during the New Kingdom,* Hildesheimer ägyptologische Beiträge, 27, Hildesheim: Gerstenberg Verlag, 1987

**Sales, 1999**
José das Candeias Sales, *As Divindades Egípcias. Uma Chave para a Compreensão do Egipto Antigo,* Col. Nova História, Lisbon: Editorial Estampa, 1999

**Sales, 2000**
José das Candeias Sales, *A Arte do Antigo Egipto. Uma Arte para a Eternidade,* Lisbon: Universidade Aberta, 2000

**Sales, 2005**
José das Candeias Sales, *Ideologia e Propaganda Real no Egipto Ptolomaico (305-30 a. C.),* Lisbon: Fundação Calouste Gulbenkian & Fundação para a Ciência e a Tecnologia, 2005

**Schäffer, 1986**
Heinrich Schäffer, *Principles of Egyptian Art,* Griffith Institute, revised edition, Oxford: Oxford University Press, 1986 (translation of the German original)

**Schilck-Nolte, 1977**
Birgit Schilck-Nolte, "Fayence", *in* Wolfgang Helck & Wolfhart Westendorf (eds.), *Lexikon der Ägyptologie,* II, Wiesbaden: Otto Harrassowitz, 1977, cols. 138-142

**Schneider, 1977**
Hans D. Schneider, *Shabtis. An introduction to the history of ancient Egyptian funerary statuettes with a catalogue of the collection of shabtis in the National Museum of Antiquities at Leiden,* 3 vols., Leiden: Rijksmuseum van Oudheden te Leiden, 1977

**Seidlmayer, 2000**
Stephan Seidlmayer, "The First Intermediate Period (c. 2160-2055 BC)", *in* Ian Shaw (ed.), *The Oxford History of Ancient Egypt,* Oxford: Oxford University Press, 2000, pp. 118-147

**Seipel, 1980**
Wilfried Seipel, "Königinnentitel", *in* Wolfgang Helck & Wolfhart Westendorf (eds.), *Lexikon der Ägyptologie,* III, Wiesbaden: Otto Harrassowitz, 1980, cols. 473-475

**Shaw, 2000**
Ian Shaw (ed.), *The Oxford History of Ancient Egypt,* Oxford: Oxford University Press, 2000

**Shinnie, 1995**
Peter L. Shinnie, *Ancient Nubia,* London: Kegan Paul International, 1995

**Smith, 1949**
William S. Smith, *A History of Egyptian Sculpture and Painting in the Old Kingdom,* London: Oxford University Press, 1949

**Sousa, 2001**
Rogério Ferreira de Sousa, "Morte", *in* Luís Manuel de Araújo (dir.), *Dicionário do Antigo Egipto,* Lisbon: Editorial Caminho, 2001, pp. 584-585

**Sousa, 2002**
Rogério Ferreira de Sousa, *Os Doces Versos. Poemas de Amor no Antigo Egipto,* Fafe: Editorial Labirinto, 2002

**Spencer, 1993**
A. J. Spencer, *Early Egypt. The Rise of Civilisation in the Nile Valley,* London: The British Museum Press, 1993

**Taylor, 2000**
John Taylor, "The Third Intermediate Period (1069-664 BC)", *in* Ian Shaw (ed.), *The Oxford History of Ancient Egypt,* Oxford: Oxford University Press, 2000, pp. 330-368

**Tefnin, 1988**
Roland Tefnin, *Statues et Statuettes de l'Ancienne Égypte,* Brussels: Museés Royaux d'Art et d'Histoire, 1988

**Théodoridès, 1977**
Aristide Théodoridès, "Frau", *in* Wolfgang Helck & Wolfhart Westendorf (eds.), *Lexikon der Ägyptologie,* II, Wiesbaden: Otto Harrassowitz, 1977, cols. 280-295

**Trépanier & Noppen, 1992**
Paul Trépanier & Luc Noppen, "L'objet de musée: de l'objet témoin à l'objet dialogue", in *Forces,* 98, Montreal, 1992, pp. 13-16

**Vandier, 1958**
Jacques Vandier, *Manuel d'Archéologie Égyptienne,* vol. III, *Les Grandes Époques – La Statuaire,* Paris: Éditions A. et J. Picard, 1958

**Vernus & Yoyotte, 1988**
Pascal Vernus & Jean Yoyotte, *Les Pharaons,* Col. Les noms, les thèmes, les lieux, Paris: MA Éditions, 1988

**Vogelsang-Eastwood, 1992**
Gillian Vogelsang-Eastwood, *Patterns for Ancient Egyptian Clothing,* Leiden: Textile Research Centre, 1992

**Walker, 1983**
John Walker, *Portraits: 5000 Years,* New York: Harry N. Abrahms, 1983

**Wildung, 1984**
Dietrich Wildung, *L'Âge d'Or de l'Égypte. Le Moyen Empire,* Col. l'Âge d'Or des Civilisations, Paris: Presses Universitaires de France, 1984 (translation of the German original)

**Wilkinson, 1992**
Richard Wilkinson, *Reading Egyptian Art. A Hieroglyphic Guide to Ancient Egyptian Painting and Sculpture,* London: Thames & Hudson, 1992

**Wilson, 1953**
John A. Wilson, *La Cultura Egipcia,* Breviarios del Fondo de Cultura Economica, 86, México, 1953 (translation of the English original, USA)

**Yoyotte, 1968**
Jean Yoyotte, *Les Trésors des Pharaons,* Geneva: Éditions Skira, 1968

**Yoyotte, 1970**
Jean Yoyotte, "Art", *in* Georges Posener (dir.), *Dictionnaire de la Civilisation Égyptienne,* Paris: Fernand Hazan, 1970, pp. 24-28

**Ziegler, 1987**
Christiane Ziegler, "Les arts du métal à la Troisième Période Intermédiaire", in *Tanis: L'Or des Pharaons,* exhibition catalogue, Paris and Marseille, Paris: 1987, pp. 85-101

# INDEX

## INVENTORY NUMBER / CATALOGUE NUMBER

## PROVENANCE

| COLLECTION | CATALOGUE NUMBER |
| --- | --- |
| Amherst | 5, 12, 13 |
| Carmichael | 11, 30 |
| Count Grégoire Stroganoff, Roma | 16 |
| Dr. Eddé, Alexandria | 27 |
| Dr. Fouquet, Cairo | 8, 25, 39 |
| Durighello | 31 |
| Hope | 34 |
| John Maxwell | 32 |
| Lord Grenfell | 14 |
| MacGregor | 1, 2, 4, 7, 9, 10, 17, 18, 19, 20, 21, 22, 23, 24, 26, 28, 35, 37, 40, 41, 42, 43, 44, 45, 46, 47 |
| Paul Mallon | 3 |
| Vicount Rothermere | 53, 54 |

## GENERAL INDEX

## Luís Manuel de Araújo

PhD in History and Pre-classical Culture, University of Lisbon.
Professor at the Faculdade de Letras, University of Lisbon (Oriental Institute).

Postgraduate internship in Egyptology, Faculty of Archaeology, University of Cairo (1984-1985).

Participation in congresses, seminars and archaeological meetings. Over sixty lectures given in Portugal (1986-2005) and two in Barcelona (1998 and 2003).

Participation in Egyptology congresses in Cairo (1988 and 2000), Cambridge (1995) and Grenoble (2004), and the conferences of the International Committee for Egyptology in Leiden and The Hague (1989), Budapest (1990), Moscow (1991), Quebec (1992), Madrid (1994) and Barcelona (2001).

Participation in the Egyptology Meetings in Horssen (Holland), part of the Champollion Project (1998 and 1999), with the support of the European Commission, the 2nd Iberian Egyptology Congress, Barcelona (2000), and in the 3rd Iberian Egyptology Congress, Tenerife (2006).

Secretary of the Portuguese Association of Orientalism, secretary general of the Portugal-Egypt Friendship Association, and senior member of the 'Confraria Queirosiana'.

Secretary of *Cadmo*, journal of the Oriental Institute (Faculdade de Letras), University of Lisbon (fifteen issues published).

Member of the Portuguese Association of Writers, the Association of History Teachers, the Portuguese Museology Association, the International Association of Egyptologists, Sociedade de Geografia, Lisbon, the International Council of Museums and the International Committee for Egyptology.
Director of the *Dicionário do Antigo Egipto*, Lisbon: Editorial Caminho, 2001 (twenty contributors and some 900 pages).

Director of the *Revista de Portugal,* 'Confraria Queirosiana'.

Besides numerous articles, he has published the following books:

*Eça de Queirós e o Egipto Faraónico*, Lisbon: Editorial Comunicação, 1987; *Antiguidades Egípcias* I, Museu Nacional de Arqueologia, Lisbon: Instituto Português de Museus, 1993; *Estudos sobre Erotismo no Antigo Egipto*, Lisbon: Edições Colibri, 1995; *O Clero do Deus Amon no Antigo Egipto*, Lisbon: Edições Cosmos, 1999; *Imagens do Egipto Queirosiano*, Vila Nova de Gaia: Gaianima, 2002; *Egipto: As Pirâmides do Império Antigo*, 2nd edition, revised and expanded, Lisbon: Edições Colibri, 2003; *Estatuetas Funerárias Egípcias da XXI Dinastia*, Lisbon: Fundação Calouste Gulbenkian and Fundação para a Ciência e a Tecnologia, 2003; *Mitos e Lendas do Antigo Egipto*, Lisbon: Centralivros, 2005